Resolving Water Conflicts Workbook

Social–Environmental Sustainability

Series Editor **Chris Maser**

Published Titles

Biosequestration and Ecological Diversity
Mitigating and Adapting to Climate Change and Environmental Degradation
Wayne A. White

Insects and Sustainability of Ecosystem Services
Timothy D. Schowalter

Land-Use Planning for Sustainable Development, Second Edition
Jane Silberstein and Chris Maser

Interactions of Land, Ocean and Humans
A Global Perspective
Chris Maser

Sustainability and the Rights of Nature
An Introduction
Cameron La Follette and Chris Maser

Fundamentals of Practical Environmentalism
Mark B. Weldon

Economics and Ecology
United for a Sustainable World
Charles R. Beaton and Chris Maser

Resolving Environmental Conflicts
Principles and Concepts, Third Edition
Chris Maser and Lynette de Silva

Sustainability and the Rights of Nature in Practice
Cameron La Follette and Chris Maser

Resolving Water Conflicts Workbook
Edited by Lynette de Silva and Chris Maser

For more information on this series, please visit: www.routledge.com/Social-Environmental-Sustainability/book-series/CRCSOCENVSUS

Resolving Water Conflicts Workbook

Edited by
Lynette de Silva and Chris Maser

CRC Press is an imprint of the
Taylor & Francis Group, an **informa** business

First edition published 2022
by CRC Press
6000 Broken Sound Parkway NW, Suite 300, Boca Raton, FL 33487–2742

and by CRC Press
2 Park Square, Milton Park, Abingdon, Oxon, OX14 4RN

© 2022 Taylor & Francis Group, LLC

CRC Press is an imprint of Taylor & Francis Group, LLC

Reasonable efforts have been made to publish reliable data and information, but the author and publisher cannot assume responsibility for the validity of all materials or the consequences of their use. The authors and publishers have attempted to trace the copyright holders of all material reproduced in this publication and apologize to copyright holders if permission to publish in this form has not been obtained. If any copyright material has not been acknowledged please write and let us know so we may rectify in any future reprint.

Except as permitted under U.S. Copyright Law, no part of this book may be reprinted, reproduced, transmitted, or utilized in any form by any electronic, mechanical, or other means, now known or hereafter invented, including photocopying, microfilming, and recording, or in any information storage or retrieval system, without written permission from the publishers.

For permission to photocopy or use material electronically from this work, access www.copyright.com or contact the Copyright Clearance Center, Inc. (CCC), 222 Rosewood Drive, Danvers, MA 01923, 978–750–8400. For works that are not available on CCC please contact mpkbookspermissions@tandf.co.uk

Trademark notice: Product or corporate names may be trademarks or registered trademarks and are used only for identification and explanation without intent to infringe.

Library of Congress Cataloging-in-Publication Data
Names: De Silva, Lynette, editor. | Maser, Chris, editor.
Title: Resolving water conflicts workbook / [edited by] Lynette de Silva and Chris Maser.
Description: First edition. | Boca Raton, FL : CRC Press, 2022. | Includes bibliographical references and index.
Identifiers: LCCN 2021026432 | ISBN 9780367469849 (hbk) | ISBN 9781032134178 (pbk) | ISBN 9781003032533 (ebk)
Subjects: LCSH: Water security. | Water rights. | Conflict management. | Environmental mediation. | Water-supply—Political aspects.
Classification: LCC HD1691 .R468 2021 | DDC 333.91—dc23
LC record available at https://lccn.loc.gov/2021026432

ISBN: 978-0-367-46984-9 (hbk)
ISBN: 978-1-032-13417-8 (pbk)
ISBN: 978-1-003-03253-3 (ebk)

DOI: 10.1201/9781003032533

Typeset in Times
by Apex CoVantage, LLC

Contents

Foreword vii
Preface ix
About the Editors xi
List of Contributors xiii
Acknowledgments xv

Introduction 1
Lynette de Silva

Chapter 1 The Consequence of a Decision and the Case of the Aswan High Dam 11
  Chris Maser

Chapter 2 Water Conflict Transformation 33
  Lynette de Silva

Chapter 3 Evolving Water Governance under United States Law 49
  Holly V. Campbell

Chapter 4 Different Systems, Common Conflicts 61
  Holly V. Campbell and Liliana Pimentel

Chapter 5 Rights of Nature: The Relationship between Water and People 85
  Cameron La Follette

Chapter 6 Intertribal Fishing Conflicts and Federal Obstruction in Oregon 103
  David G. Lewis

Chapter 7 The Role of Gender in Water Conflicts 123
  Jaclyn Best and Jahan Taganova

Chapter 8 Water Insecurities in Two African–American Communities 149
  Lynette de Silva

Chapter 9 A Global Water Solution: An Example of the Sustainable Development Goal Target 6.5.. 179

Melissa McCracken

Chapter 10 Religious Worldviews, Environmental Values, and Conflict-Management Traditions..205

Josiah J. Shaver

Conclusion 239

Lynette de Silva

Index..241

Foreword

In an increasingly globalized and interconnected world, societies have become less resilient with respect to water resources. Long-term developments such as population growth, urbanization, increasing standards of living and related consumption, natural resource degradation and pollution, and the impacts of climate change have resulted in numerous impacts on water resources. As a result, their availability in the long term is at the risk of becoming unsustainable. Decision making on how to manage, allocate, and use them has become progressively complex as diversity of views on what should be sustained and how, and over what period of time, differs across sectors and actors and varies over time.

Resolving Water Conflicts Workbook focuses on social and environmental sustainability. It is rich in examples and reflections. It analyzes in depth how institutions, legal, and policy instruments, as important as they are in terms of governance, are many times slow to respond, with the consequent negative impacts on disadvantaged populations. The case studies are robust and present in detail short- and long-term effects of human activities and institutional responses on specific sectors of society and on the environment on which their livelihoods depend.

The text transmits the urgency to develop frameworks to manage water resources that are more comprehensive such as river basin management and integrated water resources management. As certain as this is, these paradigms have not yet delivered what has been expected from them because of political, policy, and administrative constraints in most of the world. The time has come for institutions to identify the advantages of these paradigms in practice, the reasons why their implementation has been hampered, and either address the concerns or change the paradigms to more practical ones.

Finally, the workbook emphasizes the relevance of using water conflict management frameworks to build trust, improve understanding of common problems and possible alternatives, and encourage collaboration. It is rightly argued that this is essential to move forward and transform conflicts into opportunities for cooperation. Approaches that are more comprehensive and that take into consideration broader aspects of development are needed.

Dr Cecilia Tortajada
Professor in practice
School of Interdisciplinary Studies
University of Glasgow, UK

Preface

The last winter I snowshoed in the high Cascade Mountains of western Oregon was in 1958. I was 19 years old. I spent several days and nights living in a cave I made in a bank of snow at the edge of North Santiam Lake. The snow on the lake's surface was 15 feet deep, and the bank was at least 5 feet deeper. That was 63 years ago. From 1970 to 2019, 11 stations in the snow-telemetry-observation network of Oregon, Washington, and Idaho had decreasing accumulations.

> Analyzing 50 years of data shows snow amounts declined 91% at 11 stations in the Northwest during the fall. Snowfall increased 36% at 7 [stations] during the winter, but decreased 64% again during the spring season. This is a region where accumulated winter snowpack in the mountainous areas is essential to the annual water cycle, as snowmelt supplies freshwater that sustains local watersheds through the drier summer months. A growing share of the West has endured worsening droughts since the beginning of the 20th century, straining water supplies and increasing the risk for wildfires.
>
> . . .
>
> A 2019 study by researchers at Portland State University found that snowfall frequency in the mountainous Northwest declined the most at low- and mid-elevation sites. The study also projected that by the end of the 21st century, many of the sites in the [snow-telemetry-observation] network will experience more precipitation falling as rain than snow.[1,2]

And, it is not just in the northwestern United States. Glaciers are melting all over the world. The Arctic is warming faster than anywhere else on Earth, and Antarctica ice shelves are calving into the ocean. The marine world is changing dramatically, shifting its currents, thereby altering the wind patterns that affect global climate and, consequently, the amount and distribution of rain and snow—the *effect* of which is the amount of water available for human use throughout different parts of the world.[3] These fluctuating changes are not only irreversibly affecting local and regional river basins but also stimulating conflicts among differing social interests and progressively threatening the wellbeing of all generations. In addition to the growing decline of and unpredictability in the amount of available water, the incalculable degradation of water quality through worldwide chemical pollution, among other forms, is accelerating the limitation of good-quality, usable water—increasing the contention over who gets to use what water, how much, and for how long.

The resolution of such a conflict is based on the art of serving people, with disparate points of view, to find enough common ground to ease their fears, sheath their weapons, and listen to one another for their mutual good, which ultimately translates into social-environmental sustainability for all generations. If those in opposition can be helped to understand and move toward the heart of their agreement, the differences entrenched in their quarrel are more easily negotiated. Ultimately, it is necessary for the participants to formulate a shared vision toward which to strive, one that accommodates the personalized perceptions for everyone's long-term benefit.

Only then can the barriers among those concerned be dissolved into mutual respect, acceptance, and potential friendship—only then is a conflict truly resolved.

This workbook examines human activities that strain the planet in terms of demands on land, water, energy, and other resources; climate change that forces people to undertake mass movements in search of better living conditions; and humanity's contributions to extinction of species and degradation of ecosystems. The complexities of these challenges are assessed to bring about more sustainable, effective, and efficient water solutions for an improved ecological and socio-economic future. Given the impacts of climate change and its particular consequences on vulnerable communities, the workbook explores ways in which social difference, political power, and discrimination disproportionately impact nature, as well as women, indigenous peoples of the Americas, and other marginalized communities.

Through a water conflict management framework designed to bolster collaborative skills, the book opens out a *middle way* to build trust and consensus through enhanced understanding, case study analysis, and hands-on application. An overview of the chapters is provided in the Introduction. Business leaders, policy makers, mediators, and other professionals, as well as academics and university students, can benefit greatly from this book.

Chris Maser, Series Editor

NOTES

1. The Case of Shifting Snow. 2020. *Research Brief by Climate Central.* www.climatecentral.org/news/report-the-case-of-the-shifting-snow (accessed March 2, 2021).
2. Catalano, A.J., Loikith, P.C., and Aragon, C.M. 2019. Spatiotemporal Variability of Twenty-First-Century Changes in Site-Specific Snowfall Frequency Over the Northwest United States. *Geophysical Research Letters*, 46 (16):10122–10131.
3. Maser, Chris. 2014. *Interactions of Land, Ocean and Humans: A Global Perspective.* CRC Press, Boca Raton, FL. 308 pp.

About the Editors

Lynette de Silva is Co-director of the Program in Water Conflict Management and Transformation at Oregon State University. She teaches courses in water resources management and transforming water conflicts. She has acted as a consultant to United Nations Educational, Scientific and Cultural Organization (UNESCO), offering training to senior water professionals. Over the past 20 years, she has worked in areas emphasizing water resources and land management practices. In 2019, de Silva co-authored the book titled *Resolving Environmental Conflicts: Principles and Concepts*, third edition, through CRC/Taylor and Francis Publishers.

Chris Maser spent over 25 years as a research scientist in natural history and ecology in forest, shrub steppe, subarctic, desert, coastal, and agricultural settings. He has lived, worked, consulted, and/or lectured in Austria, Canada, Chile, Egypt, France, Germany, Japan, Malaysia, Mexico, Nepal, Slovakia, Switzerland, and various settings in the United States. Today, he is an independent author as well as an international lecturer, facilitator in resolving environmental conflicts, vision statements, and sustainable community development. He is also an international consultant in forest ecology and sustainable forestry practices.

Contributors

Jaclyn Best is a PhD student in the Integrated Coastal Studies program at East Carolina University in North Carolina. She holds a master's degree in water resources management and policy from the University for Peace in Costa Rica, IHE Delft Institute for Water Education in the Netherlands, and Oregon State University, where she conducted research on women's representation and the ways that gender is conceptualized in water governance organizations.

Holly V. Campbell conducts interdisciplinary research and teaches courses bridging environmental and ocean science and policy at Oregon State University.

Cameron La Follette is an independent scholar who researches and writes on Oregon coastal history, Rights of Nature, and sustainability. She lead-authored two books with Chris Maser: *Sustainability and the Rights of Nature: An Introduction* (2017), and *Sustainability and the Rights of Nature in Practice* (2019), both published by Taylor and Francis. She also was the lead author and researcher on the Summer 2018 special issue of *Oregon Historical Quarterly* on the Manila galleon wrecked on the Oregon coast in 1693. She is also executive director of an Oregon coastal conservation organization.

David G. Lewis is a member of the Grand Ronde tribe, a descendant of the Santiam, Chinook, and Takelma peoples of western Oregon. He has a PhD in anthropology from the University of Oregon and is faculty in the anthropology and Ethnic Studies departments at OSU. He currently lives in Salem, Oregon, with his family and researches the colonial histories of the Oregon tribes, writing numerous essays for journals and for his blog The Quartux Journal at ndnhistoryresearch.com

Melissa McCracken is Assistant Professor of international environmental policy. Her research focuses on international water policy and management, cooperation and conflict over shared surface and groundwaters, and conflict transformation surrounding environmental resources, and she teaches courses in water resources management and water security. Prior to joining The Fletcher School at Tufts University, McCracken was a Post-Doctoral Scholar with the Program in Water Conflict Management and Transformation and the Manager of the Transboundary Freshwater Dispute Database housed at Oregon State University.

Liliana Pimentel is PhD Candidate at the Program of Postgraduation in Geography at the Universidade de Brasilia. She teaches courses in Urban Planning and Landscape Architecture at Universidade Paulista. She is a public officer currently working at the Brazilian National Secretariat of Water Security. In the last 30 years, she has worked at different institutions in the private and public sectors in areas such as environmental policy, licensing, environmental assessment, management and conservation, water resources, sanitation, landscape architecture, climate change, infrastructure development, and education. Liliana is a former Humphrey Fellow and a trained mediator and peacebuilder activist volunteering for several organizations.

Josiah J. Shaver earned a BS in Geology from Oregon State University (OSU) in 2019 and is expecting to graduate with a MS in Water Resources Policy & Management from OSU in 2022. He is the visionary founder of a student group called Oregon Climate Change NEXUS: Need for Extreme Unity towards Sustainability. He is also earning a graduate certificate in Water Conflict Management & Transformation from OSU. Shaver is a member of Young Evangelicals for Climate Action and a leader in his local Christian community. He plans to launch a career trajectory focused on collaborative water management.

Jahan Taganova is a development professional working at the intersection of gender, disability, water, and climate change. She holds a master's degree in water resources policy and management from the University for Peace in Costa Rica, IHE Delft Institute for Water Education in the Netherlands, and Oregon State University.

Acknowledgments

Chris, this opportunity to write and work with you, on an interactive approach to water conflict management has been an honor. Your unwavering support and encouragement have inspired me (Lynette) as a writer to take on new tasks with bravery. Thank you.

A big note of gratitude to the following individuals for their chapter contributions to this book: Jaclyn Best, Holly V. Campbell, Cameron La Follette, David G. Lewis, Melissa McCracken, Liliana Pimentel, Josiah J. Shaver, and Jahan Taganova. Please know that your hard work, dedication, patience, and commitment to this endeavor are deeply appreciated. Thank you for believing in what we could do together. It has been a pleasure to work with you!

To all the chapter reviewers, thank you for your suggestions, early reads, professional content assessment, wordsmithing, paragraph reordering, and constructive comments. Because of your generosity of time and resources, the quality of each individual chapter is considerably enhanced. Sami Al-AbdRabbuh, Michael Campana, Evandro Cruz, Jane Darbyshire, Susan Eriksson, Todd Jarvis, David Lewis, Richard Meganck, Mekan Narliyev, Jacob Petersen-Perlman, Silena Pimentel, Janine Salwasser, Greta Smith, Joshua Stutzman, Abby Terris, Blaine Vogt, Aaron T. Wolf, and Annagul Yaryyeva, thank you. And, last but not least, a special thanks to Brook Colley and the Grand Ronde tribe.

I am especially indebted to Lucia De Stefano (Complutense University of Madrid) and Cecilia Tortajada (University of Glasgow), who both agreed to edit the entire book, at short notice. Thank you, sincerely. Your guidance and critical review benefit not only this book, but also me (Lynette), immensely. Thank you for your graciousness, professionalism, and expertise. Lucia De Stefano, I am immensely grateful for your detailed and constructive comments. I look forward to more authentic bouillabaisse with you! A special acknowledgment to Cecilia Tortajada for an outstanding Foreword. It warms my heart, thank you.

Julie Donovan, your friendship and professional opinion means the world to me. Special thanks for your willingness to take a look at the combined chapters.

Dear Mark Giordano and Scott Jones, please know I am most appreciative of the outstanding back-cover blurbs you both provided. From Oregon State University, I express thanks to Nancy Steinberg for her editorial suggestions and guidance, and to David E. Reinert for assistance with re-drafting maps and imagery. Additional gratitude, to the Transboundary Freshwater Dispute Database team, and to Aaron Wolf, as ever, for your mentorship and support.

To my parents, Gwendoline and Cyril Oscar Lucas, and my brother, Kwesi, thank you for your unconditional love and acceptance. To my husband and mate, Shanaka de Silva, and daughter, Chiara, I relish in your love and humor.

Finally, special thanks to Irma Britton who suggested we write this workbook. And, to Shannon Welch and Rebecca Pringle for their editorial assistance and to the entire CRC Publishing team.

Lynette, I am deeply grateful to you for accepting my request—a total stranger when we first met—to join me as a coauthor in the 3rd edition of *Resolving Environmental Conflict: Principle and Concepts*. Because of your knowledge concerning the management of water conflicts and the way you presented it, this workbook came into being. Working with you has been a pure joy, in addition to which you have greatly expanded my knowledge. Thank you.

Irma, working with you and the entire CRC team these past 12 years, continues to be one of the highlights of my life. Because of you, and CRC, this workbook has been made available for the benefit of all generations—present and future.

With respect to you, authors and reviewers, who have helped to make this book possible, "Thank you for your commitment, time, and expertise," which you have cast into the ethers of time as an unconditional gift of social-environmental sustainability for all life and its generations into the unforeseeable future. On behalf of those generations who cannot yet speak, I say, "Thank you."

And, finally, it is with deep gratitude and love for her understanding and patience while I worked on this book that I thank my wife, Zane.

Respectfully, Lynette and Chris.

Introduction

Lynette de Silva

CONTENTS

Water: The Irreplaceable Resource 1
   A River and Its Tributaries 3
   The Geopolitics of Water 3
   The Challenges of a Rapidly Changing Climate 6
The Book's Structure 7
Notes 9

WATER: THE IRREPLACEABLE RESOURCE

Apart from air, which humans cannot live without for more than a few minutes, there is no resource that meets or matches water's life-supporting and sustaining properties. For this reason, Aulenbach considers water "our second most important natural resource."[1] It sustains all life, our socio-ecological functions and services, and Earth systems. It is a primary ingredient for industrial and energy production, as well as being critical to the development of other resources.[2] And, unlike other resources—such as some forests that can be renewed; and minerals, such as bauxite and copper, that once utilized will not return in our lifetime—Earth's supply of water is regarded as fixed. It is a foundation resource. As a result, humans move in tandem with it; relentlessly tracing its movement by drilling through Earth's subsurface to saturated zones; fetching it on foot for miles per day; using vertical meshes to harvest fog; stimulating precipitation from clouds; engineering reservoirs and conduits; and praying and dancing for rain.

The flow of this vital resource is a cyclical process from oceans, to the atmosphere as water vapor; to the land as rain, snow, or ice; and back again to the oceans. The hydrologic cycle has been continual since oceans formed almost 4 billion years ago.[3] Since then, the quantity of water circulating through Earth's system has been approximately 332.5 million cubic miles (mi^3) or 1,386 million cubic kilometers (km^3). It is essentially the same water that quenched the thirst of dinosaurs during the Triassic Period and that coursed through the tributaries of China's Huang He (Yellow River) in 1100 BC, and was enjoyed within the Manden Kurufaba (Mali Empire) in the 14th Century.

Of Earth's water distribution, humans depend on freshwater in lakes, rivers, and wetlands, which accounts for 0.01 percent, as well as fresh groundwater, which amounts to 0.76 percent, while total groundwater (fresh and saline) is estimated at 1.7 percent. More challenging for humans to acquire is freshwater trapped in icecaps and glaciers. In total, ice and snow, which also includes ground ice and permafrost,

DOI: 10.1201/9781003032533-1

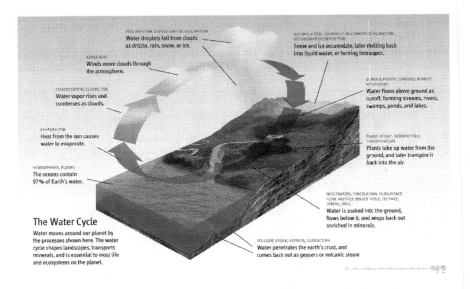

FIGURE 0.1 Diagram of the water cycle, showing how water is stored and transported across the planet.

Source: (Ehud Tal, Wikimedia, 2016).

accounts for 1.76 percent. Other freshwater reserves include soil moisture (0.001 percent) and atmospheric water (0.001 percent). However, the bulk of the planet's water (96.5 percent) is oceanic. These saltwater bodies are of particular significance because lifeforms first originated in them.[4]

Water in the sea comes from rivers and lakes, groundwater, glaciers, and the atmosphere. Conversely, the only pathway from oceans is through the atmosphere via evaporation, which involves both solar energy converting seawater into vapor and winds that distribute it worldwide. This oceanic evaporation is facilitated by the fact that the world's oceans cover more than 70 percent of Earth's surface (Figure 0.1).

Whereas land-based evaporation and evapotranspiration (water vapor from plants) both contribute to atmospheric moisture, evaporation from the world's oceans exceeds both. Nevertheless, the combination of evaporation and evapotranspiration forms clouds that become precipitation (snow, hail, sleet, or rain) when atmospheric temperatures cool. Some precipitation contributes to glaciers; snow-capped mountains; lakes and rivers, as it flows to oceans; and/or soil moisture on the ground that often connects to groundwater flowing to oceans.[5] This process is important because freshwater is renewable only by precipitation.[6]

Oceans help moderate global climate, absorbing solar energy and redistributing heat from the equator toward the poles. Both the sun and gravity play a major role in the water cycle: the sun by helping with the vertical movement of water into the atmosphere and gravity in driving the water cycle. As such, the ocean is credited with providing a continual supply of water throughout the global ecosystem.

The complexity of this moving resource, as it relates to ecosystem dynamics, sustainability, and the availability of freshwater, has led to the measurements and various scales of observation, to determine the timing of water inputs, outputs, and storage.

A River and Its Tributaries

Water storage, pathways, and rates of movement can be studied on the surface of the ocean, a wetland, glacier, in a garden, or on an outdoor table; in fact, any regional area in which quantities of water arrive, accumulate, and/or leave over a given timeframe can be measured. However, a network of rivers and their tributaries, bounded by higher topography, typically make a distinct unit (a river basin) wherein to study the water cycle over varying time intervals. Topographic boundaries, such as mountain ridges, form a natural divide between river basins because they contain and connect all the water reservoirs (glaciers, biomass, soil moisture, streams and lakes, and oceans) via pathways (infiltration, snowmelt, and overland flow) across a particular landscape, with just a few pathways capable of extending beyond the boundaries (such as precipitation and evaporation).

This level of interconnectivity means that within these natural boundaries, a biophysical ecosystem (fungi, plants, animals, and humans) shares the same water, ecosystem services (food and oxygen production), and river basin dynamics. Much of this basin-related water flow (including its connectivity with groundwater) is governed by long-term weather patterns, Earth's physical structure and processes, soil, vegetation, both natural and human-made physical features, and human activities. These variables make each basin unique. However, when there is similarity among basins in size and stream characteristics, along with the aforementioned variables, basin waters are more likely to behave in a similar manner.

Human activities also influence basin dynamics, among the most unnerving ways include when hazardous waste spills occur from industrial facilities in the upstream reaches of a basin, detrimentally impacting the ecosystem, especially water quality downstream. Even planned structures, such as the placement of dams and reservoirs, can influence aquatic passage by cutting off spawning grounds to anadromous fish; altering water chemistry and temperature; and changing culturally specific ways of life for dislocated riparian communities. This kind of interconnectivity means that any changes in the basin, "like revitalizing a wetland, building a factory, or flushing pharmaceutical drugs into the toilet, will either positively or negatively impact the capacity for a river-basin system to be resilient, sustainable, and healthy."[7]

The Geopolitics of Water

If the movement of water is not complicated enough, water crossing political boundaries adds another layer of complexity—geopolitics. This complexity arises because estate-, city-, county-, and nation-building requires sustainable access to water, but these invisible property lines and country borders do not restrict the passage of water. As a result, there is often a tendency to want to control water flow, because without a dependable water supply, ecosystems and human populations cannot thrive. This is true at every spatial scale. However, controlling the ownership and movement of water can be counter to a shared approach.

A more integrated mechanism to water management, not limited to territorial boundaries, is to focus on the hydrological unit, at the river-basin scale. This allows for planning and policies defined by the physical attributes of the basin; resource-driven requirements of the ecosystem and humans, as well as the political conditions of the region. In the best of circumstances, such planning and policies must provide resources in an institutionally equitable manner among hierarchical agencies; with broad stakeholder input; employing reliable scientific findings relevant to the specific topic; economic considerations that reflect societal attitudes and modest risk; and sufficient political will to provide inter-governmental directives, process, financial support, and partnerships, along with measurable outcomes and standards.[8]

While an integrated, basin-wide approach to water resource management has its foundation in centuries-old planning processes, it is regarded as a "relatively recent approach to water resources planning."[9] Spain makes for a good case study, since it has implemented river basin management, and adaptation of integrated water resources management is underway.[10] Nonetheless, "management is based on the assumption that today's decisions have future consequences;"[11] as such integrated water resources management is thought to provide a comprehensive view of the basin-scale hydrologic system beyond incrementalism and short-term planning.[12]

Integrated water resources management is established in a holistic approach to environmental management, incorporating both the human and the natural world for long-term sustainable and equitably effective conditions. It is a process wherein water is considered in terms of its cyclical storage reservoirs and pathways; its quality, quantity, and natural ebb and flow; its critical environmental and natural resource aspects; with consideration given to different stretches of the river system,[13] while simultaneously incorporating the political concerns of stakeholders.

While sound in concept, the U.S. National Research Council states that combining an understanding of basin dynamics with the benefits provided by integrated water management is challenging to actualize.[14] Despite this, as early as the 1920s, Spain was adapting to a river-basin approach to water management[15]—though they are still working toward an integrated approach. Early adaptive management was also employed by the Ruhr River Association in Germany and the UK River Basin Authorities.[16]

In 1933, the U.S. established a regional, multipurpose water entity, the Tennessee Valley Authority, which is considered both federal and public. It is a regional agency and a federal corporation based on the Tennessee River Basin system[17]—creating infrastructure for flood management, energy, environmental services, and irrigation, in addition to navigation and industry along the Tennessee River. Regarded as having "a high level of formal authority: in a sense, it is one of the most integrated and powerful examples of what today we call integrated water resources management."[18] However, duplication of the Tennessee Valley Authority, in other parts of the U.S., has not been realized. Nevertheless, as a river basin organization, it provides a basin-wide approach that seems less likely to be restricted by legal and political demarcations. Over a generation after its establishment, the basin showed noticeable gains; though to be clear, not all growth can solely be attributed to the presence of a river

Introduction

basin authority. Among the gains are improved health and life expectancy of the basin's residents, greater personal literacy, greater percentages of homes with access to water, lower percentages of flood damage, and higher industrial production and commerce.[19] But, there were notable losses, among them the over 3,000 families in eastern Tennessee who were displaced, losing their homes in the process.

The United States Geological Survey tends to classify river basins by grouping some and subdividing others for *convenience*, forming a hierarchical system of nested hydrologic units. As a result, hydrologic-unit codes do not always represent discrete basins. Within the U.S., over 20 states have adopted a statewide basin approach. And, since 1996, the U.S. Environmental Protection Agency has a visionary Watershed Approach Framework for the country (see Chapter 3 for additional details; in this book, the term "river basin" and "watershed" will be used interchangeably).

The river basin approach has energized other nations, notably Indonesia and Jordan, to implement this mechanism. New Zealand has also established basin-wide environmental policies at the national level, through legislation of the 1991 Resource Management Act. And in the European Union, the 2000 Water Framework Directive emphasizes water management by river basin.

At the international level, actualizing water cooperation among nations becomes even more critical when considering that two out of five people in the world live in a river basin shared by two or more countries (Figure 0.2). For example, as many as

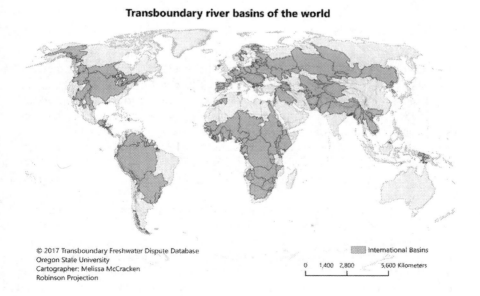

FIGURE 0.2 A map of the world's transboundary river basins.

Source: (Transboundary Freshwater Dispute Database, 2017. Product of the Transboundary Freshwater Dispute Database, College of Earth, Ocean, and Atmospheric Sciences, Oregon State University. Additional information about the TFDD can be found at: http://transboundarywaters.science.oregonstate.edu).

5 countries share the La Plata River Basin (South America); 6 countries share the Ganges-Brahmaputra-Meghna Basin (Asia); 9 countries comprise the Rhine River Basin (Europe); and 11 countries are part of the Congo River Basin (Africa).[20] And, within North America, the Red River of the North is made up of the Province of Manitoba (Canada), as well as Minnesota and North Dakota (United States). Sharing international transboundary waters becomes even more challenging with the increasing numbers of human inhabitants worldwide.

As the human population mushrooms, accessibility to readily available water is running out,[21] requiring greater deliberation to access other water storages. The United Nations projects there will be close to 9 billion humans by 2037,[22] and approximately 11 billion by the end of the century.[23] This increased demand for water stresses the global environment and places greater demands on food productivity (fishing, hunting, and farming); energy supplies (nuclear, wind, hydro, and logging and the burning of fossil fuels), and construction (housing and municipal infrastructure). Such growth in population will necessitate more of Earth's productive capacity than Earth can replenish in the time required.[24]

In this sense, humans are impoverishing Earth, while simultaneously jeopardizing the planet's ability to sustain our own existence. This dichotomy places the actions of *Homo sapiens* at odds with the planet's biophysical principles (the laws that govern biology and physics of Earth's systems), resulting in the soaring population of humans, while other species, such as whales, wolves, spotted owls, and salmon, diminish in population at an alarming rate.[25]

THE CHALLENGES OF A RAPIDLY CHANGING CLIMATE

An additional complexity is our rapidly changing climate. The Intergovernmental Panel on Climate Change projects that, within the 21st Century, climate change will exacerbate weather and climate events.[26] This will impact the water-resources sector in that the projected increase in the number of warmer days and nights will result in less available snowmelt as a usable source of water during the summer. With increased frequency of warmer temperatures, there is greater demand for water by humans for domestic, municipal, agricultural, and productive needs—heightening the chances of forest fires and impacting mountain tourism. Heat stress reduces land productivity and can result in crop failure, causing food shortages, hunger, and malnutrition.

At the other extreme, areas susceptible to heavy precipitation and flooding have greater likelihood of experiencing it with increased frequency, in more veracious ways. Flooding can impact the quality of both groundwater and surface water, which, in turn, can be detrimental to wildlife, the ecosystem, and human health. Beyond polluted waters, flooding can also cause loss of life and damage property and infrastructure, thereby resulting in forced migrations. It also ruins crops and can cause soil erosion. In short, there can be far-reaching, projected impacts that extend beyond the water-resources sector into all aspects of life: ecosystem services, agriculture, forestry, open-range livestock grazing, ocean fisheries, human health, and industry.

Ultimately, our social-environmental practices are impacting Earth's biophysical systems. This leaves us wondering how to resolve the strain between human actions and the biophysical integrity of Earth, to bring about more socially and environmentally sustainable ways of existing in harmony with the planet. Through this book, the authors will shed light on case studies and ways of raising our level of consciousness with respect to the decisions we make and their long-term, irreversible consequences.

THE BOOK'S STRUCTURE

Everything that exists, whether an object or living being, has its own inherent potential.[27] Therefore, everything has intrinsic value solely through its existence, regardless of how we humans perceive it. However, we see ourselves as the arbitrators of what that value is. We may describe it through beauty, comfort, joy, security, fulfilling our basic needs, or offering economic returns; nevertheless, its perceived value is based on our various cultural judgments.

Often, the measure by which we assess nature and other humans is so deeply entrenched in the fabric of our society that we do not realize the foundations of our thoughts may be socially conditioned. This means that our individual and collective thinking is based on false premises that unconsciously (and sometimes consciously) are taken as truths. And, with every additional thought, we may perpetuate—even contribute—to more falsehoods, further deluding our individual self and humankind. Examples of this play out when we answer such questions as:

1. "Is ours the only species fairly able to claim air, water, territory, and other necessities of life?"[28]
2. "Whose goals and purposes on Earth count most, and in particular, whose water use matters?"
3. "Who should decide water allocation?"

Our responses to such questions may reveal biases, because some of us depend on objects and living beings to show us what value they offer. Should this be the prerequisite? Even when a perceived value is intrinsic or extrinsic, we may not see it, because, as judges, our understanding depends on our awareness. For example, while economics is wholly extrinsic in its valuation, Nature is wholly intrinsic in its functional existence. This dichotomy is not restricted to relationships between humans and nature. It can equally apply to men (dominant) and women (subordinate), slave owners (entitled) and captives (substandard), industrialized nation (developed—civilized) and the non-industrial nations (underdeveloped, uncivilized), and among white (superior) and non-white peoples (inferior). So, our socially conditioned perspective shapes how we treat each other and water.[29]

This book explores these very principles of shared and coveted waters, recognizing water as a resource on the move, vital to life, ecosystem services, and the running of Earth's biophysical systems, with its distribution often shaped by social values and geopolitics. Through the utilization and application of dispute resolution tools and practices, conflict management frameworks, and traditional indigenous knowledge, the authors explore constructive avenues to healthier social-environmental outcomes.

Following this introduction, Chapter 1 characterizes the impact and result of a choice, indicating that a decision can have rippling effects across wide expanses and into the future. Illustrated is the reality that *not* choosing is still a choice. Emphasized are rules to consider in decision making, with the High Aswan Dam exemplified as a primary example.

Chapter 2 introduces different types of water conflict and their causes. Conflict resolution and transformation are described as remedies for environmental disharmony. A water conflict framework is introduced, along with tools and techniques to reinforce helpful, interest-based connections.

Chapters 3 and 4 are about the governance and management of water, with each chapter providing case studies. Chapter 3 is an overview of water management in the United States (U.S.) and the most widely recognized causes for strife. Described is the watershed approach. Highlighted is the need for constant improvement of the watershed approach in order to balance water quality, accessibility, wellbeing, and equity within and across communities and sectors. Chapter 4 provides a comparison between water management in the U.S. and Brazil. The case studies provide realities of how institutional structures of governance perform and respond to water conflicts, opening the opportunity to consider other viable procedures to manage contentious waters.

Chapters 5–8 cover disenfranchisement and processes to fairness. Chapter 5 focusses on the rights of nature and how humans treat the environment. Examples are from river systems in New Zealand and Pennsylvania (U.S). The reader is challenged to think of the river as a living entity capable of relationship. Chapter 6 is about conflicts surrounding intertribal fishing and federal barriers in Oregon (U.S). Provided are historical context and contemporary water issues and perspectives. Readers also learn about tribal traditions toward reconciliation. Chapter 7 is about women and their roles in water management. Case studies are from Oregon and the Ferghana Valley in Central Asia. These examples provide contemplation toward a gendered approach to water transformation. Chapter 8 is about two distinct water conflicts experienced in African-American society: one in the Pacific Northwest and the other in the Midwest, U.S. Conflict analysis tools are applied to these cases to provide alternative paths for future scenarios.

Chapter 9 combines two approaches to assess the global water crisis: the concept of sustainable development, through the Sustainable Development Goal (SDG) Framework; and a water conflict framework. This is done using Uganda and its transboundary river basins and aquifers, as a case study.

Chapter 10 is about faith-based practices and how they offer conflict resolution and transformation in the way of technique and tools. The reader also gains perspective as to how this may align with the Water Conflict Transformation Framework.

Finally, the concluding chapter encapsulates the essence of the book and provides parting words.

Introduction

NOTES

1. Aulenbach, Donald B. 1968. Water—Our Second Most Important Natural Resource. *Boston College Law Review*, 9(3):535–552.
2. Brown, Peter G., and Jeremy Schmidt, editors. 2010. *Water Ethics: Foundational Readings for Students and Professionals*. Island Press, Washington, DC. 320 pp.
3. Nutman, Allen P. 2006. Antiquity of the Oceans and Continents. *Elements*, 2(4):223–227. Mineralogical Association of Canada.
4. Shiklomanov, Igor. 1993. World Fresh Water Resources. In Peter H. Gleick (editor), *Water in Crisis: A Guide to the World's Fresh Water Resources*. Oxford University Press, New York.
5. Maser, Chris. 2014. *Interactions of Land, Ocean and Humans: A Global Perspective*. CRC Press, Boca Raton, FL. 308 pp.
6. Barlow, Maude, and Tony Clarke. 2002. *Blue Gold: The Fight to Stop the Corporate Theft of the World's Water*. The New Press, New York, NY. 304 pp.
7. Maser, Chris, and Lynette de Silva. 2019. *Resolving Environmental Conflicts: Principles and Concepts*. 3rd ed. CRC Taylor and Francis Group, LLC, Boca Raton, FL. 234 pp.
8. National Research Council. 1999. *New Strategies for America's Watersheds*. National Academies Press, Washington, DC. 333 pp.
9. Dzurik, Andrew Albert. 2003. *Water Resources Planning*. 3rd ed. Rowman & Littlefield, Totowa, NJ. p. 102.
10. Brown, Peter G., and Jeremy Schmidt, editors. *Water Ethics: Foundational Readings for Students and Professionals. Op. cit.*, p. 8.
11. Dzurik, Andrew Albert. 2003. *Water Resources Planning*. 3rd ed. *Op. cit.*, p. 83.
12. Ibid.
13. Ibid.
14. National Research Council. *New Strategies for America's Watersheds. Op. cit.*
15. Brown, Peter G., and Jeremy Schmidt, editors. *Water Ethics: Foundational Readings for Students and Professionals. Op. cit*
16. Allouche, Jeremy. 2016. The Birth and Spread of IWRM—A Case Study of Global Policy Diffusion and Translation. *Water Alternatives*, 9(3):412–433.
17. Priscoli, Jerome Delli, and Aaron T. Wolf. 2009. *Managing and Transforming Water Conflicts*. Cambridge University Press, Cambridge. 354 pp.
18. Ibid., p. 141.
19. Ibid.
20. Wolf, Aaron T., Annika Kramer, Alexander Carius, and Geoffrey D. Dabelko. 2005. Managing Water Conflict and Cooperation. In *State of the World 2005: Redefining Global Security*. W. W. Norton & Company, New York. pp. 80–95.
21. Priscoli, Jerome Delli, and Aaron T. Wolf. *Managing and Transforming Water Conflicts. Op. cit.*
22. The World Bank. 2020. *Total Population*. https://data.worldbank.org/indicator/SP.POP.TOTL (accessed July 21, 2020).
23. Rosling, Hans. 2010. Global Population Growth, Box by Box. *TED* (Technology, Entertainment and Design converged), June. www.youtube.com/watch?v=fTznEIZRkLg (accessed July 15, 2020).
24. Carroll, Sean B. 2017. *The Serengeti Rules: The Quest to Discover How Life Works and Why It Matters*. Princeton University Press, Princeton. 280 pp.
25. Brown, Peter G., and Jeremy Schmidt, editors. *Water Ethics: Foundational Readings for Students and Professionals. Op. cit.*

26 Intergovernmental Panel on Climate Change. 2007. Climate Change 2007: Synthesis Report. *Contribution of Working Groups I, II and III to the Fourth Assessment Report of the Intergovernmental Panel on Climate Change.* IPCC, Geneva, Switzerland. www.ipcc.ch/report/ar4/syr/ (accessed July 1, 2020).
27 Rolston, Holmes. 1993. Value in Nature and the Nature of Value. In Robin Attfield and Andrew Belsey (editors), *Philosophy and the Natural Environment*, Royal Institute of Philosophy Supplement, Series Number 36. Cambridge University Press, Cambridge, pp. 13–30.
28 Brown, Peter G. 2004. Are There Any Natural Resources? *Politics and the Life Sciences*, 23(1):12–21. BioOne.
29 Gaard, Greta. 2001. Women, Water, Energy: An Ecofeminist Approach. *Organization & Environment*, 14(2):157–172.

1 The Consequence of a Decision and the Case of the Aswan High Dam

Chris Maser

CONTENTS

The Inviolable Rules of Decision Making 12
    Rule 1—Everything Is a Relationship 13
        Intra-personal 13
        Inter-personal 13
        Between People and the Environment 14
        Between People in the Present and Those of the Future 15
    Rule 2—All Relationships Are All Inclusive and Productive of an Outcome 16
    Rule 3—The Only True Investment Is Energy from Sunlight 17
    Rule 4—All Relationships Involve a Transfer of Energy 17
    Rule 5—All Systems Are Based on Composition, Structure, and Function 18
    Rule 6—All Relationships Have One or More Trade-offs 18
    Rule 7—All Systems Have Cumulative Effects, Lag Periods, and Thresholds 18
    Rule 8—Change Is an Irreversible Process of Eternal Becoming 19
    Rule 9—Systemic Change Is Based on Self-Organized Criticality 20
    Rule 10—Dynamic Disequilibrium Rules All Systems 22
    Rule 11—Success or Failure Lies in the Interpretation of an Event ... 23
    Rule 12—People Must Be Equally Informed If They Are to Function as a Truly Democratic Society 23
    Rule 13—We Must Consciously Limit Our "Wants" 24
    Rule 14—Simplicity Is the Key to Contentment, Adaptability, and Survival 25
    Rule 15—Nature, Environmental/Cultural Wisdom, and Human Well-Being Are Paramount 25
    Rule 16—Every Legal Citizen Deserves the Right to Vote 26
    Rule 17—This Present Moment, the Here and Now, Is All We Ever Have 26
The Aswan High Dam—A Case Study Illustrating the Irreversible Consequences of a Single Decision 27
Conclusion 29

DOI: 10.1201/9781003032533-2

Questions..30
Notes 30

> No person, institution, or nation has the right to . . . contribute to irreversible changes of the Earth's biogeochemical cycles or undermine the integrity . . . of the Earth's ecologies—the consequences of which . . . [pass to] succeeding generations as an irrevocable form of remote tyranny.
>
> —David Orr[1]

Are we deluding ourselves about the availability of clean water? Our earthly survival, and that of our children, their children, and all generations, ultimately depends on clean water. Water is an interactive thread connecting air, soil, biodiversity, human population density, sunlight, and climate. (Biodiversity refers to the variety of living species and their biophysical functions and processes.) Think of this interconnectedness as the "waterbed principle," which simply demonstrates that you cannot touch any part of a filled waterbed without simultaneously affecting the whole of it.

In other words, the magnitude of a decision's outcome is based either on the relative sustainability of its biophysical consequences or on the contrived political/economic promises. Either way, it is the compounding effect of a decision's multifaceted outcome that we bestow on all generations—present and future.

Yet, with our myriad data points and statistics, economists and politicians are subjected to accessing the complexities of air, soil, water, sunlight, biodiversity, and climate through economic equations and models and, to a large extent, through planning models.[2] Often, lost in this process are intangibles and ecological variables—including air, soil, water, sunlight, biodiversity, and climate, which are more challenging to convert into economic externalities. Their omission results in unforeseen biophysical consequences. Unless required by law, biodiversity is discounted when its consideration interferes with monetary profits.[3]

THE INVIOLABLE RULES OF DECISION MAKING

With the foregoing in mind, it is critical to understand that just as there are inviolable biophysical principles that govern nature and the universe, so there are inviolable rules of decision making; for example, change is a constant, irreversible process with ever-novel outcomes. Here the term *inviolable* means that, if one circumvents the biophysical principles and rules of decision making, all future life forms will bear the irreversible consequences. To put it plainly, there are no problems in the world or the universe outside our own thinking, which prompted Winston Churchill to say:

> When the situation was manageable it was neglected, and now that it is thoroughly out of hand we apply too late the remedies which then might have effected a cure. There is nothing new in the story. . . . It falls into that long, dismal catalogue of the fruitlessness of experience and the confirmed unteachability of mankind.
>
> Want of foresight, unwillingness to act when action would be simple and effective, lack of clear thinking, confusion of counsel until the emergency comes, until self-preservation strikes its jarring gong—these are the features which constitute the endless repetition of history.[4]

This quotation is part of Winston Churchill's speech to the British Parliament in 1935, as he saw with clear foreboding the onrushing threat of Nazi Germany.

Rule 1—Everything Is a Relationship

From a decision-making perspective, there are four basic relationships that must be consciously accounted for because they are interactive in space through time: (1) intra-personal, (2) inter-personal, (3) between people and the environment, and (4) between people in the present and those of the future.

Intra-personal

An *intra-personal* relationship is an individual's inner sense of self-worth, personal growth, authenticity, and so on. In short, it is the degree of psychological maturity that makes a person conscious of and accountable for his or her own behavior and its consequences. The more conscious we are, the more other-centered we are, the more self-controlled our behavior, and the greater our willingness to be personally accountable for the outcomes of our behavior with respect to the welfare of fellow citizens, present and future, and Earth as a whole.

Each decision is a fork in the road of life; each presents at least two choices—right-hand fork or left-hand fork. Whichever fork we choose determines what we get, whereas everything encompassed in the fork not taken is foregone. In this sense, the direction of our lives is determined by cumulative results of many little decisions. Some are remembered, but most are not because they were made unconsciously. We tend to remember the "big decisions," while seldom realizing that a single, big decision is merely the sum of the many little decisions made along the way. We give just a little here and again a little there, and eventually we have pointed ourselves in a new direction.

Therefore, taking personal responsibility for our thoughts, words, and deeds reflects both our self-respect and the quality of care we give ourselves, becoming a critical first step toward social-environmental sustainability. Extending this to others provides a heightened level of sustainability within a community, as measured by how people treat one another and protect nature and the global commons—such as clean water, clean air, and fertile soil—as everyone's birthright.[5]

Inter-personal

Not enough can be said for civility, respect, and hospitality toward other people. If we use these basic human behaviors to frame our decision making, we can focus more on the mutual values that bind us and less on the dividing tensions between our beliefs and attitudes.

While we always have a choice, we must choose—in that we have no choice. We are not, therefore, the victim of our circumstances but rather the consequential product of our choices and decisions. And the more we are able to choose love and peace over fear and violence, the more we gain in wisdom and the more we live in harmony and social-environmental sustainability. This is true because what we choose to think about determines how we choose to act, and our thoughts and actions set up self-reinforcing feedback loops—or self-fulfilling prophecies, as it were—that become our individual and collective material realities.

It is just such self-reinforcing-behavioral feedback loops based on competition for money through the exploitation of resources—often including one another—that are destroying our environment and thus our society. As long as competition is the overriding principle of our social-economic system, we can only destroy our supportive environment because it has become the commercial battlefield in which the material war is fought. Our *overemphasis* on rivalry in nearly everything fosters insecurity that manifests as greed, which is just the fear of not having enough to feel personally secure—and thus is the cause of conflicts.

Our obsession with having to be "right" at the expense of someone else having to be "wrong" brings forth another human tendency—defending a point of view when faced with a perceived threat to our sense of material survival. There are, however, as many points of view as there are people, and each person is indeed right from his or her vantage point. Therefore, no resolution is possible when people are committed only to winning agreement with their respective intellectual positions.

Setting aside egos and accepting points of view as negotiable differences, while striving for the common good over the longer term, are necessary for teamwork. Unyielding self-centeredness represents a narrowness of thinking that prevents cooperation, coordination, collaboration, possibility thinking, and the resolution of issues. Teamwork demands the utmost personal discipline of a true democracy, which is the common denominator for lasting success in any social endeavor.

But, even if we exercise personal discipline in dealing with current social-environmental problems, most of us have become so far removed from the land that sustains us that we no longer appreciate it as the embodiment of continuous processes and self-reinforcing, social-biophysical feedback loops. Attention is focused instead on a chosen product and its conversion potential to monetary profit, and anything diverted to a different outcome is considered a challenge to the economic bottom line. It is time, therefore, to reevaluate the nature of decision making, how it can be sustainably integrated into the common future that lies ahead—generation after generation.[6]

Between People and the Environment

Sustainability means that development programs must, to the extent possible, integrate the local people's requirements, desires, motivations, and identity in relation to the surrounding landscape. It also means that local people, those responsible for development initiatives and their effect on the immediate environment and the surrounding landscape design, must participate equally and fully in all debates and discussions, from the local level to the national. Here, a basic principle is that programs must be founded on local requirements and cultural values *in balance* with those of the broader outside world, which includes understanding environmental issues, long-term ecological trends, and their social-environmental ramifications—all the while honoring the limitations of nature's inviolable biophysical principles[7] and their counterpart, inviolable rules of decision making.[8] After all, social-environmental sustainability is a reciprocal relationship between people and the land. As we nurture the land, we nurture ourselves. As we abuse the land, we abuse ourselves and threaten the future of all generations, beginning with ours.

Short-term trends must be viewed in relation to long-term trends, and long-term trends in relation to even longer-term trends. The more we trace the present into the past, the better we understand the present. The more we project the present into the future, the humbler we need to be in our notion that we understand the present. Knowledge of the past tells us what the present is built on and what the future may be projected on. But this is true *only* if we accept past and present as a cumulative collection of our understanding of a few finite points along an infinite continuum—the trends that may, and likely do, point to the future.

Failing to account for a community's long-term supply of water in the face of short-term dollars to be made by a few people is dangerous because changes in the spatial patterns of land use, which grossly alter habitats through time, may well be crucial to understanding the dynamics of landscape design and will have implications for many biophysical processes. Changes in landscape patterns also relate to the flow of materials and energy, such as the processes of erosion, the movement of water and sediments, and the trapping of heat by urban areas as heat islands.

Beyond this, the power of sustainable development comes from the local people as they move forward through a process of growing self-realization, self-definition, self-determination, and the evolution of their consciousness in decision making. Such personal growth opens the community to its own evolution within the context of the people's sense of place, as opposed to coercive pressures applied from the outside.

Sustainable development encompasses any process that helps people meet their requirements, from self-worth to food on the table, simultaneously creating a more biophysically and culturally sustainable and just society for the current generation *and* those that follow. Due to its flexibility and openness, sustainable community development is perhaps more capable than other forms of development of creating such outcomes because it integrates the requirements of a local community with those of the immediate environment and surrounding landscape, as well as neighboring communities.[9]

Between People in the Present and Those of the Future

As a global citizen, consider the question of human consciousness: Do those living today owe anything to the future? If the answer is "Yes," then we must determine what and how much we owe because our present, *non-sustainable* course is rapidly destroying the environmental options for all generations to come. Meeting the acknowledged obligation will require a renewed sense of consciousness—to be other-centered in caring for the welfare of those to come, as we wish vastly more of those before us had considered our welfare as an outcome of their environmental decisions and actions.[10]

To change anything, we must reach beyond where we are, beyond where we feel safe. We must dare to move ahead, even if we do not fully understand where we are going, because we will never have perfect knowledge. We must ask innovative, other-centered, future-oriented questions to make necessary changes for a higher level of social-environmental consciousness.

True progress toward an ecologically sound environment and an equitable world society will be expensive in both money and effort. The longer we wait, however, the more unlikely success becomes, as the environmental condition continues to deteriorate, and the more expensive, difficult, and improbable become the necessary social changes—until the situation becomes so dire it is "do or die."

FIGURE 1.1 Portrait of a laughing girl and a smiling boy in Don Som (Si Phan Don), Laos. (Photograph by Basile Morin. *Source*: https://commons.wikimedia.org/wiki/File:Laughing_girl_and_smiling_boy_in_Laos.jpg).

No biological shortcuts, technological quick fixes, or political promises can mend what is increasingly broken. Dramatic, fundamental change—frightening, painful, and increasingly expensive—is necessary if we are really committed to the world's children, present and future (Figure 1.1). It is not a physical question of whether we can change, but rather one of whether we will choose to change *and do so*. Whatever our decisions, we, the adults of the world, pass on to our successors the consequences of those decisions and their resultant actions for which *we are all responsible, whether we consciously choose to participate or not*.[11]

Rule 2—All Relationships Are All Inclusive and Productive of an Outcome

Clearly, all relationships are productive simply because they produce an outcome of some sort. The challenge for humanity, and thus its decision making, is what kind of outcome will result. Every functional part of a government, from communities to nations, is influenced by how every other part of the government functions—the waterbed principle.

Remembering—dredging the recesses of memory for things long forgotten—and the development of things new is an ongoing process of multidimensional learning. Such learning encompasses both theoretical and practical conceptualization, decision making, action, and the deeper aspects of reflection—including the intellect, intuition (spirituality), and imagination. Multidimensional learning is important because overemphasis on achievement—one part of which is competition—simply reinforces fixation on short-term, quantifiable results. Our overemphasis on success can preclude reflection, a persistent practice of deeper learning that can produce wiser decisions and thus far better outcomes over time. That said, many of today's problems resulted from yesterday's solutions, and many of today's solutions are destined to become tomorrow's problems because we too frequently insist on little, *symptomatic* approaches that yield *immediate* results without regard for what happens to productive sustainability of the social-environmental system itself.

For a different outcome, a different approach is needed—one that offers a *systemic* understanding and ideas that promote and safeguard social-environmental sustainability. At the same time, we must understand that any "fix" is only as good as the integrity of its biophysical foundation and must be subject to alteration based on experience and new knowledge.

When people speak from and listen with their hearts (by having open and honest communication), they are more likely to unite and produce tremendous power to formulate new realities and bring them into being through collective decisions and actions. Focusing on special interests leaves many unresolved biophysical necessities to be addressed for the continued productivity of global ecosystems. After all, social-environmental sustainability is only a choice—our choice, but one that must be carefully and humbly planned if it is to endure the ongoing, shortsighted, contradicting political vagaries of human decisions and actions.

To protect the best of what we have in the present—for the present *and* the future—we must continually adjust our thinking and behavior to accommodate new circumstances, knowledge, and understanding. Society's saving grace is that we have choices. Accordingly, much of what needs to be done *can* be—if enough people want it to be done *and decide to do it*.

RULE 3—THE ONLY TRUE INVESTMENT IS ENERGY FROM SUNLIGHT

The only true investment of energy in our world is light from the sun, which is 93,205,679 miles from Earth. It takes sunlight about 8.3 minutes to reach us and deliver 120 trillion watts of energy to Earth's surface—thereby providing enough energy in a single hour to satisfy the requirements of the global human society for an entire year.[12] Everything else is either a *re-allocation* or a *re-investment* of energy—including every coinage that exchanges hands in the global marketplace. This makes solar energy the only truly renewable resource. Moreover, capturing this energy and converting it to usable forms is dependent on viable communities of green plants worldwide. In this sense, fossil fuels are at least partly ancient solar radiation archived over millennia in the Earth. All other earthly resources, such as water, are limited because they already exist and obey the three thermodynamic laws, which make *them both finite and locally exhaustable*.

RULE 4—ALL RELATIONSHIPS INVOLVE A TRANSFER OF ENERGY

All we humans ever do is transfer energy from one place to another, from one level of intensity to another. A wise decision, therefore, is to use energy carefully because the conservation of energy allows more work to be done with a minimum of disruption to the functional processes. Such care simultaneously constrains material costs while allowing each individual to be fully valued for the energy he or she expends in the furtherance of a shared vision. Many of today's decisions, however, are based on quick fixes rather than the wisdom of long-term biophysical sustainability.

RULE 5—ALL SYSTEMS ARE BASED ON COMPOSITION, STRUCTURE, AND FUNCTION

It is imperative to understand that any organizational outcome of a resolved conflict is based on the composition of people and their various areas of expertise and levels of psychological maturity, which defines how the organizational system can and will function and what it allows to be accomplished. Grasping this dynamic is critical because the degree to which organizational members are behaviorally functional or dysfunctional, systemic or myopic in their points of view, team players or grandstanders, will determine the nature of the team and the kind and quality of its products. Therefore, a leader, who is conscious enough to make social-environmental sustainability the bedrock of his or her administration, begins with the necessary team function and works backwards to find the interdisciplinary expertise (composition) required for creating the indispensable structure that, in turn, will allow the functional fulfillment of the vision, such as the purposeful protection of water quality and quantity for all generations.

RULE 6—ALL RELATIONSHIPS HAVE ONE OR MORE TRADE-OFFS

Every decision has its trade-offs. Let us take a simple example from a city park. The challenge for the city council's leadership is to determine what kind of recreation will take place, considering that different factions of the community want different things: Some want to play baseball, which requires a diamond of bases, a backstop, and a wide-open space; some want soccer, which requires a wide-open space and goals at both ends of the field. Others desire volleyball, which requires a relatively small space filled with sand or asphalt, two poles, and a net stretched between them; and then there is tennis, which, like volleyball, requires a relatively small space, but an asphalt foundation with a low net in the middle, as well as a high, surrounding fence to prevent the ball from escaping. Since space is limited, how might more than one group be accommodated?

Each of these decisions represents a self-reinforcing feedback loop in terms of a living system. In that sense, each decision is the beginning of a never-ending story of cause and effect, which touches all local generations throughout time.

RULE 7—ALL SYSTEMS HAVE CUMULATIVE EFFECTS, LAG PERIODS, AND THRESHOLDS

A conflict teacher/mediator must help the participants to understand that all systems have incremental, *cumulative effects* that occur below our level of awareness (*lag period*) until such a time that sufficient change has taken place to cross a *threshold of visiblity*. In a human sense, this often means accepting the delayed gratification of a vision's outcome, despite wanting to see immediate results. Herein lies a major challenge for leaders of industrialized countries, where the citizenry insists on and uses technology that constantly ramps up the speed of transactions.

Unfortunately, we in the Western industrialized countries—and the United States in particular—are too often like the rich but foolish man in the Buddha's parable who wanted instant results:

> Once there was a wealthy but foolish man. When he saw the beautiful three-story house of another man, he envied it and made up his mind to have one built just like it, thinking himself just as wealthy. He called a carpenter and ordered him to build it. The carpenter consented and immediately began to construct the foundation, the first story, the second story, and then the third story. The wealthy man noticed this with irritation and said: "I don't want a foundation or a first story or a second story; I just want the beautiful third story. Build it quickly."[13]

Everything in nature has its own timing, and we would be wise to accept that timing with patience, including the patience of achieving consensus prior to committing an action that will affect all generations. Most people in the industrialized West seem to have the attitude that "time is money" and so are in a hurry to act, often without thinking through the potential consequences of their actions on either people or the environment.

Some years ago, while working with the Shinto priests in Japan, I learned a valuable lesson. The priests spent much time discussing the pros and cons of various decisions, as well as the potential outcomes of this choice or that. While the meetings seemed interminable and inefficient to me, when the priests came to consensus, they acted correctly with their collective wisdom the first time because they had winnowed the possibilities and probabilities through an informal, but very effective, risk analysis. This experience taught me that patience and delayed gratification are often more efficient than instant gratification because doing it right the first time is both effective *and* efficient since it precludes the necessity of having to do it over at the extra cost of time, labor, money, and potentially undesirable social-environmental consequences.

We, too, would have a far greater probability of achieving our desired outcome, both efficiently *and* effectively, by doing whatever we do correctly the first time. But first, we have to properly understand the notion of *leisure*.

Whereas we tend to think of leisure as the privilege of the well-to-do, Brother David Steindl-Rast (a Benedictine monk) reminds us that leisure

> is a virtue, not a luxury. Leisure is the virtue of those who take their time in order to give to each task as much time as it deserves. . . . Giving and taking, play and work, meaning and purpose are perfectly balanced in leisure. We learn to live fully in the measure in which we learn to live leisurely.[14]

Therefore, teachers and practitioners of conflict resolution must teach leisure and patience by example if their legacy is going to be a true benefit for all generations.

RULE 8—CHANGE IS AN IRREVERSIBLE PROCESS OF ETERNAL BECOMING

One of the more complex issues of decision making—especially social-environmental decisions—is dealing with the irreversibility of change as a process of eternal novelty. Moreover, all systems are cyclical, but none are perfect circles, which often confronts decision makers with perplexing choices because most people seem to want everything to go perpetually their way. For example, Wall Street, the U.S. government, and the majority of the citizenry insist that our economic system be linear and ever-growing. This myopic economic view has produced a symptomatic configuration based so completely on competition and mesmerizing advertisments to foster continual comsumerism that it is destroying the global environment's ability to serve humanity as a viable life-support system, of which the availability of good-quality water is a prime example. This legacy, from many centuries of humanity's persistent form of decision making, cannot continue unabated if we are to avoid becoming the authors of our own demise—as a viable society in the short term or even as a species in the long run.

It is imperative that people become aware of the long-term effects of their decisions. I say this because children are one of the five silent parties in all social-environmental decisions; air, water, soil, the general landscape, and its productive capacity are the others. Leaders at every level of society must understand the social, environmental, and economic circumstances to which they are committing future generations through their decisions of today. If the outcome of their decisions and actions is a deficit in terms of the future options for humanity, the productive capacity of ecosystems to serve human necessities, or both, it is analogous to "taxation without representation," and that goes against everything a true democracy stands for.

Rule 9—Systemic Change Is Based on Self-Organized Criticality

According to the theory termed "self-organized criticality,"[15] the mechanism that leads to a minor event, such as a drop of rain (Figure 1.2), is the same mechanism, drops of rain, that leads to a major event, for example, a flash flood (Figure 1.3). Not understanding this, analysts have typically and erroneously blamed some rare set of circumstances (some exception to the rule) or some powerful combination of mechanisms when catastrophe strikes.

Yet, having learned little or nothing from history, today's rich, industrialized nations are increasingly engaged in a competitive race, wherein *more* is always better and *enough* does not exist, which fosters the destruction of the very environments from which society sprang. With this in mind, sociologists might think of self-organized criticality as the *butterfly effect*, so-called because it is analogous to the flapping wings of a butterfly, which represents a small change in the initial condition of a social system, which in turn causes a chain of events that ultimately leads to large-scale cultural alterations.

For example, earlier civilizations were marked by birth, maturation, and demise, the last commonly caused by uncontrolled population growth that eventually outstripped its sources of available energy, especially during times of climate stress, which initiated internal and external conflicts. In some cases, survivors moved on to less-populated, more fertile areas as their civilizations collapsed. Today, however, there are few places left on Earth to go.

FIGURE 1.2 A drop of rain.

(Photograph by Kazimua. *Source*: https://commons.wikimedia.org/wiki/File:Rain_Drop,_Drop_Top.jpg).

FIGURE 1.3 A flash flood.

(Photograph by Paulsmithrj. *Source*: https://commons.wikimedia.org/wiki/File:Iphiclides_podalirius.jpg).

Because civilizations have much in common, their evolutionary stages being somewhat similar in their sequences of cultural development, self-organized criticality is an important concept for decision makers to understand when addressing conflicts because most—but not all—current leaders base their decisions on linear, syptomatic thinking. They do not realize that virtually all social collapses are initiated from within. Consider that all past civilizations—and present societies—evolved by: growth of knowledge and technology through discoveries and inventions and through the ideas of government, family, and property, all of which are based on observation and the accumulation of experimental knowledge.

Such understanding is important because, when framed in the positive sense, it means that what a few influential, psychologically mature teachers, conflict mediators, and leaders think and say can spread and bring about significant changes in the thinking and behavior of large numbers of people, which in turn would affect the social-environmental sustainability and inheritance of all generations.[16] But, what does psychologically maturity mean? As the Buddha said, "Though he should conquer a thousand men in the battlefield a thousand times, yet he, indeed, who would conquer himself is the noblest victor."[17] That is psychologically maturity.

Rule 10—Dynamic Disequilibrium Rules All Systems

All social systems, like those of nature, are ruled by dynamic *disequilibrium*, which simply means that the universally constant process of change, with its ever-novel outcomes, precludes a state of lasting balance. Therefore, the notion of any kind of "steady-state economics," as it is known on the Internet, is impossible. Here, the abiding paradox of life is that we have a choice in everything we think and almost everything we do—except practicing relationships, experiencing ourselves as we experience relationships, choosing, changing the world, living without killing, and dying. In those we have *no* choice, but we *do* have a choice of how we do it—and we *must* choose. Not choosing *is still a choice*. In addition, we make a new choice (even if it is doing nothing) each time a circumstance in our life changes, which, of course, is an ongoing process, be it the outworking of biophysical principles that govern life or how we view life-changes as we mature in years.

The consistency of change dictates the infinity of choice. Life can therefore be viewed as an eternal parade of decisions, each of which marks a fork in the path we follow. Each time a decision is made, others are foregone—whatever they might be. Nevertheless, each decision creates a kaleidoscope of additional choices, some leading to wisdom and others to folly because, as Israeli statesman Abba Eban observed, "History teaches us that men and nations behave wisely once they have exhausted all other alternatives."[18]

In this sense, everything we think and do is a fork in the road of consequences at the time a thought is formed, a decision made, and a choice of action selected and implemented. Hence, each decision—and the subsequent action—involves the hoped-for outcomes amid the irreversibility of life's unknowns and uncertainties that are the essence of *dynamic disequilibrium*.

Rule 11—Success or Failure Lies in the Interpretation of an Event

All relationships are self-reinforcing feedback loops that, in nature, are neutral in valuation because all values are intrinsic. Yet, when these same feedback loops carry either a positive or a negative extrinsic emphasis in human valuation because we want a specific, predetermined outcome to provide the illusion of being in control of circumstances, they become a *comparison* of right vs wrong, good vs bad, socially acceptable vs socially unacceptable, and so on, which fosters competition. This human dynamic is the same that drives the notion of success or failure, which lies in the human interpretation of an event—but not in the neutrality of the event itself.

To illustrate, I was once asked to mediate a conflict in Northern California over how to "restore" the Mattole River. During the process, some of the long-time, older residents began lamenting how newcomers into "their valley" had destroyed "their river" through years of overuse and abuse. Finally, a youth in his late teens, who was in juvenile detention, spoke up and said: "I don't know what you're talking about. I've been working for 3 years with a crew to improve the river's condition. The river is so much better than when I started. What's your problem?"

Where the old-timers could only see the loss of what, to them, had been a "pristine condition," the boy perceived a vast improvement in a short period of time. The success or failure of the efforts to revitalize the river was clearly perceived differently, depending on the life experiences of those involved. In this case, the old-timers constantly reinforced their collective grief over the *negative* changes for which they blamed others, although they had been complicit in rendering the changes they perceived through their own actions. The boy, on the other hand, was encouraged by his ability to produce a *positive* change in the river's condition—to which the old-timers were blind but for which he gladly took responsibility. In this case, to the old-timers the glass was half empty (failure), whereas the boy saw the same glass as half full (success), while the level of water in the proverbial glass had not changed in either case (Figure 1.4).

With the foregoing in mind, there is one aspect of conflict most people seem either not to understand or to ignore, and that is the unifying similarities of their innate human values as opposed to their competitive comparisons of right vs wrong, good vs bad, this is mine not yours, and so on.

Rule 12—People Must Be Equally Informed If They Are to Function as a Truly Democratic Society

For a group of people to be socially functional, they must be given the opportunity to be equally informed about what is going on and how it is projected to affect them. In other words, there must be no secrets that are or can be potentially detrimental to any member. Inequality of any kind within the group related to gender, race, social class, or education is merely the fear of inadequacy disguised as privilege by those who would impose their will.

FIGURE 1.4 Is the glass half empty or half full?
(Photograph by Derek Jensen. *Source*: https://commons.wikimedia.org/wiki/File:Glass-of-water.jpg).

Rule 13—We Must Consciously Limit Our "Wants"

We in the world today are so ensnared in the process of buying and selling things in the market place that we cannot imagine human life being otherwise. Even our notions of well-being and of despair are wedded to the ebb and flow of the markets. Why is this so much a part of our lives? It is largely because people have yet to understand the notion of conscious simplicity, which is based on the realization that there are two ways to riches: want less or work more. Put differently, wealth lies in the scarcity of one's wants as opposed to the hard work required to increase the abundance of one's possessions.

Author James B. Twitchell puts it nicely:

> Once we are fed and sheltered, our needs are and have always been cultural, not natural. Until there is some other system to codify and satisfy those needs and yearnings, commercialism [consumerism]—and the culture it carries with it—will continue not just to thrive but to triumph.[19]

By consciously limiting our wants, it is likely that we can have enough to provide comfortably for our necessities, as well as some of our most ardent desires—and leave more for other people to do the same. Unfortunately, capitalistic systems are based on advertising dissatisfaction and a continual stimulus to purchase superfluous items at the risk of personal debt, the long-term expense of the environment—especially the availability of pure water—and the growing impoverishment for *all* generations. Herein lies one of the greatest challenges for the contemporary teachers, conflict mediators, and leaders, a challenge that must be met if our society—and the environment that supports it—is to survive the 21st century with any kind of dignity and well-being for more than the top 1 percent of the monetarily wealthy.

RULE 14—SIMPLICITY IS THE KEY TO CONTENTMENT, ADAPTABILITY, AND SURVIVAL

Anyone can complicate life, but it requires genius to keep things simple. Simplicity depends on appreciating things simple, small, sublime, and sustainable. What is more, simplicity is the key to contentment, adaptability, and survival as a culture. Beyond some point, complexity becomes a decided disadvantage with respect to cultural longevity, just as it is to the evolutionary longevity of a species. As artist Hans Hoffman puts it, "The ability to simplify means to eliminate the unnecessary so that the necessary may speak."[20] To this, His Holiness the 17th Gyalwang Karmapa Ogyen Trinley Dorje (head of the Karma Kagyu School, one of the four main schools of Tibetan Buddhism) would add,

> A life full of material goods and barren of compassion is quite unsustainable from an ecological and karmic point of view. Of course, advertisements are always telling us that the path to happiness lies in purchasing the goods they sell. . . . We don't have to live a life that is sold to us—we can make the brave choice to live simply.[21]

RULE 15—NATURE, ENVIRONMENTAL/CULTURAL WISDOM, AND HUMAN WELL-BEING ARE PARAMOUNT

Placing material riches, as symbolized by the money chase, above the wealth of nature, spirituality, and human well-being is the road to social impoverishment, environmental degradation, and the collapse of societies and their life-support systems. We must, therefore, rethink our priorities and place the viability of ecosystems at least on par with economics of "natural capital," which means reconnecting with nature, if our own well-being is to prevail.[22]

Here, it is instructive to consider the difference between money and the true wealth of nature's services and our personal well-being. Conventional money knows no loyalty to a sense of place, a person, a local community, a landscape, a region, or even a nation, so it flows toward a global economy in which traditional social bonds give way to a rootless quest for the highest monetary return at virtually any social-environmental cost. The real price we pay for money is the hold it has on our sense of what is possible—the prison it builds around our imaginations, which American journalist Sydney J. Harris captured in a few words: "Men make counterfeit money; [but] in many more cases, money makes counterfeit men."[23]

One of the most important indicators of economic well-being is social-environmental sustainability, which means not only quality interpersonal relationships but also quality reciprocal relationships between people and their environment. A truly viable economy is based on love and reciprocity, where people do kind and useful things for one another with no expectation of financial gain. Such mutual caring is the soft social capital that both creates and maintains the fabric of trust, which in turn is the glue of functional families, communities, societies, and productively sustainable ecosystems.

RULE 16—EVERY LEGAL CITIZEN DESERVES THE RIGHT TO VOTE

Every legal citizen of every country deserves the right to an equal vote of their conscience on how their country is to be governed because they and their children and their children's children must live with the consequences of the collective choices and actions.

RULE 17—THIS PRESENT MOMENT, THE HERE AND NOW, IS ALL WE EVER HAVE

This eternal, present moment is all we ever have in which to act. The past is a memory, and the future never comes. *Now* is the *eternal moment*. Therefore, being grounded in the present can reduce fear.

With respect to an appointed leader, perhaps the toughest decision she or he will be confronted with is to bear, unflinchingly, all the abuses that the disagreeing parties normally hurl at one another. In effect, a person, such as a mediator who serves the people, must pass the tests described in the eulogy that Senator William Pitt Fessenden of Maine delivered on the death of Senator Foot of Vermont in 1866:

> When, Mr. President, a man becomes a member of this body [the senate] he cannot even dream of the ordeal to which he cannot fail to be exposed;
> of how much courage he must possess to resist the
> temptations which daily beset him;
> of that sensitive shrinking from undeserved censure
> which he must learn to control;
> of the ever-recurring contest between a natural desire for public approbation and
> a sense of public duty;
> of the load of injustice he must be content to bear, even
> from those who should be his friends;
> the imputations of his motives;

the sneers and sarcasms of ignorance and malice;
all the manifold injuries which partisan or private
malignity, disappointed of its objects, may shower upon his unprotected head.

All this, Mr. President, if he would retain his integrity, he must learn to bear unmoved, and walk steadily onward in the path of duty, sustained only by the reflection that time may do him justice, or if not, that after all his individual hopes and aspirations, and even his name among men, should be of little account to him when weighed in the balance against the welfare of a people of whose destiny he is a constituted guardian and defender.[24]

Such is the price of true social-environmental leadership, whatever the social level—to be the keeper of everyone else's dignity by keeping one's own in the eternal, present moment—*leading by example*.

THE ASWAN HIGH DAM—A CASE STUDY ILLUSTRATING THE IRREVERSIBLE CONSEQUENCES OF A SINGLE DECISION

Global biodiversity in river and riparian ecosystems is created and maintained by the geographic variation in stream processes and fluvial disturbance regimes, which, in turn, largely reflect regional differences in geology and climate. The extensive network of dams constructed by humans has greatly diminished the seasonal and year-to-year variability in the streamflow of rivers, thereby altering ecologically important biophysical dynamics in continental drainage basins. The cumulative effects of modifying regional-scale environmental templates are largely unexplored.

Although dams can provide considerable economic and social benefits, their placement and construction must be grounded in sufficient knowledge of the river and its catchment basin to account for long-term ecological consequences. Dams are highly individualistic, and similar physical circumstances may elicit dramatically different responses. The effects of a dam in time and space can be considerable and may become apparent only after a long time.[25] For purposes of illustration, I (Chris) shall discuss one dam with which I have some personal experience, the Aswan High Dam in Egypt, with additional examples from other places.

While I was working as a vertebrate zoologist with the Peabody Museum, Yale University, prehistoric expedition to Nubia, Egypt, in 1963 and 1964,[26] a representative of the Egyptian Ministry of Agriculture spent time with us as we worked just north of the Sudanese border along the Nile. One day, three of us from the expedition discussed with the minister the ecological implications of building the Aswan High Dam across the Nile River. He could not, however, see beyond the generation of electricity and irrigation, which was the official argument of the government for constructing the dam, behind which would be Lake Nasser—named after Gamal Abdel Nasser, then president of Egypt.

We explained that building the dam would increase the geographical distribution of "schistosomiasis," also known as "bilharzia," a debilitating disease. This would occur when freshwater snails carrying the tiny, parasitic worms that cause the disease made their way from below the existing Low Aswan Dam (built by the British in the early 1930s at the town of Aswan) over the yet-to-be-completed Aswan High

Dam south to at least Khartoum in the Sudan, several hundred miles away. At that time, it was still safe to swim above the Low Aswan Dam, where the water was too swift and too cold for the snails to live, but it was not safe to swim, or even catch frogs, in the slower, warmer water below the dam, where the snails and their parasitic worms already thrived.

We told him that the Nile above the high dam would fill with silt, which would starve the Nile Delta of its annual supply of nutrient-rich sediment and affect farming in a deleterious way. We even conveyed to him that the dam could easily become a military target for the Israelis, as German dams were targets for the British during World War II. However, all our arguments were to no avail.

The engineers building the Aswan High Dam had intended only to store additional water and to produce electricity, which they did. Nevertheless, deprived of the nutrient-rich silt of the Nile's annual floodwaters, the population of sardines off the coast of the Nile Delta in the Mediterranean diminished by 97 percent within 2 years.[27] (A similar dynamic is occurring in the East China Sea due to the Three Gorges Dam in the Yangtze River of China.)[28] In addition, the rich delta, which had been growing in size for thousands of years, is now being rapidly eroded by the Mediterranean because the Nile is no longer depositing river sediment at its mouth.[29]

To return to the Aswan High Dam, until it was built, the annual sediment-laden waters of the Nile added a little less than a sixteenth of an inch of nutrient-rich silt to the farms along the river each year. Now that the new dam has stopped the floods, the silt not only is collecting upriver behind the dam, thus diminishing its water-holding capacity, but also is no longer being deposited on the riverside farms, thus decreasing their fertility. In addition, because irrigation without flooding causes the soil to become saline, parts of the Nile Valley, which had been farmed continuously for 5,000 years, may have to be abandoned within a few centuries. Also, bilharzia has indeed spread southward to Khartoum in the Sudan.

The Nubian people, whom I got to know, were a community of black people living many miles south of Aswan on small farms sandwiched between the east bank of the Nile and the Eastern Desert of restless sand and outcroppings of ironstone. The people had a wonderful sense of humor, were quick to laugh, and seemed genuinely pleased that I delighted in playing with their children and vice versa. For their part, the children had a good sense of self and of each day as an adventure to be lived to the fullest.

But the Aswan High Dam changed all that. The Egyptian Government moved the Nubians to Cairo from the bank of the Nile, whose quiet flowing waters and silent guardian desert had been a part of their lives for centuries. In place of their freely spaced, cool, self-designed, and self-constructed mud-brick homes, the Nubians were put into government-built, look-alike, minimum-quality housing. Gone was the peaceful silence of the desert and its clean air. Gone were the songs of the birds in the shrubs along the Nile's banks. Vanished was their experience of the still, black nights, ablaze with crisply visible stars, including the magnificent Southern Cross. Their freedom of choice stolen, many of them could not adjust to the loss of their culture and their gentle way life, and simply died.

The same thing is happening to the indigenous peoples who live in the jungle of the Malaysian state of Sarawak on the island of Borneo, where thousands are being relocated to accommodate the government's race to generate quick profits. For example, 10,000 Indigenous people were displaced to make way for the Bakun Dam.[30] Moreover, the Iban people near Lubok Antu had to ritually exhume and move their ancestral graves in order to prevent them from being submerged by the lake created by the Batang Ai Dam.[31]

There is another consequence of the Aswan High Dam, one I would never have thought of, even though I had studied the mammals along the Nile. The Nile annually flooded the many nooks, crannies, and caves along its edge, killing the rats whose fleas carry bubonic plague. Because the floods no longer occur, the rat population soared, and bubonic plague once again poses a potential threat.

I learned about this unexpected consequence from Wulf Killmann of the Deutsche Gesellschaft für Technische Zusammerarbeit, whom I met in Malaysia. As we talked about the effects of dams on rivers and oceans, I told him about my experience in Egypt. Killmann then told me that he had been part of a project to figure out how to control the ever-growing population of rats, which had become a serious health threat.

I find in this scenario an interesting problem, one I see arising again and again. We humans introduce something, such as the Aswan High Dam, into the environment, where it provides some benefits to humanity (electricity and additional irrigation) while simultaneously causing untold, unknown, even unimaginable problems. But when the problems begin to manifest themselves, rather than removing the cause—the dam—we propose to remedy the problems by introducing more of the same—another dam—into the environment. I have never seen a second dam fix the ecological problems created by the first dam.

Even if all conceivable questions could be answered and most of the perceived negative effects could be reversed to some extent, there is at least one effect of the dam that is final. The way of life enjoyed by the Nubian people along the Nile north of the Sudan border, in which I found such beauty and joy, would still be extinct. Therefore, the question is, how reversible—in reality—are the effects of the Aswan High Dam? The answer: *they are irreversible* because change is a constant process of eternal novelty.

CONCLUSION

In Chapter 1, we discussed the understanding and application of the inviolable rules for decision making and how they determine the irreversible, social-environmental consequences for all generations. If we, the adult decision makers of today, honor the biophysical-social rules of decision making, we will bequeath our children, grandchildren, and beyond the greatest legacy possible. The endowment of viable choices and things of value from which to choose in a sustainably cooperative, productive world, where the quality of life takes precedence over the fearful, competitive accumulation of materiality, is the greatest gift we, the authors of this book, have to offer.

In Chapter 2, we explore the four-stage approach to water conflict and management and transformation.

QUESTIONS

1. Of the inviolable rules of decision making listed in Chapter 1, name three that resonated with you? In your mind, what makes the three rules you chose significant?
2. Are there any rules of decision making that you would add to the list in Chapter 1? If so, please explain what your addition is, and why you are adding it?
3. In light of the irreversible consequences of the Aswan High Dam, how would you, in retrospect, propose to resolve Egypt's need for more electricity and a wider distribution of water throughout the populated region of the country?
4. In Chapter 1, we learned about the impacts of a single decision, as it relates to the Aswan High Dam. Do you know of any other case studies that illustrate irreversible, environmental consequences based on short-term, quick-fix decision making?

NOTES

1 Orr, David. A Proposal. *Conservation Biology*, 14 (2000):338–341.
2 Beaton, Russ and Chris Maser. *Economics and Ecology: United for a Sustainable World*. 2012. CRC Press, Boca Raton, FL. 191 pp.
3 Ibid.
4 Churchill, Winston. Pp. 10–12. In T. A. Warren. Leaders Need Followers. *The Rotarian*, 1945 October.
5 The foregoing discussion is based on: Maser, Chris. *Sustainable Community Development: Principles and Concepts*. 1997. St. Lucie Press, Delray Beach, FL. 257 pp.
6 Ibid.
7 Maser, Chris. *Social-Environmental Planning: The Design Interface Between Everyforest and Everycity*. 2009. CRC Press, Boca Raton, FL. 321 pp.
8 Maser, Chris. *Decision Making for a Sustainable Environment: A Systemic Approach*. 2013. CRC Press, Boca Raton, FL. 304 pp. (with a chapter by Jessica K. La Porte).
9 Maser, Chris. *Sustainable Community Development: Principles and Concepts*. 1997. Op cit.
10 Maser, Chris. Do We Owe Anything to the Future? 1992. Pp. 195–213. In *Multiple Use and Sustained Yield: Changing Philosophies for Federal Land Management? Proceedings and Summary of a Workshop Convened on March 5 and 6, 1992, Washington, D.C. Congressional Research Service, Library of Congress. Committee Print No. 11*. US Government Printing Office, Washington, DC.
11 Maser, Chris. *Sustainable Community Development: Principles and Concepts*. 1997. Op cit.
12 **(1)** Petit, Charles. Cold Panacea. *Science News*, 175 (2009):20–23 and **(2)** Dave Kornreich. How Long Does It Take for the Sun's Light to Reach Us? (Beginner). http://curious.astro.cornell.edu/about-us/49-our-solar-system/the-sun/general-questions/197-how-long-does-it-take-for-the-sun-s-light-to-reach-us-beginner (accessed October 17, 2019).
13 *The Teaching of Buddha*. Bukkyo Dendo Kyokai, Tokyo, Japan. 1985.
14 Brother Steindl-Rast, David. *Gratefulness and the Heart of Prayer: An Approach to Life in Fullness*. 1984. Paulist Press, Ransey, NJ.
15 Bak, Per and Kan Chen. Self-Organizing Criticality. *Scientific American*, January (1991):46–53.
16 Butterfly Effect. **(1)** http://en.wikipedia.org/wiki/Butterfly_effect and **(2)** www.news.cornell.edu/releases/Feb04/AAAS.Kleinberg.ws.html (accessed February 4, 2011).

17 *The Teaching of Buddha. op. cit.*
18 Eban, Abba. *The Quotations Page.* www.quotationspage.com/quote/298.html (accessed September 25, 2019).
19 Lehmann-Haupt, Christopher. Sales Pitches That Put the M (for Mega) in Madison Ave. *The New York Times,* January 3, 2001.
20 Hoffman, Hans. http://quotationsbook.com/author/3495/ (accessed January 7, 2011).
21 H.H. [His Highness] 17th Gyalwang Karmapa Ogyen Trinley Dorje. Walking the Path of Environmental Buddhism through Compassion and Emptiness. *Conservation Biology,* 25 (2011):1094–1097.
22 Beaton, Russ and Chris Maser. *Economics and Ecology: United for a Sustainable World.* 2012. *Op. cit.*
23 Harris, Sydney J. www.brainyquote.com/quotes/sydney_j_harris_121037 (accessed May 25, 2019).
24 Kennedy, John F. *Profiles in Courage.* 1961. Harper & Row, New York, NY.
25 The previous two paragraphs are based on Poff, N. LeRoy, Julian D. Olden, David M. Merritt, and David M. Pepin. Homogenization of Regional River Dynamics by Dams and Global Biodiversity Implications. *Proceedings of the National Academy of Sciences,* 104 (2007):5732–5737.
26 Dornburg, Alex, Jordan G. Colosie, Chris Maser, and others. A Survey of the Yale Peabody Museum Collection of Egyptian Mammals Collected during Construction of the Aswan High Dam, with an Emphasis on Material from the 1962–1965 Yale University Prehistoric Expedition to Nubia. *Bulletin of the Peabody Museum of Natural History,* 52 (2011):255–272.
27 George, C. J. The Role of the Aswan Dam in Changing Fisheries of the South-Western Mediterranean. Pp. 179–188. In M. T. Farvar and J. P. Milton (editors), *The Careless Technology.* 1972. Natural History Press, New York.
28 (1) Park, Young-Seuk, Jianbo Chang, Sovan Lek, and others. Conservation Strategies for Endemic Fish Species Threatened by the Three Gorges Dam. *Conservation Biology,* 17 (2003):1748–1758, and (2) Gong, G.-C., J. Chang, K.-P. Chiang, and others. Reduction of Primary Production and Changing of Nutrient Ratio in the East China Sea: Effect of the Three Gorges Dam? *Geophysical Research Letters,* 33 (2006):L07610, doi:10.1029/2006GL025800.
29 (1) Quelennec, R. E. and C. B. Kruk. Nile Suspended Load and Its Importance for the Nile Delta Morphology. Pp. 130–144. In *Proceedings of the Seminar on Nile Delta Sedimentology.* 1976. UNDP/UNESCO Project, Coastal Protection Studies, Alexandria, VA; (2) Summerhayes, C. and N. Marks. Nile Delta Nature Evolution and Collapse of Continental Shelf Sediment System. Pp. 162–190. In *Proceedings of the Seminar on Nile Delta Sedimentology.* 1976. UNDP/UNESCO Project, Coastal Protection Studies, Alexandria, VA; and (3) Toma, S. A. and M. S. Salama. Changes *in* Bottom Topography of the Western Shelf of the Nile Delta since 1922. *Marine Geology,* 36 (1980):325–339.
30 (1) The Resettlement of Indigenous People affected by the Bakun Hydro-Electric Project, Sarawak, Malaysia. *A Working Paper of the World Commission on Dams* (1999):1–16. www.internationalrivers.org/sites/default/files/attached-files/resettlement_of_indigenous_people_at_bakun.pdf (accessed October 27, 2019), (2) Bakun Dam. *International Rivers People – Water – Life.* www.internationalrivers.org/campaigns/bakun-dam (accessed October 26, 2019), and (3) Sarawak, Malaysia. www.internationalrivers.org/campaigns/sarawak-malaysia (accessed October 26, 2019).
31 Taswell, Ruth. Dam in Sarawak Forces 3,000 Iban to Resettle. *Cultural Survival Quarterly Magazine.* 1986. www.culturalsurvival.org/publications/cultural-survival-quarterly/dam-sarawak-forces-3000-iban-resettle (accessed October 26, 2019).

2 Water Conflict Transformation

Lynette de Silva

CONTENTS

Introduction 33
    Degrees of Remedy 34
    Interests 34
Conflict Transformation 36
    Adversarial Stage 37
    Reflective Stage 39
    Integrative Stage 39
    Action Stage 40
    Transformative Processes and Examples 42
Concluding Remarks 44
Exercises 45
Notes 45

INTRODUCTION

Water conflicts transcend geography, occurring anywhere from local streets to the international stage. Some examples are: (1) downstream Egypt and upstream Ethiopia (and Sudan to a lesser degree) in dispute over Nile River waters, with water quantity claims made even more contentious by Ethiopia's completion of the Renaissance Dam, in July 2020;[1] (2) when, in 2018, it looked as though the drought in Cape Town, South Africa, would result in daily water rationing; (3) when, in 2016, parents in Newark, New Jersey (USA), learned that their school-aged children were exposed to lead in their drinking water;[2] and (4) the privatization of water in Cochabamba, Bolivia, in 2000, which raised water rates, creating substantial hardships for the financially impoverished, resulting in violent protests.[3] This chapter provides an understanding of what water conflicts are, how they can be transformed, and what benefits transformation provides.

Conflicts are centered around issues related to disagreements over information and data, relationship problems, assumed competing interests and/or incompatible values, or political hierarchies.[4] Conflict tends to increase when there is a change in a familiar system (community, city, country, river basin) to which the institutional response (by government agency, organization, watershed council) is too slow to adequately alleviate the crisis and accommodate the affected people.[5]

Degrees of Remedy

Just as clashes over water can take many forms, there is a spectrum of approaches that can achieve degrees of remedy. For example, traditional litigation includes the court system with its established rules and legal precedence. Through this mechanism, disputing parties relinquish power to appointed people who act as judge and jury, thereby determining victors and losers.

However, an alternative form of dispute resolution is preferred by those interested in self-determination with respect to both the process and final decision. Such an approach can include parties working unassisted. Yet assistance from a neutral, third-party facilitator, negotiator, or mediator can help set the tone for greater discussion through implementation of agreed-upon ground rules among disputants, thereby increasing the chances of an effective process, without violating such established rules as strict privacy concerning the meetings. The end result, which may be disclosed, provides the likelihood of parties having their individual interests heard and possibly met through defining a cooperative future. This said, the outcome of a water conflict is often described as the management of water in a sustainable, efficient, and effective way that addresses stakeholder needs and political actualities.[6]

When students, laypeople, or water ministers study water disputes and perform a fictitious water negotiation, a common community vision emerges, no matter where in the world participants live, whether they are in Oregon's temperate Klamath River Basin or Uzbekistan's arid grassland plains. Here, it is important to understand that a conflict arises because people are individually focused on what they do not want to have happen in the present that will affect their chosen concept of the future. A vision, on the other hand, is a cooperative agreement among participants to focus collectively on what they do want in the present that will, to the best of their knowledge, affirm their desired future.

Yet, in real life, one cannot walk into a stakeholder meeting as an outsider and set the goals for a group with contentious water issues. Why? Because, each individual or group, regardless of location, needs to come to their own realization in their own time of what interests and resulting vision form the core of cooperation.

Although water is central to the vision, the outlook of all things hoped for stretches into every aspect of life. The list will often include: clean drinking water and air, a healthy ecosystem, rich biodiversity, and safe and enduring aquifer systems, together with effective conservation and restorative projects. Beyond emphasis on resilient ecosystems, there may also be the collective vision for creating a certain legacy for the next generation, as well as regional economic prosperity and sustainable forestry, agriculture, commerce, and other practices. Since water is imbedded in all aspects of life, these broad strokes typically include fostering good relationships and peace for the purpose of maintaining healthy families and communities.

Interests

In conflict resolution, the term *interest* generally refers to a want and need. Getting to the heart of a matter is to determine the underlying cause of *why* a disputant needs and/or wants a specific thing.[7] While it explains motivation, neither the purpose nor

Water Conflict Transformation

FIGURE 2.1 A photomontage of what a whole iceberg might look like. Here the image is used as an analogy, where ice above sea level represents known "positions" held in a negotiation and ice below sea level serves as vast "interests," generally not revealed in the early stages of a negotiation.

Source: (Created by Uwe Kils and Wiska Bodo, Wikimedia, 2005).

the reason for its perceived need may be obvious to the opposing party. Those details are usually obscured in the secrecy of an emotional cloak. It is through the development of trust and deeper conversation that interests are revealed.

What is most obvious is a party's position, represented both by physical posturing and by bargaining stance, which tells *what* a party wants.[8] An analogy that may help with understanding positions and interests is an iceberg. Figure 2.1 represents the cross section of an iceberg floating in open waters, with its considerably larger, unseen mass below the surface. In this analogy, the exposed ice represents *positions* and the much larger segment below the surface represents the vast extent of unknown *interests*.

So, interests tend to be hidden and not unveiled until levels of trust are established, which is built through listening and actions. None of this is easy. There is a delicate balancing act of opening up to listen, while *gently* trusting. Listening, as part of a conversation, requires one's entire focus (five senses, including mind and spirit)—without interruption and judgment. It is as though one surrenders to the moment. Such focus is achieved with time set aside for private discussion in a quiet setting fully dedicated to this activity.

Only when a speaker has fully expressed their thoughts, can the listener ask a question for clarity. In this way, the original speaker can communicate their own thoughts, feelings, and information without interruption. The listener may also paraphrase to ensure an accurate understanding of the content. Once the original speaker feels heard, the roles are reversed. This process is reiterative.[9] It is also a form of both learning about each other and learning together in a nonthreatening way. Building trust through a sincere discussion is the physical manifestation of opening the door to resolution and transformation.

Resolution is thought of as a superficial, symptomatic solution that addresses the immediacy of the problem, but does not address the underlying, systemic cause that created the current problematic dynamics. It tends to focus on the dispute, with a goal of ending the undesirable conflict and tension.[10] The specific content of a resolution makes it a subset of conflict transformation.

CONFLICT TRANSFORMATION

Within this context of water disputes, transformation is about raising the level of personal consciousness through relationship-building. It not only explores the interconnectivity and boundaries of the relationship, as a system, but also explores the outward appearances of the conflict. In this respect, it goes beyond the problem at hand, building a foundation to strengthen the relationship through time.[11]

There is, within the transformative perspective, the recognition that relationships have an ebb and flow, and that conflicts are a natural part of that dynamic. In that sense, conflicts are to be expected from time to time, as an opportunity for growth—an opening for constructive change through which to increase justice and peace.

Conflict transformation is designed to replace outdated activities with constructive behavior toward a united mission, in which the behavior is directed toward authentic, genuine, and voluntary cooperation. And, since life is a constant process of novelty, the aim is for a transformational shift that is always in motion and needs nurturing to raise the level of consciousness and potentiality.

There are many ways to approach this outcome and many tools to assist. Among them are water conflict frameworks such as:

1. *The Water Event Intensity Scale of the Basins at Risk*, which employs a linear system to assess one water event at a time, characterizing a hydrocircumstance across a scale where −7 means all-out war, +7 signifies

Water Conflict Transformation

unification by choice, and 0 implies a neutral encounter.[12] This assessment is derived from communication and/or actions or the lack thereof, giving insight into a water interaction within a specific snapshot in time.

2. The *Transboundary Water Interactions Nexus (TWINS) Matrix* helps map relationship dynamics over time. Each interaction has its own pair of coordinates, illustrated on a cooperation- and conflict-intensity axis. For example, in 2008, one encounter between Party A and Party B could result in both a high cooperative intensity and a high conflict intensity, characterized as: "unstable, intense, sometimes creative." Whereas, another event between the same two parties, in 2015, might be assessed as low cooperation intensity and high conflict intensity, characterized as: "unstable relations."[13]

3. The *Hydro-Trifecta Framework* addresses disputes over groundwater and aquifers. It navigates disputants during a negotiation, as to when it is necessary to bolster their cooperative skills, while having them query resources and strategy through questions like: "What is the current circumstance?" "What are we capable of doing?" "What do we want to do?" and "What must we do?"[14]

4. Sadoff and Grey's (2002) *Cooperation Benefits on International Rivers* showcases different types of benefits at various levels of interaction, indicting what might be lost or gained regarding the health of the environment, economy, and geopolitics.[15]

5. *The Four Stages of Water Conflict Transformation* assesses conflict in terms of stages of negotiation (adversarial, reflexive, integrative, and action), where descriptions of disputant's allegations suggest which collaborative skills need to be enhanced.[16]

This last tool, the Four Stages of Water Conflict Transformation, is particularly helpful because it not only divides the negotiation into discernible phases, with descriptions that shed light on what may be occurring in a particular segment of the process, but also informs what kind of skillset is needed to move through it. It also complements many frameworks, allowing some to be used in combination depending upon the situation. And, this framework functions well for addressing the diversity of natural resource challenges at the country, state, and local scales. In the following, the individual stages (adversarial, reflexive, integrative, and action) are presented in Table 2.1. In this book, this author uses the term "reflective" stage rather than "reflexive" stage, finding it more descriptive for our objectives.

ADVERSARIAL STAGE

Antagonistic displays of engagement among water stakeholders represent the adversarial stage of conflict management. Challengers may refuse to listen to each other, spreading rhetoric often shaped by supremacy, authority, and/or geographic claims based on political dominance. In this space, historical events choke present and future interactions, where rights-based processes may give way to legal authority. The outcome is about winners and losers, with emphasis on individual party interests rather than gaining mutual understanding, leaving no room for building trust.[23]

TABLE 2.1
Four Stages of Water Conflict Transformation

Negotiation Stage[a]	Common Water Claims[b]	Collaborative Skills[c]	Geographic Scope
Adversarial	Rights	Trust-building	Nations
Reflexive	Needs	Skills-building	Watersheds
Integrative	Benefits	Consensus-building	"Benefit-sheds"
Action	Equity	Capacity-building	Region

Source: This framework is built mainly on the works of Jay Rothman,[17,18] Kaufman,[19,20] and Wolf.[21] This table is modified from Figure 6.1, in Jerome Delli Priscoli and Aaron T. Wolf. *Managing and Transforming Water Conflicts.* Cambridge University Press, New York, New York, 2009, 354 pp.

[a] These stages build primarily on the work of Jay Rothman, who initially described his stages as ARI—Adversarial, Reflexive, and Integrative.[17] When ARI become ARIA, adding Action, Rothman's terminology[19] also evolved to Antagonism, Resonance, Invention, and Action. We retain the former terms, feeling they are more descriptive for our purposes.

[b] These claims stem from an assessment of 145 treaty deliberations described in Wolf.[22] Rothman[22] also uses the terms rights, interests, and needs, in that order, arguing that "needs" are motivation for "interests," rather than the other way round, as we use it here. For our purposes, our order feels more intuitive, especially for natural resources.

[c] These sets of skills draw from Kaufman,[20,21] who ties each set of dynamics specifically to Rothman's ARIA model in great detail, based on his extensive work conducting "Innovative Problem Solving Workshops" for "partners in conflict" around the world.

Establishing trust is crucial and cannot be rushed. It is formed gradually by each party demonstrating trustworthiness through their own individual behavior, which over time may be reflected through the actions of other community members. Moreover, trustworthiness calls for levels of vulnerability, since the response one wishes to experience cannot be guaranteed. Here a note of caution is in order: placing oneself in vulnerable situations must be done only when one feels safe. Where the stakes are low and the meeting place is secure, one can begin with small gestures of openness at levels that are not too compromising. Of course, each individual will have to determine for themselves what that scenario would look like.

Meetings must take place in secure, nonpartisan settings (such as public libraries, coffee houses, or outside by a river) preferably hosted and facilitated by a neutral third party, where rules for cordial rhetoric and acceptable behavior are agreed on, ahead of the meeting. Recognizing contrasts in cultural differences and perspectives around nature, water, and life, the aim is to allow multiple perceptions to be heard with respect for everyone's point of view. Building trust opens us to listen, through which we hear and understand one another's interests.

REFLECTIVE STAGE

Nonjudgmental listening is a lifelong discipline. While all stages benefit from it, it is vital that the practice be rooted during the adversarial phase, which affords disputants the opportunity to move beyond entrenched positions, to the freedom of articulating interests. Given enough time (days, weeks, sometimes years), the process can be done in such a way that stakeholders feel that their concerns about water—and more importantly, the contextual history of their relationship with nature, biophysical, and cultural necessities, and one another—are heard. The impression of previously unknown interests may present each disputant with greater understanding and thoughtful moments.

Reflective listening allows for paraphrasing to ensure the clear understanding of what was heard. In this way, participants can gain an enhanced perspective of one another's interests and needs—without ridicule and/or vocal interruptions. Listening is done with tactful respect, giving the speaker sufficient space to fully express complete thoughts, with minimum questioning by the listener.[24] A question (such as: "How did that make you feel?") allows the speaker to provide further understanding, while leaving pauses for silence and thought.

INTEGRATIVE STAGE

Now, engaging in conversation, parties are continuing to build trust with those once considered adversaries. Worldviews are being joined through personal connections on a path toward a more compassionate future with mutual values through a sharing of knowledge, ideas, resources, and the allocation of water.[25,26] Once interests are heard and clarity surrounding the conflict's history is understood, moments to brainstorm possible solutions can be organized.

A joint exercise of structured brainstorming, with all stakeholders involved, provides an opportunity for associated interests to surface by encouraging everyone to think out loud, placing all possible benefits on a whiteboard—without criticism, no matter how eccentric a concept may seem. Once ideas are on the whiteboard, participants are asked to build on one another's thoughts, incorporating reciprocal interests. This practice can give rise to spontaneous group discussions toward common goals. On the whiteboard, circles are drawn around ideas that might address multiple-party interests. This process is based on the emotional aspect of thinking beyond one's own wants, thereby stimulating creative views and stronger bonds.

Reframing is another technique often employed at this stage, which involves looking at a problem in a new way, with the hope of sparking innovation. One way of reframing is to have disputants formulate their dilemma by merging their opposing viewpoints, which requires changing from the "Either/Or" thought process to "Both/And." Here is an example: *How can we address "A" and at the same time build "B"?*[27] Two formulated sentences are given in the following:

(1) How can we address the sedimentation problems in the river caused by logging and at the same time build a robust logging industry?
(2) How can we address the need to let migrating Chinook salmon return to their native spawning grounds and at the same time reap the benefits building a dam would provide?

Lederach says this exercise helps build our "capacity to live with apparent contradictions and paradoxes,"[28] which seems to be at the core of our evolving consciousness and the very nature of transformation. Reframing allows us to shift a conceived problem to a different scale. Depending on what the circumstance requires, one can either amplify the issue to magnify its details or reduce it through a broader, more systemic view, garnering more observations.

Simply formulating a question, as stated, does not mean it should be answered or that the correct question has even been asked. The critical element is time for the stakeholders to determine if the question incorporates everyone's needs.

Timing is also critical from another point of view, namely, it allows joint discovery and consensus-building and is a source for greater creativity and non-linear expression. On the other hand, when an answer or solution is preconceived, the continued, mutual learning is terminated.

At this integrative stage, breaking boundaries goes beyond reframing questions at different social scales. It can extend across geospatial boundaries, shifting, for example, from national demarcations to transboundary river basins with mutual benefits becoming more evident.[29]

ACTION STAGE

This dynamic stage of water transformation is for joint gains with the possibility of dividends extending beyond the negotiated benefits, even broadening economic corridors across regions and political borders. It requires buy-in at multiple scales of governance (village, province, and sometime across nations). Obtaining maximum benefits may require new associations, additional resources, and even new institutions. Although water would be the primary driver for cooperation, the agreements might add value beyond that one resource.[30,31]

Creative water arrangements can go beyond direct payment for water delivery or utilization. One example of an approach to sharing benefits that extends beyond a straight money transaction can be seen in the 1964 Columbia River Treaty. This treaty is between the US and Canada, and was designed for flood control and to generate hydroelectric power. In this arrangement:

1. Canada agreed to construct three storage reservoirs (behind Mica, Arrow, and Duncan Dams) within its territory and operate them to meet the needs of the US. This arrangement includes optimizing the generation of hydro-energy, for which each country receives half of the downstream power resulting from water storage.
2. From the US, Canada received an upfront, lump-sum payment for both half the cost of averted flood damages once the dams were completed and subsequent flood control for 60 years.
3. US built the Libby Dam, in Montana. In the treaty, each country keeps the benefits accrued within its own country.[32]

To be clear, while this treaty offers negotiation ingenuity, the agreement failed in offering equity to actors who have relationship with and interests in the Columbia River; among them are the indigenous communities, the ecosystem, and river species (particularly, salmon). Opportunity exists to rectify this, since the treaty stipulates that, after September 16, 2024 with 10-year prior notice, this arrangement can be subject to change, if either country wishes.[33]

The aforementioned frameworks are by no means a complete list. While these, and many others, can be used to address contested waters of any size, and/or can be modified to meet the needs of disputants, there is no prototype for resolving conflicts. Nevertheless, water conflict-related frameworks provide loose guidelines. Table 2.2 is a detailed version of Table 2.1. This comprehensive tabulation provides indicators that can help in determining which stage within the framework a conflict is in.

Regarding the Four Stages of Water Conflict Transformation Framework, it should not be adopted blindly. Nor should it necessarily be thought of as a stepwise

TABLE 2.2
A Detailed Version of Four Stages of Water Conflict Transformation

Type of Process/ Negotiation Stage[a]	Focus of Process	Collaborative and Transformational Skills[b]	Context, Geographic Scope, or Framing for Outcomes
Adversarial	Rights	Trust-building; deepening understanding of conflict	State, federal, tribal land, and water laws; priority, jurisdiction, and supremacy/sovereignty of rights
Reflective	Needs and interests	Skills-building in listening for and identifying positions, needs, and interests	Watersheds/basins
Integrative	Benefits/values/ reframing	Consensus-building; relationship-building	"Problemshed"/ "Benefit-shed"
Action	Governance in relationship to dynamic systems; equity	Capacity-building; community-building	Networked systems across state, region, and/ or country

Communication Style	Goal of Conflict Resolution Process[c]	Focus of Process and Participants	View of Conflict
Defend; debate; deliberate	Make decision: often win/lose among parties who differ	Apply laws and policies to reach a decision; control information to be selective and tactical	Competitive; polarize; desire to bring pain, anxiety, and difficulties to an end
Listen without resistance; causes, beliefs, and assumptions	Reach an agreement among parties about the presenting problem	Content-centered	Need to de-escalate

(Continued)

TABLE 2.2 (Continued)

Communication Style	Goal of Conflict Resolution Process[c]	Focus of Process and Participants	View of Conflict
Generative dialogue; collectively invent new possibilities and new insights	Promote constructive change processes; uncover and form a base of shared meaning that can help coordinate and align actions and values; solve and dissolve problems[d]	Relationship-centered; engages the systems within which relationships are embedded; focus shifts to listening/sensing an already existing wholeness; share information	Collaborative; envisions conflict as an ecology that is relationally dynamic, all of which is normal and results in constructive change
Network information and communication to maintain collective flow and opportunity	Facilitate people thinking and acting together in relationship within reframed context from which new agreements can come	Create or re-create institutions, policies, structures, and networks from which communities/society can express their new basis of shared meaning, goals, and principles	Conflict leads to new capacity, and a shared vision reflecting new understanding to improve quality of life

Sources: This table is from Doermann and Wolf[34] and is built from the same sources as Table 2.1 (labeled superscript a, b, c in both iterations). An additional source is William Isaacs. Dialogue: The Art of Thinking Together. DoubleDay. New York, NY. 1999, identified as superscript d, in this table.

process, because more than one stage can occur at a given time.[35] It should be used with a great deal of thought but also with the collaborative skills designed to accommodate community involvement, even if a neutral, third party (facilitator or mediator) is part of the process.

TRANSFORMATIVE PROCESSES AND EXAMPLES

Transformative processes and tools are recognized through several disciplines and traditions. Among them are ancient spiritual and faith-based practices, indigenous and local knowledge for restorative justice and resilience, and community-based mediation training and scholarly conflict management frameworks. Moreover, many of the modern-day approaches and tools used to address disputes are borrowed from historical methods.

These time-tested approaches, a few of which are expressed in de Silva and Wolf's *Transformative Practices for Water Diplomacy*,[36] correlate faith-based practices from Sufi Muslim, Buddhism, and Jewish/Catholic texts. Included are

TABLE 2.3
Examples of Practice Incorporated into the Four Stages of Water Conflict Transformation Framework.

Here the shaded parts represent when a particular practice might best support a negotiation stage. Interpretation by lynette de silva

Negotiation Stage	Examples of Practices						
	Talking Stick	Ho'oponopono	Contemplative Movement	Yes, And	Portmanteau	Building Consensus
Adversarial	■	■				
Reflective	■	■				
Integrative			■	■	■	■
Action					■	■

Indigenous people of the Americas, with social frameworks from Maslow, Rothman, and Wolf.

Here are examples of techniques that come from all walks of life (Table 2.3). The first example pertains to negotiation in the adversarial and reflective stages of the water conflict framework, where listening is especially crucial.

One strategy, employed by some Indigenous people of North America, is the use of a talking stick. "The talking stick is a sacred symbol of authority and power. When utilized within talking circles during council meetings, there are specific rules for communicating,"[37] one being that whoever is given the stick has the right to speak, while all the others respectfully listen. The sacredness of the moment honors both listener and speaker. As such, adopting this approach within a gathering for mediation or a town hall meeting can bring a sense of calm.

The second example also seems most fitting for the adversarial and reflective stages of the water conflict framework. It comes from a Hawaiian Tradition. It is the practice to make things right, "Ho'oponopono". It has specific spiritual and cultural significance and is for reconciliation within a family. Components of the practice include a form of restorative justice with all parties present for grace, conversation, admission, atonement, and shared compensation and absolution.[38,39] Associated with the practice is this four-part statement, said with sincerity within these gatherings, "I am sorry, forgive me, thank you, I love you."[40] This assertion can also be repeatedly uttered internally to heal oneself, or as a universal gesture to heal humanity, because "practitioners believe that, when conflict exists in the world, this strife is not only outside themselves but also within, since all beings are connected and all memory is collective. Everyone is responsible for transgressions and for reconciliation."[41]

The third example is for the integrative stage requiring tools that blend interests and build relationship and consensus. From Zen Buddhism and other faith-based traditions comes meditation in motion, "contemplative movement,"[42] that can awaken deeper streams of consciousness. This contemplative movement provides stakeholders an opportunity to leave the confines of the meeting room and venture together into nature to visit the disputed resource. Both movement and the added perspective of seeing the area can bring the group to greater awareness and understanding, individually and collectively.

A fourth example, also involving the integrative stage, advances constructive change. Improvisational exercises, such as "Yes, And," offer techniques that keep people open to acceptance and creativity. The way this exercise works is that whatever is said by one person, the next speaker must begin the conversation with "Yes, And," which tends to affirm what was said by building on it.[43] This technique reinforces trust through collaboration rather than the alternative response of "But, No" that terminates discussion.

A fifth example employs the linguistic fusion of words to form a new concept, portmanteau;[44] often found in pop culture. It could be applied to the integrative and action stages, where details are beginning to be crafted. Imagine one party in an agreement wanting "compulsory" procedures, while others want the agreement to stipulate "optional" approaches. Yet both parties agree in principle. Moving forward might result in a group creating and defining their own word, one that best meets their mutual understanding by blending "compulsory" and "optional," to form, for example, "Opulsory" or "Comptional."

A sixth example involves building consensus that is especially crucial in the integrative and action stages. A useful tool from conflict resolution training is the art of getting the support of all stakeholders, even though all may not agree on the decision.[45] In this process, all perspectives of the topic are heard through an open forum in which each person gets to speak in turn, to discuss concerns, though no vote is taken. What is sought is permission to move forward with the decision. The permission would come from those with a differing perspective than those in the larger group. Among the benefits of this approach are that richer discussions ensue, there is the possibility of keeping constructive relationships intact, and the likelihood that everyone shares in the final decision. To be clear, it does not mean that everyone is in full agreement with the decision. Crucial to this process is a good understanding of what consensus means within the group.

In fact, there are no limitations to where tools can come from. What is essential to this process, however, is that exercises meet the background and relevance of the community—drawing from concepts meaningful to that setting and executing them in the most appropriate stage and manner.

CONCLUDING REMARKS

Water conflicts can be characterized as clashes centered around relationships, data, infrastructure, interests, and values. These contentions are heightened by blundered communication, misunderstandings, and entrenched beliefs, all of which transcend geography.

No matter the scale of a water brawl, conflict transformation is about approaches to strengthen cooperative, interest-based relationships. Such possibilities await when appropriate tools can be effectively employed by stakeholders toward more collectively determined outcomes.

Emphasis is on honing the application of transformative processes, rather than dwelling on entrenched, power-based arrangements. So, regardless of where on the dimensional spectrum parties are in relationship, they may do well to focus on applying skillsets toward effective, sustainable, water management for equitable outcomes, as discussed and demonstrated through examples in the following chapters.

EXERCISES

1. Find opportunities to practice the art of listening during an observed conflict. What different perspectives did you hear?
2. Try one of the transformative processes in an everyday situation. Which one did you select? What was the situation you used it in? How effective was the approach?
3. Think of a personal conflict. At what stage in *The Four Stages of Water Conflict Transformation* would you characterize this conflict? Use Table 2.2 to explain your answer.
4. Think of an environmental conflict. At what stage in *The Four Stages of Water Conflict Transformation* would you characterize this conflict? Use Table 2.2 to explain your answer.
5. Can you think of any practices that come from any aspect of your culture that could be utilized as transformative tools? If so, explain them and indicate at which stage in the process you think it might best be used?

NOTES

1 Loulichki, Mohammed. 2020. "The Grand Ethiopian Renaissance Dam: Between the Burdens of Sovereignty and the Constraints of Neighborhood." Policy Centre for the New South. Policy Brief July 2020, PB-20/62. https://media.africaportal.org/documents/Grand_Ethiopian_Renaissnce_dam.pdf (accessed on December 26, 2020).
2 The Associated Press. "Elevated Lead Levels Found in Newark Schools' Drinking Water." www.nytimes.com/2016/03/10/nyregion/elevated-lead-levels-found-in-newark-schools-drinking-water.html (accessed on December 26, 2020).
3 Lobina, Emanuele. 2000. "Cochabamba—Water War." *FOCUS on the Public Services* 7 (2): 5–10.
4 Delli Priscoli, J., and C. Moore. 1985. *Executive Training Couse in Conflict Management*. Institute for Water Resources, USACE, Alexandria, VA.
5 Barbezat, Daniel, and Mirabai Bush. 2014. *Contemplative Practices in Higher Education: Powerful Methods to Transform Teaching and Learning*. Jossey-Bass, San Francisco, CA. 231 pp.
6 Ibid.
7 Lederach, John. 2015. *Little Book of Conflict Transformation: Clear Articulation of the Guiding Principles by a Pioneer in the Field*. Simon and Schuster, New York. 74 pp.
8 Wolf, Aaron T. 2010. *Sharing Water, Sharing Benefits: Working towards Effective Transboundary Water Resources Management*. UNESCO, Paris. 280 pp.
9 Ibid.

10 Lederach, John. 2015. *Little Book of Conflict Transformation: Clear Articulation of the Guiding Principles by a Pioneer in the Field. Op. cit.*
11 Ibid.
12 Wolf, Aaron T., Shira B. Yoffe, and Mark Giordano. 2003. "International Waters: Identifying Basins at Risk." *Water Policy* 5 (1): 29–60.
13 Zeitoun, Mark, and Naho Mirumachi. 2008. "Transboundary Water Interaction I: Reconsidering Conflict and Cooperation." *International Environmental Agreements: Politics, Law and Economics* 8 (4). Springer: 297.
14 Jarvis, Todd W. 2014. *Contesting Hidden Waters: Conflict Resolution for Groundwater and Aquifers.* Routledge, New York. 192 pp.
15 Sadoff, Claudia W., and David Grey. 2002. "Beyond the River: The Benefits of Cooperation on International Rivers." *Water Policy* 4 (5): 389–403.
16 Wolf, Aaron T. 2010. *Sharing Water, Sharing Benefits: Working towards Effective Transboundary Water Resources Management. Op. cit.*
17 Rothman, Jay. 1989. "Supplementing Tradition: A Theoretical and Practical Typology for International Conflict Management." *Negotiation Journal*, 5: 265–277.
18 Rothman, Jay. 1997. *Resolving Identity-Based Conflicts in Nations, Organizations, and Communities.* Jossey-Bass, San Francisco, CA. 224 pp.
19 Kaufman, Edward. 2002. "Chapter 9: Sharing the Experience of Citizen Diplomacy with Partners in Conflict." Pp. 183–222. In John Davies and Edward Kaufman (Eds.), *Second Track/Citizens' Diplomacy.* Rowman & Littlefield, Lanham, MD.
20 Kaufman, Edward. 2002. "Chapter 10: Toward Innovative Solutions." Pp. 223–264. In John Davies and Edward Kaufman (Eds.), *Second Track/Citizens' Diplomacy: Concepts and Techniques for Conflict Transformation.* Rowman & Littlefield, Lanham, MD.
21 Wolf, Aaron T. 1999. "Criteria for Equitable Allocations: The Heart of International Water Conflict." *Natural Resources Forum*, 23: 3–30.
22 Rothman, Jay. 1995. "Pre-Negotiation in Water Disputes: Where Culture is Core." *Cultural Survival Quarterly*, 19: 19–22.
23 Doermann, Julia, and Aaron T. Wolf (Eds.). 2012. "Sharing Water, Building Relations: Managing and Transforming Water Disputes in the US West." In *Companion Instructor Manual to Professional Skills-Building Workbook.* Oregon State University and US Bureau of Reclamation. U.S. Department of the Interior Bureau of Reclamation Technical Service Center, Denver, Colorado. 192 pp.
24 Wolf, Aaron T. 2010. *Sharing Water, Sharing Benefits: Working towards Effective Transboundary Water Resources Management. Op. cit.*
25 Maser, Chris, and Lynette de Silva. 2019. *Resolving Environmental Conflicts: Principles and Concepts.* 3rd ed. Social-Environmental Sustainability. CRC Taylor and Francis Group, LLC, Boca Raton, FL. 234 pp.
26 Sadoff, Claudia W., and David Grey. 2002. "Beyond the River: The Benefits of Cooperation on International Rivers." *Op. cit.*
27 Wolf, Aaron T. 2010. *Sharing Water, Sharing Benefits: Working towards Effective Transboundary Water Resources Management. Op. cit.*
28 Lederach, John. 2015. *Little Book of Conflict Transformation: Clear Articulation of the Guiding Principles by a Pioneer in the Field. Op. cit.*
29 Ibid.
30 Wolf, Aaron T. 2010. *Sharing Water, Sharing Benefits: Working towards Effective Transboundary Water Resources Management. Op. cit.*
31 Sadoff, Claudia W., and David Grey. 2002. "Beyond the River: The Benefits of Cooperation on International Rivers." *Op. cit.*

32 Sadoff, Claudia W., and David Grey. 2005. "Cooperation on International Rivers: A Continuum for Securing and Sharing Benefits." *Water International* 30 (4): 420–427.
33 Government of B.C. 2020. "About the Columbia River Treaty." https://engage.gov.bc.ca/columbiarivertreaty/about/ (accessed on December 26, 2020).
34 Ibid.
35 Wolf, Aaron T. 2010. *Sharing Water, Sharing Benefits: Working towards Effective Transboundary Water Resources Management. Op. cit.*
36 de Silva, Lynette, and Aaron T. Wolf. 2021. "Chapter 7.10: Transformative Practices for Water Diplomacy." Pp 195–200. In Janos J. Bogardi, Joyeeta Gupta, K. D. Wasantha Nandalal, Léna Salamé, Ronald R. P. van Nooijen, Navneet Kumar, Tawatchai Tingsanchali, Anik Bhaduri, Alla G. Kolechkina (Eds.), *Springer Handbook of Water Resources Management: Discourses, Concepts and Examples.* Springer Nature, Cham, Switzerland. 810pp.
37 Ibid.
38 Phillips, Peters F. 2011. "Alternatives to Interest-Based Problem-Solving: Ho'oponopono." www.mediate.com/articles/PhillipsPbl20110328.cfm (accessed on March 7, 2021)
39 Brinson, Jesse, and Teresa A. Fisher. 1999. "The Ho'oponopono Group: A Conflict Resolution Model for School Counselors." *Journal for Specialists in Group Work*, 24 (4): 369–382.
40 Braley, Susan. 2018. "'A Saying Forth': Rebecca Horne's art Pono; Final and Susan Braley's poem 'Ho'oponopono'." *Canadian Review of Art Education*, 45 (1): 4–8.
41 Ibid.
42 Barbezat, Daniel, and Mirabai Bush. 2014. *Contemplative Practices in Higher Education: Powerful Methods to Transform Teaching and Learning. Op. cit.*
43 Rossing, Jonathan P., and Krista Hoffmann-Longtin. 2016. "Improv (Ing) the Academy: Applied Improvisation as a Strategy for Educational Development." *To Improve the Academy* 35 (2). Wiley Online Library: 303–325.
44 Roudavski, Stanislav. 2013. "Portmanteau Worlds: Hosting Multiple Worldviews in Virtual Environments." Pp. 1–7 In K. Cleland, L. Fisher, and R. Harley (Eds.), *Proceedings of the 19th International Symposium of Electronic Art, ISEA2013 ISEA International, the Australian Network for Art & Technology, the University of Sydney.* ISEA International, the Australian Network for Art & Technology and the University of Sydney, Sydney.
45 Susskind, Lawrence, S. McKearnan, and J. Thomas-Lamar. 1999. "A Short Guide to Consensus Building." Pp. 3–57. In *The Consensus Building Handbook: A Comprehensive Guide to Reaching Agreement.* Safe Publications, London.

3 Evolving Water Governance under United States Law

Holly V. Campbell

CONTENTS

Introduction 49
Synopsis of Water Governance in the United States 50
    Legal Rights to the Use of Surface and Groundwater 50
    The Focus and Purpose of the U.S. Clean Water Act 51
    The Watershed Approach Framework Milestone 52
    Elaborating an Advanced Watershed Approach Through 2030—Three
    Pillars of Sustainability 54
Case Study 55
    The Chesapeake Bay Watershed 55
    Lessons Learned 56
Conclusion 56
Questions 58
Notes 58

INTRODUCTION

As the world further advances the pragmatic structures and practices inherent in integrated water resources management, in the United States water quantity and quality are largely managed separately, as are surface waters and groundwater. The efficiency of water use is similarly attended in a fragmented and mainly voluntary manner. Except for basic goals of water quality embedded in the Clean Water Act of 1972[1] and enforced by the states, management of water within the United States is not fully invested in a holistic assessment, long-range planning, or goals for quantity and quality—either at the national scale or at a level sufficient to meet growing risks of pollution and shortages, among other things.

    The U.S. has decades of scientific data available on water supply and consumption, because the United States Geological Service attempts to quantify it across categories every five years. In 2015, this use was estimated to be 322 billion gallons per day (USGS 2015). Although recent data suggest water withdrawals are trending downward, data from the United States Geological Service indicated fresh groundwater withdrawals were above 2010 level by about 8 percent.

As with other nations, the larger picture of water consumption since 1950 indicates withdrawals rising, regardless of sector (domestic, industrial, agricultural). For a general idea, every 1°F of increase in temperature results in a 4 percent increase in evaporation in terms of how much water the atmosphere can hold. Different regions of the U.S. will continue to experience diverse effects from a warming climate, including increased flooding or severe drought, affecting both water quantity and quality.

Two of the most prevalent drivers of water conflict are: (1) increased withdrawals due to such cases as increased population; changes in use/application; or lack of metering, as is common in irrigation, and (2) changes in the availability and quality of clean water because of shifts in precipitation patterns and the overall climate over time. These factors are present on every continent, not just North America.

The structures, institutions, and legal system that evolved over the past two centuries in the United States' water governance and provision are well established and stable. The U.S. system is replete with model laws and regulations, science, technology, and interdisciplinary personnel for water resources management.

Traditionally, the law provides remedies after harm occurs. In this role, as a system to seek redress or compensation after the fact, our legal system and environmental laws have served us well. Litigation is also available to compel enforcement of the law in civil and criminal disputes and within environmental controversies, when enforcement by authorities is lax or lagging. At least eight U.S. environmental statutes contain provisions authorizing citizens to sue to compel the government to enforce a statute (among the eight is the Clean Water Act).

Mediation and alternative dispute resolution, like our common law, also date back to Roman law. Alternative dispute resolution has played an increasingly prominent role over the past 30 years in helping parties resolve disagreements with the aid of a neutral third-party facilitator. Legal processes and alternative dispute resolution are limited in that they focus on addressing—not preventing—conflict and, therefore, are critically important but one part of a much larger toolbox for cooperative, collaborative management.

The next two centuries will bring the development, articulation, refinement, and fruition of imaginative new tools necessary not only to address harmful impacts and damages but also to foresee and prevent them.

SYNOPSIS OF WATER GOVERNANCE IN THE UNITED STATES

LEGAL RIGHTS TO THE USE OF SURFACE AND GROUNDWATER

Two systems, based on geography, govern the legal right to use water in the U.S. Property holders in the eastern half of the nation abide by the riparian system of water rights, whereby landowners whose land is situated adjacent to freshwater bodies have the right to access and consume the water for themselves, their livestock, and/or crops. The right is held in common, with no right to exclude others.

However, the western states adhere to a rule derived in 1855, known as the *prior appropriations doctrine*. The landowner with the oldest recorded used of the water has a senior right to continue using water up to his legally recorded limit. Those who settled after him or her are junior rights holders. Drought means that some junior rights holders may go without water or with a greatly reduced share. There are three exceptions: federally reserved rights on federal lands, Tribal rights, and groundwater. Groundwater management is of increasing interest.

Groundwater is not managed by the federal government, except for the enforcement of drinking water standards via the Safe Drinking Water Act of 1974[2] pertaining to an aquifer and wells that supply public water. Only two other federal statutes protect groundwater in the U.S.: (1) the Resource Conservation and Recovery Act of 1976[3] and (2) the Comprehensive Environmental Response, Compensation, and Liability Act of 1980, better known as the Superfund law (42 USC § 9601 et seq.).

About a third of the population (115 million) in the U.S. derives its public drinking water from groundwater wells (USGS 2015) and, of that population, 43 million are dependent on groundwater from private wells on their property. In general, rights to groundwater are attached to property and are governed, if at all, by individual states.

THE FOCUS AND PURPOSE OF THE U.S. CLEAN WATER ACT

The major statute governing water quality in the U.S. is the Clean Water Act of 1972. The Act contains both *numeric* and *narrative* water quality standards.[4] The purpose of the Act (in § 101(a)) is to restore and maintain the chemical, physical, and biological integrity of the nation's waters to a basic condition that supports "the protection and propagation of fish, shellfish, and wildlife and provides for recreation in and on the water." This statement is statutory origin of the Act's famous "fishable and swimmable" *narrative* water-quality standards for "conventional pollutants," as defined in the Act (§101(a)(2)). Moreover, the Act specifically requires that effluents from sewage-treatment facilities meet the norms of conventional pollutants, which form the basis of fishable and swimmable:

- Biological oxygen demand or dissolved oxygen required by organisms
- Fecal coliform bacteria
- Oil and grease
- pH over regulatory limits
- Total suspended solids

The Act also required the Environmental Protection Agency to list and adopt standards for toxic pollutants within a 90-day window. Lacking information on known methods of treating toxics at the time the statute was promulgated, the Agency missed its 90-day deadline. Consequently, litigation and a consent decree followed in the case *National Resources Defense Council et al. v Train*,[5] which resulted in the Agency proposing three items: (1) 65 toxic pollutants on the original control list, (2) a list of the main industries required to meet the relevant standards, and (3) regulatory methods to control toxic discharges. These changes were eventually absorbed into the Clean Water Act: with toxic pollutants listed in §307(a), and the statute's National Pollution Discharge Elimination System (NPDES) for point sources (effluent that is discharged from a pipe or similar discrete conveyance).

The NPDES program led to the Clean Water Act's crowning glory, the concept of holistic management of aggregate contaminants across watersheds: the Total

Maximum Daily Load Program. In both large and small watersheds impacted by multiple discharges from various sources, each permit contains its own calculated pollution discharge limit so that the entire watershed stays within water quality compliance—the legally quantifiable, standards assigned. The numeric, science-based total maximum daily loads are sometimes defined as a "prescribed pollution diet" for the recovery of a waterbody, which is further discussed in the Case Study.

Thus, the only thing remaining to be controlled after the Clean Water Act's regulatory approach to conventional and toxic pollutants was nonpoint source pollution. Nonpoint source pollution is any polluted water that does not come from a pipe, generally referring to runoff caused by heavy precipitation. Unless storm water flows into a street sewer grate in a community that is lucky enough to have facilities that treat combined sewage and storm water (called combined sewer systems), runoff is not covered (nor required to be treated) under the Clean Water Act. However, it is important to understand that heavy rains in regions served by combined sewer systems can result in sewage overflows[6] when the system becomes overwhelmed by water volume and velocity. In these cases, the overflow of sewage causes frequently severe pollution that requires the closure of waterways—including local beaches—to swimming, fishing, and even pets such as dogs due to high bacterial and pathogen loads.

THE WATERSHED APPROACH FRAMEWORK MILESTONE

In 1996, the U.S. Environmental Protection Agency announced a vision for the nation called the Watershed Approach Framework (EPA 1996). Several factors in play at the time influenced the development of this innovative vision. For example, as many as 40 percent of water surveys compiled during the 1994 National Water Quality Inventory (also known as the § 305(b) report to Congress every 5 years) reflected measurements of water quality that were inadequate to support the Clean Water Act's basic requirements of fishable and swimmable.

At the time the Agency developed and promoted the Watershed Approach Framework, the nation was embroiled in a protracted, controversial discussion about the loss of wetlands and how to protect those remaining, which are a powerful resource in the mosaic of nature-based opportunities for water quality and water quantity. The Watershed Approach Framework is defined as:

> The watershed approach is a coordinating framework for environmental management that focuses public and private sector efforts to address the highest priority problems within hydrologically defined geographic areas, taking into consideration both ground and surface water flow.[7]

Informing and shaping this approach is the breakthrough recognition that the landscape and all watersheds are continually influenced on by thousands of decisions. Watersheds and their ultimate drainage such as the coastal zone frequently involve the management of legacy pollutants from former technologies (polychlorinated biphenyls or PCBs, for example)[8] and former land uses, including coal mining, extraction of oil and gas, agriculture, and logging.

In essence, landscape and watershed conditions and quality are continually impacted by individual, local, state, and national decisions that may appear discrete but are never accounted for as a whole. This fragmented, death-by-a-thousand-blows has profound, cumulative effects on air, soil, water quality and quantity, and availability. Add the additional effects of population growth, sprawl, and climate change, and the enormity of influences on a region, regardless of its size, and limited water become starkly clear.

This basic overview is, of course, not limited to specific watersheds, but is a bird's eye view that naturally applies everywhere people rely on water in any form. Imagining this scope is staggeringly informative. By enhancing our humility, and systems-based knowledge by way of technologies that were never before available, we can change the management and planning paradigms through more integrated, long-term, systemic-oriented discussions.

The Environmental Protection Agency labels three principles that guide the watershed approach:

1. Partnerships (those who are affected are involved in determining environmental objectives and community/economic goals)
2. Geographic focus
3. Science-based management in an iterative process based on shared information (EPA 1996)

The third principle (a science-based, iterative process) includes the following steps:

1. Assessment and characterization of the natural resources and the communities that depend upon them
2. Goal setting and identification of environmental objectives based on the condition or vulnerability of resources and the needs of the aquatic ecosystem and the people within the community
3. Identification of priority problems (EPA 1996)
4. Evaluation of effectiveness and revision of plans, as needed (EPA 1996), to which should be added: *as well as a review of conflict-oriented inflection points and the need for proactive conversations*

Page 4 of the 1996 document alludes to conflict reduction but the guidelines do not elaborate. In order to be most proactive, the author suggests that a working group engaged in watershed planning might consider inserting two additional steps:

Step 5: a discussion and determination of a set of specific and logical guidelines for preventing and mitigating conflict in their watershed at any point in the planning, decision-making, or management, leading up to the adoption and ongoing implementation of the plan. Furthermore, regular stakeholder-group checkpoints might be considered, perhaps annual, detailed discussions about the prevention and mitigation of conflicts to be held during Step 6: evaluation and revision.

In a September 2014 handbook on the watershed approach, experts from the Environmental Law Institute and the Nature Conservancy recommend that stakeholders focus on ecological and hydrological processes, not structures in the system.[9]

This is wise counsel, and the same could likely be said of the people inhabiting the system (residents, landowners, businesses, and water consumers) who are, after all, an integral part of the landscape's ecology.

Elaborating an Advanced Watershed Approach Through 2030—Three Pillars of Sustainability

The breakthrough of the Watershed Approach Framework reflects the adoption of comprehensive, holistic (less fragmented), ecosystem-based management by the United States to be applied generally to watersheds, each of which is unique, and their processes.

Ecosystem-based management applies not only to the environment but also to agencies and non-government organizations who, as managers, are stewards in charge of conservation, provisioning, and planning.

Ecosystem-based management is an integrated, science-based systems approach to managing natural systems that seeks to identify and incorporate the major interactions in an ecosystem, including human beings, in contrast to traditional approaches that considered individual impacts, species, issues, industrial sectors, or ecosystem services (such as water in a watershed) in isolation.[10] Over the past 30 years, ecosystem-based management has gained currency globally as the preferred contemporary management approach. At the same time, the approach is constantly evolving: it seeks to see the forest for the trees, to quote an old adage.

In the administrative realm, horizontal ecosystem-based management refers to entities of equivalent authority. For example, state agencies involved in a watershed plan are engaged in horizontal ecosystem-based management. In contrast, government agencies working together in scales that span city, county, state, and regional through national and/or international are engage in vertical, ecosystem-based management.

In the application of either horizontal or vertical ecosystem-based management, the goal is coordinated and consistent processes and actions that avoid duplication and/or gaps. Administrative ecosystem-based management seeks to unify goals and approaches, establish non-duplicative roles, transparency, evaluation, and accountability through regular public reports. In many ways, the evolution in applied concepts over the past 30-plus years, such as ecosystem-based management and the watershed approach framework, represents a revolution in worldviews that may be summarized as moving from a hierarchy to a network, something predicted by various authors, including Austrian-American physicist Fritjof Capra (Capra 1997).[11]

The network, as a model of durable governance, takes time to build thoughtfully (perhaps generations) and succeeds by having countless connections linking knowledge and communication with far greater equity. Hierarchies, being more familiar, seem to be a twentieth-century social reaction to a problem. Hierarchies may seem superficially easy to establish and maintain but are ultimately less effective in building cooperation and community and sustaining the integrity of their inherent networks. Hierarchies may be more prone to waste, corruption, and failing bureaucracies.

Evolving Water Governance Under United States Law

Ecosystem-based management fits well with planning for the sustainable use of water and other natural resources. In this context, "sustainable" means planning water quality and quantity for present generations and the environment in such a way that today's decisions include conserving and providing for future generations and the environment they will inherit. Sustainable refers to resource management methods and tools that are capable of maintaining the resources in states that are ecologically, socially, and economically sound into the indefinite future, with all three criteria being equally required.

CASE STUDY

THE CHESAPEAKE BAY WATERSHED

The most ambitious—geographically large and complex—example of a total maximum daily load of pollutants is perhaps Chesapeake Bay in the southeastern United States. The reason Chesapeake Bay makes a valuable case study is its inherent scale and complexity, which includes rivers and streams spanning the boundaries of six states (Delaware, Maryland, New York, Pennsylvania, Virginia, West Virginia, and the District of Columbia with a total of 18 million residents) that participate in the watershed.

The region covered by Chesapeake Bay's total maximum daily load[12] of pollutants is the 200-mile-long Bay and a 64,000 square mile watershed. In turn, the Bay watershed's total, overarching maximum daily load consists of 92 smaller total maximum daily loads of pollutants, from a spectrum of sources including: agriculture, transportation exhaust, industrial facilities, power generation, and other emissions. The Chesapeake Bay states and partners managing the maximum daily load of pollutants represent a real, working network.

The complexity of the region required an enormous, decades-long process in order to put the total maximum daily loads for the watershed in place, as well as investing in collaboration for the coming decades. This teamwork is necessary because the Bay's total maximum daily loads from development and maintenance are impacted by the presence of many complicating and unique factors:

- Hydrological and geological scale and complexity
- Complex and constricted tidal volume of water and its turnover
- Diverse land-use factors (and impervious vs pervious surfaces)
- Diverse point and nonpoint sources of contaminants, effluents, and air emissions
- Diverse stakeholders
- Diverse, multi-jurisdictional, governmental, and nongovernmental participation at various levels of authority.

The water quality of the Bay is largely impaired by contamination from excess nitrogen, phosphorus (nutrients), and sediment from runoff. The Chesapeake Bay Program established restoration goals in the form of reduction targets for nutrients and sediment in each of the watershed's states and the District of Columbia, stemming from sources including runoff from agriculture and storm water, as well as discharges of treated wastewater in order to restore habitats, fisheries, and the communities dependent on the Bay ecosystem.

The Bay's total maximum daily load of pollutants has 2-year milestones containing short-term goals, as part of the Bay's accountability framework in which the partners and the Environmental Protection Agency evaluate progress. The midpoint assessment (EPA 2017) indicates that implementation of the application of the Bay's total maximum daily load has successfully recovered a record number of acres of sea grasses (66,387 acres, 26,866 hectares) in the Bay and its tidal tributaries, a 70 percent increase from the first survey in 1984. Reductions in phosphorus and sediment exceeded the 60 percent goals, but did not meet the 2017 goal for nitrogen reduction.[13]

Efforts by the upstream states directly affect the Bay, and successes, such as in Maryland, make a difference to all. From 2010 through 2017, Maryland's streams and lakes, impaired by phosphorus and total suspended solids, are evidenced higher levels of dissolved oxygen and submerged vegetation. In addition, 17 waterbodies were removed from the Clean Water Act's §303(d) list of impaired waters in Pennsylvania's Susquehanna River watershed since 2014.

Lessons Learned

Restoration of watersheds, their habitats, and species assemblages takes a long time. The time required is directly related to: (1) how altered the system is as a whole, (2) how complex the system being restored is—hydrogeologic factors in the watershed, such as shallow water with low turnover, constricted tidal influence, and so on, and (3) the time lag from the beginning of restoration to signs of progress. The time lag is very much a part of the watershed itself (its geological, hydrological, and geomorphological features and soils) and this inherent time lag is referred to as hysteresis. This time lag must be taken realistically into account and honestly communicated to partners, funders, and the general public. For example, if a restoration of a large, complex watershed will take 80 years, that estimate should be plainly communicated in order to establish realistic expectations.

Transparency, monitoring, reporting, and evaluation are all critical to accurately determining whether objectives are being met or if adjustments to methods are necessary.

CONCLUSION

As with most other forms of environmental governance in the United States, the governance of water is fragmented. For example, even while many experts agree that sources of freshwater are threatened or dwindling, water quantity and quality are conceptually treated and regulated separately, although they are strongly related. Conflicts over water management are traditionally, and by necessity, recognized and approached after a problem arises. Like environmental law itself, solutions can result in decades-long debates and negotiations that are debilitating and costly, even as the social-environmental landscape keeps changing.

As a thought experiment, imagine if we were to invite an interdisciplinary group of experts to wide-ranging discussions challenging traditional approaches to water management in order to theorize fresh ideas that are more preventative in application. Even while each watershed and its controversies are unique, looking broadly at water conflicts over the past century across the United States, certain patterns become apparent. For these patterns to become fully discernible, the discussion would have to include: water resource managers, state and federal scientists, hydrologists and engineers, ecologists and public health representatives, water quality experts, consumers from every sector, zoning and land-use planners, developers, university faculty and students, and the water-conflict mitigation community.

Elaborating on the watershed approach with knowledge gained since studied and discussed throughout the 1990s (EPA 1996, NRC 1999) and adopted in 2000 (FR65 No. 202, 62566, October 18, 2000), the U.S. could potentially modernize water conflict management by promoting further integration within the systems-based, holistic concept. Simultaneously integrating data, planning, and policy goals for sustainable flows; equitable distribution; restoration, where appropriate; and improved water quality over the coming century could yield multiple, long-term, money-saving co-benefits.

Further developing a state-of-the-art, federally supported watershed evaluation and strategic approach could greatly aid the states in sharing information and deriving more consistent cooperative processes aimed at coherent management paradigms that combine multiple goals. This approach would, however, require the joint participation of state, local, and non-governmental organization partners representing each region and appropriate watershed scale. In essence, this would amount to ecosystem-based management for watersheds, which recognizes people as an integral part of the ecosystem. Many states, such as Oregon, have already elaborated individual watershed frameworks within their states.[14]

The rights to access and use water would be directly tied to its quantity, quality, and the sustainable maintenance of its watershed for future generations. The approach would supply tools and other support for states to begin prioritizing nationwide reduction of mindless, immeasurable, wasteful use of resources within and across sectors (agriculture, residential and urban, power generation, and water infrastructure itself).

In U.S. law (derived from English common law), the doctrine of waste enshrines waste reduction as an affirmative responsibility. Under the Public Trust Doctrine, federal and state sovereigns are the Trustees of assets (natural resources, such as water). The governments, as trustees acting on behalf of citizens—the beneficiaries of the trust for whom the resources are a necessity—have the affirmative, legal duty to conserve and protect the natural resources, a role that is similar to any other trustee at law.

A holistic, national, watershed approach would have multiple goals to achieve increased efficiency *and* effectiveness in tandem with improved social, economic, and ecological outcomes (the three pillars of sustainability)[15] in the supply and distribution of water in the U.S. This achievement requires that systems for planning and delivery become more adaptive and resilient to disruption from both drought and flooding. It is my hope that an integrated, systems-view of water management can contribute to the sustainable, equitable advancement of the Watershed Approach Framework and to ongoing national discussions about the development of proactive ways and means to effectively improve the prevention and/or resolution of water conflicts.

QUESTIONS

1. Assume that most people in the United States do not know where their water comes from. How can they find this information? What are the benefits for a town, state, and region when water consumers (residents and businesses) are actively engaged in water literacy?
2. In your opinion, which institutions or corporations are leaders in water literacy and conservation? What actions are they taking that leads you to believe that they are water stewards?
3. Assume that supplies of freshwater are decreasing over time due to rising consumption, leaking infrastructure, over-application, or other forms of waste, exacerbated by shifting patterns of precipitation and increased frequency and potential severity of drought. What creative, wide-ranging, collaborative conservation initiatives can you design to address these dire challenges?

   In brainstorming, think across scales from local to national or international and across contexts: social and cultural, governance/policy, and technical/engineering, as well as across sectors: food, energy, manufacturing, landscaping, and recreation (golf courses, parks, and so forth).
4. What are the potential benefits of allowing limited or regulated investment in and purchase of water rights? What type of policy framework is necessary and at what level? Consider watershed or state levels. Should the rights that were purchased revert to the state after 5 or 10 years? What are the enforcement and regulatory dangers, and what are the ethical and equity concerns?

NOTES

1 The United States Clean Water Act of 1972 (33 USC Ch. 23 §1151 et seq.).
2 The United States Safe Drinking Water Act of 1974 (42 USC §300f et seq.).
3 Water Resources Reform and Development Act of 2014, Public Law 113–121 (42 USC Ch. 82 § 6901 et seq.).
4 The CWA's water quality criteria are explained by the United States Environmental Protection Agency, Key Concepts Module 3: Criteria, available at www.epa.gov/wqs-tech/key-concepts-module-3-criteria
5 *National Resources Defense Council et al. v Train* (8 ERC 2120, DDC 1976).
6 The EPA explains CSOs in the National Pollutant Discharge System, Combined Sewer Overflows (CSOs), United States Environmental Protection Agency, available at www.epa.gov/npdes/combined-sewer-overflows-csos
7 Federal Register, Unified Federal Policy for a Watershed Approach to Federal Land and Resource Management, *Notice*, Vol. 65, No. 202, October 18, 2000, accessed December 15, 2020, available at www.govinfo.gov/content/pkg/FR-2000-10-18/pdf/00-26566.pdf. See also: National Research Council, *New Strategies for America's Watersheds*,

The National Academies Press, Washington, DC, 1999, available at www.nap.edu/catalog/6020/new-strategies-for-americas-watersheds
8 The EPA explains polychlorinated biphenyls (PCBs), United States Environmental Protection Agency, available at www.epa.gov/pcbs/learn-about-polychlorinated-biphenyls-pcbs
9 Environmental Law Institute and The Nature Conservancy, *Watershed Approach Handbook: Improving Outcomes and Increasing Benefits Associated with Wetland and Stream Restoration Protection Projects, and Case Studies Included*, September 2014, available at www.eli.org/sites/default/files/eli-pubs/watershed-approach-handbook-improving-outcomes-and-increasing-benefits-associated-wetland-and-stream_0.pdf
10 National Oceanic and Atmospheric Administration, *Ecosystem Based Management 101*, available at https://ecosystems.noaa.gov/EBM101/WhatisEcosystem-BasedManagement.aspx
11 Capra, F., *The Web of Life: A New Scientific Understanding of Living Systems*, Anchor Books/Random House, New York, 1997.
12 The United States Environmental Protection Agency, *Chesapeake Bay Total Maximum Daily Load (TMDL) and Regional Watershed Implementation Plans (WIPs)*, accessed December 22, 2020, available at www.epa.gov/chesapeake-bay-tmdl
13 The United States Environmental Protection Agency. 2017. *Midpoint Assessment of the Chesapeake Bay Total Maximum Daily Load (TMDL)*, available at www.epa.gov/sites/production/files/2018-07/documents/factsheet-epa-midpoint-assessment-chesapeake-bay-tmdl.pdf
14 State of Oregon, *Watershed Approach Framework*, available at www.oregon.gov/deq/wq/Pages/Watershed-Framework.aspx
15 The United States Environmental Protection Agency, *Sustainability Primer Version 9* (n.d.), available at www.epa.gov/sites/production/files/2015-05/documents/sustainability_primer_v9.pdf

4 Different Systems, Common Conflicts

Holly V. Campbell and Liliana Pimentel

CONTENTS

Introduction 61
Water Management in Brazil 63
Case Studies from Brazil 68
    The Water Crisis in the São Paulo Metropolitan Region (2014–2016) 69
        Context 69
        Conflict 71
        Main Results and Lessons Learned 72
    The Water Crisis in the Federal District (2016–2018) 73
        Context 73
        Conflict 74
        Main Results and Lessons Learned 75
Water Management in the United States 76
    Florida V Georgia 78
        Context 78
        Conflict 78
        Results, Lessons Learned, and Lessons Suggesting Design of New Approaches 79
    Mexican Water Treaty of 1944 80
        Context 80
        Conflict 80
        Main Results and Lessons Learned 81
Conclusion 81
Questions 82
Notes 82

INTRODUCTION

Regardless of geopolitical setting or scale, understanding the causes and history of conflict is essential for an accurate and meaningful assessment of the full context of disputes and underlying negotiations. Like the United States, Brazil is politically structured using a federal governance system. Differences stemming from the evolution of the two nations are apparent in their institutional structures and management practices, but they share the attributes of States having substantially more autonomy and Governors more power than in other organizational models where the central government has pre-eminent authority.

Brazil's federative pact was imposed by the 1891 Constitution, which determined the unbreakable union of its federative units. The concentration of decision-making authority in the highest levels of the Brazilian Government remained in force for a long time and discouraged broad participation of civil society in decision-making. After several Constitutional revisions, triggered at times by rather complex political movements that had to be navigated to strengthen democracy in the country, the 1988 Constitution consolidated the prominent role of local governments and paved the way to broader participation of civil society in decision- and policymaking. This evolution to broader societal involvement across all sectors included environment and water management policies, particularly since the early 1990s when Brazil's profile in international environmental issues was catalyzed by hosting the Earth Summit in 1992. The attention brought to Brazil as a result of this Conference has continued as manifested by its hosting the 8th World Water Forum in 2018 in Brasilia and its increasingly visible role in global and regional fora with a focus on water and the environment.

This chapter briefly describes the Brazilian Water Management System ("Singreh" for Portuguese acronym), which contains common directives that the States follow when designing and implementing their own management, policy, and regulatory systems. Aspects of how Brazil built a non-hierarchical, National and State-level water-resources management system will be discussed further in the next section.

Among many cases of water conflict in Brazil, two examples were selected for this chapter, a sectorial conflict and a locational conflict. The Brazilian case studies cover conflicts that affected the water supply of two of Brazil's most important cities. Both cases happened after a water crisis that hit São Paulo State from 2014 to 2016, which accounts for 33 percent of the country's Gross Domestic Product[1] and a similar one affecting the Federal District of Brasilia in 2016 to 2018, which is the center of the political power in Brazil.

Although quite different in terms of dimensions and geography, both the State of São Paulo and the Federal District have their own water management systems formed by State agencies, legislation, and mechanisms for implementation and monitoring, following national guidelines. The comparison between these two federative units reveals systems at different stages of consolidation, as their respective crises happened sequentially—the Federal District in 2016–2018 benefitted from some lessons already learned in São Paulo in 2014–2016.

At that time, the crisis seriously impacted water supplied to the largest urban area in South America,[2] São Paulo Metropolitan Region (RMSP in Portuguese), which is surrounded by other metropolitan areas that together consolidate into a macrometropolitan region[3] comprising a total of 174 municipalities and almost 34 million inhabitants equivalent to 73.5 percent of the State of São Paulo's and around 16 percent of the entire country's population. In the case of São Paulo, it is possible to identify a history of cross-sector and cross-institution water conflicts that resurfaced after being resolved at some level in the past, as with the 2016–2018 crisis. Public water supplied to the São Paulo Metropolitan Region (RMSP) is ensured by water-basin transfers and a complex network of reservoirs, pumps, and pipelines fraught with many ongoing technical and political issues. The 2014–2016 water crisis, caused by the State-wide drought, simultaneously affected all basins providing water to the greater RMSP. The response to the crisis was an overlay on the ordinary, individual water supply and water regulatory compliance issues that each basin was confronting.

In the Federal District, the dispute over the needs of local farmers versus prioritizing water for human consumption dominated the crisis. The importance of and interdependence between water and food and the seriousness of the imbalance of that relationship in central Brazil become evident when we consider that the region is home to the Country's second-largest biome and is also the headwaters of three of Brazil's largest rivers (São Francisco, Paraná, and Tocantins) as well as of the Country's capital city Brasilia.

Both Brazilian cases (presented in this chapter) are related to water crises caused by sudden, unexpected changes in rain patterns, aggravated by gaps in the integration of public policies related to land use and planning. Similar circumstances are increasing in both frequency and their impact on society.

WATER MANAGEMENT IN BRAZIL

The freshwater in Brazil accounts for 12 percent of the world's surface water resources. This highlights the importance of proper management of this strategic resource beyond national interests. The biodiversity and the environmental wealth linked to this resource have also boosted water management in the country.

Water scientist Dr. R. Meganck[4] wrote about the importance of the Brazilian water management system: On one hand, the tremendous water resources provide the basis for analyzing a wide range of problems and potential solutions. On the other hand, it is a responsibility for Brazil to share its management experience as its system could serve as a model for many countries in how conflicts can be equitably resolved nationally.

Meganck highlighted the Country's increasingly important role in South America that places Brazil as a focal point of many regional Treaties, Agreements, and Conventions such as the Treaty of the Río de la Plata (*Prata* in Portuguese) that has been in force since the mid-1970s and the Amazon Cooperation Treaty since 1978. Additionally, he evaluates that Brazil will continue to develop its understanding of water conflict resolution based on both its national and international experience fostered by the research sector to share this wealth with the world.

But Brazil worked over many years to develop its water management expertise. The social relationship with bodies of water in Brazil was initially utilitarian, based on notions of abundance and perceived ownership of the resource. That attitude, at first, led to inefficient water use and the dismissal of water's intrinsic value. Water was considered a "given," a resource never in short supply.

Water quality was the first concern to emerge in the Brazilian legal system: the 1916 Civil Law Code determined punishment for polluters. However, the first specific water law passed in 1934, as concerns about water quality also arose. The so-called 1934 Water Code aimed more to establish State control over the use of water as a public asset than conserving water or improving its management. Some states, even as early as the turn of the previous century, faced challenges in managing both water quality and increasing demand.

Isolated disputes, driven by water scarcity or quality, were starting to emerge—leading some States, such as São Paulo, Rio de Janeiro, and Ceará, to consider management models and laws. After more than 50 years since the Water Code was passed, the political scenario has changed, and a new democracy emerged in the country as reflected in the 1988 Constitution. Among many civil rights, the new Constitution established a different approach to solve environmental issues and the importance of local decision-making and management systems.

The 1988 Constitution determined when a given water body is under the protection of the Union or a State. Basically, watercourses or water bodies defining or crossing federative boundaries are under the dominium of the Union; all the others, including groundwater, are under the dominium of the States.

This definition has huge importance for the design of the integrated water management framework in Brazil as we explain later. Following the constitutional requirements, the Federal Law 9433 of March 20, 1997, replaced the 1934 Water Code and become popularly called the National Water Law.

This law reflected the Dublin Principles and contemplated participatory management as well as the shared responsibility, as outlined in the 1992 Rio Earth Summit Convention, and supported by national and international financing institutions, especially for non-industrialized countries. Established by the Law, Brazil's National Water Policy defines water as a "public good" and recognizes it as a "limited natural resource that has economic value." Because of these principles, the law also states that multiple water uses must be assured and defines the watershed as the territorial unit for water planning and management.

The 1997 Water Law established the National Water Resources Policy, five instruments for its implementation, and a governance framework called Water Resources Management System (Singreh from the Portuguese acronym).

This management system was designed to enable regulation and participatory management in a tripartite model. These two elements help offset the force of economic and political power in decision-making by defining human consumption as the "main priority" followed by "animal consumption." Including these accesses and use priorities in legislation directly impacts the dynamics of any negotiations involving water resources.

Based on the French model, the Brazilian system (Singreh) is a non-hierarchical structure designed to manage water in the country, while respecting the different water domains (State and Federal). Figure 4.1 illustrates this framework; the columns establish the role and competencies an entity has regarding water management and the lines explain its jurisdiction.

As Figure 4.1 shows, there are three levels of planning and decision-making regarding the management of water in Brazil: (1) watershed; (2) State level; and (3) National level. Because of the dominium over the water bodies defined in the 1988 Constitution, some watershed committees work at National level and others at the State level.

The watershed committees form a tripartite collaborative entity, comprising representatives from the: (1) water user sector; (2) government; and (3) organized civil society. This tripartite structure also applies to the Councils working both at the State and the National levels.

Different Systems, Common Conflicts

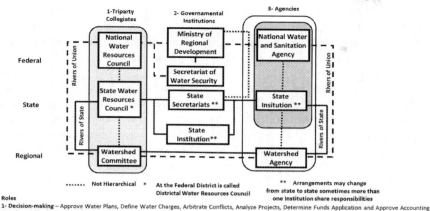

FIGURE 4.1 The Brazil water management system framework.

Source: (Designed by Liliana Pimentel based on the 9433 Brazilian Federal Law).

In the first column, Figure 4.1 shows that committees and Councils oversee the decision-making process; in the second column, there are the administrative governmental entities in charge of policymaking and administrative support to their respective Councils; and in the third column, the agencies or similar entities at the National or State level carry out regulation and enforcement activities and provide technical information and support to Committees and Councils respecting its jurisdiction. They can delegate some of their responsibilities to the agencies serving committees as technical and administrative support, but not in a regulatory or enforcement capacity.

The logical, interrelated structure of the Brazilian water management system noted previously and involving institutions, committees, and councils at various administrative scales naturally supports their utility in applying the conflict transformation framework. This is evident in the cases that follow.

While in some countries watershed committees or entities are created only by popular initiative, in Brazil they are prefigured and stated in the law. The Committees were conceived as a context for democratic participation in decision-making: the basis for Brazil's water management system, making it responsible not only for the decision-making and planning, but also for moderating negotiations and conflict resolution.

However, the lengthy time for committees to be created, to mature, to function, and to achieve practical results, in addition to other frailties described by Abbers and Kerk in the results of the Water Mark Project,[5] had adverse effects on the consolidation of Singreh as they should be the basis to the whole water management system. Almost 25 years after the system creation, a large portion of the country's territory is still not served by Committees.

As mentioned before, the 1997 Water Law established five instruments to assure the National Water Policy implementation and organize water management at all levels: (1) classification of the water bodies, related to a desired target of quality based on planned future uses; (2) water resources plans, intended to reach the desired class in a given time; (3) water grants, granted by the agencies taking into account the priority uses established by the committee, the water balance and the uses already established in a watershed; (4) water charges, revenue generated (when users pay for water used) is returned to the watershed to keep the water management system financially sustainable, and (5) the water resources information system to guarantee transparency and provide data to support decision- and policy-making processes. Those instruments should work in an integrated manner and mainstream the National Water Resources Policy with other related public policies, such as environmental management, land use, occupation, and sanitation and health.

The National Information System on Water Resources (SNIRH in Portuguese, carried out by the National Agency) was created to assure water resources data-sharing. Additionally, the Ministry of the Environment carried out the Information System for Follow-Up and Assessment of the Water Management Policy Implementation (Siapreh in Portuguese) for designing and monitoring the implementation of the National Water Management Policy. Until 2018, the Ministry of Environment staff, in collaboration with the other actors involved in integrated water resources management in Brazil (including academia, non-government organizations, university research centers, and subnational agencies and institutions), was in charge to maintain accurate records about the water management system aiming to improve water governance. This record should include information about the implementation of those five instruments and the profile of the committee members to guide National Water Council decision-making regarding financial resources investments needed in each watershed to strengthen and foster the Singreh implementation, which, in turn, would guide the operation of the National Water Agency.

However, the development of Siapreh as the system to monitor the Water Policy Implementation was discontinued about a decade ago and the results of the evaluation made by the Ministry were never published. Therefore, the aspiration that the information flow between the committee-national council would be seamless did not come to fruition. Over time, without the Siapreh results to inform its activities, the National Water Management Council (CNRH from Portuguese) lost prominence, and today the whole system is much weaker than as originally conceived. As a result, today, nearly 25 years after the Water Law was passed, the management instruments that it embodied are not fully implemented nationally, the number of committees is growing at a much slower pace, and the political influence of the National Water Council itself has been severely diminished and surpassed by the National Water Agency.

The National Water Agency (ANA in Portuguese) was created by Federal Law 9984 on July 17, 2000. After an administrative reshuffle of the federal government in 2019, the entire water management system, including ANA, now reports to the Regional Development Ministry instead of the Environment Ministry. The scope of ANA's responsibility and its official name was changed to National Agency of Water and Basic Sanitation by Law 14.026 (July 15, 2020) to include regulation of the basic sanitation sector. While the scope of sanitation services goes beyond water supply and sewage collection and treatment systems, this chapter focuses on those two services, which are usually provided in an integrated fashion, being now regulated by ANA at the Federal level.

Basic sanitation services are also the responsibility of the State in Brazil, per the Constitution, and are assigned to local governments, which may grant authorization to private or state companies, form joint ventures and consortiums, or set up dedicated municipal entities. When authorization is granted for a given period of time, the related management responsibility of the State remains in force, and the concession contract stipulates the compliance standards the grantees must meet. These requirements are applicable for water supply, such as affordability, regularity, and quality, among others.

Because provision of water is a public service, the grantees' activities have to comply with the Transparency Law to make data and information available to the public. Consumers pay for such services. The Federal Consumers' Rights Law, combined with other regulations, requires water-sanitation companies to openly release water quality data and information. Minimum-quality parameters for potable water use in the distribution network are issued by Brazil's health authorities, while the quality standards at the water source are controlled by the environmental authorities. Those standards are accounted for when the agency in charge releases water grants for the sanitation companies to withdraw water from any water body.

Human settlements and economic activity along waterways led to watercourses being modified, channeled, and violated, with a sense of entitlement on the part of decision-makers, who frequently failed to derive substantive inputs from the supposed beneficiaries. This alteration of water movement compounded landscape changes and sanitation challenges, which have always been problematic in Brazil. To this day, there are large areas where basic sanitation services are not available. In fact, 16 percent of the country's population has no access to the public-water network,[6] and 45 percent lacks access to a public sewerage system,[7] all within a context of considerable inequality and regional differences.

Brazil's power generation is based on hydraulic systems (where water is used to drive technology), and hydroelectric generation accounts for 65 percent of the electricity production.[8] In 2012, a water crisis affected the electricity production of the entire country. As a result, the investment in alternative sources of energy, including solar and wind power, has increased notably, reducing by about 15 percent the Country's dependence on hydroelectricity. However, control of the river flow and management of reservoirs are still essential to the country while attending to increased demands for multiple uses, such as sanitation services.

In 2019, the total water withdrawal in Brazil was 458,196 gallons/s, while the total consumption was 247,465 gallons/s. Irrigation consumed 66 percent of this total, while urban supply consumed 9 percent and rural supply 2.4 percent. About the withdrawal volume, we can notice that irrigation accounts for 50 percent and urban supply 24.3 percent, indicating the need to improve efficiency on basic sanitation services. There is an estimated increase in water demand in Brazil, indicating that withdrawal might rise by 23 percent by 2030.[9]

The regional differences in water availability and the concentration of human settlements contribute to significant gaps in income levels and the availability of public services and infrastructure at the national and regional scales.

Logically, these variations also impact the existence and maintenance of water collection and distribution infrastructure as well as the laws and regulatory framework that underpin the long-term management and sustainability of communities dependent on water resources. As has been frequently stated, water is a renewable, but not an inexhaustible, resource; and like any natural resource, water requires careful planning and management at all levels of governance.

In Brazil, in contrast to many other countries, litigation rarely arises from disputes over water rights. This is because water rights are not related to the date a grant is issued, but rather are subject to change based on quantity and priority uses established in the law. Some committees also have effective mechanisms in place to prevent overallocation, setting aside water or legal devices from precluding any user requesting and obtaining access to higher water volumes than their known requirement.

Brazil's size naturally creates regional differences that affect management systems. As a result, it is challenging to describe the entirety of the specific details of the country's water management system. Instead, this chapter's goal is to present an overview and main points to support the analysis of the included case studies. The choice of case studies is based on the degree of involvement by the sanitation segment and the perceived need for a change in water grants, a change that does not routinely occur.

Changes in land use, combined with changes in precipitation and weather patterns, highlight the need for a nationwide reconsideration of the way water is accessed and used in Brazil. From 2012 through 2017, the country faced a severe water crisis in the normally drier northeast, making the region particularly vulnerable. The crisis has now reached places that were not usually impacted by drought. For example, the water crisis affected São Paulo Metropolitan Region in 2014–2016 and Brasilia in 2016–2018. Since 2018, severe conditions impact southern Brazil and in 2020 even threatened the Parana River Basin that flows to neighboring countries in South America. This situation affects a long list of regional water uses, including navigation, hydropower, irrigation, tourism, and fishing, and importantly also has international implications to existing accords and agreements with neighboring, downstream countries.

Despite the complexities of the Brazilian case studies presented in this chapter, it is important to note that the Country has made substantial progress in developing a cadre of first-class water scientists. It has also supported the development of several world-class research institutes that are helping to ensure that quality science is the foundation for institutional and infrastructure development as well as policy advances in the sector. In this regard, Brazil has also increased its international profile in water with prominent roles in the World Water Council, the UNESCO Intergovernmental Hydrological Programme, and the UN Sustainable Development Commission.

CASE STUDIES FROM BRAZIL

There are many ongoing water conflicts in Brazil, few of which have been analyzed, particularly by the international scientific community. The two cases included here are selected because of their relationship to the change in the Sanitation Law, which

Different Systems, Common Conflicts

FIGURE 4.2 Brazilian case study locations.
Source: (Created by Liliana Pimentel).

in July 2020 assigned partial regulation (supply and sewage) of the sanitation segment to the National Water and Sanitation Agency (ANA).

Both case studies involve negotiations about sanitation, but occurred at different times and places (refer to Figure 4.2). They resulted from a water crisis caused by unexpected, sharp fluctuations in rain patterns that affected the availability of water for all uses in their respective basins. The reduction in availability required existing water grants to be revised to ensure the supply of water would meet the required priorities, standards, and regulations. In both cases, simultaneous compliance with various legislations had to be considered. Additionally, all parties involved in the water management system had to act swiftly and in a coordinated manner. The São Paulo case happened at the federative union level, while the Brasilia case was addressed within the federative jurisdiction.

THE WATER CRISIS IN THE SÃO PAULO METROPOLITAN REGION (2014–2016)

Context

São Paulo City was founded in 1554 and is one of the oldest in Brazil. As one of the cradles of colonization, São Paulo developed into an important trade and financial hub. Industrialization and the favorable location for the distribution of produced goods turned the capital city into a magnet for labor. Migrants and immigrants came seeking opportunities at a time when Europe was dealing with the aftermath of World War II and the Brazilian northeastern states were suffering from a prolonged drought.

The population skyrocketed, urbanization was quick and chaotic, and the city grew from 2 million inhabitants in 1950 to 12 million in 2020. Industrial pollution and unregulated disposal of non-treated domestic sewage rose on a collision course with the growing demand for water in a territory where unplanned occupation contributed to the degradation of water sources.

Despite concentrating the most important Brazilian centers for education and research, a solid technology sector, and finance conglomerates, São Paulo State has not managed to avoid the consequences of its biggest weakness—the negative impact of unregulated human activity on its supporting ecosystems, especially around the capital. São Paulo, in the 1970s, was one of the first federative states to develop and implement a state law to prioritize and protect the water sources for human use. That pioneering approach was driven by the need to preserve supply sources and to allay rising tensions among sectors, such as sanitation and electric power.

São Paulo State has large volumes of groundwater and an extensive network of waterways. Some of this resource is used for electric power generation, essential for urban expansion and a thriving economy. In 1991, the State introduced one of the first participatory water management systems in Brazil. This system was mostly based on the French model. This model was the inspiration for today's Brazilian Water Law—its structure and most of its instruments.

Since the beginning of industrialization, global challenges have arisen related to the effects of the use of natural resources and to exploitative practices, which exacerbate inequality. Such effects were seen when a sudden change in rain patterns almost paralyzed the largest economy in Latin America. In addition to social inequality, it revealed the difficulty of the State to address and meet water demands in a scenario of natural changes in rain cycle trends. The 2014 drought negatively impacted the navigational system in São Paulo State for almost 5 years.

Southeast Brazil holds about 77 percent of the entire population, in 11 percent of the nation's territory with only 7 percent of the available water. As we mentioned, the major population is concentrated around São Paulo City, located in the central portion of the macro-metropolitan area known as São Paulo Metropolitan Region (RMSP in Portuguese). The RMSP is formed by 39 municipalities and almost triple the number of inhabitants of the capital, who rely on eight different water supply systems working in an integrated fashion. Some systems used to supply RMSP depend on watersheds located in more than one state, and some of the water bodies also supply other Metropolitan Regions such as Rio de Janeiro or Campinas. Notably, ANA classified all of these watersheds as water-scarce, in consideration of demand and availability projections. The main system to supply RMSP is called Cantareira. After a 5-year series of declining rainfall patterns, in 2014 the most severe drought to hit the state since 1953 led to a drop in the hydrological capacity of the river system in the region to just 25 percent of the average annual volume, which led some reservoirs such as Cantareira to drop down more than 10 percent of their total volume.

Conflict

The Cantareira reservoir is supplied by a complex system of water transfers, channels, and pumps, which include water bodies under Union, São Paulo State, and Minas Gerais State jurisdiction. Therefore, the evaluations and the regulations governing the water collection and distribution system in São Paulo are made jointly by institutions from both levels of government as discussed previously, the ANA, the Department of Water and Energy of São Paulo State (DAEE in Portuguese), and the Institute of Water Management of Minas Gerais (Igam in Portuguese).

The two main basins supplying water for the Cantareira System are Upper Tietê River and the Piracicaba, Capivari, and Jundiaí Watershed (PCJ). As mentioned before, financial mechanisms preclude the reservation of rights for future use of water, as that would reduce availability and increase the financial risk for immediate needs and water grants. That financial device in the case of the Piracicaba, Capivari, and Jundiai Rivers Basin Committee is the applicability of heavy fines when measured water catchment is not equivalent to at least 70 percent of the volume granted by the Agency.

When the water crisis occurred, the PCJ basin and the Upper Tietê river region were severely impacted. This jeopardized the Cantareira system in two ways: (1) Within a short timeframe, the drought depleted the water source from the Campinas area; and (2) the Upper Tietê system, the alternate water supply to the capital, could not fully serve its purpose. According to data from the DAEE, the basins are under the recommended annual availability of water per inhabitant equivalent to 241,966 gallons/inhab/year, although Tietê has about 44,214 gallons/inhab/year and Piracicaba, Capivari, and Jundiai about 105,580 gallons/inhab/year.[10] Those values were recorded during non-crisis periods but indicate that water demands exceeded availability.

In 2014, the ANA added a special group to the monitoring headquarters, already jointly established in 2009. The involved parties could appoint representatives to the special group to help work on water quality and volume indicators, negotiate agreements, and find solutions for shared challenges related to the crisis.

At that time, the operational costs of Sabesp, a São Paulo State utility company for water supply and sanitation serving the majority of the cities of São Paulo Metropolitan Region, including the capital, increased considerably. The utility had to maintain standards for drinking water and the availability of service, as per the Consumer Law and existing contracts granting rights of usage. The situation also required negotiations for further investments to keep catchments feasible and expand the treatment of wastewater and sewerage systems. The utility company simultaneously faced reduced revenue, increased expenses, and changes in licenses over the water catchment in the PCJ basin and its transfer to the Cantareira complex. The most serious conflict had to do with water allocation to different regions and companies.

Even though Sabesp abided by all agreements, upon receiving the bill for the volume in the subsequent period, it was fined for the deployment of the device used to protect against water reservation by the users because the utility had not met the minimum volume (equivalent to 6,820 gallons/s) in the catchment, as determined in the license, but rather the one defined in an agreement, around 3,520 gallons/s.

Sabesp appealed to the National Water Council, the supposed highest arena for water conflict resolution in Brazil's Water Management System. However, the Council did not even analyze the matter, as the understanding of the Water Law and resolutions by its Secretariat was that Committees oversee rulings of unsolved conflicts between members. Therefore, the Committee itself should have requested the Council's intervention, not the company.

The Federal Piracicaba, Capivari, and Jundiai Committees should have worked as a forum for the resolution of conflicts arising from decisions and negotiations taking place in the monitoring headquarters. This is part of their directive; besides, collected billing funds are reinvested in the original basin, so the fine value goes to the Committee. Given the complexity of the situation, the National Water Management Council should have been involved throughout negotiations, at least as an observer, and should not have allowed the ANA, whose role is distinctly different, to take the lead. No doubt, the ANA staff are more than qualified, but this action does not comply with the water management system in place—when one entity gains so much power, there is no positive effect for the improvement of governance.

Main Results and Lessons Learned
- The water grants were revised. The new documents jointly released by the DAEE and ANA now include previsions about extreme events.
- Several agreements still fail to include unusual situations and preview roles for future rounds of negotiation.
- More easily written than applied to real situations, an agreement is beneficial when everything is clearly stated, and all parties explicitly understand the agreement's terms.
- The experience in São Paulo helped things go smoothly in Brasilia years later, based on such tools as contingency fees, programmed shortages, incentives for the acquisition of water-efficiency equipment, donation of water tanks for the poorest, and public education, among others.
- Integrated Water Resources Management must better assess the availability to properly balance the potable water demand and supply capacity, including different approaches and actions.
- Crisis can be addressed temporarily, but complex problems require negotiation to continue enhancing proactive partnerships toward conflict prevention and resolution.
- In 2020, a contingency plan was released[11] involving three states, three committees, and agencies toward improving resiliency in a meaningful way during water scarcity.
- Many short-, medium-, and long-term infrastructure/building measures are being taken toward water security (National Water Security Plan 2019).
- During a crisis, involved parties commonly focus on ongoing problems more than the future consequences of their decisions.
- The agent in charge of moderating a conflict should be a neutral party, not one with a vested interest in the outcome.

- Some systems are well planned, thoroughly thought out, and debated for years; however, the world is dynamic, and there will always be challenges and unexpected circumstances.

THE WATER CRISIS IN THE FEDERAL DISTRICT (2016–2018)

Context

Brasilia was inaugurated in 1960 when the Brazilian capital was moved from Rio de Janeiro. By moving the entire core of the federal government to central Brazil in a process of interiorization, incentives were given to an already privileged and highly paid class of civil servants. The federal workers were placed on land surrounded by poor communities of workers who came to help build the new capital. This dynamic caused a concentration of wealthy residents amid the poor, creating a huge social gap across the new federal unit that persists to today.

Before 1960, that entire area was covered by the Brazilian Savannah (*Cerrado*), sparsely inhabited by traditional indigenous groups, small farms, and livestock. This tropical savanna is typically affected by long periods of drought and temperatures ranging between 82° to 89°F.

Located in the highlands, this central portion of Brazil is the headwaters for three main river basins in the country (São Francisco, Paraná, and the Tocantins). Upstream waters can be more pristine than in lower parts of the river system. However, being up-gradient, these watercourses, located in the plateau, tend to have less volume and reduced capacity for the removal of contaminants, compared with tributaries further downstream.

After the transfer of the Federal Government, and the construction and 1960 inauguration of Brasilia, the region had a thriving economy. Roads were built to integrate the new capital with other important southeast cities, such as Sao Paulo and Rio de Janeiro around 650 miles away. Attracted by new opportunities, people from north and northeast Brazil arrived in search of jobs and better living conditions.

The new capital was planned for around 500,000 inhabitants; yet, 60 years later, it has around 3 million people. Even as a modern, planned city, disorganized urbanization spread into Brasilia's surroundings. The lands that became occupied by unplanned communities underwent further deforestation and somewhat chaotic development of the supporting infrastructure. Construction in environmentally sensitive areas led to changes in vegetation and increased impervious pavement—both of which altered runoff, stream flows, groundwater recharge, and water quality.

At the same time, the new communities also increased demand for livestock and food production in the region, straining the government and institutional capacity to meet rising demands for infrastructure and public services.

The imbalance of power among the residents of this area is one of the most notable in Brazil. To establish the Federal District in Brazil, a huge portion of the land was expropriated by the Union or the Federal District, which makes it even more difficult for people to access legal property rights and housing. This informal market of land is still growing, and threatens springs, groundwater recharge, biodiversity, and vegetation.

Over the past 60 years, Brazil experienced significant political and economic changes. With the end of the military dictatorship in the mid-1980s, Brazil reestablished commercial relations with several countries. Globalization and new international trade fostered changes in land use, driving monoculture and funneling international capital through central Brazil, with effects spilling over into Cerrado and the Amazon. This transformation followed on adjacent lands with access to the roads and other infrastructure, and several changes were brought about by the construction of the new Capital. The small farmers near Brasilia were already fighting against big corporations to keep their land and local production. At the same time, large volumes of groundwater were withdrawn from the subsurface to irrigate monocultures.

Since the 1960s, the population growth rate in the Federal District continues to rise, reaching 2.25 percent per year in 2018, which means that the local water-supply company has to accommodate growth in the demand for drinking water equivalent to 60,000 new water consumers every year. And, like São Paulo, Brasilia also has a false sense of water security. Water consumption in Brazil is reported to be 243,946 gallons/inhab/year, more water than the Federal District can supply.

The main uses of water in the Brasilia area follow Brazil's average total consumption of water, consisting of irrigation (68 percent), livestock (11 percent), urban uses (9 percent), and rural households (2.3 percent). Industries and mining activities make up the remainder of the used water.

The water-management structure has been consolidated; there are citizen watershed committees to facilitate decision-making and conflict resolution. The local Water and Sanitation Agency (Adasa) is technically strong, with effective legal instruments to enforce the law, such as: inform, monitor, and comply with allocation and negotiation among water users.

The difference, in this case, is that the conflict is localized, with fewer actors involved. Even if the Integrated Water Resources Management rules are similar, the two parties involved in this case have different legal priority rights. But similar to what happened in São Paulo where the National Agency took the lead on negotiations, in this case, the local Water Agency negotiated and moderated the conflict; this role put them out of compliance, as defined by the 1997 National Water Law.

Conflict

Between 2016 and 2018, the region's rainfall dropped from an average of 56.3 in/year to less than 47.2 in/year, causing a 34 percent reduction in the average annual streamflow. This reduction matters greatly in terms of human water supply, the priority-use established under Brazilian law. Also, note that the water supply company grants come first, before other uses, such as the small farmers' irrigation needs.

Under *normal* conditions, the local water supply company (Caesb) has permission to withdraw a maximum of about 13,737 gallons/s. During the crises, however, permitted withdrawal was reduced to 9,774 gallons/s in January 2017 and to 9,243 gallons/s in March 2018. Because of this reduction, and to foster more efficient water consumption, Caesb raised contingency fees for consumers and implemented alternating daily supply cuts for different neighborhoods in the form of programmed water outages.

This process exposed several urban challenges. For example, several households do not comply with urban regulations and they do not have water tanks in their houses to cope with days with no running water from the pipes; several households and businesses, even in central Brasilia, had to deal with consecutive days without water. The crisis resulted in the Federal District water and sanitation agency, Adasa, and the committees conducting joint reviews to assess water allocation as a means to conflict resolution between farmers and the water supply company.

The water withdrawal grants were reduced for the company and the farmers. The usual permits for their groundwater withdrawals also dropped from 6,604 gallons/s to 3,170 gallons/s in January 2017 to 1,585 gallons/s in March 2018. This was particularly devastating for the poorest families, who were least able to invest in water-efficient appliances.

The farming community, reliant on water availability, was also severely affected by the water shortage. Furthermore, the water scarcity triggered a reduction in water withdrawals and raised water prices, which meant that farmers could not afford to install or improve irrigation systems. As a result, the government intervened to subsidize costs and institute price-control measures. Many farmers received government loans and technical assistance to improve water efficiency.

The Water Producer Project in the Pipiripau Watershed (inspired by the Extrema-MG) that pays rural property holders to implement spring and stream conservation gained international recognition. The conservation effort was key in promoting understanding among the different actors and in gaining participation of farmers in addressing the conflicts in the Federal District.

Over time, the flow of information, transparency, and trust increased. To date, a new water information system exists; this includes technical articles and reports, at least one book, and other publications.[12]

Main Results and Lessons Learned

- Communities were involved in the efforts to address this water crisis.
- Increasing participation strengthened the water committees.
- Norms and regulations were reviewed and adjusted to address critical issues.
- Transparency and Communication Campaigns resulted in greater awareness, and reducing wasteful water usage, with lasting positive effects.
- Alternative water sources, improvements in infrastructure, and the conclusion of channeling systems helped build water resilience.
- Water monitoring and data collection improved because of greater social involvement.
- Technical support from state agencies improved efficiency regarding water use and conservation in agriculture.
- Water allocations and permits were reviewed and water users were registered, which also facilitated monitoring and enforcement.

- Integrated Water Resources Management now means that land use, rural and urban water consumption, and water policies are integrated.
- Improvements were made on alert systems, monitoring, data acquisition, and planning.
- The efficacy of the governance system strengthened trust between government agencies and civil society, making reaching consensus easier.
- An established priority helps start the negotiation and move it forward.
- Resources invested in education and information have long-term benefits—facilitating conversations during times of crisis; balancing power; and creating boundaries, and partnerships that will ease the success of future negotiations.

WATER MANAGEMENT IN THE UNITED STATES

Chapter 3 provides an overview of water management in the United States (US), making it unnecessary to repeat it here. Most pertinent to the comparison between water management in Brazil and the US is: (1) the similarity of a federal system with watershed-based, on-the-ground management, (2) water quality enforcement and decision-making in the 50 individual States and 5 U.S. Territories, and (3) federally approved state plans for managing water quality standards. Should states fail to maintain water quality standards outlined in the US Clean Water Act of 1972 (CWA, 33 USC Ch. 23 §1151 et seq.),[13] the federal government retains "back-stop" authority, authorizing federal intervention to compel states to fulfill their statutory obligations under the Act. Should the federal government (US Environmental Protection Agency) fail to enforce the law, section 505 of the Clean Water Act contains a citizen-suit provision enabling *any citizen* to sue to compel compliance with the provisions of the Act (33 USC § 1365); this empowerment of citizens to enforce the law is a vestige of English common law.

According to the United States Environmental Protection Agency Watershed Protection Approach Framework[14]

> The watershed approach is a coordinating framework for environmental management that focuses public and private sector efforts to address the highest priority problems within hydrologically-defined geographic areas, taking into consideration both ground and surface water flow.

As in Brazil, in the United States water use is prioritized for human consumption followed by beneficial application for livestock and crops. This value hierarchy is derived from English common law roots. Water, as a right, is not enshrined in the US Constitution. Rights to water and how they are legally determined *is* enshrined in the constitutions of some individual states, particularly those of western states.

Property rights to all water are known as *use* rights (usufructuary rights), to distinguish them from the rights of property *ownership* (as in land). Rights to surface waters in the U.S. exist in two distinct forms: (1) *Riparian* water rights stem from common law inherited by the American colonies from England, and apply geographically to the eastern half of the US (and Hawaii), and (2) The *prior appropriations doctrine* applies in the western half of the US, where it arose in response to property notions inherent in the historic period.

In the relatively well watered eastern states that follow the riparian doctrine, owners directly adjacent to a waterbody generally have the right to access and consume the water. Riparian landowners' rights are held and enjoyed in common, meaning there is no right to exclude others.

In contrast, the arid western states follow the prior appropriation doctrine, thought to have originated in the case of *Irwin v Phillips* (5 Cal. 140, 1855)[15] during the California Gold Rush. Under prior appropriation, the nature and quantity of the water right is determined when each right was established or "proved." This is often referred to as a system of "first in time, first in right." When comparing landowners' rights within a western watershed, the rights are described as "senior" or "junior" rights in water. The senior rights holder has the lawful ability to consume first and to the full extent of his recorded right; thus, a junior rights holder may go without water during a drought. In the lore of western water law, the saying goes that, "whiskey is for drinking, water is for fighting."

There are three exceptions to the bifurcated rights system in the US. The first pertains to the water rights of Native American Tribes, which are neither riparian nor prior appropriation but are *reserved* water rights, as decided by the 1908 United States Supreme Court case *Winters v. the United States* (207 US 564).[16]

Second, all federal lands and enclaves have *federally reserved water rights*, such as: national parks and monuments, national forests, the National Wildlife Refuge system, lands overseen by the Bureau of Land Management, and so on.

Finally, groundwater management represents the third exception to the riparian or prior appropriations water-rights system. Groundwater is managed individually by the 50 states and the 5 major Territories. For example, if a landowner drills a well on his or her property, he/she has the right to withdraw water according to whatever parameters exist within the groundwater laws in the particular state. There is no federal management of groundwater (quantity or quality) except within the context of public drinking water derived from wells. The federal Safe Drinking Water Act of 1974 (SDWA 42 USC §300f et seq.)[17] defines the legal water quality standards with which all public water supplies (including those from groundwater) must be in compliance. Federal (and state) agencies provide assistance, testing, and training on the proper maintenance of wells and well fields wherein landowners can voluntarily participate. In some states such as Oregon, wells must be inspected and certified to be in compliance prior to sale of the subject real estate.

As in many parts of the world, surface and groundwater supplies are increasingly fragile—subject to contamination and over-withdrawal due to myriad, complex causes, including a growing population and associated urban sprawl, drought, waste of resources, flooding, and climate disruption.

While the US Clean Water and Clean Air Acts have made historic, well-documented strides in reducing pollution since the early 1970s, water is subject not only to over-withdrawal but also simultaneously to increasingly complex, even synergistic, contaminations by chemicals deposited from a wide variety of sources due to terrestrial flow (runoff via ditches, streams, and rivers), withdrawal of polluted groundwater (wells, drilling, and pumping), pollution from atmospheric deposition air (dry, wind borne), and precipitation (wet, rain, and snow).

The largest sources of contaminated surface and groundwater are agriculture, transportation emissions, industrial emissions, and stormwater. Reassuringly, innovative and interdisciplinary solutions toward the reduction of contaminants in these sectors continue to evolve. In contrast, the profoundly important goal of adequate water quantity in the US is challengingly elusive, even as water policy and technology innovate to advance water quality for the future.

The two case studies described in this section deal with water quantity in transboundary settings.

Florida V Georgia

The first case study in the US involves an ongoing, interstate water dispute begun in 2013 by Florida (the downstream state) against Georgia (the upstream state) in the United States Supreme Court. In February 2021, the Court heard oral arguments. All of the ongoing developments are available in the High Court's blog.[18] (See also 2018 slip opinion of remand on exceptions of the report of the Special Master in the case.)[19]

Context

At the center of *Florida v Georgia* are three rivers that form a Y shape in the region (Chattahoochee, Flint, and Apalachicola Rivers flowing south from Georgia into Florida; the basin is larger than 20,000 square miles, or 51,800 km^2). Florida's ongoing complaint alleges that Georgia's over-consumption of the water is denying Florida its legal (and equal) sovereign right to an equitable portion.

Conflict

Because this conflict is between two states, the U.S. Supreme Court has original jurisdiction under its "redressability" through "equitable apportionment" jurisdiction, according to the Constitution. In this controversy between two sovereign states, original jurisdiction means that procedurally Florida did not have to file a complaint "below" in the Federal District Court for Florida, but was allowed to file directly with the high court.

Notably, throughout this long-lived dispute, there were two significant attempts at agreement: a 1992 memorandum of agreement, followed by a Congressionally approved interstate compact in 1997 (a multistate type of agreement that the Constitution authorizes). The two agreements required equal, cooperative management and the development of a formula to equitably allocate the water supplies among the two states. The states' negotiations failed and the compact expired in 2003.

In 2014, Congress passed Public Law 113–121, the Water Resources Reform and Development Act,[20] partly to address the Florida-Georgia controversy. Still, the two states could not reach an agreement, leading Florida to sue Georgia, demanding a judicial intervention to limit or cap Georgia's water withdrawals. Consequently, the U.S. Supreme Court appointed a special master that same year to undertake the gathering of evidence and to issue reports on the findings.

During the Court's October 2017 term, and following the amassment of mountains of documents, the Court reviewed the key question as to whether Florida had proven "clear and convincing evidence" that equitable apportionment of the basin's waters would provide the remedy the state was seeking (*Florida v. Georgia* slip opinion No. 142, originally argued January 8, 2018—Decided June 27, 2018). The Court noted that, according to case precedent, both states have equal right to make *reasonable use* of the water that is commensurate with responsibilities that include *affirmative duties to take steps to conserve and even increase the resource for the benefit of other states* (common-pool resources). According to precedent (*Nebraska v Wyoming*, 325 US 589, at 618, 1945),[21] the factors the Court must analyze include biophysical and climate conditions, consumption and established uses, return flows, storage, waste, and potential detriment to the upstream user if they are faced with a usage limit.

Finding that the special master's determinations were too strict, and remanding the case for further proceedings, in 2018 the Court said:

> In our view, unless and until the Special Master makes the findings of fact necessary to determine the nature and scope of likely harm caused by the absence of water and the amount of additional water necessary to ameliorate that harm significantly, the complaining State should not have to prove with specificity the details of an eventually workable decree by "clear and convincing" evidence. Rather, the complaining State should have to show that, applying the principles of "flexibility" and "approximation" . . ., it is likely to prove possible to fashion such a decree. . . . [in other words] To require "clear and convincing evidence" about the workability of a decree before the Court or a Special Master has a view about likely harms and likely amelioration is, at least in this case, to put the cart before the horse.[22]

Following the above-quoted reasoning, in the remand the Court proceeds to finely dissect various realistic scenarios involving how the US Army Corps of Engineers (Corps) applies drought operations based on hard data rather than discretionary authority, drawing on historic examples. The Court undertook this analytical exercise in order to effectively apprehend the key question at the heart of the case: Would placing a cap on Georgia's consumption from the Basin, in fact, result in the actual remedy Florida sought through the restoration of flow in the range of an increased 1500–2000 cubic feet per second from the Basin across an array of possible conditions?

The Court found that such a cap or limit on Georgia was a reasonable route to the remedy Florida was seeking. The *Florida v Georgia* proceedings continue into 2021.

Results, Lessons Learned, and Lessons Suggesting Design of New Approaches

- Consumers of adjoining states have reasonable rights to the use of water.
- As with other "rights," responsibilities to conserve common-pool resources are equal.

- It takes several years to adjudicate long-term, multi-state water conflicts, and such adjudication is costly.
- Multiple examples of regional, federally authorized, multi-state commissions exist, which could be analyzed (administrative mechanisms, such as interstate compacts and commissions) by students, managers, and practitioners from a database of freshwater disputes curated at Oregon State University.[23]
- Investigating, indexing, and analyzing common themes of inter-state water conflicts' structures, parties, and approaches has the potential to yield data to construct an adaptable model, step-wise water-conflict methodology for earliest intervention in such conflicts: involving managers, agencies, consumers, and regional representatives of major water-use sectors, like agriculture, cities, and power.
- Such a proactive, contemporary model and management tool for water-conflict intervention could potentially save parties up to hundreds of thousands of hours and dollars by shortening the conflict.
- A customizable and proactive tool is urgently needed in response to shifting populations, land uses, and precipitation patterns attributable to changing climate.

MEXICAN WATER TREATY OF 1944

The second U.S. case study regards the Mexican Water Treaty of 1944[24] and the search for water equity in the desert. The Mexican Water Treaty of 1944 covers the Colorado, Tijuana, and Rio Grande Rivers. This case, also, involves ongoing negotiations. But, as a transnational boundary case, it might suggest innovations for multi-state conflict resolution.

Context

Under the 1944 agreement, Mexico releases around 512 million cubic meters of water every 5 years in October, as repayment of its treaty obligations. The debt stems from the fact that Mexico's share of water from the Colorado River is four times the quantity it gives to the US from the Rio Grande River. As other examples of international law, treaties are agreements between the parties. In the case of noncompliance, the treaty has neither penalties nor other enforcement mechanisms.[25]

Due perhaps to predictable increases in temperatures and demands for the resource, Mexico fell behind in its obligations. Because this contemporary conflict involves an international treaty, the management issues surrounding arid lands in a changing climate, and significant questions of equity and comity (an association of nations for their mutual benefit) among the parties, this transboundary conflict makes a good case study—for reasons somewhat similar to *Florida v Georgia*, but in terms of two nations instead of two states.

Conflict

Persistent drought in the autumn of 2020 caused farmers in northern Mexico (Chihuahua) to occupy the La Boquilla dam prior to the treaty's annual deadline for Mexico to pay its water debt to the United States for use of the Colorado and Rio Grande Rivers. In this case, Texas received abundant rainfall in 2020, while the drought in northern Mexico persisted. At the last minute, while Mexico deployed troops to quell the dam's occupation, and after one farmer was killed, the two countries came to an agreement.[26]

Felbab-Brown (2020) set forth the flexibilities and innovations inherent in the approach that ended the standoff. These include more adaptable options for the delivery of water to farmers, a wider range of sources for the US to take pressure off the Chihuahua growers, and two other developments. The solution posits a Mexican water reserve, whereby Mexico can store its water in Lake Mead for future use, as well as a water right for the environment that is similar to Oregon's statutory, instream rights[27] to provide flows that would restore some of Mexico's riverine flow.

Felbab-Brown's analysis concludes by outlining a compelling list of policy actions, among them: scientific measurement and monitoring of ground and surface water supplies, increased application of conservation techniques in agriculture, increased conscious understanding and tailoring of the informed connection between sustainability evaluations and economic decisions, and implementing more precise management and application via the technical advances continually coming on line. While Felbab-Brown's list concludes with recommendations on penalties and enforcement, notably many of the suggestions in her list were borne of collaboration and modernization.

Conflicts (either local, regional, interstate, or transboundary international) are necessarily unique, and one-size solutions to conflict prevention, management, or resolution do not fit all contexts—just as a fixed, historical agreement might not continue to be effective between 1944 and 2020 if not updated for current conditions. Nevertheless, certain overarching principles may be derived that are compelling for adaptation to a wide range of water conflicts in the United States and elsewhere. Upcoming students and practitioners seeking to understand the greater implications of water conflict will no doubt help pioneer thoughtful, positive, and profound change.

Main Results and Lessons Learned
- The flexibility of agreements to share water is increasingly fundamental to the reduction of conflicts.
- Flexibility is not only the foundation for systematic annual or periodic adjustments necessary but also to *a priori* authorize inclusion of innovative solutions that make agreements alive and responsive, instead of moribund.

CONCLUSION

The systems of water governance in Brazil and the United States are works in progress, constantly evolving to balance increased multiple uses, contrasts in developing rural and urban needs and applications, and rapid global change.

Key to the success of both systems are national and state leadership, scientific data and modeling, effective contemporary law and policy, the prioritization of human rights and environmental justice, and the intensive participation of citizens and sectoral representatives at linked, nested geographic and regional scales. The future success of both nations and their water systems will depend on these, but also on the ability to conserve water, which will be led by technological advances, outreach, and education to ensure that expectations of demand are realistically and expressly tied to fluctuating water supplies that support not only people but also ecosystems and the planetary biome.

QUESTIONS

1. What are the main differences between the water management system in Brazil and in the United States?
2. What do you see as the challenges in applying the conflict transformation framework to the water management system in Brazil? What are the advantages?
3. What do you see as the challenges in applying the conflict transformation framework to the water management system in United States? What are the advantages?
4. If you were to file a friend-of-the-Court (*amicus*) brief in the *Florida v Georgia* case before the US Supreme Court, what would be your top three points you would like the Court to consider? What is your rationale for those points?
5. What considerations appear to be completely omitted from both intra-state and international transboundary water disputes? What are some innovative ways to bring the forgotten considerations to the table?
6. Based on what you have learned, what are some ways that (as a society and as practitioners) can we begin to transform conflict into constructive dialogue, revolutionizing the very approach we use toward water and other natural resource decisions?

NOTES

1 IBGE. 2019. "Sistema de Contas Regionais: Brasil—2017 Principais Destaques Por Unidade Da Federação." 2020. Accessible at https://agenciadenoticias.ibge.gov.br/media/com_mediaibge/arquivos/77e8b10de4ed9e8125968e56d9d720b7.pdf. For a 2021 update on the effects of climate change on São Paulo's water resources, see: Pooler, Michael, and Carolina Pulice. 2021. "Climate Change Poses Theat to Thirsty São Paulo." *Financial Times*, May 10, 2021.
2 CDRMSP. 2019. "Plano de Desenvolvimento Urbano Integrado—RMSP Diagnóstico Final, Setembro 2019." Accessible at www.pdui.sp.gov.br/rmsp/?page_id=755
3 EMPLASA. 2020. "Macrometrópole Paulista." Accessible at https://emplasa.sp.gov.br/MMP
4 Meganck, Richard wrote to the authors via email on March 28, 2021.
5 Abers, Rebecca, and Margaret E. Keck. 2015. "Comitês de Bacia no Brasil, Uma Abordagem Política no Estudo da Participação Social." no. June. Accessible at https://doi.org/10.13061/rbeur.v6i1.104.
6 ANA—Agência Nacional de Águas (Brasil). 2010. "Atlas Brasil: Abastecimento Urbano de Água." Ano 1: 1–72. Accessible at http://atlas.ana.gov.br/Atlas/downloads/atlas/Resumo%20Executivo/Atlas%20Brasil%20-%20Volume%202%20-%20Resultados%20por%20Estado.pdf
7 ANA. 2017. "Agência Nacional de Águas (ANA)—Atlas Esgotos—Despoluição de Bacias Hidrográficas." Accessible at http://arquivos.ana.gov.br/imprensa/publicacoes/ATLASeESGOTOSDespoluicaodeBaciasHidrograficas-ResumoExecutivo_livro.pdf.

8 BEN, Balanço Energético Nacional. 2020. "Relatório Síntese: BEN 2020—Ano Base 2019." 73. Accessible at www.epe.gov.br/sites-pt/publicacoes-dados-abertos/publicacoes/PublicacoesArquivos/publicacao-479/topico-528/BEN2020_sp.pdf
9 ANA. 2020. "Conjuntura Dos Recursos Hídricos No Brasil 202020: Informe Anual / Agência Nacional de Águas." *Agência Nacional de Águas*, 100. Accessible at http://conjuntura.ana.gov.br/static/media/conjuntura-completo.23309814.pdf
10 Cesar Neto, J.C. 2015. "A Crise Hídrica No Estado de São Paulo." *GEOUSP: Espaço e Tempo (Online)*, 19 (3): 479. Accessible at https://doi.org/10.11606/issn.2179-0892.geousp.2015.101113.
11 SABESP. 2020. "Estratégias Resilientes Um Plano De Adaptação Às Variações Climáticas Na Gestão De Recursos Hídricos Para O Abastecimento Da Região Metropolitana De São Paulo." Accessible at www.sabesp.com.br/estrategias_resilientes/pdf/SAB03_completo-V2.pdf
12 Werneck de Lima, J.E.F., G.K. Freitas, M.A. Teixeira Pinto, and P.S.B. Almeida Salles. 2018. "Gestão Da Crise Hídrica 2016–2018." Accessible at www.adasa.df.gov.br/images/banners/alta.pdf
13 United States Clean Water Act of 1972 (33 USC Ch. 23 §1151 et seq.).
14 United States Environmental Protection Agency. "Watershed Protection Approach Framework, 1996." Accessible at www.epa.gov/sites/production/files/2015-06/documents/watershed-approach-framework.pdf
15 *Irwin v Phillips* (5 Cal. 140, 1855).
16 *Winters v. the United States* (207 US 564, 1908).
17 US Safe Drinking Water Act of 1974 (42 USC §300f et seq.).
18 *Florida v Georgia* case document record, US Supreme Court blog. Accessible at www.scotusblog.com/case-files/cases/florida-v-georgia-2/
19 *Florida v Georgia* (ongoing before the United States Supreme Court upon 2018 remand, docket number 22o142). Accessible at www.supremecourt.gov/opinions/17pdf/142%20orig_new_3ebh.pdf
20 Water Resources Reform and Development Act of 2014, Public Law 113–121
21 *Nebraska v Wyoming* (325 US 589, 1945)
22 *Florida v Georgia* (ongoing before the United States Supreme Court upon 2018 remand, docket number 22o142 at page 3). Accessible at www.supremecourt.gov/opinions/17pdf/142%20orig_new_3ebh.pdf
23 Transboundary Freshwater Dispute Database, Oregon State University College of Earth, Ocean and Atmospheric Sciences. (n.d.). Accessible at https://transboundarywaters.science.oregonstate.edu/content/transboundary-freshwater-dispute-database
24 Treaty Concerning the Utilization of Waters of the Colorado and Tijuana Rivers and of the Rio Grande of 1944. Washington, D.C.
25 Mackinnon A. 2020. "The Water War on the US-Mexico Border Has Just Begun." *Foreign Policy*, While You Weren't Looking (October 19, 2020). Accessible at https://foreignpolicy.com/2020/10/19/water-war-us-mexico-border-just-begun-chihuahua-boquilla-dam-farmers-drought/
See also Nusser, N. 2020. "A Water Treaty Has Aided Mexican and US Farmers for Decades. This Year, It's Wreaking Havoc." *Texas Monthly*. Accessible at www.texasmonthly.com/news-politics/water-farmers-rio-grande-valley-mexico/
26 Felbab-Brown, V. 2020. "Not Dried Up: US-Mexico Water Cooperation." *The Brookings Institution, Washington D.C.* (October 26, 2020). Accessible at www.brookings.edu/blog/order-from-chaos/2020/10/26/not-dried-up-us-mexico-water-cooperation/ last visited 12.14.2020.
27 Oregon Revised Statutes (ORS) In-Stream Water Rights §§537.332–537.360.

5 Rights of Nature
The Relationship between Water and People

Cameron La Follette

CONTENTS

Overview	85
How Will the Relationship between Nature and Humans Work?	87
Case Study: New Zealand's Whanganui River	89
Case Study: Grant Township and Highland Township, Pennsylvania	90
Highland Township	91
Grant Township	91
The Legal System and the Rights of Nature	92
Moving Beyond Relationships of Destruction with Rivers	93
Local and Worldwide River Protection	96
If I Am the River and the River Is Me: Water Conflict and Ecological Governance	98
Conclusion	98
Questions and Exercises	99
Notes	100

OVERVIEW

It seems absurdly trite to say water is important to life or even that water is life. But, in a world where water scarcity bleaches entire landscapes and forces communities to move, or pollution is so severe it chokes rivers until they literally die, the banal suddenly becomes the supremely critical.

Water scarcity due to drought, shifting weather patterns, or overuse is nothing new in human history worldwide. Pollution so invisible, long-lasting, and irreversible that it poisons waters, turning them into the enemies of life, is fairly new: an outcome of the Industrial Revolution. This revolution changed businesses, the workplace, and the use of natural resources to an intensity never before seen or sustained for long periods and/or over large landscapes. As a result, entire cultures, and even nations, now have serious issues with their water supply or water purity.[1] Polarized struggles over the use of water, its regulation, cleanup, and oversight erupt time after time in urban and rural settings, both in the United States and worldwide. An ever more intricate structure of bureaucratic regulation grows up to keep tabs on new, more potently poisonous chemicals—but despite passage of the Clean Water Act in 1972, more than half of the nation's water bodies continue to struggle with heavy pollution loads.[2]

The current system of oversight and permits is clearly failing; making it even more complex and top-heavy will not add to its already feeble and diminishing successes. Only a new paradigm, one that does not promote escalating human use, can restore our waters worldwide. How can this be done? The root of the industrial paradigm is the rupture of relationship between humans and their environment, leaping over all boundaries of restraint, sustainability, and environmental integrity for the sake of constant economic growth and short-term gain.[3] This is clearly an economics framework that will not provide the food, water, or air humans need to maintain the ecological resilience on which all life depends.

The only way to ameliorate today's use of the world's water is to forge a new relationship with it. The basis of human use must be *based on relationship*, not merely industrial plundering for profit, if the many challenges within the current system are to be repaired. But how? It requires some form of what is often called "ecological governance"—that is, forging a reciprocal relationship with the ecosystem, watershed, and regional landscape in which one lives. As in any relationship, there are duties and reciprocities on both sides, with an overall aim of allowing all life to flourish. It means retooling human use to live respectfully within the biophysical limits of land, sea, and air. There are many possible ways to reestablish this once-universal, and now very often broken, sense of relationship. Starting mainly in the 21st century, various alternatives have been discussed in different communities. But the first crystallization of the concept in modern industrial culture came in 1972.

Walt Disney Enterprises aimed to build a resort, complete with hotels, restaurants, and recreation facilities, in Mineral King Valley in the High Sierras of California. The Forest Service had granted the lease. The Sierra Club Legal Defense Fund sued to stop the project. But a lower court held that the Legal Defense Fund did not have standing to sue—that its members would not be adversely affected if the resort were built. The United States Supreme Court decided to hear the case. The problem of who would really be "aggrieved" if the resort project went ahead caught the eye of Christopher Stone, a law professor at the University of Southern California School of Law. He authored a law review article arguing that natural areas and objects should have legal rights.[4] They would be the ones truly injured in developments like the Disney resort.

The Supreme Court majority agreed that the Legal Defense Fund did not have standing to sue—but Justice William O. Douglas dissented. In his now-famous words, "Contemporary public concern for protecting nature's ecological equilibrium should lead to the conferral of standing upon environmental objects to sue for their own preservation."[5] Justice Douglas's words, and the Stone law review article, from which Douglas took many of his ideas, percolated quietly among environmental activists during the decades of growing public concern over degradation of the world's ecosystems, as it became clear the permit-and-oversight system was failing.[6]

Then, in 2008, Ecuador adopted a new Constitution. To the world's shock, Ecuador enshrined the Rights of Nature directly, unequivocally, and openly in its supreme governing document. Suddenly, the Rights of Nature became a legitimate, new way to conceptualize relationship between humans and Nature, a way to end the blistering cycles of extractive industry, environmental degradation, permanently damaged lands, and the ensuing human despair. Article 71 of the Constitution states, "Nature, or Pacha Mama, where life is reproduced and occurs, has the right to integral respect for its existence and for the maintenance and regeneration of its life cycles, structure, functions and evolutionary processes."[7] Nature also has the right to be restored, and its integral restoration is held to be independent of "natural persons or legal entities."[8] Moreover, the state has to restrict activities that would lead to species extinction, ecosystem destruction, and the permanent alteration of Nature's biophysical cycles.[9]

Since Ecuador's bold step, municipalities, courts, and countries have been, and continue to, experiment with the Rights of Nature. The most notable, initially at least, was Bolivia, which passed a unique law in 2012 called the "Framework Law on Mother Earth and Integral Development for Living Well." The law's scope was sweeping: "This Act is intended to recognize the rights of Mother Earth, and obligations and duties of the Multinational State and society to ensure respect for these rights."[10] This law required human activities to achieve balance with Mother Earth's processes, and required the state to ensure the Earth's living systems can regenerate without altering their fundamental characteristics. The state and its citizens are required to protect and guarantee the rights of Mother Earth for the wellbeing of current and future generations. The rights of Mother Earth included the right to life, to the diversity of life, to water, to clean air, to equilibrium, to restoration, and to pollution-free living.[11]

Bolivia has not advanced its own environmental program much under this law. Nevertheless, President Evo Morales, who has advocated for the Rights of Nature in many international forums and become a worldwide spokesman for this paradigm change, was the catalyst for a major international conference on the Rights of Nature in 2010. The World People's Conference on Climate Change and the Rights of Mother Earth attracted delegates from all over the world, including many nations that have suffered heavily from corporate depredations. This group promulgated the Universal Declaration of the Rights of Mother Earth, modeled on Bolivia's law—framing humans' relationship to Earth as one of respect and responsibility to protect the living Earth.[12]

The concept has metamorphosed into unique new forms as it confronts situations as diverse as a major waterway that millions depend on choked by severe pollution and a country in need of a new concept for treaty negotiations with its indigenous peoples. Not surprisingly, many of the new faces of the conceptual Rights of Nature focus on waterways, because water is essential, and the degradation of rivers and watersheds has caused, and continues to cause, unspeakable misery for millions.

HOW WILL THE RELATIONSHIP BETWEEN NATURE AND HUMANS WORK?

Rights of Nature is so new and innovative a concept—requiring such a dramatic and deep-rooted change from the popular industrial paradigm—that it is in danger of degenerating into just another pretty idea that sounds promising, but alters nothing in practice, while miseries continue. In other words, it is profoundly vulnerable to green-washing by those whose extraction of (or profiting from) the world's resources would be curtailed by a true Rights of Nature relationship.

Despite sounding legal, the Rights of Nature concept is less about court battles than it is about *relationship*. What is new is refining the ideals of relationship in law so that either party, if injured, can seek redress, as would be the case in any relationship. It is also the opportunity to spell out the responsibilities of both parties. Nature's responsibilities to humankind, whatever they might be, are not exactly humanity's concern. On the other hand, humanity's responsibility to Nature is essential for humans to grapple with, and that is where the relationship is broken. It was once commonplace in all preindustrial cultures, shaped in a staggering variety of ways; but ideals of sacredness, reciprocity, and respect for a local landscape have withered under the glare of industrialization, leading to an ever-worsening degradation of the environment.

To actually work in practice, within communities and countries worldwide, the Rights of Nature must be embedded in conflict-management strategies. If Nature is in a relationship with humans in a world that has lost most guidance for sustaining such a relationship, many questions arise.[13] A few of these are:

- What are the Rights of Nature that humans must respect: the right to flourish, the right to be restored, the right to uninterrupted ecological cycles, the right to live without pollution?
- How does a court or conflict-management group determine what harm Nature has suffered—and, specifically, how is it to be quantified?
- What restoration is required for harm to Nature: the merest minimal amount or complete restoration?
- Who will pay for repairing the harm caused to Nature?
- How to weigh the harm to humans by restricting the use of Nature? This is a question of environmental justice: if a group of people depend on Nature for their food, thereby extirpating a species, or a timber company completely clear-cuts a watershed, how can the human needs be balanced with Nature's own right to flourish?
- If Nature and humans are once again in a relationship (rather than mere human exploitation of "natural resources"), how must humans treat a living entity, such as an ecosystem, on which they also depend?
- How does a group of people revive concepts of the sacred once they have been cast off, as such concepts are the precursor to respect of Nature for its own sake and as the progenitor of life?
- Who will monitor and adjust a relationship with Nature if people in a particular area are in danger of overusing, polluting, or otherwise threatening Nature's integrity?
- What are the boundaries for acceptable behavior toward Nature with respect to Nature's right to flourish? The answer might differ greatly when considering a local watershed versus climate change, the latter requiring actions by all humans worldwide.

However, questions in the abstract are less helpful than actual case studies. The two cases (New Zealand's Whanganui River and Pennsylvania's Grant and Highland Townships) explore how the Rights of Nature, brought to the problems with a

Rights of Nature

waterbody—a river in one instance, and local springs in the other—changed the outcome of the conflict, in one case successfully, but not in the other.

CASE STUDY: NEW ZEALAND'S WHANGANUI RIVER

The Whanganui River, which flows through part of North Island into the Tasman Sea, was the home of the Whanganui Iwi, the tribe of indigenous Māori who were living along its banks when the British took over New Zealand and for centuries before. This group of Māori, living in a narrow territory alongside the Whanganui, was known as the River People.[14]

The root of the problem that ultimately led to bestowing the Rights of Nature upon the Whanganui lay in the 1840 Treaty of Waitangi between the British and the Māori. In this treaty, the Māori became British citizens and the British Crown agreed to safeguard the lands, forests, and other treasures of the Māori. But, over time, New Zealand's government and settlers breached parts of the treaty. The Whanganui, for example, was damaged by mining, flood control, waste disposal, and diversion for hydroelectric schemes. The River People tried for many years, and in many different forums, to have their grievances about the abuse of the river corrected. Serious negotiations on many Māori claims began in the 1990s, but they went slowly, due to the necessity of defining terms and finding "agreements in principle" as to what would constitute the elements of a settlement.

What, in general, would the elements of a settlement be? They included acknowledgment of the Crown's actions, which resulted in loss to the Māori of tribal lands, loss of access to forests, waterways, and sacred places; an apology for the Crown's actions; commercial redress in a manner that augmented an iwi's assets; a return to the iwi of culturally significant lands owned by the Crown; and designing a post-settlement relationship.

Every settlement claims process with the Māori differed. But the Whanganui settlement became internationally famous, because it vested the Whanganui River with its own rights. New Zealand already had a precedent for this: the area known as Te Urewara National Park, which was the traditional home of the Tuhoe people, was also part of a claims-settlement process. In that case, New Zealand took the National Park (created in 1954) out of Crown ownership, and made the land its own owner, so to speak—the land owned itself. It was then governed by a board made up of a majority of Tuhoe people.

Using this precedent, and the concept Christopher Stone had laid out in his famous law article of 1972, New Zealand and the Whanganui Iwi crafted a settlement in which the River was recognized as an "indivisible and living whole" from the mountains to the sea. The settlement gave the River status of a legal person, with all the rights, powers, and duties of a legal person. A board, comprised of members of the Crown and the Whanganui Iwi, would represent the River, promote the health and wellbeing of the River, and uphold its intrinsic values. All parties signed the Whanganui River Claims Settlement Agreement in August, 2014, later ratified by legislation. The two representatives were appointed in 2018.

This settlement is justifiably famous for several reasons. First, it was a model collaborative proceeding, in which all parties worked together to create a solution.

FIGURE 5.1 The Whanganui River on the North Island of New Zealand.

Source: (Photograph by James Shook; https://commons.wikimedia.org/wiki/File:Whanganui_River.jpg; Photo modified from color to a black and white image).

Second, it involved a major waterway—the Whanganui is New Zealand's third-longest river, 180 miles long (Figure 5.1). Most intriguing, this settlement process married novel Western legal concepts with indigenous understanding of the River as an ancestor and living entity. The result was a successful settlement of the longest-running litigation in New Zealand. But more than that, the Whanganui settlement has opened the door to understanding how water can be an important part of human communities and still keep its own integrity.

Because the Whanganui is its own legal entity, with its integrity overseen by a board committed to maintain it, the River's right to flourish comes before all human claims. Once the River has its own presence, human uses that the river can sustain without being damaged come into play. No human right to use the river takes precedence over the River's own needs. New Zealand, through a technical and specific settlement process, has pioneered a methodology of having the Rights of Nature function as a means of tempering human use of a river for the sake of the river's integrity. The key elements included not only a collaboration between the parties but also the willingness of the Crown negotiators to see the Whanganui in a new way: not as a "watershed" but as a living entity with integrity of its own. The law could then protect the river via a new guardianship structure.

CASE STUDY: GRANT TOWNSHIP AND HIGHLAND TOWNSHIP, PENNSYLVANIA

The struggle in Highland Township and Grant Township for either the protection of or the industrial use of a local water source in rural Pennsylvania presents an exact

Rights of Nature

opposite situation to the Whanganui of New Zealand. In these linked and similar struggles, the long-running discord, still unresolved as of 2020, provides a history of conflict, bitter legal fights, political upheaval, corporate jockeying, and continuous citizen activism.

Highland Township

The citizens of Highland Township passed a Community Bill of Rights ordinance in 2013, becoming one of the earliest in the United States to adopt language granting Rights of Nature. They did so because they were concerned about the plans of Seneca Resources, a gas-drilling company, to site a hydraulic fracturing wastewater-injection well less than a mile from Crystal Springs, the township's water source. These wastewaters contain toxic and hazardous materials, but are exempt from most environmental restrictions and are very poorly regulated. As such, the residents were concerned about contamination of their water supply, all the more so given that Seneca had a history of permit violations.

Consequently, their new ordinance stressed the rights of ecosystems to flourish, thereby banning the injection of wastewater and the extraction of fossil fuels. Seneca Resources promptly filed suit against the township. The Western District Court of Pennsylvania barred a local citizens' group—Citizens Advocating for Clean Healthy Environment—from intervening on behalf of Crystal Springs watershed, on grounds that the township's litigation adequately represented its interests. The Highland Board of Supervisors subsequently signed a "consent decree" with Seneca, and in 2016 rescinded the offending ordinance, allowing the company to proceed with their plans to inject the wastewater.

The residents then voted for a Home Rule Charter, over the objections of the Board of Supervisors, giving themselves greater legal power and flexibility to protect their watershed. It specifically included the ecosystem's right to flourish and exist. Seneca Resources then filed a second suit against the Charter, arguing, among other things, that a local charter could not grant rights to an ecosystem, and that state law provides for the disposal of wastewaters from hydraulic fracturing. But, once again, the Western District of Pennsylvania struck down the peoples' efforts, ruling the Home Rule Charter's banning of waste disposal was invalid and unenforceable, as state and federal law preempted local efforts to control oil and gas activity. Sued also by the Pennsylvania Department of Environmental Protection over the Charter—ironically, as the Department of Environmental Protection proposed to permit the wastewater wells, rather than protect the local watershed—the Highland Board of Supervisors settled the lawsuit. The Department promptly issued a permit for Seneca's disposal well.[15]

Grant Township

Grant Township adopted an ordinance containing a Community Bill of Rights, including a Rights of Nature clause, in June 2014. Their Board of Supervisors was more congenial to protecting the local water supply of Little Mahoning watershed, but the community faced the same legal roadblocks as Highland. Pennsylvania General Electric Company, which wanted to inject hydraulic fracturing wastewater into a well in the area, immediately sued Grant Township over the new ordinance, arguing that state law regulated wastewater wells and thereby preempted the township's efforts to protect its own water supply. The Electric Company also argued that the township had overstepped the powers allowed to it under the constitution. The township counterclaimed that the Electric Company's challenge robbed them of self-government. They also argued for the Rights of Nature to protect the Little Mahoning watershed, as well as the people's right to clean water and a safe environment.

The Western District Court of Pennsylvania disagreed. The court held that the watershed had no standing of its own in court because its interests were vicariously and indirectly being "represented" by the municipality. Having lost the first round, the citizens of Grant Township passed a Home Rule Charter, at the same time repealing its Bill of Rights. The Charter gave Grant Township greater legal flexibility to bar the wastewater-injection wells by specifically granting Nature rights: "Natural communities and ecosystems within Grant Township, including but not limited to, rivers, streams, and aquifers, possess the right to exist, flourish, and naturally evolve." (Section 106). Nature also had the right to be free of such threats as waste from the extraction of oil and gas.

The Pennsylvania Department of Environmental Protection sued Grant Township in 2017, as they had in Highland Township, arguing against the legality of the Home Rule Charter. However, in a stunning reversal in March 2020, the Department revoked the injection well permit, citing Grant Township's Charter as grounds for their reversal. The agency's action followed on a ruling by the Commonwealth Court of Pennsylvania refusing the Department's request for summary relief to prevent the Township from mounting a defense on the nature of hydraulic fracturing.[16] There may be further lawsuits, but this unprecedented milestone—the first local success of a Rights of Nature law—has brought law-making for the Rights of Nature to the forefront of struggles to protect local watersheds in the United States.

The Legal System and the Rights of Nature

These two cases, of townships forced to deal with the same problem, but ending with different outcomes, show the raw and unsettled side of the Rights of Nature concept. In the United States, the legal system is hierarchical, with more wide-ranging regulatory powers limited to state and federal levels of government. Local ordinances can, in general, only regulate local matters that are not preempted by higher levels of government, and this is the root of the problem in both Highland and Grant Townships.

Western legal thought subsequent to the Industrial Revolution has largely conceptualized Nature and its components, whether watersheds, animals, or ecosystem processes, as "things" owned by humans, not entities with rights to exist and flourish. The irony of such a perception is that humans are entirely, unavoidably, and wholly dependent on Nature for all aspects of life and life itself. To intellectualize that which provides life as property to be unconditionally exploited seems the height of folly, yet the perils of such a blinkered system did not become apparent until aggressive industrialization began to threaten the integrity of ecosystems and their ability to support life worldwide.

Only since the now-famous Stone article, and Justice Douglas's equally famous dissent opining that Nature should have standing to sue, has American jurisprudence timidly begun to explore the idea of granting rights to ecosystems. Specific American laws, dating from the early 1970s, were already moving in this direction, especially those dealing with classes of animals or endangered species. These laws protect their subject species and require habitat to be set aside for them, as in the Endangered Species Act and Marine Mammal Protection Act.

Granting rights to Nature would be a much larger enterprise than either of those landmark laws, with enormous consequences for industrial capitalism. The industrial paradigm relies on constant growth and unlimited exploitation to provide a steady, rising stream of profits. It thus requires unfettered access to "natural resources," and cannot tolerate much restraint to that access. The current permit-granting system in the United States does provide minimal restraint to protect human health and safety and allows for—often hotly contested—opportunities to protect a minimal level of ecosystem function. Nonetheless, it offers no true change in economic or ethical values, nor offers grounds for forging relationship with the natural world.

MOVING BEYOND RELATIONSHIPS OF DESTRUCTION WITH RIVERS

Restoring the relationship between humans and Nature will have to be a many-faceted enterprise, including both changes in the law to codify relationships of mutual respect and many long-term projects on land and in the waters to restore ecosystems too damaged from industrial activity to flourish on their own. It is commonly thought that restoration literally restores an environment to its pre-damaged state. But this is neither true nor even possible. Even if an environment were restored to a pristine state, the world around it has changed enormously, which would affect its functioning.

Restoration can and does, however, repair ecosystem function. Nature is highly resilient in many ecosystems, and restoration aids Nature in its self-repair, thus revitalizing ecosystem productivity that industrial use or abuse damaged or even destroyed. The larger the scale of restoration, the larger the effects it will have on regaining the integrity of natural processes. Thus, landscape-scale restoration is almost a shorthand for the Rights of Nature in practice. This is true even where, as in the United States, there is no Rights of Nature provision in law and even less in contemporary legal thought. Nevertheless, landscape-scale restoration is continuing apace with such projects as the American Prairie Reserve, which aims to create a full-scale prairie ecosystem on millions of acres of restored grasslands.

Most importantly, recent landscape-scale restoration is often focused on rivers. This might be expected, as a river can extend a very long distance and encompass many ecosystems dependent on and tributary to it, as well as being a complex ecosystem of its own. Historically, the ambivalence in the United States about rivers is astonishing, even unsettling. In the 20th century, the United States led the world in building massive dams on large rivers—on top of the many smaller dams for such purposes as irrigation, water supply, and hydroelectric power. There are at least 90,000 dams above six feet high on the country's waterways, as well as thousands upon thousands of smaller ones throughout the nation across streams, creeks, brooks, smaller rivers, and even headwaters. These dams, whether for hydropower, irrigation, flood control, or other purposes, destroy fish runs, degrade riverine and riparian ecosystems, and eliminate the rivers' ability to self-regulate ecologically.

However, beginning in the 1990s, Americans began a dam removal movement. It has intensified, broadened, and grown so much that, by 2018, the organization American Rivers estimated some 1,480 dams had been breached or removed nationwide, and the trend continues.[17] Exactly the opposite of its 20th century reputation, the United States now leads the world in dam removal. Thus far, the two largest dam removals in the world are the now-demolished Elwha and Glines dams in Washington state. Glines was more than 200 feet high and Elwha 100 feet in height. Removing both restored the Elwha River and, incidentally, its once-famous salmon runs (see Figures 5.2, 5.3, and 5.4).[18]

An even larger dam removal project is in the works: bringing down the four PacifiCorp dams in the Klamath River basin, built between 1908 and 1962. Under a newly amended Klamath Hydropower Settlement Agreement, signed by the Governors of Oregon and California, the four dams will be removed once they are transferred to the nonprofit Klamath River Renewal Corporation and receive the necessary federal and California state approvals. Together these dams block some 400 miles of salmon habitat on the Klamath River (California's second largest). This

FIGURE 5.2 Elwha Dam, Washington State, in 2006. The dam was removed in 2012.

Source: (Photograph by Larry Ward).

FIGURE 5.3 Glines Dam on the Elwha River before removal.
Source: (Photograph by National Park Service).

FIGURE 5.4 Glines Dam removal process, 2012.
Source: (Photograph by National Park Service).

project, the largest dam removal in United States history, will probably begin in 2022 and cost some $40 million.[19]

The project, as it moves ahead, will not only restore hundreds of miles of riverine ecosystem, but also highlight questions of environmental justice that must be answered when landscape-scale restoration takes place: those who relied on the damaged ecosystem must be compensated in some way for all they will lose. That can include farms, ranches, homes, and a cherished lifestyle. How best to undertake this compensation, in a situation where environmental restoration is desperately needed, is a central question for the Rights of Nature paradigm, whether it is changing the law or working on the ground to restore entire landscapes or river systems.

LOCAL AND WORLDWIDE RIVER PROTECTION

The concept of "Rights of Nature" requires relationship, but no relationship is possible with an entity incapable of it. At best, there would be only a one-sided relationship, as with (for example) a lump of plastic or a factory building. The philosophical and spiritual underpinnings of the Rights of Nature paradigm are profound, but not all people, or cultures, wish to embrace or expand them. What would that reluctance mean for implementing ecological governance?

One answer could be to design interlocking levels of human use and biophysical consequences, based on the best available knowledge from all reliable sources. This would not require individuals to change personal belief systems, though it would necessitate adjusting public policy and philosophy to understand that ecosystems are dynamic, resilient, all-encompassing—and have biophysical limitations. That change in perspective would trigger major adjustments in an economic system designed to extract maximum "natural resources" for human use regardless of ecological consequences. There is no way to avoid such a change, however, without serious consequences to people and the environment.

One of the likeliest ways to design interlocking ecological governance is by rivers. The largest rivers begin in distant mountains and flow through vast territories, fabulously unique landscapes, and multiple cultures before emptying into the sea, often hundreds or thousands of miles away. Ecological governance, based on local watersheds within a collective drainage basin, would have far-reaching and colossal influence on many communities. Following the nature of rivers, it would easily organize into local levels of governance and higher, federal ones with greater power and oversight—just as a river begins in tiny rivulets at the headwaters, joining into a single massive river by the time it reaches the sea.

Initiating ecological governance based on one or another discrete feature is difficult, as ecosystems interlock and shape one another. However, rivers offer fairly discrete features government can focus on, and they have the added advantage that a river's influence can be mapped and delineated to some extent. It is no coincidence that most of the successful Rights of Nature efforts, as well as the most powerful political campaigns, focus on granting rights to a river. There is also no question that people living in the vicinity of a river have a relationship with it, whether they conceptualize it in sacral or secular terms.

Ecological governance seems to be successful on the Atrato River in Colombia, severely degraded by irresponsible mining, which has affected the Chocó region that most closely depends on the river, as well as the indigenous and Afro-Colombian communities for whom the river is part of their lifeway. The Colombia Constitutional Court, in 2016, recognized the Atrato's rights. But, equally importantly, the Court held that Rights of Nature are part of "biocultural rights" that apply to the human communities and the ecological communities of the Chocó region, as well the river, grounded in rights granted by the Constitution of Colombia.[20]

In other words, the Court found a new way to bring *relationship* into policy-making decisions about a river. This new legal territory could have far-reaching effects on how to approach snarled and intractable problems concerning water conflicts worldwide. The decision is recent, so how it will affect resolution of water conflicts in practice is not yet clear, though the Court directed immediate creation of an oversight, guardian body to begin restoration and conflict management, assisted by a body of experts. Most importantly, the judgment designed the work going forward as an integrated watershed plan; to that end, the court followed the river in designing the relationships between the Atrato, its dependent communities, and the attendant responsibilities.

Another high-profile river case with a successful outcome on paper, but much less so in practice, concerns the Ganges River in India. The Ganges, sacred to millions of Hindus, passes through at least 30 cities and towns as it flows from the high Himalayas to the Bay of Bengal. Some parts of its watershed are highly industrialized, especially in the state of Uttar Pradesh, where numerous factories discharge wastewater into the river, as do thermal plants, whose wastewater is hotter than the river's own water. Large amounts of untreated municipal sewage from many urban areas pour into the river as well. The result is that the Ganges River is in a dire state of pollution.[21]

Citizen efforts to force cleanups, especially of the municipal sewage, had frequently centered on lawsuits filed under India's National Green Tribunal. Then the High Court of Uttarakhand ruled, in March 2017, that the Ganges, its principal tributary the Yamuna, and all the other tributaries "were living entities having the status of a legal person with all corresponding rights, duties and liabilities of a living person." The Court appointed three guardians to oversee protection and restoration of the rivers. However, this sweeping judgment produced no victory, except on paper; indeed, India's Supreme Court quashed the ruling a few months later, so local governments would not be burdened with the accountability and responsibilities required by the Rights of Nature ruling.

Unlike in Colombia, the court's effort in India failed, because the politics of the Ganges' cleanup are so fraught. The National Green Tribunal, India's environmental court, has done most of the burdensome work of sorting through the responsibilities of parties that pollute the Ganges and its tributaries. The Uttarakhand case sought to leapfrog over the court and state efforts and centralize Ganges cleanup. However, Indian courts have rather frequently applied ecological standards to enforcement of constitutionally guaranteed rights, creating a new bureaucratic level of guardianship composed of officials whose efforts have largely failed. The Ganges Rights of Nature case merely tried to reignite these similar failed efforts under a new legal umbrella.[22]

If I Am the River and the River Is Me: Water Conflict and Ecological Governance

These contrasting results point to a few important facets of the ecological governance debate and the ways that water conflict management will be shaped, where it is in use in disputes over a river.

First, if society places the cause of a water conflict in an ecological governance framework, the conflict automatically migrates to a higher level than the needs of the contestants. The river's own ability to flourish will be the first concern, because the river has personhood and must seek for its own integrity, as living beings do. The first basis of all relationship is that both parties are equally *capable* of relationship. If the river is not a living entity with personal needs, there is no reciprocity and, thus, no relationship.

Second, once the issues rearrange themselves into a two-party conflict between the river and the humans, the next step is for both parties to see how they have failed each other in a mutually beneficial relationship. A river speaks in many ways that humans can easily understand: the water's clarity, its plenitude of life or lack thereof, its oxygen levels, the richness of its riparian forest, the amount of its water available to the river before and after human use. If the humans have degraded and defiled the river, the first step in repairing the relationship must be for the humans to restore the river and heal its ills. This might include (for example) replanting the native riparian forest; removing dams; using less water; restoring native fish; ending the pollution from factories, municipal sewage, and agricultural runoff; and protecting springs and/or headwaters from clear-cut logging, roads, and other human-caused erosion.

Third, at the same time as humans are taking responsibility for mending their end of the broken relationship—which has caused the river to be unable to meet its own needs, much less those of humans—the people must work on changing how they use the water, so the river can flourish. This elevated consciousness ultimately allows the people to flourish as well, though it may require wrenching changes in economic systems, as well as patterns or traditions of use. Squabbling over human needs while the river fades from ill health and overuse is not a relationship, except of the most selfish and unheeding kind.

Fourth, in the shift to a system of ecological governance, in which rivers have the right to flourish, all other human rights will need to be reorganized. Justice in water conflict is difficult because water is life, and traditional patterns of use are usually codified in law, court decisions, and in the very structures of daily life in that region. The required changes will take collaboration much deeper than usual in conflict cases, but could potentially lead to substantially bigger breakthroughs. Consciously working in relationship allows the people to see not only how they might become better friends with the river on *whom* they depend for sustenance but also what changes they need to make.

CONCLUSION

A Rights of Nature approach to water conflict requires depths of skill, compassion, scientific knowledge, and local understanding that are not usually drawn together.

However, as conflicts escalate and the waters dwindle, it is clear that a new way of thinking is essential. Relationships only flourish when there is abiding respect on both sides. In current water conflicts, that is too often missing. Still, that essential respect, the bedrock of all relationship, can easily be restored. We, the people, just have to take the first step.

It is not necessary to enter into theological debates over the ways a body of water might be living. People's perceptions of that will differ, yet all can agree that there is a relationship between the people and (for example) the river. Whether people are vital to the river is unknown; but the river is unquestionably vital to people, and thus a critical relationship is born, has been broken, and can be repaired through mutual understanding and respect.

Conflicts over water are among the most ancient causes of strife between individuals, towns, kingdoms, and nations. This is not surprising, since water is life. But the Industrial Revolution has vastly increased water conflicts as industrial and municipal needs—often much larger and more polluting—shoulder their way in among other, smaller-scale uses. The need for a new way of thinking has become dire, as entire river systems die, including the groundwater and springs. Rights of Nature, or a similar form of ecological governance, provides this new template. It allows humans to step back and evaluate whether the use of a water body is wise and sustainable in the only way truth can be ascertained: by placing humans and the water in relationship.

Only then, seeking to honor a relationship of respect, will humans take actions that place the needs of the water body first. This allows humans to listen to the river or lake and learn what it needs to flourish. As the water flourishes, humans can do likewise. By the greed of escalating use relationship is broken, nobody listens for and seeks to restore the integrity of the water, and both humans and the water suffer ever-greater problems. No relationship of respect is ever based on one party taking all, or most, of what the other party is able to give. The true foundation of resolving water conflicts is this: listen to the water and respect humanity's ancient relationship with it.

QUESTIONS AND EXERCISES

1. What is a paradigm shift? Is there a compelling reason for humans to change their water use to a Rights of Nature form of governance?
2. In a world where governance is based on the Rights of Nature, what actions would your community need to take to restore the integrity of the river, lake, or springs your community depends on?
3. How would Rights of Nature governance be different from the way water is now governed in your state or community? Would it change how water is used, or who is allowed to use it, from the way water is now used?
4. Draft a Rights of Nature ordinance for your community's water source that lays out the relationship between the people and the water, and the responsibilities people have to respect the water's right to flourish free of pollution and other problems.

5. How can people listen to the river or lake, be able to tell that humans are not respecting the water's right to flourish, and need to take steps to restore the relationship?
6. In a Rights of Nature form of governance, who will be responsible for helping the water regain its integrity if it is polluted or used too much? How will the community decide who is responsible, and who will pay for the work?
7. What things can members of the community do for the river, lake, springs, or groundwater to show their respect for the water?

NOTES

1 See, e.g., Alley, K. 2002. *On the Banks of the Ganga: When Wastewater Meets a Sacred River*. Ann Arbor, MI: University of Michigan Press; Micklin, P., N.V. Aladin, and I. Plotnikov (eds.). 2014. *The Aral Sea: The Devastation and Partial Rehabilitation of a Great Lake*. Berlin Heidelberg: Springer-Verlag.
2 (a) U.S. Environmental Protection Agency, Office of Water and Office of Research and Development. 2016. *National Rivers and Streams Assessment 2008–2009: A Collaborative Survey* (EPA/841/R-16/007). Washington, DC. (b) U.S. Environmental Protection Agency. 2017. *National Water Quality Inventory: Report to Congress* (EPA 841-R-16-011). Washington, DC.
3 Ito, M. 2019. "Nature's Rights: Why the European Union Needs a Paradigm Shift in Law to Achieve Its 2050 Vision." In La Follette, C. and C. Maser (eds.), *Sustainability and the Rights of Nature in Practice*. Boca Raton, FL: CRC Press.
4 Stone, Christopher D. 1972. "Should Trees Have Standing?—Toward Legal Rights for Natural Objects." *Southern California Law Review*, 45: 450–501.
5 Stone, Christopher D. 2010. *Should Trees Have Standing? Law, Morality and the Environment*. 3rd ed. New York: Oxford University Press, p. xiv.
6 Nash, Roderick F. 1989. *The Rights of Nature: A History of Environmental Ethics*. Madison: University of Wisconsin Press.
7 Ecuadorian Constitution, Title II, Chapter 7, Article 71.
8 Ibid., Article 72
9 Ibid., Article 73.
10 Bolivian Law, Complete Text (English). www.worldfuturefund.org/Projects/Indicators/motherearthbolivia.html (accessed May 19, 2020).
11 Ibid.
12 La Follette, C., and C. Maser. 2017. *Sustainability and the Rights of Nature: An Introduction*. Boca Raton, FL: CRC Press.
13 For an overview of the restraint that is needed to sustain a relationship with Nature (in the United States), see La Follette, C., and C. Maser. 2017. *Sustainability and the Rights of Nature: An Introduction*. Boca Raton, FL: CRC Press. For a good discussion of the environmental justice questions involved, see Gwiazdon, Kathryn A. 2019. "Defending the Tree of Life: The Ethical Justification for the Rights of Nature in a Theory of Justice." In La Follette, C. and C. Maser (eds.), *Sustainability and the Rights of Nature in Practice*. Boca Raton, FL: CRC Press.
14 All information in this summary taken from Finlayson, C. 2019. "A River is Born: New Zealand Confers Legal Personhood on the Whanganui to Protect It and Its Native People." In La Follette, C. and C. Maser (eds.), *Sustainability and the Rights of Nature in Practice*. Boca Raton, FL: CRC Press.

15 Schromen-Wawrin, L., and M. Newman. 2019. "Nature's Rights Through Lawmaking in the United States." In La Follette C. and C. Maser (eds.), *Sustainability and the Rights of Nature in Practice*. Boca Raton, FL: CRC Press.
16 Nobel, Justin. 2020. "Nature Scores a Big Win Against Fracking in a Small Pennsylvania Town." *Rolling Stone* (April 1, 2020). www.rollingstone.com/politics/politics-news/Rights of Nature-beats-fracking-in-small-pennsylvania-town-976159/ (accessed June 25, 2020); Hess, David E. 2020. "DEP Revokes Drilling Waste Injection Well Permit in Grant Twp., Indiana County After Environmental Rights Amendment Court Ruling." *PA Environmental Digest Blog* (March 26, 2020). http://paenvironmentdaily.blogspot.com/2020/03/dep-revokes-drilling-waste-injection.html (accessed August 20, 2020).
17 American Rivers. https://figshare.com/articles/American_Rivers_Dam_Removal_Database/5234068 (accessed May 19, 2020).
18 (a) Nijhuis, Michelle. 2014. "World's Largest Dam Removal Unleashes U.S. River After Century of Electric Production." *National Geographic* (August 27, 2014). https://news.nationalgeographic.com/news/2014/08/140826-elwha-river-dam-removal-salmon-science-olympic/ (accessed May 19,2020); (b) Mapes, Lynda V. 2013. *Elwha: A River Reborn*. Seattle, WA: The Mountaineers Books.
19 Jacobs, Jeremy P. 2020. "Calif. greenlights massive Klamath River dam removal." *E&E News* (April 9, 2020). www.eenews.net/stories/1062829919 (accessed May 19, 2020).
20 Judgment T-622/16 (The Atrato River Case) Constitutional Court of Colombia (2016). Translation: Dignity Rights Project, Delaware Law School, USA. Available at Dignity Rights Project, 2019. http://files.harmonywithnatureun.org/uploads/upload838.pdf (accessed June 23, 2010).
21 Information on the Ganges personhood struggle and history of the Ganges pollution problem from Alley, Kelly D., and Tarini Mehta. 2019. "The Experiment with Rights of Nature in India." In La Follette, C. and C. Maser (eds.), *Sustainability and the Rights of Nature in Practice*. Boca Raton, FL: CRC Press. See also Alley, Kelly D. 2002. *On the Banks of the Ganga: When Wastewater Meets a Sacred River*. Ann Arbor, MI: University of Michigan Press.
22 Alley, Kelly D., and Tarini Mehta. 2019. "The Experiment with Rights of Nature in India." In La Follette, C. and C. Maser (eds.), *Sustainability and the Rights of Nature in Practice*. Boca Raton, FL: CRC Press.

6 Intertribal Fishing Conflicts and Federal Obstruction in Oregon

David G. Lewis

CONTENTS

Introduction 103
Change Comes 105
Contemporary Era 106
    Grand Ronde 110
    Contemporary Water Issues 113
        Finding Good Faith in a Middle Ground 114
        Why Would the Other Tribes Need to Fish at Willamette Falls? 115
Questions 118
Notes 119

INTRODUCTION

The following descriptions of context and contest over traditional resources of several Oregon tribes are told by a member of the Grand Ronde Tribe and a former manager of the Cultural Department of the tribe. As a scholar, I have experienced and studied many of the situations as a manager at the Grand Ronde Tribe and have continued to follow the actions and reactions of Oregon tribes for the past seven years. The cultural connections to many of the locations mentioned are a significant concern, and this has led to more than 20 years of historic research concerning all the tribes of Oregon. It is with no small amount of trepidation to tell this series of stories from my perspective, but I do so in the hope that, with greater dialogue and discussion about the various tribal perspectives, the tribes may one day find an equitable resolution. Oregon's tribes have collectively undergone an incredibly divisive colonization, and I believe the continued conflicts about fishing and territorial rights are another symptom of that colonization.

    The tribes of Oregon, like many others in the region, were dependent on the vast network of rivers that drained the area's many mountain ranges. Fishing was the way of life for many tribal people, as they occupied villages centered on access to highly productive areas, like Celilo Falls in the Columbia River at The Dalles; the rapids at the Cascades, also known as the "Lower Falls of the Columbia"; and Willamette Falls in the Willamette River between Oregon City and West Linn.[1] Over the past

FIGURE 6.1 Indians fishing at Willamette Falls, Alfred Agate 1841 U.S. exploring expedition (1845).

70 years, there have been numerous conflicts concerning water resources and Native American tribal nations. Tribal nations in Oregon have enduring substantial issues with access to fishing areas, which they have occupied for more than 10,000 years. These conflicts are due to the way the United States government has mismanaged tribal rights since the beginning of the reservations, creating numerous jurisdictional conflicts between tribes (Figure 6.1).

In this region, salmon was the major fish, with numerous runs of various species reentering the river systems of their birth, like the Columbia, to spawn in the upland tributaries, creeks, and streams. Four or more runs a year made the fish a significant part of the lifeways and economies of all tribal peoples during all seasons. The oily ooligan[2] smelt came in vast numbers to rivers like the Cowlitz (Washington) and Sandy (Oregon), and were highly sought for their unique properties; and the lamprey with its strong, oily flavor also had runs at the major falls in the region, climbing up the rocks in their particular manner to reach the upper, navigable waters where they would spawn. In addition, species of fish such as steelhead trout and sturgeon were constantly available in the landscape's rivers and lakes.

Fishing nations of the Columbia River system lived well, thriving off their vast catches of salmon and other species, which they wind dried, smoked, and traded to other tribes. The Columbia River was the center-point in a vast trading zone, called the Columbia River Trade Network, of tribes interacting at trading centers like Celilo Village at The Dalles. At locations like this, many tribal people who specialized in unique woven and carved products were able to bring their products and trade their craftwork for dried salmon from the prosperous villages around fishing falls.

The trading network extended across half of the North American continent, as tribes in the west, the Tillamook and Chinookans (both in Oregon), accessed commodities from the Pacific Ocean, like seashells and whale products. In turn, tribes farther east, the Nez Perce (Nimiipuu), fished for salmon in their rivers part of the year and then travelled to the Great Plains, where they hunted bison, and brought bison robes and horns back to their homelands for trading.[3]

The tribal nations of the Columbia also had many intermarriages between the tribal leaders. High-born men and women were subject to arranged marriages designed to form kinship bonds between tribes. This method was enforced as cultural policy in all tribes in the region and was responsible for generations of peace among kin-related tribes. Tribal leaders knew that keeping the peace and connecting the tribes aided in trade relations, which would help the leaders accumulate wealth and provide for their community. The best leaders were raised up by their tribal members and used their wealth to help their people. In addition, since many fishing locations at falls were claimed by families, in effect owned and protected by them, and only those of their kin relations could fish at these sites.

Others, wishing to fish in a claimed location, would have to request permission from the local chief or headman and give presents representing their respect and honor of the rights of the resident tribe, for the privilege to fish. The trading-tribe peoples of the region knew tribal diplomacy and would ask permission to land their canoes at villages, present themselves to the tribal leaders, professing their respect for the tribal rights; state their peaceful intentions; as well as respectfully follow the ceremonial ways of the resident tribe to gain mutual respect and trust.[4] White settlers rarely respected this diplomacy when they settled the land, causing conflicts for generations.

Nevertheless, conflicts between tribes were many. When conflicts erupted, they were generally between distant, unrelated tribes. Tribes would call on their group of allies and affiliated tribes for help during wars and skirmishes and could generally count on aid from their blood relatives in other tribes. This is the case with a skirmish between Chief Kiesno, an important Multnomah-Wakanasissi Chinookan leader, and the Cowlitz peoples in 1814.[5] Members of the Pacific Fur Traders at Astoria (Oregon) recorded that the Cowlitz, with their allies, sought to occupy a part of the Columbia River and came down into the Columbia with many canoes of warriors. They were met by Chief Kiesno who called on his allied tribes to send their canoes to his aid. Kiesno's allies, likely the Tualatin Kalapuyans, Clowewallas, Clackamas, and Cascades, came in their canoes to support the Chief, who won the standoff and forced the Cowlitz to return upriver.[6]

CHANGE COMES

Tribal culture changed significantly in the middle of the 19th century due to colonization of the region by the European-Americans. Tribes on the brink of genocide signed treaties with the United States and agreed to move to reservations, thus severing many connections with their traditional territories. Tribal members were made to take up farming and ranching, as their new culture; and over generations, many adapted to the new way of life on the reservation. This forced adaptation, called assimilation, was pushed by federal agents, as a way to integrate tribal adults into the American farming culture. In addition, tribal children were forced to attend on-reservation schools and off-reservation boarding schools, where they were exposed to a Christian education—forcing further assimilation. Finally, missionaries were assigned to each reservation by the Federal government to further convert the people into Christianity and the American ideal.[7]

Many of the tribal cultures changed significantly between 1856 and 1924, when tribal peoples were given U.S. citizenship. In 1935, under the Wheeler-Howard Act,[8] the federal government allowed tribes to become self-governing—if they changed their government to a constitutional democracy with elected leadership. Numerous legislative acts passed under Indian Superintendent John Collier in the 1930s, and programs like the Indian Rehabilitation Project not only gave tribal people on reservations a way to make money but also gave more control to the tribal governments.[9] But, in the 1950s, Indian policy changed to "Termination."

Termination Policy was originally meant to terminate all tribal treaties in the United States and eliminate the need for federal support for reservations. In total, 109 tribes were terminated nationally. All western Oregon tribes, including those on the Grand Ronde and Siletz reservations, and the Klamath Tribe lost their treaties and reservations—under the guise of freedom and equality. Warm Springs and Umatilla effectively fought against termination and were never affected. Besides sovereignty and land rights, termination heavily affected tribal cultures, and numerous tribal languages were lost. In the 1970s and 1980s, however, many tribes worked to reverse termination and become restored. As a result, seven tribes in Oregon were reinstated: Burns Paiute (1973), Siletz (1977), Cow Creek (1982), Grand Ronde (1983), Coos Lower Umpqua and Siuslaw (1984), Klamath (1986), and Coquille (1989). Today, the nine tribes of Oregon are confederations of many of the original tribes, as they struggle to maintain their rights to fish in their cultural ways.[10]

CONTEMPORARY ERA

In the 1950s, tribal nations on reservations were quite different from what they had been a century earlier, when they had been removed from their traditional lands. Consequently, many tribes had spent some 80 years without full rights to fish or hunt, even though these rights were promised in treaties. By the 20th century, tribes were learning how to defend their rights through legal battles.[11] Some tribes had more rights because their treaties expressed rights to fish. People of the Warm Springs Reservation in Oregon and the Yakima Reservation in Washington maintained their relationships with the Columbia River and their rights to fish in a traditional manner.

Celilo, a traditional fishing village, remained as a semi-autonomous Native village, and the Native peoples who lived there were members of the two or more reservations and continued taking salmon. But this lifeway changed with the damming of the Columbia by the Army Corps of Engineers. The Corps placed numerous dams in the Columbia and its tributaries to control runoff and capture power generated by hydroelectric turbines. The Dalles Dam, completed by the Corps in 1957, caused the inundation of much of Celilo Falls and its fishery and the near destruction of the tribal culture.

Due to flooding behind the dam, Celilo Village had to be moved uphill above the reservoir level, and the people were promised new housing, which for over 50 years is a promise that has never been kept by the Federal government. Tribal fishermen were eventually given alternative fishing sites, called "in-lieu" sites, further downriver—in the original territory of the Cascades peoples—to replace the loss of their Celilo fishery, along with promises of money for the tribes. The money, coming from the Bonneville Power Administration, funds organizations like the Columbia River Intertribal Fish Commission, which represents four tribes with fishing rights on the river because of their treaties: Warm Springs, Yakima, Umatilla, and Nez Perce.[12]

There is one other ratified treaty on the lower Columbia, the Willamette Valley Treaty of 1855, also called the Kalapuya Etc. Treaty[13] (Figure 6.2). The Confederated Tribes of Grand Ronde and the Confederated Tribes of the Siletz claim this treaty. Most of the people who signed the Willamette Valley Treaty were moved to the Grand Ronde Indian Reservation in 1856. Through time, because of the close proximity of the two reservations, many members of the Grand Ronde and Siletz Tribes inter-married, and now there are joint ancestral claims to the Willamette Valley tribal lands on both reservations. In addition, the Rogue River and Umpqua Valley tribes were moved to the Grand Ronde and the Coast Reservation in 1856. Then, in 1857, many of these people originally resettled at Grand Ronde were moved to the Siletz valley due to administrative decisions of the United States Indian agents.

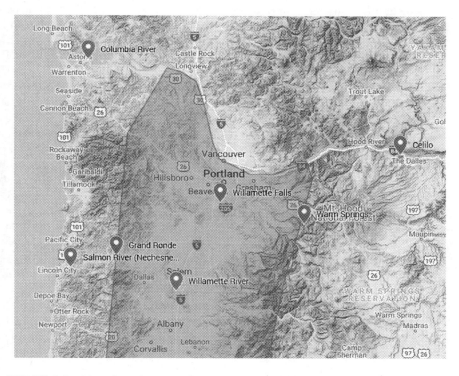

FIGURE 6.2 Map of northwestern Oregon showing Willamette Treaty outline and important river locations.

Source: (Created by David G. Lewis, 2020. Google My Maps).

Today, there is a shared cultural relationship among approximately 60 tribes from western Oregon that were relocated to the two original reservations, with additional kinships with the people at Cow Creek Band of Umpqua Indians, the Coquille Indian Tribe, and the Confederated Tribes of Coos, Lower Umpqua, and Siuslaw tribes. There are also interfamilial kinships with other reservations in the west, including Warm Springs, Yakima, Klamath, Burns Paiute, and Umatilla.

Unfortunately, the Willamette Valley Treaty does not have any rights written into it for fishing, hunting, or gathering. This presents a weaker case for the tribal descendants of the signatories to this treaty when they seek the right to fish or hunt. Nevertheless, the tribes were granted some rights for fishing and other activities on their reservations into the 20th century.[14] In addition, many tribes lacking expressed rights for fishing in their treaties maintain these rights were never expressly taken away, so they insist they have rights to fish because these were sovereign rights they possessed for thousands of years before the United States was a country.

In 1954, when the two western Oregon reservations were being terminated by the federal government under PL 588 (the Western Oregon Indian Termination Act), there was no mention of the right to fish or hunt being eliminated. This was the case not only with tribes in Washington State but also nationally, where some 109 tribes were terminated, but their hunting and fishing rights were not mentioned. Following termination, state governments simply assumed that, since the terminated tribes were no longer recognized, they did not have fishing rights. In Washington, for example, Native fishermen, like David Sohappy,[15] were being arrested for fishing if they were from terminated tribes. This began the era called "the fishing wars" that involved political and legal battles about the rights of Native people to fish, a conflict that took place within three decades 1960s–1980s.

The fact is that terminated tribes in states like Washington and Oregon did not lose their fishing rights. Fishing, as stated previously, was originally a sovereign activity; therefore, nothing could legally take it away without tribal agreement. Since there is no mention of this in their termination legislation, the members of the terminated tribes retain these rights to fish in their usual and accustomed places and ways. Two court cases, informally called the 1974 Boldt[16] and 1969 Belloni[17] decisions, certified that tribal fishing rights were never taken away, that tribal members could fish in their usual and accustomed ways and won the right to half of the catch in Washington State. These decisions were important in maintaining the rights of tribal fishermen who were members of tribes that had ratified treaties granting the usual and accustomed rights to the tribes.[18]

Many tribes that had been federally terminated in the 1950s and 1960s gained restoration in the 1970s and 1980s under Congressional bills. Tribal restoration was aided by the findings of the Task Force Ten Commission (1975), that termination of tribal treaties and reservations had been a disaster.[19] It was concluded by the commission that terminated tribes had experienced social, political, cultural, and economic declines, and that tribal cultures were dying while communities suffered crippling social ills, such as poverty, alcohol, drug abuse, and racism.[20]

In the 1970s, the Grand Ronde and Siletz tribal councils amid termination began to seek a solution to the social ills their people were experiencing and sought political restoration. During this same period, the "fishing wars" were won in favor of the tribal rights, and many Americans, wary of "special" Indian rights, cast a critical eye on restoration of more tribes who could further complicate the fishing issues. Numerous people assumed that, once Siletz Tribal rights were restored, sport fishing would be "destroyed." Because of this, dozens of Oregonians sent letters of opposition to the Governors of Oregon Robert Straub (1975–1979) and Victor Atiyeh (1979–1987) detailing many reasons why not to support tribal restoration, many of them based on misunderstandings and racial stereotypes of "Indians."[21] After years of fighting for tribal restoration, Governor Robert Straub forced the Siletz to give up hunting and fishing in their tribal restoration bill, and they were restored by Congress in 1977.[22] The Siletz did not lose fishing or hunting through termination but instead through restoration. Similarly, the people of the Confederated Tribes of Grand Ronde, a neighboring reservation in Western Oregon, faced restoration a few years later. They too were forced to give up hunting and fishing to gain the support of Governor Vic Atiyeh.[23] As a result, the Grand Ronde tribal government was restored in 1983 without fishing and hunting rights.[24] In addition, in 1988 the tribe received a 9,811-acre reservation under the Grand Ronde Reservation Act, with a proviso that they do not manage their own timber sales for 25 years. Presently, 43 years after Siletz was restored and 37 years after Grand Ronde was restored, we can safely say their restorations had no detrimental impact on non-native fishing, hunting, or logging even though the tribes have engaged in all these activities.[25]

Nevertheless, there currently are numerous conflicting viewpoints regarding the fishing rights of tribes in Oregon and throughout the Pacific Northwest. Tribes continue to struggle with federal administration of hydroelectric dams, causing crippling effects on annual fish runs. The federal government seems to continually question and obfuscate the rights of tribes, pitting them against one another over declining natural resources. In addition, in-stream flows for fish habitat and seasonal migrations in some basins are not always assured, which does not account for the fact that water is increasingly polluted with runoff from agriculture, industry, and human development. The most recent example of problems with in-stream flows involved several tribes along the Klamath River, including the Klamath Tribe of Oregon.[26] Newly re-established tribes not only have to manage this set of problems but also must navigate their traditional rights within an increasingly complex tribal-rights matrix. Therefore, tribes along the Columbia River with expressed fishing rights now call themselves the "treaty tribes" as they possess greater rights than tribes who are struggling to recover from termination and have no treaty rights to fish.

Grand Ronde is also a treaty tribe, in fact claiming seven ratified treaties, and yet none of the treaties of western Oregon include the right to fish, including the Willamette Valley Treaty (ratified March 3, 1855) which includes land on the Columbia River from Cascade Rapids to Oak Point, the whole of the Portland basin. In addition, during the time that Grand Ronde was being restored, the tribe had little opportunity to become more deeply involved with fish rights on the Columbia River. During restoration, while the tribe was still getting organized in the 1980s, federal discussions about the formation of the Columbia Gorge National Scenic Area (created by law in 1986)[27] were addressed, but only with tribes that had never been terminated and could mount an organized response to the act, like Warm Springs and Yakima. Consequently, there was little or no opportunity for Grand Ronde to join the act and thereby gain any additional rights in areas of the Columbia River Gorge.[28] In recent years, the Columbia River Intertribal Fish Commission has extended their influence west of the Gorge and begun addressing issues in the Portland Basin and on the Willamette River. This area is of special interest to the Grand Ronde tribe because these are the central homelands of Chinookan tribes, Multnomah, Clackamas, Clowewalla, and Cascades, all of whom signed the Willamette Valley Treaty and came to Grand Ronde during removal in 1856. Therefore, there are additional territorial issues concerning intertribal rights to fishing and relate to other federal projects like the superfund cleanup project at the Portland Harbor site.[29]

While the Grand Ronde Tribe was not involved in the Columbia Gorge National Scenic Act, a Grand Ronde tribal member, Chuck Williams, a Cascades native, environmental activist, and artist, was involved. In fact, he initiated the project to protect the environment of the Columbia River Gorge from destructive industrial development. Chuck worked for years as an environmental activist with the tribes, other activists, and regional politicians to get the legislation passed, but has gotten little credit for his actions, which protected the Gorge—the homelands of his Cascades tribe and other tribes of the Columbia—from industrialization.[30]

Many of the people at Grand Ronde descended from the Columbia River tribes, Clackamas, Clowewalla, Wapato Island (Multnomah), and Cascades peoples, are, in turn, directly related to other tribal peoples from the upper and lower Columbia River. As tribal people, many at Grand Ronde want to go back to their ancestral fishing areas and fish again, but they do not possess rights for fishing on the Columbia, where many of the Chinookans had permanent or seasonal fishing villages. The Cascades, for example, were well known for moving into the Wapato Valley, the Columbia River between Sauvie Island and the Sandy River, to fish and gather wapato through the winter, and then moved back to their villages at Cascade Rapids in April in time for the spring salmon run in early May.[31] Gaining fishing rights for Grand Ronde on the river would be today a serious political issue among tribes in the region. Not only are there federal issues regarding fishing rights, stated or not stated in treaties, but also two sovereign entities now administer their own halves of the upper and lower Columbia—the rights of Canada on the upper Columbia across the border (the Columbia River Treaty of 1964) and "treaty" tribes. The latter, however, are attempting to stop Grand Ronde from joining the treaty re-negotiations in an attempt to limit the access of the tribe to fishing on the river, regardless of the fact that parts of the Columbia is the original territory of many of the tribes who came to Grand Ronde. Grand Ronde has successfully pushed back and is part of the re-negotiations for the Columbia River Treaty between the United States and Canada.[32]

GRAND RONDE

When the Grand Ronde Tribe was restored in 1983, one of seven tribes restored in Oregon between 1973 and 1989, most members did not understand why the tribe had been terminated in the first place. The U.S. federal government initially removed the tribes from their original territories in 1856 and then disallowed them from leaving the reservation. This policy dissociated many Native people from their original lands. In addition, the federal government's policy toward tribes was to assimilate them into American culture. Assimilation involved exposing all native peoples to Christian missionaries, forcing children into boarding schools, and making the adults take up American lifestyles, like being farmers and ranchers. After over 100 years of federal assimilation policies, many tribal members lost a deep understanding of the history of their tribes. Federal policies, which included the aforementioned tribal termination in the 1950s, compounded tribal members' lack of knowledge concerning their cultural past and history of how the reservation was formed.

It has taken some 37 years for tribal scholars to reveal the history of the tribe, how the reservation was originally formed and what has happened to the people over the past 170 years. Tribal scholars are still uncovering the stories about the tribe from distant federal archival repositories. Many tribal records are buried within vast federal collections that are not easily accessed by tribal people unfamiliar with such archives. However, tribal scholars today are revealing histories that are helping to re-associate the tribe with the locations of their ancestors, including Willamette Falls in the lower Willamette River.[33]

The Willamette Falls is probably one of the most important natural resources for the tribes of western Oregon. It was a very productive fishery prior to colonization, as the Clowewalla people lived in villages around the base of the falls. The related Clackamas people, in the vicinity of the falls and up the Clackamas River, also had rights to fish at the falls. Cascades people, kin with the Clowewalla, would come to the falls in May for the spring run of salmon. The Kalapuyans and Molallans of the Willamette Valley traded at the falls for dried and smoked fish in exchange for cooked camas, wapato roots, and other trade resources. It was an exceedingly valuable resource for salmon and lamprey and created a trading hub for various tribes in this area of the river. All the Clowewalla and Clackamas peoples, living in villages close to the falls, were removed to the Grand Ronde Indian Reservation in 1856. Therefore, the fishing culture of the falls is significant to a great number of people at the tribe today, because this is their traditional homeland, where their ancestors lived for more than 10,000 years.[34]

The Grand Ronde Reservation was liquidated in 1956 after the termination of the treaties of western Oregon including the Willamette Valley Treaty in 1954 under Public Law 588.[35] Tribal members were paid $35 for their share of the reservation and released to freely integrate with the white population in Oregon. In the 29 years the tribe was terminated, many tribal members lost languages and knowledge of their traditional lands and history. Some families were able to pass on tribal traditions and have worked to revitalize tribal traditions. The tribe was restored in 1983 after gaining the support of Oregon's politicians.

The Grand Ronde Tribe, since restoration, has pushed for ever-increasing rights for its members to return to fishing in the Willamette River. They have fostered good relationships with the state to accomplish their goals. It has taken years for the tribe to gain the trust and goodwill of the Oregon Department of Fish and Wildlife to once again be allowed to fish in the Willamette. Part of this endeavor had been educating the state leaders about Grand Ronde's treaties and their tribal culture. The tribe has also proven to be a good steward of its own creeks and streams in the upper Yamhill River on their small reservation by establishing a weir for management, turning over roadway culverts for better fish passage, and establishing green forest corridor "buffer zones" where streams and creeks will not be affected by logging activities.

Fishing for many in the tribe is an essential part of the culture because we are also a river people. When the tribe was restored, the government sought on-reservation fishing rights for members. Today, the tribe has had rights for some 25 years to fish on the north side of the Salmon River and on the little Nestucca River under a tribal fishing license in an agreement with the state. Consequently, many tribal members are returning to fishing after generations without ancestral rights. Information about the tribe's deep history in the region has proven invaluable to the tribe's efforts.[36]

After much work, in 2016 the tribe obtained an agreement with the Oregon Department of Fish and Wildlife to fish in a discrete area around Willamette Falls, as a ceremonial right.[37] The tribe has a similar agreement with hunting rights in the Trask Wildlife Unit, to the north of the reservation, for year-round ceremonial hunts since about 2008.[38] These arrangements under state laws and jurisdictions sidestep the need to gain rights under federal laws, which are difficult to change.

Historically, fishing rights for Native people in Oregon were not controlled by state laws until the 1930s, as it was assumed by many administrators at the state level that Native peoples had the right to fish wherever they wished. The State of Oregon had no jurisdiction on federal Indian reservations at that time. If there was an issue with tribal fishing rights, the state officials had to ask federal officials about the jurisdictions with regard to native rights to fish. Because tribal people mainly lived on federal reservations, it was the federal government that determined and set the laws and policies regarding their fishing rights.[39] Even so, in correspondence and reports, many federal officials appeared uninformed about tribal rights because of the diverse and sometimes confusing entitlements stated in numerous treaties. For fishing rights, state officials generally allowed native people broad discretion. Hunting rights for tribal people were more tightly controlled and were only allowed on reservations. There are state court records of Native men being caught hunting off-reservation and fined under state hunting laws.[40]

In the first years at the reservation, most of the 1,200 Native people were living in poverty with bad housing, no resources, no land, and insufficient services, such as health care, due to a lack of consistency in federal funding, services, and supply of food. To alleviate this situation and keep the people on the reservation,[41] Indian agents at Grand Ronde developed a fishery at the Salmon River in about 1860. The fishery, roughly 20 miles west from the reservation on the coastal Salmon River (Nechesne is the original name of the river and people) along the Salmon River Wagon Road, now called the Salmon River Highway, allowed the Native people at Grand Ronde to fish and bring their own food to the reservation. The establishment of this fishery impinged upon areas of the Coast Reservation, managed by the Siletz Agency, but because Grand Ronde had a more direct route to the Salmon River fishery, the Grand Ronde Indian agent took charge of that area of the Coast Reservation between the Salmon and Siletz rivers estuaries—the area is now mainly occupied by Lincoln City and the town of Taft. This overlapping claim to a portion of the Coast Reservation was a point of some disagreement between the Siletz and Grand Ronde agencies and Indian Agents for some 20 years, which was not fully decided until the Siletz Indian Agency took full charge of the area in about 1886.[42]

Intertribal Fishing Conflicts and Federal Obstruction in Oregon 113

CONTEMPORARY WATER ISSUES

Since its restoration in 1983, the Confederated Tribes of Grand Ronde have been highly active in seeking to recover sovereign rights. While the tribe was forced to give up hunting and fishing to be reinstated, tribal members still value these cultural traditions and are working diligently to revitalize them. During termination, many families were made to move away from their former tribal reservation for jobs, education, and opportunities in far-flung cities. Since tribal restoration, families have been returning. While knowledge of tribal history and culture was limited to some, members are working diligently to restore tribal cultural traditions. Lack of access to natural-resource areas, like rivers, delays the work to restore tribal culture. Grand Ronde tribal members are devoted to restoring tribal river environments essential to the ancestral tribes, and necessary for practicing traditions of fishing and canoeing. To this end, the tribe has participated for about 20 years in the Pacific Northwest canoe journeys and collaborated with several regional tribes to restore their own traditions.

Oral histories tell us that the rivers and other landforms have spirits, that they are our brothers and sisters, and it is the duty of our people to protect and care for these things like we would our own families. Our tribes state we have been here since time immemorial, and many dozens of generations of our people lived and died here. The land and waters are full of the spirits and DNA of our people, and many in the tribe still feel a responsibility to their health and welfare. Our long-ago treaty chiefs said the land is our heart, and this is an expression repeated in stories and histories by many tribes in the region, as people seek to reconnect with their ancestral lands. The land is both the heart of the people and our truth in many ways.

Political tensions have now formed over which tribes should have access to the falls.[43] Warm Springs tribal lawyers have even tried to deny that the Grand Ronde has the right to name the Clackamas and Clowewalla peoples as having lived at this location.

In about 2013, I was party to a meeting with Warm Springs representatives, the Oregon City Cultural Coalition, and the Willamette Falls Heritage Area Coalition. These organizations were asking if Warm Springs, who had made claims to usual and accustomed fishing rights at the falls, would sign onto an agreement to help develop tourism at the falls. The Warm Springs lawyer refused to allow the coalition or Grand Ronde to state, in any agreement, that the Clackamas and Clowewalla tribes had lived at the falls. This demand was a shock to those of us from Grand Ronde, and we could not get an agreement, as we were not willing to dissociate from our traditional heritage.

What was so upsetting to us tribal members was knowing that the tribes of Oregon were fully aware that the Clowewalla and Clackamas had lived at the falls, until they were moved to the Grand Ronde Reservation.[44] This fact was well documented in hundreds of publications and reports and in oral histories. Yet the Warm Springs insisted that we omit this, which, to me, was counterproductive to our work restoring our association with the falls. They wanted us to dissociate from our tribal heritage, which is exactly what the United States government did when they removed us from our lands and worked to assimilate our people. Because we were unwilling to agree to dissociation, the negotiations went nowhere, and if this is asked of us again, we will never dissociate.

Finding Good Faith in a Middle Ground

Tribes in traditional times, before removal to the reservations and forced to adopt constitutions and bureaucratic governments, would sit with one another and negotiate in good faith for all disagreements. Any problem could be settled, and tribal leaders worked hard to be respectful in negotiations. Without good-faith discussions, negative feelings are constantly being cast back and forth, as there is little or no opportunity to find middle ground, where everyone agrees on solutions to the disagreements.

Additionally, many tribes in the Northwest feel that tribes who were terminated, like Grand Ronde, had agreed to no longer be Indians by being terminated, and so they do not deserve any Indian rights. But the termination of the tribe did not happen with the tribe's agreement, but was forced by the federal government, and so the idea the tribe had agreed to termination is not based on the truth of the termination era in Oregon (1953–1963). My doctoral research on termination revealed that there never was an agreement by the terminated tribes before termination, and that the termination bill for Grand Ronde and Siletz, PL 588, was voted on by Congress without any agreements from the tribes.[45] Therefore, termination status was forced on the peoples of Grand Ronde and Siletz.

Regardless of whether other tribes genuinely believed the people of Grand Ronde had willingly gave up their tribal identities, it is not the experience of many families at Grand Ronde. The tribe has records of constant visitations to Willamette Falls to fish by descendants of the Clackamas and Clowewalla from 1856 into the 1970s. Grand Ronde people also visited the falls after termination, because their culture did not die when the tribal status was ended without their approval. Members visited and constructed fishing scaffolds in the 1970s, and many families continued to keep their traditions alive and persist in doing so today.

In the restoration era, when Grand Ronde was being restored, Warm Springs supported the tribe's restoration, as an expression of solidarity. But, when Warm Springs was suffering in the 2000s due to poor performance of their casino at Kah-nee-ta and tribal programs lacked funding for their tribal members, they sought to build a casino in Cascade Locks. Grand Ronde did not support them and worked to counter this development politically. This is a significant area of contention between the tribes today, which continues to spoil relations between the tribes. The reason for lack of support from Grand Ronde was the closeness of the location to Portland, not only making it highly competitive with Grand Ronde's Spirit Mountain Casino but also placing it within the boundaries of the Willamette Valley Treaty. The results of the halting of the Cascades Locks Casino forced Warm Springs to pursue other locations and finally built the Indian Head Casino on the edge of their reservation on Highway 26. But the obstacles created by Grand Ronde in conjunction with several Gorge communities continue to ruin all manner of relations between the tribes for the last two decades.[46]

Why Would the Other Tribes Need to Fish at Willamette Falls?

In recent decades, members of the Warm Springs and Yakima have come to the Willamette Falls each year to collect lamprey. They now maintain that they are a people with rights at Willamette Falls.[47] Historically, these peoples did come to the falls and trade for salmon, but they did not live there. Nevertheless, they want fishing rights at the falls, and are pushing back at the rights the Grand Ronde Tribe has in connection to their ancestral lands and treaties. When Grand Ronde sought to fish at the falls in recent years, and in 2019 built a fishing scaffold at the falls, Warm Springs and allied tribes took steps to impede Grand Ronde from access to fishing in this location.[48] Council members of the Warm Springs Tribe even stated that Grand Ronde is "expanding" their influence, suggesting that Grand Ronde did not have an original stake in the falls in the first place,[49] while they want to use the expressed rights in their 1855 treaty to expand their own influence over the falls as part of their usual and accustomed places.

> That the exclusive right of taking fish in the streams running through and bordering said reservation is hereby secured to said Indians, and at all other usual and accustomed stations.
>
> (Article 1, Treaty with the tribes of Middle Oregon, 1855. June 25, 1855. | 12 Stats., 963. | Ratified Mar. 8, 1859)[50]

It is in the interest of the tribes to gain a political toehold at Willamette Falls, and they do this by declaring the falls to be part of the "usual and accustomed" areas of their tribes. The idea of *usual and accustomed* areas is written into many of the treaties in eastern Oregon and allows the tribes to fish in any location they say is usual and/or accustomed. There is little federal guidance about the concept of *usual and accustomed*; thus far, the federal government has simply decided to consult with any tribe that claims a resource in this manner.[51]

There are aspects of this policy that ring true for the tribes, with respect to their cultural land claims. Traditionally, tribes did claim lands and were especially clear about maintaining claims to highly productive salmon-fishing areas, like falls. As previously mentioned, the Clowewalla and Clackamas peoples lived near and had residence claims to fish at Willamette Falls in all the ethnographic histories. There were fishing camps on both sides of the river and above the falls, as well as along the lower Willamette and up the Clackamas River (Figure 6.1). In addition, there was intermarriage between numerous tribes in the region, and so people from relatively distant villages, like those at the Cascades Rapids villages, also possessed familial rights to fish at the falls.

Intertribal relations ran throughout the region, from tribes on the Pacific to the tribe upriver of The Dalles, and down into the Willamette Valley with the Tualatin and Santiam tribe. It is likely that there are numerous relations in all the area tribes that gave rights 180 years ago to come fish at Willamette Falls with their kinfolk.[52] It is also likely that people in the Clackamas villages had similar rights at Celilo and at fishing stations all throughout the Columbia River. There is clearly a difference today because tribes struggle to maintain their fishing rights based on treaty rights, which were created through unequal negotiations with the United States. The lack of expressed fishing rights for tribes on the west side of the Cascades causes inequality of tribes generally, and this equation is causing a lot of conflict.

During historic fish runs, the villages at the falls would swell to many times their size, as relatives and traders came from many locations to share in the bounty of the salmon catch. If tribal peoples did not have a right to fish, they would trade for smoked, dried, and fresh fish or other Columbia-River trade items from hundreds of tribes. The falls attracted visitors from hundreds of miles around. Therefore, it is entirely true that Willamette Falls was a usual and accustomed place for many families from other tribes.[53]

One of the missing pieces today in the cultures of some neighboring tribes is the adherence to established protocols for fishing. Normally, if a relative or visitor from another tribe wanted to fish at an important fishing falls, they would seek permission to do so from the local headman or chief. Such protocols were common standard rules for gaining access to fishing areas, for visiting a neighboring village, and even for traveling through another tribe's lands, as well as hunting and gathering. Gaining permission may mean meeting the headman and gifting them and professing your friendship and peaceful intentions. This is not being regularly practiced at Willamette Falls in the appropriate manner, because of the dispute over territorial ownership and treaty rights. Without this simple and appropriate ceremony of respect by the various tribes at Willamette Falls toward the Grand Ronde Tribe, it is unclear how a culture of respect between the tribes will grow.

The way the tribes were arbitrarily split up and placed on reservations by the United States is largely responsible for this unfortunate situation. Division between tribes came when the Indian superintendent, from the U.S. Bureau of Indian Affairs, noted that the boundaries of the tribes in the treaties followed the crest of the Cascade Mountains. As a result, the superintendency districts dictated that any tribe located on the west side went to Grand Ronde and tribes on the East side went to Warm Springs.

This forced removal resulted in the Cascade Tribes being divided between Warm Springs Reservation and Grand Ronde Reservation. The Hood River Wascos (formerly called Dog River Cascades) were signatories to the Treaty of Middle Oregon, but late in the process, and so were moved to the Warm Springs. Nevertheless, it was clear that they were related to the members of the Cascades Tribe. On the other hand, their brethren, the Cascades people, were signatories to the Willamette Valley Treaty, and many of these people were sent to Grand Ronde.

> We, the chiefs and headmen of the . . . Wal-lal-lah band of Tum-waters [Cascades], and the Clockamus tribe of Indians, being assembled in council, give our assent unto, and agree to the provisions of the foregoing treaty
>
> Pulk-tah, second chief, his x mark.
>
> Tum-walth, first chief, his x mark.
> O-ban-a-hah, second chief, his x mark.
> Watch-a-no, first chief, his x mark.
> Te-ap-i-nick, second chief, his x mark.
> Wal-lah-pi-cate, third chief, his x mark.
> . . .

Intertribal Fishing Conflicts and Federal Obstruction in Oregon 117

> We, the chiefs and headmen of the Clow-we-wal-la, or Willamette Tum-water band of Indians, being assembled in council, give our assent unto, and agree to the provisions of the foregoing treaty . . .
>
> Lal-bick, or John, his x mark.
> Cuck-a-man-na, or David, his x mark.
>
> (Signatories to the Willamette Valley treaty of January 22,1855, Chiefs of the Watlala, Clackamas, and Clowewalla, tribes)[54]

Additionally, the Cascade tribes on the north side of the Columbia River, near Skamania, were treated differently, as they were within the Washington Indian Superintendency District, and many of their people went first to the temporary White Salmon Reservation and then in less than 2 years to the Yakima Reservation. The division of the territorial claims suggests that the Indian agents made the choice as to where the lines would be drawn. The agents were, after all, not aware of tribal territories and simply wanted the agreements to purchase the land. It did not really matter where that land was, or which tribe claimed it, as long as 100 percent of the land was purchased under treaty and then the aboriginal claims to the land ceded.[55]

In fact, culturally, tribes did not have exclusive borders and claims into wilderness areas, many of which were jointly used by several tribes. In places like the Cascades Range, the mountains were too high and carried too much snow to have tribal villages, so most tribes lived in the valleys and foothills away from the high, cold alpine areas. The tribes only ventured into these high mountains in the summer, when the trails had opened, during the huckleberry season, when there was food to harvest or capture, or they needed to travel the mountain trails to a far-away location for trading.[56] The idea that tribes had exclusive borders and land claims is purely a colonial construct based on the needs of the United States to buy every acre of land from the tribes so that there would no longer be any aboriginal land claims. Regardless of what the cultural use of the land was, tribes now must abide by treaties to maintain their rights as domestic dependent nations within the United States. The colonial structure of tribal relations forces tribes to fight for their rights with other tribes.

Some families at the Warm Springs had rights to usual and accustomed areas like Willamette Falls based on familial relations, but treaties now tell tribes which territories are their ceded lands. The tribes work to protect their claims from the encroachment of other tribes, and there is little legal room for overlapping territorial issues, except for the four tribes already admitted to the Columbia River Inter-Tribal Fish Commission. This is the system created by the United States government based on their treaty system.

The CRITFC tribes have substantial claims to the middle and upper Columbia River, but portions of the river were obstructed by a series of dams built from the 1930s to the 1970s by the Army Corps of Engineers. These dams blocked salmon passage and caused many salmon runs to go extinct. Strategies to increase the salmons' survival rate, like salmon hatcheries and fish ladders, were established to help bring some species back. Still, the runs of salmon today are nothing like they were in the past. Furthermore, other fishes, such as lamprey, also died out because the dams prevented them from reaching their spawning grounds. As a result, Warm Springs and the other Columbia River Inter-Tribal Fish Commission tribes appear to seek rights at Willamette Falls because it has one of the last remaining healthy lamprey runs in the system. The tribes are accessing this lamprey run and by doing so expand their territorial claims. This makes Willamette Falls invaluable to the tribes who are looking to revitalize traditions and to study aquatic species.

To surmount the tribal politics around the use of Willamette Falls for fishing, the Grand Ronde Tribe has purchased the former Blue Heron paper-mill site, thereby securing an interest in the falls that other tribes cannot deny nor impinge on.[57] Still, there are rumblings of tribes being upset about the fishing scaffold at Willamette Falls, of Grand Ronde somehow taking away the rights of other tribes.[58] Grand Ronde has offered to allow other tribes to use the scaffold, but there has yet to be a positive response. The Siletz Tribe has now asserted their rights to fish at the falls, suggesting that Grand Ronde's actions have affected their rights, yet Grand Ronde has not tried to limit their rights in any way.[59] In recent opinions, the Umatilla tribe has also suggested that the Grand Ronde Tribe are expanding their territory by fishing at the falls, but this argument is not valid when we understand that the signatories of the Willamette Valley treaty, including the peoples who lived at the falls for 10,000 or more years, came to Grand Ronde.[60]

In conclusion, the conflict about fishing rights at Willamette Falls is originally caused by actions of the United States federal government. It is the federal government who arbitrarily divided tribes to make room for settlers in the 1850s, taking all the valuable land and leaving the least valuable to tribes. The United States gave tribes unequal rights for fishing, hunting, and gathering, and destroyed valuable fishing sites on the Columbia from the 1930s to the 1970s, when they built numerous dams in the river. The dams and reservoirs destroyed many fishing areas and stocks of salmon. Some species, such as the "June Hogs," a very large salmon, are no more.[61] It is the federal government who forced the tribes to adopt a new tribal government structure under the Indian Reorganization Act (1934), which has eliminated many of the original tribal approaches to negotiating conflicts. As the fishing conflicts continue, tribes will have to find ways to step outside of federal structures, to work out solutions through deep tribal connections, despite the continued obstructions of the United States and its legacy of imposing scarce resources under an administrative structure of settler colonialism. It is my belief that all the tribes in the Columbia River drainage have more to gain by committing to working out any issues and being supportive of one another outside of the divisive federal system of administration.

Contexts and conditions will likely change in the next few years until a mutual resolution is agreed to.

QUESTIONS

1. What is the responsibility of the federal government toward tribal rights to fishing and other cultural resource activities?

2. Should tribes have rights outside of regular state and federal policies to fish, hunt, and gather?
3. Tribal governments are supposed to be equal to state sovereignty. Should tribes have more administrative rights over waterways and lands in their traditional territories?
4. A possible direction has been mentioned in the text for addressing cultural resources rights. Are there other methods of handling these conflicts?
5. Envision a future that honors Native American tribal nations. At the national level, what actions could improve interactions among the tribes and federal government? How might those actions be sustained?

NOTES

1 Boyd, Robert, *People of the Dalles, the Indians of Wascopam Mission*, U. Nebraska Press 1989.; Boyd, Robert et al. *Chinookan Peoples of the Lower Columbia*, U. Washington Press, 2013.
2 Also called Eulachon or oolichan, or surf smelt, a very small anadromous fish, *Thaleichthys pacificus*.
3 Stern, Ted, "Columbia River Trade Network," in *Handbook of North American Indians*, Smithsonian Institution, Washington, DC, 1998.
4 Lewis, David, "Native Kinships and Wealth Among the Middle Chinookans." *ndnhistoryresearch.com*, https://wp.me/p2ENjV-1z0
5 Coues, Elliott, *New Light on the Early History of the Greater Northwest*. The Manuscript Journals of Alexander Henry . . . and of David Thompson . . . 1799–1814. Exploration and adventure among the Indians on the Red, Saskatchewan, Missouri and Columbia rivers, by, Henry, Alexander, 1765–1814; Thompson, David, 1770–1857, p 790.
6 Boyd, Robert et al., *Chinookan Peoples of the Lower Columbia*, U. Washington Press, 2013.
7 Lewis, David, "Enforced Assimilation in Tribal Correspondence about the Grand Ronde Boarding School," *ndnhistoryresearch.com*, https://wp.me/p2ENjV-1Wk
8 Also called the Indian Reorganization Act, one of the Indian New Deal acts.
9 Philp, Kenneth R., *John Collier's Crusade for Indian Reform: 1920–1954*, U. Arizona, 1977.
10 Lewis, David, *Termination of the Confederated Tribes of the Grand Ronde Community of Oregon: Politics, Identity, Community*. Dissertation, U. Oregon, 2009.
11 Lewis, David, "Fishery Politics with the Yakima Reservation Peoples: 1890s," *ndnhistoryresearch.com*, https://wp.me/p2ENjV-1OT. Note the essay addresses the Yakima rights which suggest that there was a real problem for some decades of tribes not getting what was promised in their treaties.
12 Dupris, Joseph et al., *The Si'lailo Way, Indians, Salmon and Law on the Columbia River*, Carolina Academic Press, 2006.
13 Lewis, David, "The Willamette Valley Treaty (Treaty with the Kalapuya, Etc.) Signed January 22 & Ratified March 3, 1855," *ndnhistoryresearch.com*, https://wp.me/p2ENjV-1g6
14 Lewis, David, "Indian Fishing rights on the Grand Ronde-Siletz Indian Agency," *ndnhistoryresearch.com*, https://ndnhistoryresearch.com/2016/12/04/indian-fishing-rights-on-the-grand-ronde-siletz-indian-agency/.
15 Sohappy, David, Sr., *Tucknashut*, https://yakamafish-nsn.gov/honor/david-sohappy

16 United States v. Washington, 384 F. Supp. 312 (W.D. Wash. 1974), aff'd, 520 F.2d 676 (9th Cir. 1975).
17 Sohappy v. Smith, 302 F. Supp. 899 (D. Or. 1969).
18 Woods, Fronda, "Who's in Charge of Fishing?" *Oregon Historical Quarterly*, Vol. 106, No. 3, The Isaac I. *Stevens and Joel Palmer Treaties, 1855–2005* (Fall, 2005), pp. 412–441.
19 Task Force Ten, *Congress of the U.S. Washington, D.C*, American Indian Policy Review Commission.
20 Task Force ten report.
21 Letters suggested that the tribal people were too mixed blooded, too white to be Indian, or that they would simply destroy fishing and hunting. See Oregon Governor collections from the 1970s-80s at the Oregon Historical Society and the Oregon State Archives.
22 Public Law 95–195, 91 Stat. 1415
23 Lewis, David, *Termination of the Confederated Tribes of the Grand Ronde Community of Oregon: Politics, Identity, Community.* Dissertation, U. Oregon, 2009.
24 97 STAT. 1064, PUBLIC LAW 98–165—NOV. 22, 1983.
25 PUBLIC LAW 100–425,102 Stat. 1594.- Sept. 9, 1988.
26 Klamath Water, Klamath Life; the Water Wars of the Northwest.
27 16 U.S.C. §§ 544–544p.
28 Several tribes claim rights on the lower Columbia, but they do not have a ratified treaty. Cowlitz has claimed rights in the vicinity of Portland, as a strategy get their casino built closer to Portland. The unrecognized Chinook Nation also would claim rights in the area, but they have been refused re-restoration up to 2020. Additionally, there is another unrecognized tribe, the Confederated tribes of the Clatsop and Nehalem, who would claim lands closer to the Pacific Ocean on the Columbia. The Willamette Valley treaty also has a sentence addressing rights of the Multnomah and Cascades who had villages and claims on the north side of the river in Washington State, a land claim that was never paid for by the federal government.
29 Negotiations over how and when to clean up the Portland harbors after more than a century and a half of toxic industrial waste buildup have been ongoing since the 1990s. This has involved dozens of tribes and local governmental organizations.
30 Gold, Pat Courtney. "The long narrows: The forgotten geographic and cultural wonder." *Oregon Historical Quarterly* 108.4 (2007): 596–605; Wilkinson, Charles. "Celilo Falls: At the Center of Western History." *Oregon Historical Quarterly* 108.4 (2007): 532–542; Benac, David. "The Value of a Historical Landscape: Heritage and Nature at Bridal Veil." *Oregon Historical Quarterly* 116.4 (2015): 448–475.
31 See the Lewis and Clark Journal volume 4, for details of the Cascades seasonal movements.
32 Note the further complications of the 1961 Columbia River Treaty, which came up for renewal in 2024, with negotiations ongoing since 2018. www.state.gov/columbia-river-treaty/. The Treaty negotiations involve tribes, and this is yet another issue which has seen barriers from "treaty tribes" to Grand Ronde joining in the negotiations because of the Willamette Valley treaty. www.govinfo.gov/content/pkg/CHRG-113shrg87345/html/CHRG-113shrg87345.htm
33 See the Southwest Oregon Research Project at the University of Oregon, for some ethnographic and government records of the tribes. Additional records are being examined by David Lewis and published on the Quartux Journal, ndnhistoryresearch.com.
34 Lewis, David et al., "Honoring our Tilixam: Chinookan People of Grand Ronde," in *Chinookan Peoples of the Lower Columbia*, Robert T. Boyd, et al. eds. U. Washington Press, 2013.
35 The Western Oregon Indian Termination Act. See Lewis, David G., *Termination of the Confederated Tribes of the Grand Ronde Community of Oregon.* Dissertation, U. Oregon, Eugene, 2009.

Intertribal Fishing Conflicts and Federal Obstruction in Oregon 121

36 I personally worked on community education efforts while employed at the tribe and attended and testified in ODFW meetings to help educate state officials about tribal culture.
37 Chapter 635, Division 41, COLUMBIA RIVER SYSTEM TREATY INDIAN FISHERIES, 635–041–0610, Ceremonial Salmon and Steelhead Harvest at Willamette Falls, https://secure.sos.state.or.us/oard/viewSingleRule.action?ruleVrsnRsn=168047
38 Chapter 635, Division 41, COLUMBIA RIVER SYSTEM TREATY INDIAN FISHERIES, 635–041–0600, Confederated Tribes of the Grand Ronde Community of Oregon; https://secure.sos.state.or.us/oard/viewSingleRule.action?ruleVrsnRsn=168045; Grand Ronde Gets Expanded Hunting Rights, Oregon live, www.oregonlive.com/breakingnews/2008/04/grand_ronde_tribe_gets_expande.html; Also see Chapter 801, Grand Ronde Fish and Wildlife Ordinance, www.grandronde.org/media/1194/10282015fish-and-wildlife-ord.pdf.
39 Lewis, David, "Indian Fishing Rights on the Grand Ronde-Siletz Indian Agency," *ndnhistoryresearch.com*, https://wp.me/p2ENjV-Pn
40 Specifically, for one example, John Wacheno was caught fishing and fined. John Wacheno on Fishing Rights and Land Inheritance, 1931, ndnhistoryresearch.com, https://ndnhistoryresearch.com/2019/07/13/john-wacheno-on-fishing-rights-and-land-inheritance-1931.
41 Besides the need for food, Indian agents felt the natives would begin to leave if they could not get food.
42 Lewis, David G., "Indian Fishing Rights on the Grand Ronde-Siletz Indian Agency," *ndnhistoryresearch.com*, https://wp.me/p2ENjV-Pn; it is not until the 1886 census of the Siletz Reservation that we see Tillamook peoples listed, and it is these people who lived at the Salmon River, before this the Tillamook people are listed as under the administrative purview of the Grand Ronde Reservation.
43 Jaquiss, Nigel, "Three Oregon Tribes Are Locked in a Dispute Over Fishing at Willamette Falls. It's About Much More Than a Few Salmon," *Willamette Week*, www.wweek.com/news/2018/09/12/three-oregon-tribes-are-locked-in-a-dispute-over-fishing-at-willamette-falls-its-about-much-more-than-a-few-salmon/, accessed 7/9/2020.
44 I was personally in a negotiation in 2010–2013 with Warm Springs lawyers who stated that we could not mention the tribes at the falls in our agreements.
45 Lewis, David, *Termination of the Confederated Tribes of the Grand Ronde Community of Oregon: Politics, Identity, Community*. Dissertation, U. Oregon, 2009.
46 Colley, Brook, *Power in the Telling: Grand Ronde, Warm Springs, and Intertribal Relations in the Casino Era*, U. Washington Press, 2018.
47 Yakama Tribal Members Cited for Fishing in a Closed Area, https://archive.seattletimes.com/archive/?date=19940503&slug=1908574.
48 Harbarger, Mary, "Grand Ronde Win Right to Keep Willamette Falls Fishing Scaffold," *Oregonlive*, www.oregonlive.com/business/2018/12/grand-ronde-win-right-to-keep-willamette-falls-fishing-scaffold.html, accessed 7/9/2020.
49 Grand Ronde want to catch 15 salmon. It's pitted Northwest tribes against each other, www.oregonlive.com/news/erry-2018/10/684a2d812f8916/grand-ronde-want-to-catch-15-s.html
50 The provision is substantially the same in both of the eastern Oregon treaties, www.fws.gov/pacific/ea/tribal/treaties/Tribes_Mid_or.pdf; www.fws.gov/pacific/ea/tribal/treaties/wallawalla.pdf
51 Harbarger, Molly, "Grand Ronde Want to Catch 15 Salmon. It's Pitted Northwest Tribes Against Each Other," *Oregonlive*, www.oregonlive.com/news/erry-2018/10/684a2d812f8916/grand-ronde-want-to-catch-15-s.html
52 Lewis, David et al., "Honoring Our Tilixam: Chinookan People of Grand Ronde," in *Chinookan Peoples of the Lower Columbia*, Robert T. Boyd et al. eds. U. Washington Press, 2013.

53 Lewis, David et al., "Honoring Our Tilixam: Chinookan People of Grand Ronde," in *Chinookan Peoples of the Lower Columbia*, Robert T. Boyd et al. eds. U. Washington Press, 2013.
54 Lewis, David, "A Startling History of the Cascades Indians, 1855–1862," *ndnhistoryresearch.org*, https://wp.me/p2ENjV-2l; Treaty with the Kalapuya etc, 1855, www.fws.gov/pacific/ea/tribal/treaties/kalapuya_1855.pdf
55 This I surmise because of irregularities in tribal territory, some overlapping areas, and likelihood that supposedly claimed areas under treaty were common-use land for tribal people. Areas like the Cascade Mountain range were thought to be claimed territories of tribes, but it is clear from ethnographic evidence that many tribes used all the Cascades as common-use lands. Indian Agents normally did not know much about tribal culture and what they did think they knew was fraught with stereotypes about savage "Indians" quite common in the era and even today.
56 Lewis, David, "Ethnographic Molalla Homelands in Historic Scholarship," *ndnhistoryresearch.org*, https://wp.me/p2ENjV-1I8
57 Rhodes, Dean, "Tribe Buys Blue Heron Paper Mill Site," *Smoke Signals*, www.smokesignals.org/articles/2019/08/15/tribe-buys-blue-heron-paper-mill-site/, accessed 7/9/2020.
58 Burke, Gary et al., "Opinion: Grand Ronde Not the Only Tribe with Willamette Falls Interests," *Oregonlive*, www.oregonlive.com/opinion/2019/05/opinion-grand-ronde-not-the-only-tribe-with-willamette-falls-interests.html
59 Opinion: Grand Ronde not the only tribe with Willamette Falls Interests, www.oregonlive.com/opinion/2019/05/opinion-grand-ronde-not-the-only-tribe-with-willamette-falls-interests.html
60 CTUIR Board of Directors. Willamette Falls is a Part of Our Heritage for Many Reasons. July 13, 2021, https://tinyurl.com/xbzjjt9n, Accessed 7/25/2021.
61 Harrison, John, *June Hogs (salmon) Oregon Encyclopedia*, https://oregonencyclopedia.org/articles/june_hogs_salmon_/#.XwfEyedlCUk

7 The Role of Gender in Water Conflicts

Jaclyn Best and Jahan Taganova

CONTENTS

Introduction	123
Defining Gender	125
Defining Conflict and Water Conflicts	125
Is the Water Sector a Man's Domain?	126
Where Are the Women, and Why Do We Need Them? A Lack of Data and Representation	127
Invisible Women of the Deschutes River Basin	128
Geography of the Deschutes River Basin	128
Styles of Water Management in the American West and the Deschutes River Basin: Shifting Away from the Masculine	130
Gender Representation of Water-Related Institutions in the Deschutes River Basin	131
Do Women Forge Peace in the Ferghana Valley?	132
Geography of the Ferghana Valley	133
Water Management in the Ferghana Valley: From Kingdoms to Independence from the Soviet Union	133
Where Are the Women? Emancipation of Central Asia's Women	135
Seeing Like a Donor	136
Transboundary Water Conflict Resolution: Whose Domain?	137
What Can We Learn from the Deschutes River Basin and Ferghana Valley?	138
How Can We Move Forward Transforming Conflicts Using a Gendered Approach?	140
Conclusion	141
Questions	142
Notes	142

INTRODUCTION

Water conflicts and contestations are about much more than water allocation to various users. Water conflicts highlight deeply ingrained societal and cultural inequities. This chapter sheds light on one of those inequities, the involvement of women in water management processes and the integration of a gendered lens in water conflict transformation. Despite recognition in global water discussions and development agendas that women have a crucial role to play in all processes of water governance and management,[1,2,3] laws and organizations responsible for water management at the state and inter-state level do not reflect a top-down gendered approach.[4] Similarly, in the development sector, there is widespread agreement that participation by both men and women as equal partners is essential for sustained interventions.

Through an examination of two case studies, one in the northwestern United States and the other in Central Asia, we illustrate gender inequities. Both cases explore how women have or have not been integrated into water resources management and governance in the two geographic settings and systems. The case studies illustrate that current policies strongly support women's empowerment and contribution to decision-making, and development agencies advocate for women's "equality" and "empowerment." However, the absence of women's participation in male-dominated spheres of the water sector directly opposes these commitments. They also elucidate that the obstacles for women's involvement in decision-making in both regions are enormous.

Guided by these findings, the larger goal of this chapter is to illustrate the necessity of systemic change to effectively address gender inequalities in water management and governance. This involves abolishing long-established, highly masculinized traditions and including women in all stages of management, including design, execution, and hiring processes. This chapter is intended to stimulate thought and open the door to discussion around development, gender, and water resources management that may lead to the realization of more inclusive and effective programs and policies.

These vastly different case studies, one in the Deschutes River Basin and the other in the Ferghana Valley, were chosen because they are illustrative of larger, pervasive, and systemic problems in water resources management. The first case is situated at a regional level—the Deschutes River Basin in Oregon, USA. Herein, the masculine, century-old "command-and-control" style of water management—centralized, anthropocentric, bureaucratic, top-down management—has led to conflicts among users over access and allocation of the river's water and associated resources. In recent years, however, the basin's management has shifted toward more collaborative systems of governance. Through document analysis and gender mapping within the organizations dealing with water resources management, this case elucidates how historically ingrained gender relations have influenced who holds decision-making positions within various types of water management organizations. Those who hold decision-making positions are more likely than not to make decisions for people who look like them, in this case, men.

The second case focuses on a transboundary dispute involving two countries in Central Asia—Kyrgyzstan and Tajikistan—as well as development agencies' efforts to address gender integration into transboundary water resources management and peacebuilding projects. The analysis suggests that external attempts to integrate women in water conflict management usually lack a deep understanding of gender injustices in the Ferghana Valley. Insufficient knowledge of the region's history, culture, and geography results in projects that merely scratch the surface of a larger systemic problem.

The final section first considers the similarities between the two seemingly different case studies and then situates both cases in the Four Stages of Water Conflict Transformation framework. The four interconnected stages, Adversarial, Reflexive, Integrative, and Action, provide a blueprint for transforming intractable, zero-sum water conflicts to solutions that are creative and positive-sum.[5] The analysis of both cases through the Four Stages offers suggestions on how and why it is important to incorporate a gender-inclusive lens at each stage.

The findings from both case studies suggest that, regardless of geographical location and the relative level of development, a gender-inclusive approach is beneficial to analyzing water conflicts and working toward transformation. Participation by both men and women as equal partners is essential for promoting effectiveness in the development project in Central Asia and for reaching societal equity, as manifested in the Deschutes River Basin.

We conclude with thoughts on the multiple themes that underscore our objective: that a gender-inclusive, contextually based approach is imperative to equitable, just, and sustainable water resources management.

DEFINING GENDER

In this chapter, we define gender, or gender identity, as performative activities, traits, and values based on ever-changing social constructs of what is associated with men and masculinities, as well as women and femininities.[6,7] It is not the same as biological sex, which is typically assigned at birth. Rather, it is how we individually behave, based on behavioral conditioning, usually during childhood. Gender is ever-changing, in that socially acceptable behaviors and traits for men and women are not necessarily the same as they were 100 years ago or even 20 years ago. For example, the color pink was associated with men just 100 years ago, and until the turn of the 20th century, it was more common to see men wearing high heels than it was for women.[8] Likewise, in the U.S., women made up the majority of the first computer programmers, and this profession was considered a women's position until the 1970s and 1980s when it switched to a male-dominated field.[9] Social precepts of gender also vary spatially, in that what is acceptable for men and/or women in one society or location may not be acceptable in another.

Gender is generally regarded as a range of behaviors, rather than a dichotomy, and there are people who do not identify with either of these concepts. Unfortunately, there is a lack of data and research on people who perform outside the boxes of male or female, especially as it relates to water resources management.[10]

Throughout this chapter, we will use the term masculine, in terms of a style of traditional, state-centric water management. The differences between *masculine* and *feminine* are not a result of gender (men/women) alone, but refer to traits that are human and are only traditionally attributed to men and women.[11] Accordingly, we oppose the notion that *masculine* and *feminine* are polar opposites on the same spectrum. Rather, they should be viewed as separate scales, in which one person (or organization) can have both masculine and feminine traits that do not have to contradict each other.[12]

DEFINING CONFLICT AND WATER CONFLICTS

Conflict is any situation in which two or more parties perceive they have mutually incompatible goals.[13] Conflicts are inevitable, and can occur at various scales: interpersonal, family, community, organizational, national, international, and global.[14] Conflicts over water can further be defined as verbal, economic, or militarily hostile actions between or among parties over shared water resources.[15]

Research on transboundary water governance between two or more countries has shown that cooperative events have reigned over conflictual events by a 2:1 ratio throughout modern history.[16] However, conflict and cooperation are not necessarily opposite ends of a continuum. Studies on transboundary water conflict and cooperation have discussed how they typically coexist; thus, not all conflicts are necessarily bad, and not all cooperative efforts are necessarily good.[17] Some cooperative arrangements end up reinforcing existing conflicts, and some conflicts may lead to more equitable cooperative arrangements.

The case studies that follow highlight two contrasting water conflicts. Both would benefit from incorporating a gendered analysis, leading to more equitable water resource allocations and conflict transformations. However, we first consider whether the water sector should be strictly a man's domain.

Is the Water Sector a Man's Domain?

When thinking of women and water, one might conjure an image of a woman carrying a bucket of water on her head or along her waist. A simple Google image search of "women water" brings up countless photos like this, often portraying women from the Global South. When one thinks of a hydrological engineer, one might think of a man, wearing a hard hat and some safety gear, working at some large water infrastructure, like a dam or a water treatment plant. A farmer might also bring to mind a man. Because gender performance and perceived limitations are constantly reinforced, masculine and feminine norms are ingrained in many professions. Careers within the water sector are no exception.

Access to water is a fundamental human right. Because of this, allocation and use of water resources as well as access to water facilities and investments should equally benefit all members of society, regardless of their gender, age, or sexual orientation.[18] Yet the field of water resources management and governance is constructed along the tenets of socially "acceptable" gender roles and relations.[19] In other words, the dominant perspectives on water infrastructure, management, and provision are associated with men.[20] Historically, male experts, scientists, engineers, and diplomats have dominated positions in the water sector.[21] The water-related institutions run by men have persistently maintained norms and practices that are associated with male supremacy, making it difficult for women to enter a field that has been historically constructed alongside norms and practices traditionally associated with men and masculinity.[22]

This gender discrepancy did not go unnoticed by academics and practitioners, and it was not solely a problem in water-related institutions and occupations. In line with feminist movements in many Western societies in the 1970s and 1980s, people began to question why most decision-making roles and organizations in fields, such as politics, engineering, and international relations, were dominated by men.

This recognition led to a shift toward including women in management of water resources and governance. For instance, the 1992 International Conference on Water and the Environment in Dublin recognized that "women play a central part in the provision, management and safeguarding of water."[23] Similarly, the Ministerial Declaration adopted at the International Conference on Freshwater in 2001 stated that: "[t]he role of women in water-related areas needs to be strengthened and their participation broadened."[24] Multinational institutions, such as the World Bank and the United Nations, have established gender mainstreaming (making all necessary accommodations to achieve gender equality) in policies and resolutions. Despite these efforts, women still make up a global fraction of the experts in the governance of shared water resources,[25,26] and women working in management have limited opportunities for participation in decision-making.

Research indicates that women's participation in water management is more prevalent at the local and community levels, whereas at the regional, state, and transboundary scales, women are underrepresented in positions with decision-making power.[27,28,29] For instance, data collected by the World Bank from 64 water and sanitation service providers in 28 economies around the world show that the percentage of female workers is considerably lower than that of men.[30] Other research corroborates this, showing that the water sector, especially in technical professions, continues to employ higher numbers of men than women.[31] The following two case studies demonstrate how persisting masculine norms and practices in the water sector lead to limited opportunities and representation for women.

Before diving into the first case study, it is important to underscore that we cannot stop at simply increasing the number of women in water-related professions. It is difficult for women to enter traditionally male-dominated spaces to begin with, especially when the cultural norms have not evolved to be inclusive of historically marginalized genders and ethnicities.

WHERE ARE THE WOMEN, AND WHY DO WE NEED THEM? A LACK OF DATA AND REPRESENTATION

Currently available gender statistics are primarily in the context of developing and emerging economies, meaning there is a data gap on gender representation in water-related professions and organizations in the United States.[32] Hence, it is unknown how many women are working in these fields in relation to men. The lack of data on gender representation creates an obstacle in achieving objectives for sustainable water management. For instance, United Nations Water states,

> The differences and inequalities between women and men influence how individuals respond to changes in water resources management. Understanding gender roles, relations, and inequalities can help explain the choices people make and their different options. Involving both women and men in integrated water resources initiatives can increase project effectiveness and efficiency.[33]

Additionally, research suggests that more substantial improvements in the governance, transparency, and sustainability of water resources are achieved when men and women are involved in equal measure.[34] Hence, the lack of data on gender representation can impede the ability to produce scientific evidence on gender inequalities related to water. Thus, without a more deliberate, data-driven focus on how water management decisions impact women and girls, progress toward a wide range of objectives is slowed down. The case study of the Deschutes River Basin addresses this lack of data and its implications, and calls for more research on the representation of women in water management and governance.

Large-scale water resources development, such as building of big dams and canals that made deserts bloom, was a defining feature of the 20th century in the Global North. This development was entrusted to powerful state-run water bureaucracies and became a symbol for political power.[35] Those who worked on such projects were tied in with power and control, features inherently associated with masculinity. Further, male water engineers of the colonial and post-colonial periods were lauded as heroes, triumphs, and pioneering champions.[36] The strong association of water bureaucracies with male engineers has made it difficult for women to enter these spheres.[37,38,39] Consequently, women need to simultaneously invest themselves in professions that are primarily occupied by men while maintaining their identities as women.[40,41] Despite a growing awareness that simply inserting women in these spaces will likely not lead to systemic change, most gender-inclusive water policies and practices stop after implementing a gender quota.

The incorporation of a *gendered lens* (the explicit acknowledgment that gender is a factor), along with increasing the number of women in water management and governance, has been shown to account for more sustainable and equitable outcomes overall. In other words, water projects are more effective when women are involved.[42] A growing body of evidence demonstrates that the participation of women can improve the effectiveness of water projects. For instance, research on 44 water projects in Asia and Africa illustrates that, when men and women are mutually engaged in creating water policies and institutions, communities use water services more and sustain them longer.[43] In fisheries management, a lack of attention to gendered roles and diversity can result in policy interventions missing their targets of creating sustainable livelihoods at the community level.[44] All genders are variously affected by different processes, so ignoring the gendered lens can have negative, unintended consequences such as exclusionary, ineffective practices and unsustainable outcomes.

As most academic research on gender is centered around "empowering" women in less industrialized countries, the first case in the Deschutes River Basin addresses the lack of data and research on the representation of women in various water sector professions in an industrialized country—the U.S.

INVISIBLE WOMEN OF THE DESCHUTES RIVER BASIN

This section addresses the data gap concerning the proportion of women working in water management and governance by providing quantitative data and analysis to understand gendered representation within industrialized nations. First, however, it is necessary to understand the geographical and historical context of current and past water contestations in this basin in order to uncover the gendered dynamics.

GEOGRAPHY OF THE DESCHUTES RIVER BASIN

The Deschutes River Basin is a tributary of the Columbia River Basin in the northwest U.S., located in central Oregon. It is classified as a mixed rain-snow basin with a majority of its inflow coming from precipitation on the volcanic Cascade Mountains

The Role of Gender in Water Conflicts

situated along the basin's western.[45] And, unlike many other river systems in Oregon and the American West that are fed by seasonal surface runoff from melting snowpack, the Deschutes River is primarily groundwater-fed from porous, volcanic soils in the upper part of the basin.[46] Thus, the river has a stable, annual, hydrologic regime,[47] making the basin a significant area of study by scientists for more than a century[48] (Figure 7.1).

Though land and water in the basin are used mainly for agriculture, there are a number of towns with rapidly growing populations, such as Bend, Redmond, and Prineville. With growth in population comes an increasing demand for municipal

FIGURE 7.1 The Deschutes River Basin.[49]

consumption of water. The river also runs through the Warm Springs Native American Reservation, which comprises the Confederated Tribes of Warm Springs.

Styles of Water Management in the American West and the Deschutes River Basin: Shifting Away from the Masculine

A defining feature of the post-colonial development in the American West has been strong management and control of unpredictable waters flowing through it.[50] Growth and development in the region have been historically dependent on the ability to manage these aquatic resources.[51,52,53] Consequently, legal structures, such as the "Prior Appropriation Doctrine," were inspired by the traditional view that all water should be used for human needs and to guide water governance of western river basins.[54] These legal structures paved the way for building diversions and dams to allocate limited water resources, mainly for agricultural uses.

Historical management of the Deschutes River Basin is an epitome of the masculine command-and-control style of the American West. Since the early 1900s, surface water in the basin has been almost entirely allocated for agriculture by eight irrigation districts.[55] Artificial storage and diversion of water to meet irrigation demand for rapidly growing human populations have dramatically altered the river's natural flow, especially in the upper parts of the basin. For example, the Wickiup Reservoir and Dam, which holds water for agricultural users of the North Unit Irrigation District, releases just 3 percent of natural flows in the winter months. In the summer growing season, the reservoir releases up to 200 percent of natural flows.[56,57,58] This drastic shift from historically stable annual flows has impacted basin ecosystems, causing a number of local species to become endangered, including four salmonid fishes, two bird species, and the Oregon spotted frog.[59]

In addition to agricultural water use, there has been growth in the municipal demand for water, caused by a massive population increase in three counties located in the upper part of the basin that include such towns as Bend and Redmond. This growth has decreased the amount of land used for farming, while increasing the demand for municipal, recreation, and environmental needs.[60] Consequently, the old system of water management is being tasked with meeting new challenges from population growth and ecological flows.[61]

To meet these changing and growing water demands, several collaborative efforts have formed, most recently and notably the Deschutes Water Alliance in 2004.[62] The Alliance brought together various stakeholders representing major user groups, including Irrigation Districts (agriculture); municipal governments; an environmental, Non-Governmental Organization (representing ecological uses); and the Confederated Tribes of Warm Springs. In 2004 and again in 2014, the Alliance convened to identify unmet water management needs and crafted plans to fulfill diverse water-resource interests.[63] The meetings in 2014 added state and federal agencies, as well as additional environmental non-profits to the original stakeholder groups.[64]

Despite stakeholder groups coming together on multiple occasions to address shifting water needs and growing demands, relationships among the relative entities were unequal in power pertaining to legal rights to the basin's waters, especially those of the irrigation districts and the environmental non-profits. The irrigation districts held substantially senior rights to a majority of the water for more than a century, allowing them to store it in reservoirs during winter for summer irrigation, thus significantly altering natural flow within the basin.

This unequal balance of power led to conflict among these groups, culminating in a legal battle in 2016 organized by an environmental non-profit and enforced by the U.S. Fish and Wildlife Service to augment in-stream flows for the protection of endangered species. Throughout the collaborative processes, until the lawsuit, power was still vested in the hands of the irrigation districts.[65] Recognizing conflict among major stakeholder groups is vital to understanding who holds authority and why. In this case, we see a shift away from the command-and-control, masculine style of water management that prioritizes human uses over ecological needs, toward one that is more collaborative and biocentric. Thus, taking into account the established importance of gender equity in sustainable and collaborative water management, an examination of who is making the decisions for the Deschutes River Basin is warranted.

GENDER REPRESENTATION OF WATER-RELATED INSTITUTIONS IN THE DESCHUTES RIVER BASIN

In the Global North, there has been little research conducted regarding gender representation in water resource organizations.[66,67,68] Most attempts at "empowering" women for water resource management have been documented in less-developed countries.[69,70]

To begin filling this informational void, we conducted research to find out what the gender representation within the Deschutes River Basin looked like. Accordingly, the employment of various water-related organizations was examined, including irrigation districts, municipal agencies, environmental non-profit organizations, private sector companies, and state and federal agencies. We wanted not only to know how many men and women were working in these organizations but also to understand who held positions of decision-making power, defined as having some level of authority within an organization and/or the basin's governance.

Our findings revealed that throughout the entire basin, which included over 700 employees and 37 organizations, 29 percent of employees involved in decision-making were women.[71] In irrigation districts, 9 percent of women held decision-making roles.[72] However, women held 93 percent of administrative—secretarial—positions in the same organizations.[73]

The organizations with the highest overall representation of women within the basin were non-partisan, political, and nonprofits, where they held 86 percent of decision-making positions.[74] In environmental non-profit organizations, women held 34 percent of decision-making roles.[75]

In terms of employees with decision-making power (e.g., Board Members, presidents, managers, CEOs), we found that, overall, women were less represented in these roles. In fact, very few irrigation districts even had women in such positions. In administrative and secretarial roles, women were overrepresented. Further, practitioners, such as ditch operators and water masters, were 99 percent occupied by men, whereas male engineers constituted 75 percent of the workforce.[76]

In the last three to four decades, there has been a shift toward sustainable watershed management in the western United States,[77] which has led to a decline in the construction of dams. Despite this shift away from the masculine command-and-control style of water management, the frequency of male irrigation engineers and decision-makers compared to women has not substantially changed. This is not to say that more equitable, collaborative, and inclusive water management processes are necessarily feminine; however, the persisting command-and-control style excludes women in the profession.

Women holding practitioner positions across eight irrigation districts represent only 1 percent. Likewise, our study further demonstrated that women hold only 3.5 percent of decision-making positions across all irrigation districts. Underrepresentation of women in both decision-making and practitioner positions at the irrigation-district level is likely related to the preconceived, century-old notion that irrigation and water bureaucracy is the domain of men.[78] However, it is recommended to not merely include gender representation, but also change the educational and hiring procedures to reflect different gendered realities, which are multiple and still largely unknown.

Power, conflict, and gender are inherently interconnected. Although control of the Deschutes River Basin has been moving away from traditional, masculine, command-and-control forms of water management, where agricultural use of water has priority, toward that of more collaborative and equitable allocations with ecological uses, this has not been without conflict. The power imbalance began to shift in 2016 when an irrigation district lawsuit forced district officials to release instream flow water from reservoirs during the winter. This directly contested and upended the traditional, masculine forms of water management that had dominated the basin for over a century.

This case study highlights not just the lack of women throughout the basin, but also how those holding traditionally powerful roles in water management are predominantly men who cling to traditional gender norms and practices, such as prioritizing water for agricultural uses through natural flow-altering dams. It is therefore vital in the analysis of any conflict to ask and examine who holds authority and what the in-place structures are that maintain it.

DO WOMEN FORGE PEACE IN THE FERGHANA VALLEY?

The case study of the Deschutes River Basin demonstrated that underrepresentation of women in the water sector is not limited to non-industrialized nations. The present case examines the Ferghana Valley, located within the Syr Darya River Basin in Central Asia. It shows how international donors and aid agencies engage with issues of gender (women's underrepresentation) and water in the transboundary conflict management.

In this section, we move beyond gender disaggregated data on women's and men's roles in water resources management to understand how external donor-agencies engage with and depict women's roles in transboundary water resources management and conflict resolution in the Ferghana Valley. We argue that despite a growing effort to improve gender equity in cross-border peacebuilding processes, imported

The Role of Gender in Water Conflicts

initiatives by donors do not support dismantling outdated gender norms and are not inclusive of women of various intersectional identities.

GEOGRAPHY OF THE FERGHANA VALLEY

The Ferghana Valley is nestled between the high mountains of the Ala-Tau Range in the north, the Tian Shan Mountains in the east, and the Alay Mountains in the south.[79] It is situated within one of the water-rich subregions of Central Asia—the Syr Darya River Basin.[80] The valley's climate is arid and sharply continental. The Naryn and the Kara Darya rivers, along with multiple tributaries, create favorable conditions for irrigation agriculture in Central Asia. Because of this, the Ferghana Valley accounts for 45 percent of the total irrigated area in the Syr Darya basin.[81] Though not always the case, the valley is currently split between three countries: Tajikistan, Kyrgyzstan, and Uzbekistan (Figure 7.2).

WATER MANAGEMENT IN THE FERGHANA VALLEY: FROM KINGDOMS TO INDEPENDENCE FROM THE SOVIET UNION

Irrigation has played a crucial role in Central Asian life and has influenced the social, political, and economic development in the region.[82] Accordingly, to understand

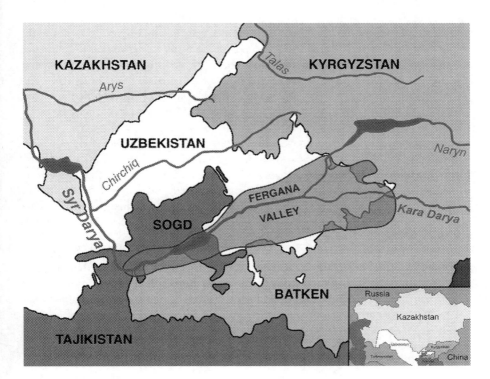

FIGURE 7.2 The Ferghana Valley.[85]

water governance and the gendered dynamics of the Ferghana Valley, it is important to analyze it in terms of political and social processes.[83] We will therefore situate our analysis in the history of the Ferghana Valley to trace how governance has shaped the direction and nature of water flow, and unpack what this means for the communities there.[84] For the purpose of this case study, a brief history of the region will be provided from the time of kingdoms (*khanates*) to the emergence of the present independent states.

From the 13th century through the 20th, the Central Asian region was divided between three kingdoms. Water management in the kingdoms was organized in a hierarchical manner, where the king (*khan*) was at the head of the water delivery hierarchy, followed by governors (*khokim* and/or *bek*) who were responsible for the management of each administrative territory, tailed by the ditch manager (*aryk bashi*). At the level of irrigation ditches, a ditch rider (*migrab*) was responsible for operating the ditches and allocating water.[86] During this period, beyond domestic use, peasant (*daykhan*) women were mainly using water for irrigation.

In 1876, the territories of the Ferghana Valley, as well as the whole of Central Asia, were conquered by Tsarist Russia. Upon colonization, the Tsarist administration remodeled the kingdoms into one administrative unit of Turkestan. In addition, agriculture was transformed into cotton-centered production. However, Central Asians adhered to traditional methods of irrigation and water management.[87]

In 1922, agriculture underwent a major restructuring after the fall of Tsarist Russia and subsequent colonization by the Soviet Union. This was part of a much larger political and economic transition that took place during this time. To begin with, the Soviet government altered the socio-spatial patterns in the region to construct the new state, as a union of nationalities: the Kyrgyz, Uzbek, Tajik, Kazakh, and Turkmen Soviet Socialist Republics. This process of redrawing the borders remains a highly controversial issue because such division completely disregarded complex identities, ethnic mixes, kinships, and clan networks.[88] For instance, in some cases, traditional, rival tribes were placed together in the same state, while major population centers of one ethnic group were divided into different republics.[89]

Furthermore, the Soviet government implemented land reorganization to transform Central Asia into a cotton-growing region. Thus, Soviet policy changed primitive, nomadic, agricultural practices into sophisticated, mechanized production in Central Asia, following the command-and-control water management style. This was done by developing large-scale hydraulic infrastructure. For instance, the big Ferghana irrigation canal, which stretches over 270 km (168 miles), was built in just 45 days.[90]

While the implementation of large irrigation innovations contributed enormously to the overall welfare of the region, including increasing energy and food generation, the infrastructural development became an end in itself, rather than the means to an end. This outcome fueled rent-seeking—symbolic masculine state power—that had devastating environmental consequences, such as the irreversible drying of the Aral Sea.[91]

Generally during the last two decades before the fall of the Soviet Union, the neighboring Kyrgyz and Tajik Republics were marred by water and land conflicts. For instance, due to disagreements over the access to irrigation water in 1975, Isfara farm, located in northern Tajikistan, was obliged to provide the Batken farm, situated in southwestern Kyrgyzstan, with water during the irrigation season.[92]

In a similar vein, a dispute in 1989 over land between the villages of Uch-Dobo in south-western Kyrgyzstan and Khodjai-Alo in Tajikistan escalated into a violent conflict, involving the villagers of Vorukh and Ak-Sai.[93,94] Several reports indicate at least 63 separate cross-border tensions—which in this case refers to a conflict between two neighboring territories over natural resources such as land and water—along the Kyrgyz-Tajik border.[95,96] These events have shaped the widespread perception that the Ferghana Valley is turning into a "host of crises," sparking a hot debate among scholars who have called for the intervention of international communities.[97]

Following the dissolution of the Soviet Union in 1991, the former administrative boundaries of the Ferghana Valley became international borders, which divided the Valley between three countries: Uzbekistan, Kyrgyzstan, and Tajikistan. This division yet again altered socio-spatial patterns, which created eight, "extra-territorial" enclaves—distinct units fully enclosed within foreign territory—within the Ferghana Valley. These new resettlements did not match well with ethnic compositions and old political boundaries.[98] As a result, new border regimes and migration regulations changed cross-border activities, restricted travel, altered kinship relationships, and made it extremely hard for residents of the enclaves to have access to the "mainland."[99] Since the collapse of the Soviet Union, the regional water governance system has been increasingly destabilized, leading to tensions among neighboring states. For these reasons, scholars discursively cast Ferghana Valley as the region that could emerge as a volatile, crisis-ridden zone, prone to violent inter-ethnic conflict because of a broken water distribution system and border demarcation.[100,101]

WHERE ARE THE WOMEN? EMANCIPATION OF CENTRAL ASIA'S WOMEN

In the previous section, we traced through the history of the Ferghana Valley. In the proceeding section, we analyze how historic developments have impacted women's roles and duties in transboundary water management. A narrow focus on their present responsibilities in public, without consideration of history, would provide a fragmented picture of women.

After the Soviet conquest of Central Asia, the Communist Party of the Soviet Union initiated a campaign to abolish "backwardness" in Central Asia in a fierce battle to "emancipate" Muslim Central Asian women.[102] The Soviets viewed the veil—burqa and hijab—as an embodiment of female inferiority, and veiled women, therefore, were perceived "as a potent symbol of Central Asian backwardness."[103] For Muslims, the campaign was an assault (*hujum*) on their way of living, culture, and traditions. For the Soviets, however, it embodied fighting against "backwardness" and "degrading" customs.[104] Therefore, in early 1919, the Communist Party created the "Zhenotdel" (Women's Department) in the Central Asian Republics to "teach, mobilize, and politicize local women and to draw them into the Party [and] trade unions."[105] As a result, there was an influx of women entering official public and governmental domains, including the water sector.

As in all other aspects of the public domain, the Soviet government tried to involve more women, on a similar basis to men, in political and economic decision-making processes within the collective farms.[106] While the representation of men and women in these farms evened up, specialization was newly split along gender lines. For instance, such tasks as planting, weeding, and harvesting became the responsibility of women. In the cotton-growing areas of Central Asia, 50 to 75 percent of a family's income came from female labor. Men, on the other hand, took over the roles in irrigation, heavy-land preparation work, and transportation.[107] This gendered segregation became a barrier to women's involvement in irrigation. While women held some managerial positions, they were reportedly at lower levels of significance and decision-making power than their male counterparts. The impact of gender segregation in the agricultural sector was also reflected by a deepening wage gap between women and men and underrepresentation of women in higher echelons of water resources decision-making professionals.[108]

The civil war that plagued Tajikistan in 1992–1993 further exacerbated the "gendered" nature of the transition. The fear among women and girls of being kidnapped and raped was so strong that it affected their freedom of movement.[109] In addition, the resurfacing of traditional gender stereotypes and calls to uphold women's "natural destiny" resulted in a sharp decline of their representation in government and other official public positions.[110,111]

Promotion of gender equality is presently reappearing, but instead of being pushed by the state (as it was during the Soviet era), it is being articulated by institutions of global governance, such as the United Nations.[112] In other words, the neoliberal and development discourse on gender equality is being reintroduced in the post-Soviet Ferghana Valley through the advocacy for women's rights, gender awareness, and gender training from international development agencies. However, this is occurring amid increasing cross-border tensions between neighboring villages and enclaves in Kyrgyzstan and Tajikistan. The following section discusses how the international development agencies incorporated women in their program.

Seeing Like a Donor

After a series of cross-border clashes in Kyrgyz and Tajik villages, the United Nations Development Programme and the United Nations Entity for Gender Equality and the Empowerment of Women, along with other development partners, launched the Cross-border Cooperation for the Sustainable Peace and Development project (hereinafter, the project) to restore stability and security in the region.[113] Following the trend of most water policies and donor-funded projects in non-industrialized nations, the project also has a mandatory gender component, which boiled down to including women in the project, though essentially as a check-marked item.[114] Since the project is funded by the United Nations Secretary General's Peacebuilding Fund, there is a mandated gender component. In line with donor requirements, the implementing agencies incorporated gender with an aim of engaging local women on both sides of the Kyrgyz-Tajik border to facilitate community dialogue and thus enhance cooperation and trust among communities.[115]

However, such prescriptive conditions often come from ideologically informed speculation about how international development should intervene, rather than from an in-depth, empirical understanding of how a particular society functions, including their water governance.[116] Thus, the integration of the gender component into the project likely happened due to necessity rather than genuine commitment.[117] In another instance, research indicates that in order to access debt-relief funds, governments in the Global South conducted national dialogues on a policy to relieve poverty.[118] Such practices were also observed in donor-funded transboundary water-cooperation efforts, which resulted only in vague declarations that women and children are most affected by water conflicts and need both special attention and rectification on the ground.[119]

Seen from this perspective, it is necessary to understand how the United Nations Development Programme, United Nations Women, and their development partners have integrated gender aspects into the project and how they define the role of women in transboundary water conflict and peacebuilding. To do so, we conducted a discourse analysis of the project description and online blog posts published by the United Nations Agencies providing insights on projects and activities, as well as women's involvement and their corresponding roles.[120]

TRANSBOUNDARY WATER CONFLICT RESOLUTION: WHOSE DOMAIN?

The analysis of five online blog posts by the United Nations Agencies showed a narrow focus on women of a certain age category and educational level. More concretely, female peace activists, who took on the role of cross-border mediators, were usually educated (such as teachers and doctors) and in their late 40s to 50s.[121] The fact that United Nations Women selected women of this age and education level as cross-border conflict mediators is not surprising. Taken in a historic perspective, women in their late 40s and 50s grew up under Soviet rule, which provided conditions for equal access to education and political empowerment, as opposed to women and girls of younger ages.[122,123,124]

Scholars have previously termed the proceeding generation of women, born between 1968 and 1990, as a "lost generation," because this age group "witnessed neither strength in state ideology nor equality in social, economic and gender roles" and received no support from neither the deteriorating Soviet government nor the newly independent republics.[125] Similar trends were captured in a survey with 150 women on the Kyrgyzstan side of the Valley, which found that women in this age group "do not see their role as engaging in peace-building: they generally wish for peace (21%), but feel their main responsibility is to raise and protect their children (19%)."[126]

A narrow focus on female mediators of a certain age and educational level raises further questions about those whose voices and opinions are heard and those who are left out. Who is included in the echelons of mediators and who is absent from the negotiation and conflict resolution? The older generation is the natural choice for the project because they had better preparation and education and grew up in a more stable period when there were more opportunities for public engagement. However, United Nations Women must involve women from all intersectional backgrounds in their cross-border peacebuilding project if they want to empower all women in the Ferghana Valley, prior to the execution of its project.

By depicting women as a single, coherent group, United Nations Women failed to acknowledge the complexities of gender intersectionality and the ways in which gender overlaps and interacts with age, class, culture, and political ideology.[127] In the context of ethnically diverse and historically colonized regions, such as the Ferghana Valley, overlooking these dynamics may omit relations among women of different age groups and levels of education with respect to authority. However, this statement is not to imply that younger women have been completely disregarded by United Nations Women. To the contrary, they have been included, but usually under the umbrella of "youth." The concept of youth, according to the United Nations definition, includes persons between the ages of 15 and 24 years, which means women born between 1968 and 1990 remain a "lost generation." Equally, younger women and ordinary village women have an important role to play in changing attitudes and maintaining ties across the border. Their role and engagement in these cross-border peacebuilding activities as mediators must be acknowledged.

Moreover, the project largely failed to recognize the role of men. Men are not explicitly mentioned in the project description, nor in the blog posts, nor acknowledged in gender mainstreaming initiatives. To address gender issues effectively, the project must include men. Specifically, men must be purposefully included to proactively promote women's empowerment, with the participation and support of male peers. Their inclusion would help to showcase that gender issues are not solely a women's problem and hence must be openly addressed. The presence of men could further assist in solidifying the notion of women's roles in transboundary water management and conflict mediation within national traditions.

Overall, the narrow focus on women, and a specific group of women at that, not only limits policy-making and implementation on the ground but also risks producing opposing results since changes in norms and behavior are tasks for the whole society. The analysis of the blog posts and accompanying photos suggests that United Nations Women see gender integration in decision-making, peacekeeping, and empowerment as a technical fix. This technocratic observation leaves out unequal power relations among women of different age groups, as well as maintaining that distinction between men and women. Instead, United Nations Women need to be more inclusive of women from various backgrounds and intersections of identities in deciding who to involve in their projects. United Nations Women "checked off" the gender requirement of the Peacebuilding Fund, which prevails in genuinely addressing the complexity of the gender dimension. In fact, the failure to account for the diversity of women may have reinforced social hierarchies of power. Gender inclusion in transboundary water resources management and water conflict resolution often remains a promise, yielding limited outcomes. While imported initiatives of United Nations agencies play an important role in debiasing and addressing gender stereotypes in their current state, they are not sufficiently inclusive and tend to be divorced from historical context.

As there is no easy solution to eliminate gender bias, there is also no quick fix to dismantle outdated social norms.

WHAT CAN WE LEARN FROM THE DESCHUTES RIVER BASIN AND FERGHANA VALLEY?

The two case studies in this chapter are vastly different in their scale, scope, geographical location, and culture. Yet there are some stark similarities. Both the

Deschutes River Basin and the Ferghana Valley have recently experienced changes in the command-and-control style of governance and management that previously dominated both regions. The administrative and political changes that upended these traditional systems have led to conflict and shifting of power relations.

In the Deschutes River Basin, the male-dominated irrigation districts have recently been challenged by environmental non-government organizations and rapidly growing municipalities with increasing water demands. Both cooperative and conflictual actions have lessened traditional control over the basin's water resources. However, women's participation in some sectors has been at best disparate, in others it has been almost entirely absent.

In the Ferghana Valley, colonization and subsequent transformation of the basin significantly altered traditional ways of living, as well as water management systems that once overlooked geopolitical boundaries. Development agencies inserted themselves into the situation under the guise of empowering women, facilitating economic development, and building peace, but without accounting for cultural and historical conceptualizations of gender.

On the surface, one might contend that the water conflicts facing these regions do not explicitly involve gender. The Deschutes River Basin is continuing to encounter disputes over water allocation and the Ferghana Valley is experiencing increased tensions in a complex, transboundary region, which is impeding cooperation over shared water resources. Further, both regions are taking part in collaborative efforts aimed at equitably sharing water resources. Unfortunately, the lack of a gendered lens in both cases actually perpetuates conflict and undermines the sustainability of water policies.

Water resources management decisions and policies are directly tied to the representation and power of stakeholders; hence, the inclusion of a broad range of voices can create more equitable and sustainable solutions and enhance cooperation.[128,129] This comprehensive approach to management strengthens the representation and capacity of women and disenfranchised communities, which can ". . . contribute to enhanced democratic norms, respect for human rights, and contribute to improved social cohesion in general."[130] Women, if included in decision-making and collaboration, bring greater diversity of experience and unique perspectives and generate new, collective outputs and measurably stronger outcomes. This addition can further address unequal power relationships that stem from gender, class, race, and ethnicity. When people in positions of power represent the majority, anyone who is deemed as "other" is opposed by social barriers, thereby preventing their participation in planning processes. This kind of obstruction results in management decisions that are less inclusive, especially when unique contexts are not recognized.[131]

There are few women in decision-making roles in the Deschutes River Basin, especially in traditionally male-dominated professions. Moreover, there are discrepancies in gender representation among types of organizations, which underscores traditional gender roles in water management. Although participatory processes are being used in an attempt to address the changing requirements of water in the basin, those involved in making management decisions are omitting people whose needs they are attempting to serve.

The women of the Ferghana Valley lost aspects of their culture, tradition, and agency (in terms of self-determination) during Soviet rule. In addition, they are currently being treated as recipients of a project by international development agencies, which perpetuates the double burden they face of managing their households while obliged to be visible in the public domain. Whereas the project funded by the United Nations Development Programme in the Ferghana Valley does have an explicit gender focus, it fails to incorporate the complex historical, cultural, and societal contexts that have disempowered these women in a multitude of ways over the last century, and lacks inclusion of men.

Therefore, while collaborative and participatory approaches are being promoted in each region, the failure to include women in positions of power is leading to less equitable, just, and sustainable solutions. Still, where so-called gender-inclusive initiatives are being implemented, the responsible institutions fail to conceptualize complex gender norms, values, and practices through space and time.

HOW CAN WE MOVE FORWARD TRANSFORMING CONFLICTS USING A GENDERED APPROACH?

It has been established in this chapter that, when more women are an active part of the choices being considered, the outcomes of water management decisions are more cooperative, sustainable, and equitable for recipient communities. Likewise, a gender-inclusive approach to water management, which effectively takes historical, ethnic, and cultural contexts into account, is imperative to any water-related project or action. How, then, can this knowledge and understanding be practically used to transform water conflicts?

We now return to the Four Stages of Water Conflict Transformation (namely, Adversarial; Reflection; Integrative; and Action) that guide the structure of this book, with an awareness that no one-size-fits-all toolkit exists and that the four stages are not linear. Each stage is addressed with a gender-focused approach, as it might be applied in the Deschutes River Basin and Ferghana Valley.

The adversarial stage focuses on rights, through trust building and a deepening understanding of conflict. Potential outcomes of this stage include establishing water laws that address sovereignty to rights over water resources.[132] Conflicts that stay in this "us-versus-them" stage are mostly about allocation and not explicitly about gender. Incorporating gender at this stage may be challenging; to date, there are few (if any) water laws that explicitly incorporate a gendered lens to governing water resources.[133]

The reflexive stage focuses on listening, identifying, and understanding each side's positions, needs, and interests. Actions taken from this stage are usually at the river-basin scale.[134] A gendered approach would open a space for women and marginalized groups to have their specific positions, interests, and needs heard and understood. The challenge here is to move beyond numbers and quotas, where so many projects and initiatives fall short.

The integrative stage focuses on benefits, values, and reframing the conflict to build consensus and relationships. In this stage, the process becomes collaborative, and engages stakeholders to think about benefits beyond water.[135] That is why actions and projects must include people of all genders, and seek to go beyond gender. However, without understanding and incorporating historical, racial, and ethnic contexts, gender-inclusive projects will not succeed. In addition, even where gender is not explicitly addressed in a water conflict, there often are underlying gendered norms and behaviors that guide decision-making, which must be made clear in order to be addressed.

The action stage is focused on building adaptive institutional capacity. This stage pushes communities to work, sometimes in new ways, with relevant institutions and agencies to meet water resources management, restoration, and sustainability goals.[136] The purpose of this chapter has been to show how external agencies insert themselves in order to achieve these goals, only to reinforce unequal gender norms and even silence the voices of specific groups. Gender inclusivity must exist at every stage, at every level, and be specific to each context in which it is used.

CONCLUSION

In our effort to operationalize a gender-inclusive approach to water resources management, we examined two contrasting cases, with different geographic and cultural contexts, to anchor our investigation concerning the role and place of women in water resources management and conflict transformation. Grounding this analysis on how societies in the Deschutes River Basin and Ferghana Valley facilitate or hinder women's involvement in water resources management, we unearthed the similarities of challenges faced by women in both industrialized and non-industrialized nations.

Interactions among individuals and their social, historical, and political environments continue to shape gender roles in society and define the roles of women in water resources management, in general.[137] The two case studies demonstrate how ingrained gender norms represent structural elements that influence entrenched regimes in water resources management. Although improvements in women's occupational standing have gained momentum in the United States since the 1970s, during which sex segregation declined by more than 14 percent,[138] the enhancement of traditional roles in water management has largely failed. Our analysis of the Ferghana Valley suggests that attempts from industrialized nations and development agencies to change traditional views regarding women's roles in water-resource management in non-industrialized nations is not being completely achieved.

Through water conflict analysis, questions emerge about, whose voices are heard, and whose are absent—even ignored; and who should be present at the negotiation table. Both case studies elucidate the challenge of broadening the range of voices and representation in decision-making processes in both in the Deschutes River Basin and the Ferghana Valley.

The Deschutes River Basin highlighted that, although collaborative, transformative efforts exist, a masculine style of water management persists, thus ignoring the voices of women. The case of the Ferghana Valley drew attention to how the decision on transboundary water management and gender mainstreaming occurs in the context of complex socio-political environments and how external actors—whether colonizers or development agencies—draw on differing perspectives, interests, and norms to frame the scope and direction of management.

By mapping the gender representation in the Deschutes River Basin and analyzing the distributions of women's voices and authority in the Ferghana Valley, we have revealed how new and inherited identities and social categories may reproduce social hierarchies of power, despite attempts to move away from masculine forms of water management and despite highlighting gender in water policies and programs. Ultimately, it requires a dramatic shift in social consciousness for women to be firmly recognized, honored, and included in the management of water resources and the resolution of conflicts. It is, after all, merely a cooperative choice.

QUESTIONS

1. In your opinion, is the water sector a man's domain? If so, why, and if not, why not? Provide at least two examples to support your claim.
2. From your perspective, how can we move forward in transforming conflict using a gendered approach?
3. In your river basin or region, how would you define the role of women in water management?

NOTES

1 International Conference on Water and the Environment. 1992. "The Dublin Statement on Water and Sustainable Development." *World Meteorological Organization.* www.wmo.int/pages/prog/hwrp/documents/english/icwedece.html. Accessed October 10, 2020.
2 Weiss, Edith Brown. 1992. "United Nations Conference on Environment and Development." *International Legal Materials* 31 (4): 814–817. Cambridge University Press.
3 United Nations Educational, Scientific and Cultural Organization. 1995. *Beijing Declaration and Platform for Action: Fourth World Conference on Women.* Beijing: United Nations Educational, Scientific and Cultural Organization.
4 Earle, Anton, and Susan Bazilli. 2013. "A Gendered Critique of Transboundary Water Management." *Feminist Review* 103 (1): 99–119.
5 Doermann, Julia, and Aaron T. Wolf. 2012. *Sharing Water, Building Relations: Managing and Transforming Water Conflict in the US West.* Denver, CO: US Bureau of Reclamation.
6 Connell, Robert William, and Raewyn Connell. 2000. *The Men and the Boys.* University of California Press, Berkeley and Los Angeles.
7 Paechter, Carrie. 2003. "Masculinities and Femininities as Communities of Practice." *Women's Studies International Forum* 26: 69–77. Elsevier.
8 Criado-Perez, Caroline. 2019. *Invisible Women: Exposing Data Bias in a World Designed for Men.* Random House, London.
9 Ibid.
10 Schilling, Janpeter, Rebecca Froese, and Jana Naujoks. 2018. "'Just Women' Is Not Enough: Towards a Gender-Relational Approach to Water and Peacebuilding." In *Water Security Across the Gender Divide,* 173–196.Springer, Cham.
11 Radu, Cătălina, Alecxandrina Deaconu, and Corina Frăsineanu. 2017. "Leadership and Gender Differences—Are Men and Women Leading in the Same Way?" In *Contemporary Leadership Challenges.* IntechOpen. https://www.intechopen.com/chapters/52779; https://doi.org/10.5772/65774.

12. Claes, Marie Thérèse. 1999. "Women, Men and Management Styles." *International Labour Review* 138 (4): 431–446.
13. Mitchell, Christopher Roger. 1981. *The Structure of International Conflict*.MacMillan Press LTD, London.
14. Abdalla, Amr, and Lilya Akay. 2016. *CR SIPPABIO—A Model for Conflict Analysis*. Ciudad Colon, Costa Rica: United Nations-mandated University for Peace (UPEACE).
15. Petersen-Perlman, Jacob, Jennifer C. Veilleux, and Aaron T. Wolf. 2017. "International Water Conflict and Cooperation: Challenges and Opportunities." *Water International* 42 (2): 105–120.
16. Wolf, Aaron T., Kerstin. Stahl, and Marcia. Macomber. 2003. "Conflict and Cooperation within International River Basins: The Importance of Institutional Capacity." *Water Resources Update* 125: 1–10.
17. Zeitoun, Mark, and Naho Mirumachi. 2008. "Transboundary Water Interaction I: Reconsidering Conflict and Cooperation." *International Environmental Agreements: Politics, Law and Economics* 8 (4): 297–316.
18. Gündüz, Zuhal Yesilyurt. 2011. "Water-on Women's Burdens, Humans' Rights, and Companies' Profits." *Monthly Review* 62 (8): 43–52. Monthly Review Press.
19. Andajani, Sari., Siriporn Chirawatkul, and Erico Saito. 2015. "Gender and Water in Northeast Thailand: Inequalities and Women's Realities." *Journal of International Women's Studies* 16 (2): 200–212. Bridgewater State University, MA.
20. Zwarteveen, Margreet. 2008. "Men, Masculinities and Water Powers in Irrigation." *Water Alternatives* 1 (1): 111–130. Water Alternatives Association.
21. Ibid.
22. Kronsell, Annica. 2005. "Gendered Practices in Institutions of Hegemonic Masculinity: Reflections from Feminist Standpoint Theory." *International Feminist Journal of Politics* 7 (2): 280–298. Taylor & Francis.
23. International Conference on Water and the Environment. 1992. "The Dublin Statement on Water and Sustainable Development." *Op. cit.*
24. Earle, Anton, and Susan Bazilli. 2013. "A Gendered Critique of Transboundary Water Management." *Op. cit.*
25. Best, Jaclyn P. 2019. "(In)Visible Women: Representation and Conceptualization of Gender in Water Governance and Management." *Master's Thesis*, Corvallis, Oregon: Oregon State University. https://ir.library.oregonstate.edu/concern/graduate_thesis_or_dissertations/n870zz023.
26. Fauconnier, Isabelle., Annemiek. Jenniskens, Page. Perry, Safa. Fanaian, Sucharita. Sen, Vishwaranjan. Sinha, and Lesha. Witmer. 2018. *Women as Change-Makers in the Governance of Shared Waters*. Gland, Switzerland: International Union for Conservation of Nature.
27. De Moraes, Andrea Ferreira Jacques. 2015. "Advances and Setbacks in Women's Participation in Brazil Part 1." In *A Political Ecology of Women, Water and Global Environmental Change*, edited by Stephanie Buechler and Anne-Marie S. Hanson, 77–96. Abingdon-on-Thames: Routledge.
28. de Silva, Lynette, Jennifer C. Veilleux, and Marian J. Neal. 2018. "The Role of Women in Transboundary Water Dispute Resolution." In *Water Security Across the Gender Divide*, edited by Christiane Fröhlich, Giovanna Gioli, Roger Cremades, and Henri Myrttinen, 211–230. Water Security in a New World. Cham: Springer International Publishing. https://doi.org/10.1007/978-3-319-64046-4_11.
29. Best, Jaclyn P. 2019. "(In)Visible Women: Representation and Conceptualization of Gender in Water Governance and Management." *Op. cit.*

30 World Bank. 2019. *Women in Water Utilities: Breaking Barriers*. World Bank. https://elibrary.worldbank.org/doi/abs/10.1596/32319. Accessed November 10, 2020.
31 International Water Association. 2016. "The Untapped Resource: Gender and Diversity in the Water Workforce." *England: International Water Association*. https://iwa-network.org/wp-content/uploads/2016/08/The_Untapped_Resource_screen.pdf. Accessed November 10, 2020.
32 Babbit, Christina. 2019. "It's Not Just Congress: More Women Are Working in the Water Sector, Too." *Environmental Defense Fund: Growing Returns*. July 19. http://blogs.edf.org/growingreturns/2018/11/19/women-in-water-sector/. Accessed November 20, 2020.
33 UN Water. 2014. "Gender and Water." October 10. www.un.org/waterforlifedecade/gender.shtml. Accessed May 11, 2021
34 Narayan, Deepa. 1995. *Monitoring Environmental Progress: A Report on Work in Progress*. Washington, DC: The World Bank.
35 Molle, François. 2009. "Water, Politics and River Basin Governance: Repoliticizing Approaches to River Basin Management." *Water International* 34 (1): 62–70. Taylor & Francis.
36 Zwarteveen, Margreet. 2017. "Hydrocracies, Engineers and Power: Questioning Masculinities in Water." *Engineering Studies* 9 (2): 78–94.
37 Kulkarni, Seema, Sneha Bhat, Sutapa Majumdar, and Chanda Gurung Goodrich. 2011. *Situational Analysis of Women Water Professionals in South Asia*. SaciWATERs, Hyderabad.
38 Gündüz, Zuhal Yesilyurt. 2011. "Water-on Women's Burdens, Humans' Rights, and Companies' Profits." *Op. cit.*
39 Liebrand, Janwillem, and Pranita Bhushan Udas. 2017. "Becoming an Engineer or a Lady Engineer: Exploring Professional Performance and Masculinity in Nepal's Department of Irrigation." *Engineering Studies* 9 (2): 120–139.
40 Ibid.
41 Faulkner, Wendy. 2007. "Nuts and Bolts and People' Gender-Troubled Engineering Identities." *Social Studies of Science* 37 (3): 331–356. London: Sage Publications Sage UK.
42 Inter-agency Task Force on Gender and Water. 2006. "Gender, Water and Sanitation: A Policy Brief." *06–24641*. United Nations-Water. www.un.org/waterforlifedecade/pdf/un_water_policy_brief_2_gender.pdf. Accessed February 14, 2021.
43 Gender and Water Alliance. 2006. *Gender, Governance and Water Resources Management*. Dieren, the Netherlands: Gender and Water Alliance.
44 Bennett, Elizabeth. 2005. "Gender, Fisheries and Development." *Marine Policy* 29 (5): 451–459. Elsevier.
45 O'Connor, Jim E., Gordon E. Grant, and Tana L. Haluska. 2003. "Overview of Geology, Hydrology, Geomorphology, and Sediment Budget of the Deschutes River Basin, Oregon." *American Geophysical Union*: 7–29.
46 Deschutes River Conservancy. 2012. *Upper Deschutes River Background Report*. Bend: Deschutes River Conservancy.
47 Ibid.
48 O'Connor, Jim E., Gordon E. Grant, and Tana L. Haluska. 2003. "Overview of Geology, Hydrology, Geomorphology, and Sediment Budget of the Deschutes River Basin, Oregon." *Op. cit.*
49 Bayramova, Sona. 2020a. "The Deschutes River Basin." https://www.behance.net/sona157/
50 McKinney, Matthew, and John E. Thorson. 2015. "Resolving Water Conflicts in the American West." *Water Policy* 17 (4): 679–706. IWA Publishing.

51 Worster, Donald. 1992. *Rivers of Empire: Water, Aridity, and the Growth of the American West*. Oxford: Oxford University Press.
52 Reisner, Marc. 1993. *Cadillac Desert: The American West and Its Disappearing Water*. Penguin, New York.
53 Molle, François, and Peter P. Mollinga. 2009. "Hydraulic Bureaucracies and the Hydraulic Mission: Flows of Water, Flows of Power." *Water Alternatives* 2 (3): 22.
54 Fort, Denise D. 2002. "Water and Population in the American West." *Human Population and Freshwater Resources: US Cases and International Perspectives 107*. Bulletin Series: Yale School of Forestry & Environmental Studies: 17.
55 Satein, Hannah. 2017. "Fighting to Cooperate: Litigation, Collaboration, and Water Management in the Upper Deschutes River Basin." *Master's Thesis*, Corvallis, Oregon: Oregon State University. https://ir.library.oregonstate.edu/concern/graduate_thesis_or_dissertations/vh53x1558?lo cale=en.
56 Deschutes River Conservancy. 2012. *Upper Deschutes River Background Report*. *Op. cit.*
57 Deschutes Water Alliance. 2006. *Instream Flow in the Deschutes Basin: Monitoring, Status and Restoration Needs*. Bend: Deschutes Water Alliance.
58 WaterWatch of Oregon v. U.S. Bureau of Reclamation, Central Oregon Irrigation District, North Unit Irrigation District, & Tumalo Irrigation District. 2016. U.S. District Court for the District of Oregon.
59 Satein, Hannah. 2017. "Fighting to Cooperate: Litigation, Collaboration, and Water Management in the Upper Deschutes River Basin." *Op. cit.*
60 Deschutes Water Alliance. 2006. *Instream Flow in the Deschutes Basin: Monitoring, Status and Restoration Needs*. *Op. cit.*
61 Satein, Hannah. 2017. "Fighting to Cooperate: Litigation, Collaboration, and Water Management in the Upper Deschutes River Basin." *Op. cit.*
62 Deschutes River Conservancy. 2012. *Upper Deschutes River Background Report*. *Op. cit.*
63 Satein, Hannah. 2017. "Fighting to Cooperate: Litigation, Collaboration, and Water Management in the Upper Deschutes River Basin." *Op. cit.*
64 Ibid.
65 Ibid.
66 Arora-Jonsson, Seema. 2014. "Forty Years of Gender Research and Environmental Policy: Where Do We Stand?" *Women's Studies International Forum* 47 (November): 295–308.
67 de Silva, Lynette, Jennifer C. Veilleux, and Marian J. Neal. 2018. "The Role of Women in Transboundary Water Dispute Resolution." *Op. cit.*
68 Fletcher, Amber J. 2018. "More than Women and Men: A Framework for Gender and Intersectionality Research on Environmental Crisis and Conflict." In *Water Security Across the Gender Divide*, 35–58. Springer, Cham.
69 Mukhopadhyay, Maitrayee. 2004. "Mainstreaming Gender or 'Streaming' Gender Away: Feminists Marooned in the Development Business." *IDS Bulletin* 35 (4): 95–103.
70 Arora-Jonsson, Seema. 2014. "Forty Years of Gender Research and Environmental Policy: Where Do We Stand?" *Op. cit.*
71 Taganova, Jahan. 2020. "MAN'aging Water Resources of the Deschutes River Basin." *Master's Thesis*, Corvallis, Oregon: Oregon State University. https://ir.library.oregonstate.edu/concern/graduate_thesis_or_dissertations/nc580t65t.
72 Ibid.
73 Ibid.
74 Ibid.
75 Best, Jaclyn P. 2019. "(In)Visible Women: Representation and Conceptualization of Gender in Water Governance and Management." *Op. cit.*

76 Taganova, Jahan. 2020. "MAN'aging Water Resources of the Deschutes River Basin." *Op. cit.*
77 Tarlock, A. Dan. 1999. "Putting Rivers Back in the Landscape: The Revival of Watershed Management in the United States." *Journal of Environmental Law & Policy* 6 (2): 167–195. HeinOnline.
78 de Silva, Lynette, Jennifer C. Veilleux, and Marian J. Neal. 2018. "The Role of Women in Transboundary Water Dispute Resolution." *Op. cit.*
79 Kenjabaev, Shavkat, and Hans-Georg Frede. 2016. "Irrigation Infrastructure in Fergana Today: Ecological Implications—Economic Necessities." In *Society-Water-Technology*, 129–148. Cham: Springer.
80 Ibid.
81 United Nations Environmental Programme, United Nations Development Programme, Organization for Security and Co-operation in Europe, North Atlantic Treaty Organization. 2005. *Environment and Security. Transforming Risks into Cooperation. Central Asia: Ferghana/Osh/Khujand Area.* Geneva: United Nations Environmental Programme.
82 Bichsel, Christine. 2009. *Conflict Transformation in Central Asia: Irrigation Disputes in the Ferghana Valley.* Routledge, London.
83 Zwarteveen, Margreet, Jeltsje S. Kemerink-Seyoum, Michelle Kooy, Jaap Evers, Tatiana Acevedo Guerrero, Bosman Batubara, Adriano Biza, Akosua Boakye-Ansah, Suzanne Faber, and Andres Cabrera Flamini. 2017. "Engaging with the Politics of Water Governance." *Wiley Interdisciplinary Reviews: Water* 4 (6): e1245. Wiley Online Library.
84 Ibid.
85 Baryamova, Sona. 2020b. "The Ferghana Valley." https://www.behance.net/sona157/
86 Abdullaev, Iskandar, and Shavkat Rakhmatullaev. 2015. "Transformation of Water Management in Central Asia: From State-Centric, Hydraulic Mission to Socio-Political Control." *Environmental Earth Sciences* 73 (2): 849–861. Springer.
87 Bichsel, Christine. 2009. *Conflict Transformation in Central Asia: Irrigation Disputes in the Ferghana Valley. Op. cit.*
88 Nourzhanov, Kirill, and Christian Bleuer. 2013. *Tajikistan: A Political and Social History.* Vol. 5. ANU E Press, Canberra.
89 Hays, Jeffrey. 2008. "Early Soviet Period in Central Asia." In *Facts and Details.* http://factsanddetails.com/central-asia/Central_Asian_Topics/sub8_8d/entry-4518.html. Accessed October 8, 2020.
90 Abdullaev, Iskandar, and Shavkat Rakhmatullaev. 2015. "Transformation of Water Management in Central Asia: From State-Centric, Hydraulic Mission to Socio-Political Control." *Op. cit.*
91 Molle, François, and Peter P. Mollinga. 2009. "Hydraulic Bureaucracies and the Hydraulic Mission: Flows of Water, Flows of Power." *Op. cit.*
92 Toktomushev, Kemel. 2017. *Promoting Social Cohesion and Conflict Mitigation: Understanding Conflict in the Cross-Border Areas of Kyrgyzstan and Tajikistan.* University of Central Asia, Institute of Public Policy and Administration, Bishkek, Working Paper, no. 40.
93 Ibid.
94 Bichsel, Christine. 2009. *Conflict Transformation in Central Asia: Irrigation Disputes in the Ferghana Valley. Op. cit.*
95 Kholiqi, Abdulkholiq, and Rahimov Nabijon. 2015. "Disputable Territories as Hotbeds of Tension on the Border." *Political Problems of International Relations; Global and Regional Development* 3: 188–196.

96 Toktomushev, Kemel. 2017. *Promoting Social Cohesion and Conflict Mitigation: Understanding Conflict in the Cross-Border Areas of Kyrgyzstan and Tajikistan. Op. cit.*
97 Ibid.
98 Reeves, Madeleine. 2005. "Locating Danger: Konfliktologiia and the Search for Fixity in the Ferghana Valley Borderlands." *Central Asian Survey* 24 (1): 67–81. Taylor & Francis.
99 Bichsel, Christine. 2009. *Conflict Transformation in Central Asia: Irrigation Disputes in the Ferghana Valley. Op. cit.*
100 Slim, Randa M. 2002. "The Ferghana Valley: In the Midst of a Host of Crises." In *Searching for Peace in Central and South Asia: An Overview of Conflict Prevention and Peace-Building Activities*, edited by Monique Mekenkamp, Paul van Tongeren, and Hans van de Veen, 67:141. Boulder, CO: Lynne Rienner.
101 Lubin, Nancy, and Barnett R. Rubin. 1999. *Calming the Ferghana Valley: Development and Dialogue in the Heart of Central Asia: Report of the Ferghana Valley Working Group of the Center for Preventive Action*. Vol. 4. The Century Foundation, New York.
102 Edgar, Adrienne Lynn. 2003. "Emancipation of the Unveiled: Turkmen Women under Soviet Rule, 1924–29." I 62 (1): 132–149. JSTOR.
103 Ibid.
104 Ibid.
105 Ishkanian, Armine. 2003. "VI. Gendered Transitions: The Impact of the Post-Soviet Transition on Women in Central Asia and the Caucasus." *Perspectives on Global Development and Technology* 2 (3): 475–496. Brill.
106 Mickiewicz, Ellen. 1977. "Regional Variation in Female Recruitment and Advancement in the Communist Party of the Soviet Union." *Slavic Review* 36 (3): 441–454. Cambridge University Press.
107 Mukhamedova, Nozilakhon, and Kai Wegerich. 2018. "The Feminization of Agriculture in Post-Soviet Tajikistan." *Journal of Rural Studies* 57: 128–139. Elsevier.
108 Ibid.
109 Ishkanian, Armine. 2003. "VI. Gendered Transitions: The Impact of the Post-Soviet Transition on Women in Central Asia and the Caucasus." *Op. cit.*
110 Ibid.
111 Kandiyoti, Deniz. 2007. "The Politics of Gender and the Soviet Paradox: Neither Colonized, nor Modern?" *Central Asian Survey* 26 (4): 601–623. Taylor & Francis.
112 Ibid.
113 United Nations Development Programme. 2016. *Cross-Border Cooperation for Sustainable Peace and Development*. United Nations Development Programme. www.tj.undp.org/content/tajikistan/en/home/operations/projects/poverty_reduction/litaca1.html. Accessed September 6, 2020.
114 Zwarteveen, Margreet. 2017. "Hydrocracies, Engineers and Power: Questioning Masculinities in Water." *Op. cit.*
115 United Nations Development Programme. 2016. *Cross-Border Cooperation for Sustainable Peace and Development. Op. cit.*
116 Zwarteveen, Margreet, Jeltsje S. Kemerink-Seyoum, Michelle Kooy, Jaap Evers, Tatiana Acevedo Guerrero, Bosman Batubara, Adriano Biza, Akosua Boakye-Ansah, Suzanne Faber, and Andres Cabrera Flamini. 2017. "Engaging with the Politics of Water Governance." *Op. cit.*
117 Best, Jaclyn P. 2019. "(In)Visible Women: Representation and Conceptualization of Gender in Water Governance and Management." *Op. cit.*

118 Whitehead, Ann. 2003. *Failing Women, Sustaining Poverty.* London: UK Gender and Development Network.
119 Von Lossow, Tobias. 2015. "Gender in Inter-State Water Conflicts." *Peace Review* 27 (2): 196–201.
120 Taganova, Jahan, and Annagul Yaryyeva. 2020. "Do Women Really Forge Peace in the Ferghana Valley? A Critical Discourse Analysis of Cross-Border Cooperation for Sustainable Peace and Development in the Fergana Valley." Manuscript submitted for review.
121 United Nations Women. 2020. *Women Forge Peace along the Kyrgyz-Tajik Border.* September 21. www.unwomen.org/en/news/stories/2017/2/feature-women-forge-peace-along-the-kyrgyz-tajik-border. Accessed September 6, 2020.
122 Ishkanian, Armine. 2003. "VI. Gendered Transitions: The Impact of the Post-Soviet Transition on Women in Central Asia and the Caucasus." *Op. cit.*
123 Dhanju, Richa. 2008. "Water and Women's Empowerment in the Ferghana Valley: Agency of Older Women from Soviet Era in Contemporary Rural Kyrgyzstan and Uzbekistan." *UCLA: Thinking Gender Papers,* 1–8.
124 Kandiyoti, Deniz. 2007. "The Politics of Gender and the Soviet Paradox: Neither Colonized, nor Modern?" *Op. cit.*
125 Dhanju, Richa. 2008. "Water and Women's Empowerment in the Ferghana Valley: Agency of Older Women from Soviet Era in Contemporary Rural Kyrgyzstan and Uzbekistan." *Op. cit.*
126 United Nations Women. 2020. *Women Forge Peace along the Kyrgyz-Tajik Border. Op. cit.*
127 Mohanty, Chandra Talpade. 1984. "Under Western Eyes: Feminist Scholarship and Colonial Discourses." *Boundary* 2: 333–358. JSTOR.
128 Butler, Cameron, and Jan Adamowski. 2015. "Empowering Marginalized Communities in Water Resources Management: Addressing Inequitable Practices in Participatory Model Building." *Journal of Environmental Management* 153: 153–162. Elsevier.
129 Kemerink-Seyoum, J. 2019. "Introduction to Voice and Authority." *PowerPoint Presentation,* IHE Delft Institute for Water Education, January.
130 de Silva, Lynette, Jennifer C. Veilleux, and Marian J. Neal. 2018. "The Role of Women in Transboundary Water Dispute Resolution." *Op. cit.*
131 Ibid.
132 Doermann, Julia, and Aaron T. Wolf. 2012. *Sharing Water, Building Relations: Managing and Transforming Water Conflict in the US West. Op. cit.*
133 Earle, Anton, and Susan Bazilli. 2013. "A Gendered Critique of Transboundary Water Management." *Op. cit.*
134 Doermann, Julia, and Aaron T. Wolf. 2012. *Sharing Water, Building Relations: Managing and Transforming Water Conflict in the US West. Op. cit.*
135 Ibid.
136 Ibid.
137 West, Candace, and Don H. Zimmerman. 1987. "Doing Gender." *Gender & Society* 1 (2): 125–151. Sage Publications.
138 Cotter, David A., Joan M. Hermsen, and Reeve Vanneman. 2004. *Gender Inequality at Work.* Russell Sage Foundation, New York.

8 Water Insecurities in Two African–American Communities

Lynette de Silva

CONTENTS

Introduction 149
The Vanport Case Study 150
   The Significance of a Location 150
   Wartime 152
   Waters Leading Up to That "Horrific Day" 154
   The Plight 155
   Transformative Analysis 156
      Mapping the Vanport Situation 157
      Relating the Water Conflict Framework to Vanport 158
   Discussion 161
      Trust Building 163
      Listening 163
The Flint Case Study 164
   Emergency 164
   "Hydro-crimes" 166
   Where Does This Leave Flint Residents? 166
   Transformative Water Conflict Analysis 167
      Strengthening Water Rights in Flint 167
   Discussion 170
Conclusion 171
Questions and Exercises 172
Notes 172

INTRODUCTION

This chapter is an exploration of two African American communities within American society impacted by environmental factors: Vanport, Oregon, and Flint, Michigan. Understanding these circumstances is of particular importance because such cases are not isolated. Moreover, the impacts of potentially dangerous environmental conditions can be far-reaching over time and space—jeopardizing the physical, emotional, and mental wellbeing of households and neighborhoods. In turn, such circumstances can diminish a population's wellness, productivity, and contributions within a nation for generations, while straining county and national health-care services.

In the first case study, the plight and devastation of Vanport, a forgotten Oregon community that was part of a 1948 river deluge, is examined, including what led up to the flood. Using decision-making and assessment frameworks, stakeholders and their relationships are identified, as well as key issues within the community, such as their needs and interests. Through analysis, we hope to expand our thinking with respect to current ways of identifying collaborative and transformative skills for more constructive paths that may inform other scenarios of a similar nature, increasing equity, and broadening inclusion through community resilience. In the second case study, current-day Flint, Michigan, is explored, where communities of low income, with a high percentage of African Americans, are burdened with lead-contaminated drinking water. Legal instrumentation and mediation tools for transformative practices are applied.

THE VANPORT CASE STUDY

This story begins in the Columbia River Basin, where the Columbia River carries on average 265,000 cubic feet per second (7,500 m³/s) of water to the Pacific Ocean.[1] Only three waterways in North America, the Mississippi, St. Lawrence, and Mackenzie, surpass the Columbia River in discharge.[2]

The Columbia River and its tributaries drain an area close to 258,000 square miles (668,000 sq. km.), as they flow through parts of the Canadian Province of British Columbia (BC) and portions of seven U.S. States: Washington, Oregon, Idaho, Montana, Wyoming, Nevada, and Utah.[3] The most distant flow begins at Columbia Lake, British Columbia; from there, it heads northwest and then southward at Big Bend, BC, eventually forming the political boundary between Washington and Oregon, as it makes its way to the Pacific Ocean, at Astoria, Oregon (Figure 8.1).

The historical city of Vanport was once positioned partway between "Van"couver (Washington) and "Port"land, on the Oregon side of the Columbia River (Figure 8.2). For thousands of years, this had been the traditional home of Native Americans—the "Chinookan-speaking peoples, including the Clackamas, Kathlamet, Multnomah, and Tualatin,"[4] until the mid-1800s, when the U.S. government forced their relocation to noncontiguous lands, within the state. But that is another story. Named as a city because of its size, rather than through administrative governance, Vanport was a federal housing project that originally went by two earlier names (the Denver Avenue Housing Project and Kaiserville, respectively).[5] In the following, we explore the geographic, hydrologic, and social context leading to the loss of this city, a loss impacting several groups of people. However, here the focus is on the African American experience.

THE SIGNIFICANCE OF A LOCATION

Vanport was nestled on a slender strip of built-up wetlands, in the Columbia Slough Watershed from 1942–1948. To understand the movement of water in this

FIGURE 8.1 A map of the Columbia River Basin with the Columbia River highlighted.
Source: (Map prepared by Kmusser, Wikimedia, 2008).

locale and why it made the community vulnerable, it is noteworthy to add that the Columbia Slough Watershed is a 19-mile stretch of low-lying land directly south of the Columbia River (Figure 8.2). Within this subbasin, the headwaters originate at Fairview Lake, flowing westward for 18 miles to the Willamette River, at the southwestern end of Kelley Point Park. From there, the confluence of the Willamette and Columbia Rivers is less than a mile at the northern-most tip of the park.

In the mid-19th century, within the Columbia Slough Watershed—which today comprises the Heron Lakes Golf Courses and the Vanport Wetlands—was a compilation of "lakes, sloughs, and marshes."[6] At that time, the low-lying ground adjacent to the Columbia River was part of the floodplain and was, in fact, below the surrounding levels of the Columbia and Willamette Rivers.[7]

To reclaim the land and keep water out for the purpose of agricultural production and to build one of Portland's commercial, radio-broadcasting station with transmitter towers, the early 20th century saw the installation of flood-protection

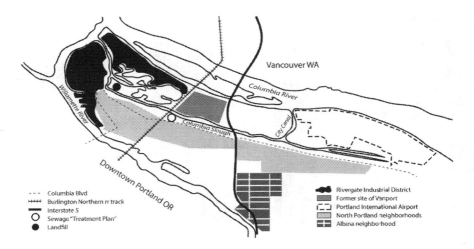

FIGURE 8.2 The historical location of Vanport city, shown in relation to the North Portland Peninsula and the lower Columbia Slough.

Source: (Map by Maria Buhigas, published in Ellen Stroud, "Troubled Waters in Ecotopia: Environmental Racism in Portland Oregon," Radical History Review (Spring 1999): 65–95).

mechanisms comprised of "a complex of dikes, drainageways, and mechanical pumping stations."[8] These were farmlands that would be used for temporary federal housing during World War II.

Wartime

Britain's war efforts needed new ships. Henry John Kaiser, an industrialist and shipbuilder, heeded the call to build them,[9] recruiting workers from around the country, some travelling directly to Portland by trains chartered by Kaiser.[10] Among the arrivals were Euro-Americans, African Americans from southern states, Mexican Americans, and Indigenous peoples.

The Housing Authority of Portland (Housing Authority), established in 1941 to address the need for wartime housing, did not act fast enough for Kaiser. So, in 1942, hampered by Portland's housing shortage and racial housing restrictions, his son, Edgar Kaiser, secured one square mile on which to build a temporary infrastructure within the Columbia River floodplain to provide housing for shipbuilders and their families,[11] on what then was the periphery of north Portland.

Over 110 days, close to 10,000 temporary, prefabricated residences were built. Many "apartments were in fourteen-unit buildings. Built of wood on wooden foundations—a challenge in the swampy site—the buildings were two-story boxes with one-story wings."[12] By December 12, 1942, though not incorporated into Portland, Vanport's population became the second-largest urban community in Oregon, "with a peak population of 42,000."[13] This entire, low-rent project came as a surprise to Portlanders. Coupled with the rapid growth of newcomers residing on the outskirts of Portland, earning a relatively good salary, the influx of African Americans sparked hostility within Portland's community.[14]

This racial sentiment was already engrained in the region. "When Oregon joined the union in 1859, it was the only state to constitutionally prohibit African Americans from living, working, or owning property there."[15] In the late 1800s, African Americans and mulatto people in Oregon could be subjected to lashes twice a year, and later subjected to "forced labor" to encourage them to leave the state.[16] In the early 1900s, in Portland, with a 9,000 Ku Klux Klan (KKK) membership wielding significant political influence, racial discrimination thrived.

Within Vanport, housing and hospital services were racially segregated,[17] but some amenities and services, such as elementary schooling (in the west district)[18] and 24-hour daycare, were shared, leading to a more progressive community than the rest of Oregon. Within Vanport, ethnic minorities worked alongside the dominant white culture in skilled trades. Vanport is where Oregon's first African American law enforcement officers, Matt Dishman and Bill Travis,[19] and school teacher, Ms. Martha Jordan, would emerge. However, even though African Americans contributed to the nation's wartime shipbuilding efforts, Portlanders continued to see them as a concern, even after the war. And though the African American community within Vanport never exceeded a third of the population, negative stereotypes prevailed, and Portland's communities continued to feel threatened.

The African American community had additional challenges in Vanport. To address broad community concerns and to recognize the racial disparities with which the Housing Authority treated non-white versus white Vanporters,[20] the Vanport Interracial Council was created by residents. It formed the basis for a call to action, which included administering written requests to the Housing Authority to bring about social and economic fairness.[21] The council also established the Portland branch of the National Urban League, a nonpartisan, historic, civil-rights organization.[22]

Once World War II was over, white residents of Vanport "were moving out by as many as 100 a day."[23] African Americans and other ethnic minority residents, who wished to live in Portland, were restricted to living in the already crowded district of Albina and Guild's Lake Courts (the other public housing facility for African Americans).[24,25] Housing options for this minority population were severely limited, resulting in many African Americans remaining in Vanport housing.

Historian Greta Smith[26] conveyed that,

> during the war, President Franklin D. Roosevelt issued Executive Order 9066, authorizing the forced removal of all Japanese-American citizens living on the West Coast—some 110,000 people—from their homes to inland internment camps. The order lapsed at the end of the war, but many Japanese Americans lost their homes and property while they were incarcerated.

Smith stated that, "as xenophobia and anti-Japanese sentiments were high during and after the war, most Japanese Americans, newly released from the internment camps, had difficulty finding new housing. Some of them moved into Vanport, one of their only available options."

In 1946, vacant residences and buildings were repurposed; this included reuse for a newly formed Vanport Extension Center. War veterans and their families moved in for college training to take advantage of the GI Bill and affordable housing, along with teachers. And, with that, the postwar population of Vanport stabilized by 1948, to about "12,600 whites, 5,000 African Americans, and 900 Japanese Americans."[27]

It was on May 30, during that same year, that waters from the upper reaches of the Columbia River and its tributaries would course along their normal route. However, the surge was beyond its usual extent, flooding low-lying areas and demolishing the wooden structures of Vanport on its way to the Pacific Ocean.

WATERS LEADING UP TO THAT "HORRIFIC DAY"

Historic records show several peak discharges in the Columbia and Willamette Rivers in 1894, 1933, 1948, 1956, 1964, and 1996. However, the magnitude of the 1948 flood in the Columbia River Basin is surpassed only by the 1894 river inundation.[28]

A combination of events brought about the May-June 1948 flood. Both the winter precipitation and accumulating mountain snowpack were high, followed by an abnormally cold spring, which delayed mountain snowmelt. Next came unusually high spring rainfalls and rapidly warming temperatures. Collectively, the combined snowmelt and precipitation contributed to twice the volume of water moving downstream than would normally occur, substantiated by records stating, "May 1, showed water contents greatly above normal for that date. Snow-survey records indicate that the water content for that date may have exceeded 200 percent of normal in some areas." By mid-May, in susceptible parts of Idaho, Montana, and Washington, officials were predicting critical flood risks and hazards.[29]

Oregon would not be spared. The flood waters moved downstream, and by May 25, 1948, waters at the confluence of the Columbia and Willamette Rivers (at Portland) reached 8 feet above what would normally not be inundated (flood stage).[30] Portland lowlands, susceptible to flooding, were evacuated, and the airport adjacent to Vanport was closed on May 30.[31] The U.S. Army Corps of Engineers informed the Housing Authority that Vanport was safe. The Housing Authority did take precautionary measures to protect its own administrative records and equipment by removing them from Vanport, in addition to hundreds of horses from the neighboring racetracks.[32] However, it did send out pamphlets to Vanport residents the morning of May 30, 1948 (Memorial Day), stating: "Remember: Dikes are safe at present. You will be warned if necessary. You will have time to leave. Don't get excited."[33]

At 4 pm, the Corps of Engineers announced that, "Vanport lay 15 feet below the level of the Columbia River," but chose to monitor Vanport embankments and levees rather than recommend evacuating.[34,35] At 4:17 pm, the first breach occurred on the west side of the city, at the western embankment.[36] Sirens blared. Within an hour, the city was engulfed with 10–20 feet of water,[37] and within 2 hours, Vanport was no more.[38] The *New York Times* (1948) described

> boat crews working under floodlights on the pool which covers the town area, reported that bodies of drowned victims were found in heaps of broken houses. The captain of one boat crew said he counted five bodies in one room. Another said he knew of two

dead in one house. One woman was brought dead to a hospital. Portland's hospitals were crowded with injured, most with broken bones.[39]

It is estimated that between 15 and 32 lives were lost.[40] Vanport city was washed away, displacing close to 18,500 people. In total, property damages were on the order of 100 million dollars.[41] The United States Geological Survey reported that: "[The] Willamette River at Portland, Oreg., backed up by the Columbia, reached peak stages of 29.95 feet on June 1 and 29.975 feet on June 14. The [flood] stage at Portland remained above 25 feet for 26 days."[42]

THE PLIGHT

The sentiment among the African American Community was that "due, at least in part, to Vanport's large African American presence, authorities were negligent toward the projects' inhabitants and failed to adequately warn and prepare residents for the real threat of flooding."[43] It was also believed that the Housing Authority "deliberately withheld warnings about the flood and the city had concealed a much higher death toll."[44] Some explain that the numbers were not higher that day because it was Memorial holiday and Vanporters were out of their homes.[45,46]

There are embankments on all sides of Vanport: north, east (Denver Avenue), south, and west. None of them were owned or maintained by the government. The government did own 80 percent of the land along with the pumping station to keep water out.[47] It was the western embankment that first failed. Its construction began with timber trestles in the early 1900s, as part of Spokane, Portland & Seattle Railway's north-south route. However, in later years, "the trestle stringers were removed but the piling [a type of deep foundation] was not. This fill [silt and clay] rests on land belonging in undivided interests to the Spokane, Portland & Seattle Railway Company and the Northern Pacific Railway Company,"[48] stated Chief Judge Fee of the U.S. District Court for the District of Oregon (1948–1954), who ruled on the Vanport case.

The Corps of Engineers, whose mission is to oversee such structural features as dams, floodplains, levees, and dikes, was monitoring Vanport's railroad embankment during the flooding event. However, the railroad embankment was not constructed to prevent flooding or to act in that capacity. It was designed to facilitate terrain adjustments for railroad operations. In fact, the embankment was constructed several decades prior to Vanport and was the responsibility of the railroad companies. "That the demands on this protective dike would increase with the construction of Vanport apparently did not occur to anybody,"[49] indicating that, perhaps, there was little or no communication between the railroad companies and the Corps of Engineers on this matter.

Skovgaard[50] recalls that on August 8, 1951, Oregon Journal reported of a federal court hearing, where John H. Suttle, an engineer for the district, testified that "he had been responsible for building the lower part of the railroad fill and said the reason it failed was because the lower part of the fill was built on soft mud."

Vanport housing was now government owned (having been sold by Kaiser),[51] and personal property were generally not insured, so Vanporters lost all their belongings.

Some 18,500 people were homeless, including some 5,000 African Americans. In the days after the demise, the Red Cross oversaw emergency relief with help of the Portland community, providing emergency accommodation in community centers, churches, schools, and homes. Vanport was not rebuilt. Overtime, many more African Americans moved to the Albina District of Portland and Guild's Lake Courts.[52] No federal agency nor company was held negligent nor legally responsible for the flood devastation.[53]

Because of the Vanport devastation, President Harry Truman instructed the Corps of Engineers to revisit earlier Columbia-River plans to ensure that, along with harnessing hydropower, provisions for flood control would mitigate future flooding of this magnitude.[54] This culminated in the 1964 Columbia River Treaty between Canada (specifically, British Columbia)[55] and the United States. The treaty resulted in the building of three dams in Canada (Duncan, Arrow, and Mica Dams) and one in the U.S. (Libby Dam).

Transformative Analysis

Although the Vanport devastation resulted in shifts in Columbia River management, it also forced the closure of Vanport and transformed the situation so that Vanport residents moved into Portland, albeit limited to the Albina and Guild's Lake Court areas. There were also short- and long-term societal changes that emerged, showcasing this African American community as courageous and resilient. It manifested because Vanport residents took elements within the social and political fabric that made them vulnerable, subjecting them to an inferior way of living and established systems of resistance for protection. African American residents formed the Vanport Interracial Council which: (1) exposed "antidemocratic actions" and hypocrisy of agencies,[56] creating administrative records of unfair practices, and challenging the system to bring about change,[57] and (2) created Portland's branch of the National Urban League, which still represents the community in Portland.[58] This illustrates that instrumental governance emerged from this small community of color that still reverberates, within Oregon—noteworthy, given Vanport's short tenure. Moreover, Vanport blazed the Oregon trail for African Americans in law enforcement and education.[59]

The Vanport case study can be explored through two techniques of a transformative water conflict lens: (1) to encourage systematic thinking by looking at the Vanport case study through a situation map, and (2) by using collaborative skills that can be applied through the Four Stages of Water Conflict Transformation Framework.[60] The Four Stages are particularly relevant because they help optimize broad-based skills for effective use in arbitrating water conflicts and social injustice. In this way, the most appropriate skills can, if circumstances are ripe, help produce a more sustainable social-environmental outcome. (See Chapter 2 to learn more about the Four Stages of Water Conflict Transformation Framework.)

Certainly, the Vanport scenario is not a dispute over the lack of access to water. Quite the opposite, it is the flooding of a community that *is* the tipping point of distress. For those experiencing injustice, the disharmony is evident. The *struggle* is between minority stakeholders (with less power) and institutional discrimination along with poor decision-making by those in power. The fight is born out of inequity and unsustainable living conditions, which leaves a group vulnerable to the second largest flood in the Pacific Northwest. So, it is for the aforementioned reasons that the author seeks to relate the water conflict framework to Vanport.

In the following, two techniques are used toward transformative water-conflict analysis. A graphic situation map is developed to display background information through a systematic lens, and a water conflict framework is used as a means to gage the kinds of skills that can improve the outcome of such conflicts.[61]

Mapping the Vanport Situation

Situation maps are used as a way of thinking about dynamic and controversial realities in terms of systems, recognizing the whole (unit) and interconnections (feedback loops). In this way, systems thinking provides a mechanism for acknowledging the complexity and fragility of systems, as "networks of relationships and causality perhaps more than either linear or nonlinear thinking tend to do."[62] As such, situation mapping is a tool to reflect on our understanding of realities, fully acknowledging that assumptions are from the perspective of the designer and are limited to a specific timeframe.[63]

Situation maps provide a flow chart or graphic of the relationship among actors regarding a central theme or topic with multi-stakeholder involvement.

> It is also a tool that can showcase types of interaction (significant or less significant to the whole system); and can be used to identify weak links in system-relationships. Consequently, situation maps are increasingly used to better understand complex, community-based water issues.[64]

Through text and illustrations, Daniels and Walker[65] break down the components that make up environmental systems thinking and mapping. Jarvis[66] applies this technique in *Contesting Hidden Waters: Conflict Resolution for Groundwater and Aquifers*, to map stakeholders and their involvement in planning processes focused on groundwater withdrawals in Oregon (see Figure 4.1)[67] and aquifer protection in Wyoming (see Figure 5.4).[68]

To map the Vanport case study, background details are reviewed specifically for Vanport, to identify primary actors and stakeholders. This information was retrieved from peer-reviewed journals, academic and government reports, and/or newspaper articles to identify organizations and communities (stakeholders). The acquired information became a primer for developing a visual interpretation of Vanport-related relationships, showcasing Vanport as the central theme, along with linkages to stakeholders with an interest in that community.

Figure 8.3 is a systematic representation of the Vanport case study. Vanport (and its impact on the African American community) is depicted as the central theme and is placed in the middle of the map. Primary places, communities, organizations, and governing bodies that make up the system are represented by shapes. Interaction, connection, and information flow are represented by arrows. And the dashed connection represents limited and/or no known information or communication between entities.

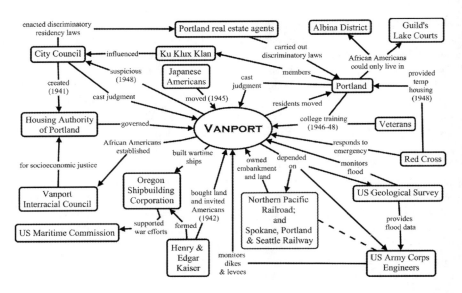

FIGURE 8.3 A graphic representation of the Vanport case study, where the central Vanport shape represents the overall Vanport history of the place, particularly as it relates to the African American experience, and the Portland shape represents the Portland location. Interpretation by Lynette de Silva.

In Figure 8.3, notice that: (1) federal and local agencies oversaw Vanport housing, governance, and flood management, (2) the KKK was influential through connections with state lawmakers and enforcers, (3) Vanport residents created agency through the Vanport Interracial Council, and (4) there appeared to be weak communication between the railroad companies and officials overseeing flood management.

Relating the Water Conflict Framework to Vanport

While somewhat distinct from developing a situation map, the water conflict framework (seen in Table 8.1) is used to gage where in the four stages of interaction (negotiation) the parties were leading up to, during and after the flood event. Interactions among primary stakeholders can be categorized as adversarial, reflective, integrative, or in the action mode, corresponding to terminology in the first column in Table 8.1.

The task is to determine which of the four negotiation processes best suits the Vanport case study. Within Table 8.1, adversarial forms of interaction among stakeholders can be described as argumentative, in which ownership is claimed with an uncompromising position, where *winners* take all—pointing to a rights-based approach. Reflective engagement implies a pause in rhetoric, allowing space for listening to the perspectives, needs, and interests of others. The integrative mode suggests the amalgamation of interests and values to benefit the collective. And, the action stage of negotiations echoes the union of ideas in the process of implementation. These stages of negotiation, however, may not necessarily happen in linearity.[69]

# Water Insecurities in Two African–American Communities

TABLE 8.1
Four Stages of Water Conflict Transformation (Part 1)

Type of Process/ Negotiation Stage[a]	Focus of Process	Collaborative and Transformational Skills[b]	Context, Geographic Scope, or Framing for Outcomes
Adversarial	Rights	Trust-building; deepening understanding of conflict	State, federal, tribal land, and water laws; priority, jurisdiction, and supremacy/sovereignty of rights
Reflexive	Needs and interests	Skills-building in listening for and identifying positions, needs and interests	Watersheds/basins
Integrative	Benefits/values/reframing	Consensus-building; relationship-building	"Problemshed"/"Benefit-shed"
Action	Governance in relationship to dynamic systems; equity	Capacity-building; community-building	Networked systems across state, region, and/or country

TABLE 8.1
Four Stages of Water Conflict Transformation (Part 2)

Communication Style	Goal of Conflict Resolution Process[c]	Focus of Process and Participants	View of Conflict
Defend; debate; deliberate	Make decision: often win/lose among parties who differ	Apply laws and policies to reach a decision; control information to be selective and tactical	Competitive; polarize; desire to bring pain, anxiety, and difficulties to an end
Listen without resistance; causes, beliefs, and assumptions	Reach an agreement among parties about the presenting problem	Content-centered	Need to de-escalate
Generative dialogue; collectively invent new possibilities and new insights	Promote constructive change processes; uncover and form a base of shared meaning that can help coordinate and align actions and values; solve and dissolve problems[d]	Relationship-centered; engages the systems within which relationships are embedded; focus shifts to listening/sensing an already existing wholeness; share information	Collaborative; envisions conflict as an ecology that is relationally dynamic, all of which is normal and results in constructive change

(Continued)

TABLE 8.1
(Continued)

Communication Style	Goal of Conflict Resolution Process[c]	Focus of Process and Participants	View of Conflict
Network information and communication to maintain collective flow and opportunity	Facilitate people thinking and acting together in relationship within reframed context from which new agreements can come	Create or re-create institutions, policies, structures, and networks from which communities/society can express their new basis of shared meaning, goals, and principles	Conflict leads to new capacity, and a shared vision reflecting new understanding to improve quality of life

Source:

a These stages build primarily on the work of Jay Rothman, who initially described his stages as ARI—Adversarial, Reflexive, and Integrative (Rothman 1989). When ARI become ARIA, adding Action, Rothman's terminology (1997) also evolved to Antagonism, Resonance, Invention, and Action. We retain the former terms, feeling they are more descriptive for our purposes.

b Expanded from and including Kaufman (2002), who ties each set of dynamics specifically to Rothman's ARIA model in great detail, based on his extensive work conducting "Innovative Problem Solving Workshops" for "partners in conflict" around the world.

c Developed from Lederach, John P. *Preparing for Peace: Conflict Transformation Across Cultures.* (Syracuse, NY: Syracuse University Press. 1995).

d Isaacs, William *Dialogue: The Art of Thinking Together.* (New York, NY: DoubleDay. 1999).

The development of the situation map helps in understanding the dynamics within a system and the negotiation stage, which categorizes a dispute. Added reassurance can come from assessing columns in Table 8.1 and interpreting where and how the Vanport situation might fit in columns, such as "Focus of Process and Participants," which provides information that can help determine if the dispute might be regarded as ego-, content-, relationship-, or union-centric. Columns like "View of Conflict" provide added descriptors that help categorize the adversarial, reflective, integrative, and action process stages as: polarizing, de-escalating, constructively participating, and sharing, respectively. The Vanport case study is placed in the Four Stages of Water Conflict Transformation framework (Table 8.1), generating Table 8.2.

Depicted in the Vanport case study is the history and pattern of issues surrounding race that reaches back to Oregon's inception and injustices that extends into the immediate aftermath of the flood. There are conflictive events, which include the housing policy, the flood disaster, and beyond the flood. The Vanport case study seems to be in line with wordage that implies that actors (Portland City Council and Housing Authority of Portland) tended to employ "laws and policies to reach a decision…[by controlling] information to be selective and tactical," listed under the

TABLE 8.2
The Water Conflict Transformation Stage That Seems Most Applicable to the Vanport Case Study.
Analysis and interpretation by Lynette de silva. Modified from Table 8.1

Type of Process/ Negotiation Stage	Collaborative and Transformational Skills	Context, Geographic Scope, or Framing for Outcome	Focus of Process and Participants
Adversarial	Trust-building; deepening understanding of conflict	State, federal, tribal land, and water laws; priority, jurisdiction, and supremacy of rights	Apply laws and policies to reach a decision; control information to be selective and tactical
		Examples include:	Examples include:
		1. In the 1940s, Portlanders were xenophobic and wanted to keep ethnic groups out of Portland.	1. From the 1940s, Housing Authority of Portland utilized discriminatory housing policies in Vanport and Portland.
		2. In the early 1900s, Ku Klux Klan (KKK) wielded significant political influence in Oregon and Portland.	2. From the 1930s, Portland City Council (and nation) utilized discriminatory housing policies and redlining practices, which segregated living spaces in Portland.
		3. In the late 1800s, African Americans were prohibited from living, working, or owning property in Oregon.	

"focus of process and participants" column in Table 8.2. A prime example of this is the discriminatory housing policy and redlining practices, which segregated living spaces, in Portland. Corroborating this decision are the items denoting a power play for "sovereignty of rights," regarding housing and districts, showing these types of actions as polarizing tactics. This allows for classifying the process/negotiation state of Vanport and surrounding communities as "adversarial" which corresponds to the need for "trust-building; [and] deepening the understanding of conflict"—which is evident in the fuller "adversarial" description (see Table 8.2).

DISCUSSION

By depicting the Vanport case study as a system (see Figure 8.3), it would appear that the movement of African Americans is restricted by decision-makers in Portland and Vanport. This is administered both formally and informally.

Consider that subsistence and security are among the most rudimentary of human needs,[70] and that the mission of public servants (Portland city council and local government officials) is to serve the necessities of all Portland and Vanport citizens, in a fair and impartial way. Therefore, had African American Vanporters been valued, their safety may have been of greater concern to appointed officials. African Americans could have had other residential options, allowing them to live in Portland, in peace, in more secure housing. At the very least, if talks had ensued among the appropriate officials and stakeholders ahead of the severe flooding, an evacuation plan might have been enacted, preserving life and safeguarding property.

When a people are banned from Oregon territory (as in the late 1800s), as African Americans were, it denotes a sense of sovereignty of rights to Oregon land among those that lay claim to it, as illustrated by the "rights" focus of process. That sovereignty of rights was in the state's constitution, conveying legal power to dispel or remove people from the state's geographic scope, making them unwelcomed, to say the least.

Decades after these rulings were removed from law, African Americans assisted the nation's World War II efforts in the shipyards, but after the war they were subjugated to other forms of discriminatory practices, such as institutions acting as barriers to everyday opportunities that the majority within society enjoyed. Their shipbuilding patriotic acts did not appear to elicit trustworthiness from the dominant culture. For example, minority groups were excluded from housing and school-age education in neighborhoods of choice, nondiscriminatory financial loans, and job opportunities of one's choosing. Under these scenarios, Portlanders could apply law to reach the outcome they desired, which was to keep Oregon white. Such strong disagreement among factions (white and non-white peoples), displays an adversarial negotiation stage, in the Four Stages of Water Conflict Transformation Framework, as illustrated in Table 8.2.

There are still vestigial thoughts that compel some to conclude that scientists, equipped with data, provide the answers to social-environmental issues. Some of this thinking may be rooted in the American Progressive Era of the early 1900s, in which "there came the concept that scientifically trained expertise...should be put to use solving society's problems."[71] Scientists must provide unbiased data, analysis, and probability. In so doing, they provide part of the solution; but one should consider that the formulation of environmental policy and decision-making may be more reliant on other factors, among them: social values, economics, and risk aversion.[72]

So, if one were to conclude that Vanport's catastrophe was merely an engineering debacle, this would be shortsighted. This line of thinking is symptomatic, rather than systematic. It assumes that science has all the answers, whereas an interdisciplinary assessment tells a more comprehensive story. A tale that includes a compromised embankment for the railroad, while recognizing Portland's underlying social construct that shaped the outcome of what transpired at Vanport. So, the water catastrophe that decimated Vanport had its origin in social injustice, at the interracial level of conflict, toward not only the African American demographic but also other minority groups and those of low socio-economic standing. Under such circumstances, it may seem trivial to think that the transformational skill needed is trust building and listening (as indicated in Table 8.2). Both will now be discussed.

Trust Building

Trust building develops through demonstrating trustworthiness. While one may want reassurances that others are trustworthy, it most often is displayed by a person through their gestures and actions, which tends to make others respond in kind. Over time, this builds confidence among parties. Though individual trust can incite mutual trust, "placing trust can be risky."[73]

Within the Vanport case study, for example, the housing restrictions placed on the African American community, as well as redlining (refusing house-related loans or insurance based on discriminatory practices), were socially unjust. The prerequisite to building social and political trust begins with fairness and nondiscrimination for all. Since transformation can only be fostered if mutual respect exists, this may seem pessimistic. Philosopher Baroness Onora O'Neill of Bengarve provides a glimmer of hope, touting that actions, such as refusing complicity even in the smallest of ways, provide an opening for the start of greater inclusion.[74]

Listening

Listening to what? To whom? And why? Because society shapes individuals, and individuals shape society, one approach toward a social transformational shift could require introspection. It starts with individuals willing to listen to themselves, examining their own conscious thoughts and feelings about race and Portland's social practices (of the day), while coming to realize that each of us, as an individual, can "choose alternative paths of action and ways of being, and in so doing exercise a degree of agency."[75] When the will is there, listening and discussion can occur, not only at the intrapersonal level but also between and among individuals within and among communities extending throughout Portland and across Oregon.

A neutral party may need to facilitate and/or mediate such listening sessions to provide a safe space for all. A series of listening sessions would be necessary within a variety of public forums (local radio, newspapers, social media, in town hall meetings, and rural and urban community settings) over an extended period of time (months and even years). Since libraries[76] and houses of worship generally prompt softer tones of speech and disciplined behavior, holding discussions in such forums may promote a more respectful exchange. It may also prove constructive to involve community leaders and well-respected stakeholders in the early stages of the listening process, to help them engage in the art of active and transformative listening, to fully hear concerns and points of contention.

A public hearing is a more formal listening process. It can be a means to restorative justice. Such an approach was administered by South Africa's Truth and Reconciliation Commission, after 43 years of apartheid laws (1948–1990), laws that subjected non-white people to institutional racism that perpetrated all aspects of society. This discrimination included "civil and political rights and instituted segregated education, health care, and all other public services."[77] These hearings helped facilitate victims and perpetrators give voice to their experiences, thereby promoting healing and reconciliation both at the individual and country levels.

THE FLINT CASE STUDY

Flint, Michigan, has compromised drinking water; we will step back in time to see how this came to be. Flint was an established fur trading post in the early 1800s and the hub for the lumber industry in late 1800s. It was this latter revenue that would fuel the horse-carriage industry from which General Motors would emerge. By mid-20th century, the city was among the leading industrial and automobile producers in the nation, including, for a short time, the manufacturing of Chevrolets and Buicks, making General Motors the leading employer. "At its peak in the 1970s when Flint's population was 190,000, General Motors GM employed 80,000 people in Flint alone."[78] Other people hired by the city included government (federal, state, and local), health care, and higher education—with employment services a distant fifth.[79]

By the close of the 20th century, the Flint automobile industry was on the decline, with automotive employment falling to less than 24,000 people by 2003.[80] By then, Flint's economy had accrued a debt estimated to be $30 million,[81] making it among the poorest cities in the country. Along with its economic decline, Flint's demographic changed, which in 1960 comprised a population of 82 percent white and 17 percent black, but by 2012, that had changed to a 39 percent white and 56 percent black population.[82] Over this same timeframe, there was a shift from a predominantly middle class to as many as 40 percent of the citizens living below the poverty level.[83]

A combination of both internal and external factors brought about the decline of the industry and with it the city. Among the causes were deindustrialization and unionization, outsourcing, a 2008 national recession, and General Motors' call for insolvency.[84] Procedurally, to bring Flint out of debt, Michigan's Governor, Rick Snyder, appointed an Emergency Manager in 2011. The idea was that a referendum (on Emergency Manager Law—Public Act 4 of 2011) would guide the common functions of the Emergency Manager, but voters killed it. However, 5 weeks later, despite public protests, a bill with similar measures (Local Financial Stability and Choice Act 436 of 2012), immune from referendums, would be signed by the governor.

EMERGENCY

Among the measures to reduce Flint's expenses, the Emergency Manager changed the water supply from pre-treated Lake Huron waters (which was through a contract the city had with Detroit Water & Sewerage Department) to one that would come from the Flint River and be treated by Flint's own treatment plant. This change was to be a temporary measure that could save the city an estimated $2 million a year, until development of a new pipeline and treatment plant that was expected by 2018. Thereafter, the Karegnondi Water Authority pipeline and the Genesee County Water Treatment Plant would connect the city to treated Lake Huron waters.

In the meantime, the Emergency Manager settled on use of the Flint River, a more corrosive source of water that would require additional procedures by the city's treatment plant. This switch was made on April 25, 2014. By that summer, community members were complaining to officials about the poor water quality, which included its discoloration, as well as bad odor and taste. But nothing would change. Early in 2015, there was an opportunity for the city to change back to its earlier water source, at no expense, but the Emergency Manager declined. By August 2015, it was determined that the anti-corrosive control step, which required adding orthophosphates to the water treatment process, was missing.

This meant that corrosive water flowing through aging lead pipes could oxidize lead compounds, making the lead dissolve, thereby increasing the chances of lead leaching into the water. Dr. Terese Olson, Associate Professor of Civil and Environmental Engineering, stated that "an average of at least 18 g of lead is predicted to have been released to individual Flint homes with a public LSL [lead service line], lead pipes undoubtedly were a major source of Flint's lead-contaminated tap water."[85]

Early on, General Motors recognized that water from the Flint River was too caustic for car manufacturing, switching its operations back to Flint's earlier water source, in 2014. It would take a Flint pediatrician (Dr. Mona Hanna-Attisha) and partners (such as Virginia Tech, among others) to connect the levels of lead in the blood of Flint's children with lead in their drinking water. In September 2015, she successfully urged the city to stop using the Flint River as its water source.[86]

Dr. Mona Hanna-Attisha estimated that as many as 14,000 children may have been exposed to lead.[87] And, since it can be transferred from mothers through pregnancy and lactation,[88] the numbers of those threatened may even be higher. Because analysis of teeth in newborns can detect the levels of lead during fetus development, scientists are seeing heightened levels in infants that correspond to the timeframe after the change in Flint's water source.[89]

This level of lead is of grave concern because lead is a health detriment to children, with irreversible consequences, because "low levels of exposure have been linked to damage to the central and peripheral nervous system, learning disabilities, shorter stature, impaired hearing, and impaired formation and function of blood cells." As such, the Safe Drinking Water Act, administered through Environmental Protection Agency, deems no amount of lead acceptable for drinking water standards.[90] Furthermore, "the Centers for Disease Control and Prevention recommends that public health actions be initiated when the level of lead in a child's blood is 5 micrograms per deciliter (μg/dL) or more."[91] Studies by the Centers for Disease Control and Prevention concluded that, of some 9,400 blood samples drawn from Flint's children below the age of 6, prior to when the water was switched in 2014, 3.1 percent of kids had levels above 5.0 μg/dL. And, after that timeframe, the number increased to 5 percent.[92] Dr. Hernán Gómez, a medical toxicology specialist, and colleagues showed supporting evidence, as far back as 2006, that lead levels in children exceeded the Centers for Disease Control and Prevention's reference level of 5.0 μg/dL, but was declining until the source of water was changed.[93]

However, a Centers for Disease Control and Prevention study and Dr. Hanna-Attish's study with Virginia Tech indicate that the water source was a contributing factor.[94] Furthermore, research conducted by Dr. David Slusky, with the University of Kansas, indicates that, "fertility rates decreased by 12 percent among Flint women, and fetal death rates increased by 58 percent."[95] In addition, at least a dozen people died from a severe form of pneumonia associated with water-borne legionella bacteria, and others have experienced sickness.

"HYDRO-CRIMES"

In addition to the failure to include orthophosphates in the water-treatment process, other offenses occurred. At least three officials were arrested for misconduct and violations under the Safe Drinking Water Act. One of them, Mike Glasgow, a supervisor at Flint's water-treatment plant "admitted to manipulating the data by removing the two results from his report and falsely stating the source of the test samples."[96] As a result, homes with the highest risk did not have adequate tap-water samples taken, thereby lowering the lead values sufficiently, so that his office would not have to inform citizens, as required by the Environmental Protection Agency.[97]

Former Department of Environmental Quality officials, Steven Busch and Michael Prysby, who took plea deals, had their charges dismissed by Judge David Goggins on December 26, 2018. Because there was no public notice that this would occur, neither victims nor the public were present at court.[98] And, after millions of tax-payer dollars had been spent on litigating these cases, the Attorney General, in the summer of 2019, ruled that all criminal charges related to Flint, Michigan's water crisis be dropped, due to investigation mismanagement, citing an interest in starting the process anew.[99]

Today, through a court order, Flint's water source is back to pre-treated Lake Huron waters, now administered through Great Lakes Water Authority. The Environmental Protection Agency assures residents that the water is safe to drink and use. Due to a loss of confidence in government, many residents refuse to use the water, relying on bottled water instead.

WHERE DOES THIS LEAVE FLINT RESIDENTS?

The mere fact that the Local Financial Stability and Choice Act 436 of 2012 was immune from referendum meant that governance and decision-making was taken away from voters and their locally elected officials. Mr. Matthew Sous, in his Michigan State University College of Law dissertation, cites this as "undemocratic" and too far-reaching an interpretation of Michigan's constitution.[100] Dr. Laura Pulido, a qualitative social scientist, minces no words in declaring that

> the people of Flint are so devalued that their lives are subordinated to the goals of municipal fiscal solvency. This constitutes racial capitalism because this devaluation is based on both their blackness and their surplus status, with the two being mutually constituted.[101]

Even when residents complained that their water quality was compromised, they were not taken seriously. And, now that tests support their claims and the water source has reverted back to treated Huron waters, residents have no confidence in the government's directives, nor the Environmental Protection Agency's assertion that the water is safe to use. Their fears may be justified. Research indicates that, even in circumstances when lead corrosion controls is added after the fact and lead plumbing is removed, there is the possibility of lead lingering within home plumbing. So, potential risks may still remain. This emphasizes the delicate nature of water chemistry and, in the case of corrosive waters, the necessity of having "uninterrupted lead corrosion control" in place from the beginning.[102]

As students of transformative analysis, now equipped with the techniques presented in the Vanport case study, you can explore the transformative practices that may be applicable in the Flint case study. You can do this by conducting your own research to tabulate actors, create a situation map, and determine what collaborative and transformational skills come from your interpretation of the events. Furthermore, under the present legal system, we will now explore acting legislation and rules to see what potential they may offer disenfranchised communities.

Transformative Water Conflict Analysis

Often, when thinking of environmental laws, what may come to mind are regulations, such as the Safe Drinking Water Act and the Endangered Species Act. Environmental laws are a system combining treaties, guidelines, rules of evidence, and even common law principles and factual conclusions. It should be thought of in the collective. In this way, combining laws can inform conduct, as a "pluralistic legal framework."

Strengthening Water Rights in Flint

Existing water laws did not protect the community, because the laws were not enforced. So, combining laws might seem futile and unrelated to transformative water conflict analysis. However, keep in mind that legal pluralism is a form of reframing, one tool in the transformational framework. Reframing creates another way of looking at a situation which could bolster leverage. After all, laws are dynamic, changing with social and political conscience. Their pluralistic nature adds complexity. As a result, legal pluralism may offer different levels of rights that can be used for effective negotiations of water use and water rights to empower marginalize groups, such as women, minorities, and poor households. Drs. Ruth Meinzen-Dick and Rajendra Pradhan, leading experts on pluralism for natural resource management, illustrate in Figure 8.4 that even when laws are overlapping, they can have varying degrees of influence and jurisdiction.[103] Because residents of Flint are experiencing physical and emotional jeopardy, with neither water security nor peace of mind, this places them somewhere on the spectrum of adversarial and reflective stages of water conflict. The collaborative skills needed are trust building and skills building, which take time. Meanwhile, the community requires water security and safe drinking

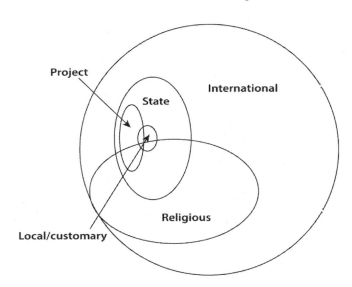

FIGURE 8.4 Illustration of overlapping legal orders related to water.
Source: (Meinzen-Dick and Pradhan 2002).

water. The key is using these legal instruments to complement each other and optimize the community's outcome.

The field of conflict management and mediation provides for parties to individually evaluate their position and to consider the spectrum of possible outcomes from a negotiation standpoint. Knowing this can provide leverage, to walk away from the process when the risk is too great or to strengthen one's solution when plausible.[104] In addition, it provides a tool to open discussion, strengthen positions, and reframe issues. So, while only partially related to the water transformation framework, the exercise of considering what the law provides should be fully explored.

Figure 8.4 demonstrates the coexistence of a number of laws that can overlap with regard to water: (1) where international and state laws are administered through government institutions, (2) religious laws are governed through doctrine and morals, (3) local and customary laws follow traditional values, and (4) project law incorporates program and project contracts.[105] To promote water equity, consider the system of laws related to water within the Flint, Michigan, domain. These combined laws can increase the "bargaining power in negotiations for resources" for underrepresented groups.[106]

Presented in Table 8.3 are some of the legal instruments that factor into the Flint story. Included are rulings and/or declarations from international and US executive, judicial, and legislative institutions. However, it is by no means exhaustive. These laws have varying geographic scope in providing degrees of water protection to Flint citizens. Among the protections are rights at the property level associated with the piping from the city connection to the place of dwelling, while city and county jurisdictions treat and supply safe drinking water through the water purveyor lines.

TABLE 8.3
A Compilation of Some Overlapping Laws Related to Flint's Water Crisis That May Inform Water Dispute Negotiations.
Interpretation by lynette de silva

Laws	Generalized Protections	Geographic Scope
Resolution 64/292 of United Nations General Assembly, July 28, 2010	• Recognizes the human right to safe and pristine drinking water and sanitation.	International
Resolution A/HRC/15/L.14 of United Nations General Assembly, September 24, 2010	• Reaffirms the human right to safe drinking water and sanitation.	International
Inter-American Court for Human Rights	• Upholds basic human rights and freedoms. • Protects religious freedom and practices.	American Continent
Fourteenth Amendment to the United States Constitution	• Prevents citizens from losing life, liberty, or property without fair procedure.	National
Executive Order 12898	• Provides environmental justice to minority and low-income populations.	National
Executive Order 13045	• Protects children from environmental health risks and safety risks.	National
Clean Water Act (1972)	• Regulates discharges of pollutants into waters of the United States. • Regulates quality standards for surface waters.	National
Safe Drinking Water Act (1974)	• Protects public health by regulating the nation's public drinking water supply. • Enforces the Lead & Copper Rule. • Enforces pollutant limits on waterways.	National
Environmental Justice	• Enforces environmental policies for fair treatment of all people regardless of race, color, national origin, or income.	National
President declares State of Emergency	• Releases federal emergency aid to help the City of Flint with lead-contaminated drinking water. (As occurred in January 2016)	State
Michigan Safe Water Drinking Act 399	• Protects public health by regulating Michigan's public drinking water supply.	State
State of Michigan Public Health Code, Public Act 368	• Protects public health.	State
Water Contracts	• Karegnondi Water Authority pipeline and the Genesee County Water Treatment Plant supply the county (except the city of Flint) with treated Lake Huron waters.	County

(Continued)

TABLE 8.3 (Continued)

Laws	Generalized Protections	Geographic Scope
Water Contracts	• A 30-year contract with Great Lakes Water Authority to supply Lake Huron waters to the city of Flint. • A contract for Great Lakes Water Authority to lease Detroit's water infrastructure from Detroit Water & Sewerage Department (as of January 1, 2016).	City
Local Financial Stability and Choice Act 436 of 2012	• Safeguards financial accountability for government sectors and school districts. • Facilitates services essential to the public health, safety, and welfare.	Local
Property Title Rights	• Protects citizens right to fully enjoy their homes. • Addresses deeds, legal registration, and easements.	Property

At the state level, there are provisions for safe water and the protection of public health, with federal-emergency funds released to the state, as occurred in January 2016 by presidential declaration. At the national level, environmental justice equality should enforce environmental policies and laws for all residents of the nation. Moreover, the Environmental Protection Agency oversees and enforces the integrity of the nation's drinking water and is supposed to keep lead and copper out of it.

There are executive orders to protect the health of children, as well as low-income and minority groups, and the United States 14th Amendment to safeguard the rights to life and equal protection of the law. International orders recognize human rights to freshwater and sanitation, as declared through United Nation resolutions. Also presented is at least one transnational ruling that serves the right to religious freedom and worship (Inter-American Court for Human Rights), which is estimated to impact at least 3 percent of the Flint community. This may be of particular interest to communities in faith-based traditions that perform purity rituals with water before worship (such as Islam and Judaism).

Discussion

Being deprived of safe public drinking water disrupts every aspect of life—hygiene, health, emotional wellbeing—and makes performing simple tasks unnecessarily burdensome. In addition, this deprivation creates hardships when performing faith-based traditions and makes productivity in other aspects of life challenging.

Government officials and water practitioners must aim to be of service, do no harm, be void of corrupt activities, and uphold professional ethical standards to provide a respectful level of quality that is open and transparent in practice and review. In the case of Flint, science reveals that the citizens of Flint are/were grossly violated, placing an already vulnerable community in physical, emotional, and mental harm, even death because of water treatment mismanagement. The ramifications will last several generations, because experiencing no justice must leave such a community untrusting of government in most or all of its phases.

The overarching mission is to meet the needs of this underrepresented sector and enforce the current laws on their behalf. Table 8.3 presents a range of laws and institutions that can be used to empower and affect dispute resolution, creating a mechanism that can work to embrace a wider social demographic. This list is not by any means comprehensive. Remember, these pluralistic legal orders are designed to challenge the system while working within jurisdictional frameworks.

One may need to consider whether these existing laws and guidance can be formulated to bring about equity and wield authority for more effectively functioning systems, if not through motivation, then with the proverbial stick. Meinzen-Dick and Pradhan suggest that, while legal pluralism can improve bargaining, "new laws aimed at strengthening the rights of the poor or other marginal groups must be accompanied by programs to create awareness by all parties, so that the new laws can be cited and accepted in the negotiation process."[107]

Enforcement mechanisms must be optimized. If such mechanisms can somehow be coupled with creative, regional, economic incentives,[108] doing the *right thing* can extend beyond Flint.

CONCLUSION

These two case studies shed light on two very distinct water experiences in the African American community: one associated with a flooding event in the Pacific Northwest, and the other on compromised water supplies in the Rust Belt. Though separated in space and time, we see how disenfranchised communities on the fringes of society find themselves in vulnerable situations. Group dynamic assessments, relationships viewed through a systematic scope, and a transformative analysis tool facilitate constructive change applicable to other scenarios.

Tools used in the Vanport case explores how the use of systematic thinking can give broader context and content to social dynamics. And, the water conflict framework provides a means to determine what collaborative skills might build and strengthen community relationships for other vulnerable communities, thereby facilitating the building of trust toward broader inclusion.

The Flint case study considers how bundled rights might strengthen the leverage inherent in negotiation, to increase bargaining strategies to underrepresented communities through laws that protect supplies of public drinking water, vulnerable citizens, environmental justice, and human rights. The goal is to provide sustainable environmental conditions of good quality for all community members—present and future.

QUESTIONS AND EXERCISES

1. How are the Vanport case study and the New Orleans case study (impacted by Hurricane Katrina and breached levees in 2005) alike?
2. Are you aware of other water injustice cases that have impacted other minority populations? If so, do your own investigation and conduct your own transformative water conflict analysis.
3. Can you think of any other laws that can be added to Table 8.3?
4. Draw a situation map based on the information provided for the Flint, Michigan, case study.

NOTES

1 Kammerer, John C. 1987. *Largest Rivers in the United States*. US Geological Survey, Department of the Interior.
2 Marts, Marion E. 2019. *Columbia River, Encyclopædia Britannica*, Published by Encyclopædia Britannica, inc., Chicago, IL. March 27, 2019. www.britannica.com/place/Columbia-River (accessed on August 17, 2019).
3 Ibid.
4 Toll, William. 2003. First Peoples in the Portland Basin. Introduction: Commerce, Climate, and Community a History of Portland and its People. In *The Oregon History Project*. www.oregonhistoryproject.org/narratives/commerce-climate-and-community-a-history-of-portland-and-its-people/introduction-3/themes-for-an-urban-history/#.X-hAji3Mx24 (accessed on December 26, 2020).
5 Podany, Zita. 2016. *Vanport*. Arcadia Publishing. Charleston, SC. 128 pp.
6 Fish, William. n.d. *Overview of the Columbia Slough*. http://web.cecs.pdx.edu/~fishw/ECR-SloughDescription.htm (accessed on December 26, 2020).
7 Ibid.
8 Dulin, Evan and C. Mirth Walker. 2018. *Vanport Wetlands Long-Term Management Plan*. https://popcdn.azureedge.net/pdfs/Miti_Vanport_Wetlands.pdf (accessed on December 26, 2020).
9 Reimann, Matt. 2017. "The Shipbuilding Town of Vanport—Home to Most of Oregon's Blacks—Was Washed Away in an Afternoon: Ten Thousand Houses in 110 Days, and Then They Were Gone." *Timeline*. Published June 8, 2017. https://timeline.com/vanport-oregon-african-american-d235eed9441c (accessed on May 29, 2020).
10 Griffith, Sarah. 2002. *Vanport Residences, 1947. The Oregon History Project*. A Project of the Oregon Historical Society. www.oregonhistoryproject.org/articles/historical-records/vanport-residences-1947/#.X-hJgiV7I24 (accessed on December 26, 2020).
11 Abbott, Carl. 2019. "Vanport." In *The Oregon Encyclopedia*. A Project of the Oregon Historical Society. Portland State University and the Oregon Historical Society. https://oregonencyclopedia.org/articles/vanport/#.XiXp2S2ZPr4 (accessed on December 26, 2020).
12 Ibid.
13 Reimann, Matt. 2017. "The Shipbuilding Town of Vanport—Home to Most of Oregon's Blacks—Was Washed Away in an Afternoon: Ten Thousand Houses in 110 Days, and Then They Were Gone." *Op. cit.*
14 Abbott, Carl. 2011. *Portland in Three Centuries: The Place and the People*. Oregon State University Press.
15 Reimann, Matt. 2017. "The Shipbuilding Town of Vanport—Home to Most of Oregon's Blacks—Was Washed Away in an Afternoon: Ten Thousand Houses in 110 Days, and Then They Were Gone." *Op. cit.*

16 Rector, Elaine. 2010. *Looking Back in Order to Move Forward an Often Untold History Affecting Oregon's Past, Present and Future.* www.osba.org/~/media/Files/Event%20Materials/AC/2009/101_History%20of%20Race%20in%20Oregon.pdf (accessed on December 26, 2020).
17 Abbott, Carl. 2019. "Vanport." *Op. cit.*
18 Harrison, James. 2020. "Vanport Day of Remembrance." *Presented at the Vanport Mosaic—2020 Virtual Festival*, Online, May 30. www.vanportmosaic.org/festival2020#may17 (accessed on May 30, 2020).
19 Moreland, Kimberly S. 1993. *History of Portland's African American Community, 1805 to the Present.* Portland, OR: Portland Bureau of Planning. https://sos.oregon.gov/archives/exhibits/black-history/Documents/flowers-portland-history.pdf (accessed on December 26, 2020).
20 Fryer, Heather. 2010. *Perimeters of Democracy: Inverse Utopias and the Wartime Social Landscape in the American West.* U of Nebraska Press.
21 Maben, Manly. 1987. *Vanport.* Oregon Historical Society Press. Portland, OR. 151 pp.
22 Pearson, Ruby. 2007. "Vanport, Oregon (1942–1948)." *Black Past.* www.blackpast.org/african-american-history/vanport-1942-1948/ (accessed on December 26, 2020).
23 Geiling, Natasha. 2015. "How Oregon's Second Largest City Vanished in a Day." *Smithsonian Magazine*, February 18. www.smithsonianmag.com/history/vanport-oregon-how-countrys-largest-housing-project-vanished-day-180954040/ (accessed on December 26, 2020).
24 Maben, Manly. 1987. *Vanport. Op. cit.*
25 March, Tanya Lyn. 2010. "Guild's Lake Courts: An Impermanent Housing Project." Doctor of Philosophy (Ph.D.) in Urban Studies, Portland, OR: Portland State University. https://pdxscholar.library.pdx.edu/cgi/viewcontent.cgi?article=3816&context=open_access_etds (accessed on December 26, 2020).
26 Smith, Greta conveyed to the author via e-mail on March 21, 2020.
27 Rubenstein, Sura. 1998. "1998 Story: Flood of Change." *Oregonlive*, May 12. www.oregonlive.com/history/2014/12/1998_story_flood_of_change.html (accessed on December 26, 2020).
28 Paulsen, C. G., S. E. Rantz, and H. C. Riggs. 1949. "Floods of May-June 1948 in Columbia River Basin, with a Section on Magnitude and Frequency of Floods." *Geological Survey Water-Supply Paper 1080.* U.S. Govt. Print. Off. https://pubs.er.usgs.gov/publication/wsp1080 (accessed on December 26, 2020).
29 Ibid.
30 Geiling, Natasha. 2015. "How Oregon's Second Largest City Vanished in a Day." *Op. cit.*
31 Paulsen, C. G., S. E. Rantz, and H. C. Riggs. 1949. "Floods of May-June 1948 in Columbia River Basin, with a Section on Magnitude and Frequency of Floods." *Op. cit.*
32 Geiling, Natasha. 2015. "How Oregon's Second Largest City Vanished in a Day." *Op. cit.*
33 Hamberg, Michael James. 2017. "Flood of Change: The Vanport Flood and Race Relations in Portland, Oregon." Master's Theses 689, Central Washington University. Ellensburg, WA. http://digitalcommons.cwu.edu/etd/689 (accessed on December 26, 2020).
34 Ott, Jennifer. 2013. "Vanport Flood Begins on Columbia River on May 30, 1948." In *HistoryLink.Org*, Essay 10473. www.historylink.org/File/10473 (accessed on December 26, 2020).
35 Maben, Manly. 1987. *Vanport. Op. cit.*
36 Ibid.
37 Ott, Jennifer. 2013. "Vanport Flood Begins on Columbia River on May 30, 1948." *Op. cit.*
38 Harrison, James. 2020. "Vanport Day of Remembrance." *Op. cit.*

39. New York Times. 1948. "The Rest of the Flooding." In *The Blanchard*, Wayne, 2017. Deadliest American Disasters and Large-Loss-of-Life Events Website. Published May 31, 1948. www.usdeadlyevents.com/1948-may-22-june-11-floodingdike-failures-pacific-northwest-esp-vanport-or1-57-77/ (accessed on December 26, 2020).
40. Kahan, James P., Mengjie Wu, Sara Hajiamiri, and Debra Knopman. 2006. *From Flood Control to Integrated Water Resource Management: Lessons for the Gulf Coast from Flooding in Other Places in the Last Sixty Years*. Rand Corporation. Santa Monica, CA. 46 pp. www.rand.org/content/dam/rand/pubs/occasional_papers/2006/RAND_OP164.pdf (accessed on December 26, 2020).
41. Paulsen, C. G., S. E. Rantz, and H. C. Riggs. 1949. "Floods of May-June 1948 in Columbia River Basin, with a Section on Magnitude and Frequency of Floods." *Op. cit.*
42. Ibid.
43. Hamberg, Michael James. 2017. "Flood of Change: The Vanport Flood and Race Relations in Portland, Oregon." *Op. cit.*
44. Abbott, Carl. 2019. "Vanport." *Op. cit.*
45. Kahan, James P., Mengjie Wu, Sara Hajiamiri, and Debra Knopman. 2006. *From Flood Control to Integrated Water Resource Management: Lessons for the Gulf Coast from Flooding in Other Places in the Last Sixty Years*. *Op. cit.*
46. Ott, Jennifer. 2013. "Vanport Flood Begins on Columbia River on May 30, 1948." *Op. cit.*
47. Fee, Jambs. 1952. *Clark v. United States, 109 F. Supp. 213 (1952)*. United States District Court for the District of Oregon.
48. Fee, Jambs. 1952. *Clark v. United States, 13 F.R.D. 342 (1952)*. United States District Court for the District of Oregon.
49. Kahan, James P., Mengjie Wu, Sara Hajiamiri, and Debra Knopman. 2006. *From Flood Control to Integrated Water Resource Management: Lessons for the Gulf Coast from Flooding in Other Places in the Last Sixty Years*. *Op. cit.*
50. Skovgaard, Dale. 2007. "Oregon Voices: Memories of the 1948 Vanport Flood." *Oregon Historical Quarterly* 108 (1). JSTOR: 88–106.
51. Harrison, James. 2020. "Vanport Day of Remembrance." *Op. cit.*
52. March, Tanya Lyn. 2010. "Guild's Lake Courts: An Impermanent Housing Project." *Op. cit.*
53. Maben, Manly. 1987. *Vanport*. *Op. cit.*
54. Ott, Jennifer. 2013. "Vanport Flood Begins on Columbia River on May 30, 1948." *Op. cit.*
55. Delli Priscoli, Jerome, and Aaron T. Wolf. 2009. *Managing and Transforming Water Conflicts*. Cambridge University Press. Cambridge, United Kingdom. 384 pp.
56. Fryer, Heather. 2010. *Perimeters of Democracy: Inverse Utopias and the Wartime Social Landscape in the American West*. U of Nebraska Press. Lincoln, NE. 412 pp.
57. Maben, Manly. 1987. *Vanport*. *Op. cit.*
58. Pearson, Ruby. 2007. "Vanport, Oregon (1942–1948)." *Op. cit.*
59. Ibid.
60. Wolf, Aaron T. 2010. *Sharing Water, Sharing Benefits: Working Towards Effective Transboundary Water Resources Management*. UNESCO. Paris, France. 278 pp. http://www.mdgfund.org/sites/default/files/ENV_BOOK_Jordan_International%20Waters.pdf (accessed on December 26, 2020).
61. Ibid.
62. Daniels, Steven E., and Gregg B. Walker. 2001. *Working through Environmental Conflict: The Collaborative Learning Approach*. Praeger Publisher, Westport, CT. 328 pp.

Water Insecurities in Two African–American Communities 175

63 Daniels, Steven E., and Gregg B. Walker. 2012. "Lessons from the Trenches: Twenty Years of Using Systems Thinking in Natural Resource, Conflict Situations." *Systems Research and Behavioral Science* 29: 104–115. https://doi.org/10.1002/sres.2100
64 Maser, Chris, and Lynette de Silva. 2019. *Resolving Environmental Conflicts: Principles and Concepts*. Third Social-Environmental Sustainability. Boca Raton, FL: CRC Taylor and Francis Group, LLC.
65 Daniels, Steven E., and Gregg B. Walker. 2001. *Working through Environmental Conflict: The Collaborative Learning Approach. Op. cit.*
66 Jarvis, W. Todd. 2014. *Contesting Hidden Waters: Conflict Resolution for Groundwater and Aquifers*. Routledge. London, United Kingdom. 210 pp.
67 Ibid.
68 Ibid.
69 Delli Priscoli, Jerome, and Aaron T. Wolf. 2009. *Managing and Transforming Water Conflicts. Op. cit.*
70 Maslow, Abraham Harold.1954. *Motivation and Personality*. Harpers. New York, NY. 369 pp.
71 Kelley, Robert. 1993. "The Context and the Process: How They Have Changed Over Time." In *Water Resources Administration in the United States: Policy, Practice, and Emerging Issues*. Michigan State University Press, East Lansing, MI. 10–22.
72 Lackey, Robert T. 2019. "Environmental Policy and Management: Understanding the Appropriate Role for Science." *Environmental Sciences* 515, October 4, 2019. Oregon State University. Lecture.
73 O'Neill, O. 2002. *A Question of Trust, in Reith Lectures 2002*, on BBC Radio 4. Lectures 1–4. May 27, 2006 transcript accessed on February 23, 2020 at https://immagic.com/eLibrary/ARCHIVES/GENERAL/BBC_UK/B020000O.pdf (accessed on December 26, 2020).
74 Ibid.
75 Robertson, Mary. 2011. "The Constraints of Colour: Popular Music Listening and the Interrogation of 'Race' in Post-apartheid South Africa." *Popular Music* 30 (3). Cambridge University Press: 455–470.
76 Wondolleck, Julia M., and Steven Lewis Yaffee. 2000. *Making Collaboration Work: Lessons from Innovation in Natural Resource Management*. Island Press.
77 U.S. Institute of Peace. 1995. *Truth Commission: South Africa*. www.usip.org/publications/1995/12/truth-commission-south-africa (accessed on December 26, 2020).
78 Bourque, Peter. 2009. "Remembering When GM Employed Half of Flint, Michigan." *Arizona Daily Star*. Published August 2, 2009. https://tucson.com/lifestyles/remembering-when-gm-employed-half-of-flint-michigan/article_e4176079-2b6b-591e-bd13-3ca041c9dcf2.html (accessed on December 26, 2020).
79 Doidge, Mary, Eric Scorsone, Tracy Taylor, Josh Sapotichne, Erika Rosebrook, and Daniella Kaminski. 2015. "The Flint Fiscal Playbook: An Assessment of Emergency Manager Years (2011–2015)." *MSU Extension White Paper*.
80 Ibid.
81 Mostafavi, Beata. 2019. "What Happened Last Time? A Look Back at Flint's 2002 State Takeover." *The Flint Journal*. Updated January 21, 2019; Posted November 10, 2011. www.mlive.com/news/flint/2011/11/what_happened_last_time_a_look.html (accessed on December 26, 2020).
82 Doidge, Mary, Eric Scorsone, Tracy Taylor, Josh Sapotichne, Erika Rosebrook, and Daniella Kaminski. 2015. "The Flint Fiscal Playbook: An Assessment of Emergency Manager Years (2011–2015)." *Op. cit.*
83 Ibid.

84 Pulido, Laura. 2016. "Flint Michigan, Environmental Racism and Racial Capitalism." *Capitalism Nature Socialism* 27 (3): 1–16.
85 Olson, Terese M., Madeleine Wax, James Yonts, Keith Heidecorn, Sarah-Jane Haig, David Yeoman, Zachary Hayes, Lutgarde Raskin, and Brian R. Ellis. 2017. "Forensic Estimates of Lead Release from Lead Service Lines during the Water Crisis in Flint, Michigan." *Environmental Science & Technology Letters* 4 (9): 356–361.
86 Alfonsi, Sharyn. 2020. "Early Results from 174 Flint Children Exposed to Lead During Water Crisis Shows 80% of Them Will Require Special Education Services. CBS. Sixty Minutes: Children of Flint." Aired March 15, 2020. *Produced by Guy Campanile and Lucy Hatcher. Broadcast associate, Cristina Gallotto. Edited by Matt Richman.* www.cbsnews.com/news/flint-water-crisis-effect-on-children-60-minutes-2020-03-15/ (accessed on December 26, 2020).
87 Ibid.
88 EPA. n.d. *Basic Information about Lead in Drinking Water.* Accessed on March 24, 2020 at www.epa.gov/ground-water-and-drinking-water/basic-information-about-lead-drinking-water#health (accessed on December 26, 2020).
89 Alfonsi, Sharyn. 2020. "Early Results from 174 Flint Children Exposed to Lead During Water Crisis Shows 80% of them Will Require Special Education Services. CBS. Sixty Minutes: Children of Flint." *Op. cit.*
90 EPA. n.d. *Basic Information about Lead in Drinking Water. Op. cit.*
91 Ibid.
92 Kennedy, Chinaro, Ellen Yard, Timothy Dignam, Sharunda Buchanan, Suzanne Condon, Mary Jean Brown, Jaime Raymond, Helen Schurz Rogers, John Sarisky, and Rey De Castro. 2016. "Blood Lead Levels among Children Aged< 6 Years—Flint, Michigan, 2013–2016." *Morbidity and Mortality Weekly Report* 65 (25): 650–654.
93 Gómez, Hernán F., Dominic A. Borgialli, Mahesh Sharman, Keneil K. Shah, Anthony J. Scolpino, James M. Oleske, and John D. Bogden. 2018. "Blood Lead Levels of Children in Flint, Michigan: 2006–2016." *The Journal of Pediatrics* 197: 158–164.
94 Alfonsi, Sharyn. 2020. "Early Results from 174 Flint Children Exposed to Lead During Water Crisis Shows 80% of Them Will Require Special Education Services. CBS. Sixty Minutes: Children of Flint." *Op. cit.*
95 KU News Service. 2017. *Flint Water Crisis Led to Lower Fertility Rates, Higher Fetal Death Rates, Researchers Find.* Published September 20, 2017. https://news.ku.edu/2017/09/15/flint-water-crisis-led-lower-fertility-rates-higher-fetal-death-rates-researchers-find (accessed on March 24, 2020).
96 Anderson, E., and J. Wisely. 2016. *Records: Falsified Report Led to Charges in Flint Water Crisis.* Detroit Free Press. Published April 22, 2016. www.freep.com/story/news/local/michigan/flint-water-crisis/2016/04/22/warrant-request-charges-flint-water-crisis/83406590/ (accessed on March 24, 2020).
97 Fonger, Ron. 2015. "Documents Show Flint Filed False Reports about Testing for Lead in Water." *The Flint Journal.* MLive Media Group, November 12, 2015. Web. February 14, 2016. www.mlive.com/news/flint/index.ssf/2015/11/documents_show_city_filed_fals.html (accessed on March 24, 2020).
98 Ahmad, Zahra. 2019. "Former State Officials Charged in Flint Water Crisis Have Criminal Cases Dismissed." Posted December 18, 2019. MLive Media Group. www.mlive.com/news/flint/2019/12/former-state-officials-charged-in-flint-water-crisis-have-criminal-cases-dismissed.html (accessed on March 24, 2020).
99 Egan, Paul. 2019. *All Flint Water Crisis Criminal Charges Dismissed by Attorney General's Office—for Now.* Detroit Free Press, Published June 13, 2019. www.freep.com/story/news/local/michigan/2019/06/13/flint-water-crisis-criminal-charges-dismissed/1445849001/ (accessed on March 24, 2020).

100 Sous, Matthew. 2016. *Restoring the Michigan Referendum*. Michigan State University. http://digitalcommons.law.msu.edu/king/265 (accessed on March 24, 2020).
101 Pulido, Laura. 2016. "Flint Michigan, Environmental Racism and Racial Capitalism." *Capitalism Nature Socialism* 27 (3): 1–16.
102 Moore, N. 2017. "'Missing Lead' in Flint Water Pipes Confirms Cause of Crisis." *Vice President for Communications—Michigan News*. University of Michigan. https://news.umich.edu/missing-lead-in-flint-water-pipes-confirms-cause-of-crisis/ (accessed on March 24, 2020).
103 Meinzen-Dick, R., and R. Pradhan. 2002. "Legal Pluralism and Dynamic Property Rights. CGIAR Systemwide Program on Collective Action and Property Rights." *International Food Policy Research Institute*. Washington, DC.
104 Delli Priscoli, Jerome, and Aaron T. Wolf. 2009. *Managing and Transforming Water Conflicts. Op. cit.*
105 Meinzen-Dick, R., and R. Pradhan. 2002. "Legal Pluralism and Dynamic Property Rights. CGIAR Systemwide Program on Collective Action and Property Rights." *Op. cit.*
106 Ibid.
107 Ibid.
108 Sadoff, Claudia W., and David Grey. 2002. "Beyond the River: The Benefits of Cooperation on International Rivers." *Water Policy* 4 (5): 389–403.

9 A Global Water Solution
An Example of the Sustainable Development Goal Target 6.5

Melissa McCracken

CONTENTS

Introduction 179
The Global Water Crisis 180
Sustainability and Sustainable Development: Foundational Concepts for
Global Solutions 181
   Sustainability 181
   Sustainable Development 181
The Sustainable Development Goal Framework 182
   Sustainable Development Goal 6 on Water and Sanitation 184
The Four Stages of Water Conflict Transformation Framework 186
   Indicator 6.5.2 Methodology 188
   Indicator 6.5.2 and the Four Stages of Water Conflict Transformation 189
Case Study: Indicator 6.5.2 and Uganda 192
   Background on Uganda's International Shared Waters
   and Cooperation 192
   Calculating SDG Indicator 6.5.2 for Uganda 194
   Applying the Water Conflict Transformation Framework
   to the Case Study 196
Summary 199
Further Reading 200
Exercises 200
Notes 201

INTRODUCTION

In 2019, the World Economic Forum identified *water crises* as the fourth highest global risk in terms of impact, after weapons of mass destruction, failure of climate-change mitigation and adaptation, and extreme weather events.[1] This macro-level water threat jeopardizes human life because it diminishes access to clean water and sanitation, creates a world health emergency, stifles education for children and women, and contributes to lost household income and regional economic potential. Such a monumental hazard calls for remedies. So, what is the global *water crisis, and what are some methods we can use to address it*?

This chapter begins with an introduction to the global water crisis and some of the potential solutions, particularly those related to water conflict management and transformation, such as the concept of sustainable development. It then shifts to introduce the Sustainable Development Goal Framework, particularly Indicator 6.5.2, which measures cooperation. Indicator 6.5.2 is then evaluated using the Four Stages of Water Conflict Transformation to understand how it can support constructive conflict transformation and ultimately support solutions to the global water crisis.

THE GLOBAL WATER CRISIS

The World Economic Forum defines a water crisis as "a significant decline in the available quality and quantity of freshwater resulting in harmful effects on human health and/or economic activity."[2] Like this definition, most understandings of the global water crisis emphasize water scarcity as the most significant challenge facing water resources globally. Water scarcity is essentially when the demand for water is greater than the supply. This discrepancy can be due to: (1) a physical lack of water (e.g., not enough precipitation), (2) the inability to store, distribute, and access water (e.g., no pipes or canals to bring water where it is needed), (3) insufficient quality (e.g., the water is available but not clean enough to use), and (4) inadequate institutional capacity to provide the water (e.g., the policy, laws, and governance bodies that manage water).

Thinking about the global water crisis only as a matter of scarcity considers the tip of the iceberg. Population growth, economic development, climate change, and socio-cultural changes are all contributing to the calamity. Social discrimination at the global, regional, and local levels also influences the lack of access and availability of water. For example, water tends to flow toward political power, money, and privilege, creating inequitable access and availability.[3]

How do we address this global water crisis? There is no one-size-fits-all solution. Resolutions could range from changing lifestyles and patterns of consumption (e.g., less meat) to recycling wastewater, addressing pollution, mitigating climate change, improving irrigation efficiency, optimizing agricultural practices, and appropriately pricing water, among many others. Yet at the core of these examples is the need for better management of our water resources and the development of laws, policies, and regulations that enable us to adapt to and address the impacts on a global basis. Although many answers can be derived at the individual, local, and within-state scales, this chapter focuses on the nation-state and international levels.

International transboundary waters are the surface- and groundwaters that cross international, political boundaries. There are 310 international transboundary river basins and nearly 600 transboundary aquifers.[4] Approximately 60 percent of the freshwater-river discharge worldwide comes from an international river basin, and about 45 percent of the world's population resides within these basins.[5] This situation makes it vital to appropriately manage and share these resources in the face of today's growing dilemma.

Political borders add a layer of complexity to the management of water resources. Most countries are dependent on another country for access to their renewable water resources,[6] which highlights the need for cooperation and water conflict transformation. The Four Stages of Water Conflict Transformation Framework can help us develop cooperation over shared waters, as well as understand how different solutions, such as the concept of sustainable development and its application through the Sustainable Development Goals, might help address part of the growing problem. The next section introduces sustainable development as a prominent framework for integrating solutions to the global water crisis, as well as other environmental and social issues.

SUSTAINABILITY AND SUSTAINABLE DEVELOPMENT: FOUNDATIONAL CONCEPTS FOR GLOBAL SOLUTIONS

Solving the global water crisis is an immense challenge, and the concept of sustainable development presents one possible means to provide solutions, particularly at the international scale. For example, "sustainability" is meant to counteract an economic system that has over-exploited natural resources, such as freshwater.[7] The terms *sustainability* and *sustainable development* are often used interchangeably; however, there are differences between the two.

SUSTAINABILITY

The term sustainability has become popular and widely used since the late 1970s.[8] The concept has been distilled into four main principles.[9] The first is that sustainability refers to more than just the natural environment; it includes human society and its economy. Second is the idea that we must live within the biophysical limits of our resources, whether they are renewable or nonrenewable. The third principle acknowledges that sustainability is intergenerational; the biophysical requirements of future generations must be considered. This principle takes inspiration from the Iroquois Confederacy's unwritten constitution, which mandates that the impact on distant generations be addressed in decisions made today. Lastly, sustainability is based on a shift back toward decentralized growth and the shared use of local resources.

SUSTAINABLE DEVELOPMENT

In 1987, the U.N. World Commission on Environment and Development published a report titled *Our Common Future* (generally known as the Brundtland Report), which not only has the most widely cited definition of "sustainable development" but also is the basis for it. The report calls for "a new era of economic growth—growth that is forceful and at the same time socially and environmentally sustainable."[10] This means that standard economic development must be converted to sustainable economic development, as the solution to the social and environmental issues created by unrestrained economic growth.[11] The Brundtland Report defines sustainable development as: ". . . development that meets the needs of the present without compromising the ability of future generations to meet their own needs."[12]

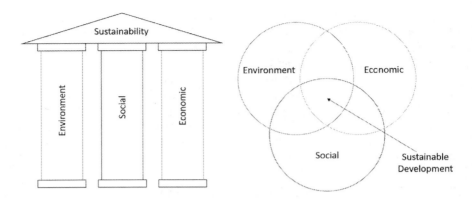

FIGURE 9.1 Pillars of sustainability adapted from Purvis et al. (2019), and tripartite Venn diagram adapted from Barbier (1987).

Today, the most common model of sustainable development is the tripartite Venn diagram or the pillars of sustainable development (Figure 9.1).[13] The three circles, or pillars, represent the three components or dimensions: environmental, economic, and social (sometimes referred to as equity). Sustainable development can only be achieved by balancing the tradeoffs of the three components, while maximizing achievement within each dimension.

The other crucial point in the discussion of sustainable development is that it must be addressed globally. "Humans are part of a single natural (global) system whose parts interact in complex ways," therefore, the national and international level of economies and societies are the most significant level of governance because our system of governance is centered around nation-states.[14] The Brundtland Report echoes this, stating that progress within the three dimensions must be focused on action at the national and international levels.[15]

Coming back to the water problem, the concept of sustainable development and the global impacts of the water crisis both function at the same scale. Thus, any achievements toward sustainable development can simultaneously address the global impacts of the water crisis.

The next section presents the Sustainable Development Goal Framework, which is a method of operationalizing sustainable development to make progress in achieving social, environmental, and economic goals while balancing the tradeoffs among them. Even though this chapter presents the Sustainable Development Goals as a means to help address the water crisis, it is not the only solution. Moreover, there are drawbacks and limitations to what it can achieve.

THE SUSTAINABLE DEVELOPMENT GOAL FRAMEWORK

In 2015, the U.N. General Assembly signed resolution A/RES/70/1 *Transforming our world: the 2030 Agenda for Sustainable Development* (2030 Agenda), which established the Sustainable Development Goal Framework.[16] This resolution was the result of 2 years of international discussions and discussions with civil society,

A Global Water Solution

following the 2012 Rio+20 Conference on Sustainable Development. The conference recognized a need to renew efforts toward sustainable development and emphasized the creation of an international institutional framework centered on the three areas of sustainable development (environmental, economic, and social), which ultimately became the Sustainable Development Goals.[17] The Sustainable Development Goal Framework runs from 2015 through 2030 and replaces and builds on the Millennium Development Goals that expired in 2015.

The Millennium Development Goals were adopted by the U.N. General Assembly through the Millennium Declaration,[18] with the aim of eradicating poverty. They contained eight goals related to poverty and hunger, education, gender equality, child mortality, maternal health, disease, environmental sustainability, and partnerships for development. While significant progress was made globally on achieving the Millennium Development Goals, it was uneven across the globe and among the goals themselves.[19] Therefore, the Sustainable Development Goals were established to both complete the unfinished Millennium Development Goals agenda and to achieve sustainable development.

The Sustainable Development Goals increased the scale, ambition, and interconnection of the international-development agenda compared to the Millennium Development Goals. For example, the Sustainable Development Goals apply to both industrialize and non-industrialize countries and, ideally, can be achieved through an integrated approach. The environmental, economic, and social development priorities are reflected in the 17 Sustainable Development Goals and the 169 targets developed within them (see Box 9.1).[20]

BOX 9.1   THE SUSTAINABLE DEVELOPMENT GOALS

Goal 1: End poverty in all its forms everywhere
Goal 2: End hunger, achieve food security and improve nutrition, and promote sustainable agriculture
Goal 3: Ensure healthy lives and promote well-being for all at all ages
Goal 4: Ensure inclusive and equitable quality education and promote lifelong learning opportunities for all
Goal 5: Achieve gender equality and empower all women and girls
Goal 6: Ensure availability and sustainable management of water and sanitation for all
Goal 7: Ensure access to affordable, reliable, sustainable, and modern energy for all
Goal 8: Promote sustained, inclusive, and sustainable economic growth, full and productive employment, and decent work for all
Goal 9: Build resilient infrastructure, promote inclusive and sustainable industrialization, and foster innovation
Goal 10: Reduce inequality within and among countries
Goal 11: Make cities and human settlements inclusive, safe, resilient, and sustainable

> Goal 12: Ensure sustainable consumption and production patterns
> Goal 13: Take urgent action to combat climate change and its impacts
> Goal 14: Conserve and sustainably use the oceans, seas, and marine resources for sustainable development
> Goal 15: Protect, restore, and promote sustainable use of terrestrial ecosystems, sustainably manage forests, combat desertification, and halt and reverse land degradation and halt biodiversity loss
> Goal 16: Promote peaceful and inclusive societies for sustainable development, provide access to justice for all, and build effective, accountable, and inclusive institutions at all levels
> Goal 17: Strengthen the means of implementation and revitalize the Global Partnership for Sustainable Development

Whereas each of the Sustainable Development Goals can be characterized as achieving environmental, economic, and social goals, they can also overlap to address more than one dimension.[21] However, the aim of the framework is to ensure integration across the interlinked goals, just as the three aspects of sustainable development are interwoven.

Each of the 17 goals has several associated targets. For example, Goal 6 on water and sanitation has six targets plus two implementation targets. These establish more specific actions for countries to achieve, as they work toward sustainability. In addition, each target has one or more indicators, which are developed to assist in the monitoring and global implementation of each target. Various U.N. agencies are responsible for collecting progress reports concerning each target and its indicator, which enables the agencies to monitor how nation-states are progressing in achieving each target and its respective, overarching goal.

Sustainable Development Goal 6 on Water and Sanitation

During the process of developing the Sustainable Development Goal Framework, there was a push to include a specific goal related to water in the 2030 Agenda, which led to Goal 6: Ensure availability and sustainable management of water and sanitation for all. The goal has six targets and two implementation targets, which are detailed in Box 9.2.[22]

> **BOX 9.2   SUSTAINABLE DEVELOPMENT GOAL 6**
>
> *Goal 6: Ensure availability and sustainable management of water and sanitation for all*
>
> 6.1. By 2030, achieve universal and equitable access to safe and affordable drinking water for all

A Global Water Solution 185

> 6.2. By 2030, achieve access to adequate and equitable sanitation and hygiene for all and end open defecation, paying special attention to the needs of women and girls and those in vulnerable situations
> 6.3. By 2030, improve water quality by reducing pollution, eliminating dumping, and minimizing release of hazardous chemicals and materials, halving the proportion of untreated wastewater and substantially increasing recycling and safe reuse globally
> 6.4. By 2030, substantially increase water use efficiency across all sectors and ensure sustainable withdrawals and supply of freshwater to address water scarcity and substantially reduce the number of people suffering from water security
> 6.5. By 2030, implement integrated water resources management at all levels, including through transboundary cooperation as appropriate
> 6.6. By 2020, protect and restore water-related ecosystems, including mountains, forests, wetlands, rivers, aquifers, and lakes
> 6.a. By 2030, expand international cooperation and capacity building support to developing countries in water- and sanitation-related activities and programs, including water harvesting, desalination, water efficiency, wastewater treatment, recycling, and reuse technologies
> 6.b. Support and strengthen the participation of local communities in improving water and sanitation management

Of these, Target 6.5 is of particular importance to our discussion of the global water crisis, the challenge of managing internationally shared waters, and the Four Stages of Water Conflict Transformation. Target 6.5 states, "By 2030, implement integrated water resources management at all levels, including through transboundary cooperation as appropriate."[23] This target was included in Goal 6 because several organizations and stakeholders argued that its inclusion would improve domestic management and transboundary water cooperation.[24] Furthermore, enhancing management and cooperation over water resources is vital to attaining the other water targets and goals.

Two indicators have been developed to help States reach Target 6.5, as well as to assist in monitoring at the international scale:

- Indicator 6.5.1: Degree of integrated water resources management implementation
- Indicator 6.5.2: Proportion of transboundary basin area with an operational arrangement for water cooperation[25]

Sustainable Development Goal Indicator 6.5.1 encourages the development of plans for implementing integrated water resources management at the basin scale, as well as the establishment of institutions.[26] It assesses four components concerning the application of such integrated management: policies, institutions, management tools, and financing. This indicator encourages states to build capacity in their water management at the national level, whereas Indicator 6.5.2 focuses on the international level.

Indicator 6.5.2 identifies the total area of a transboundary basin or aquifer that has an operational arrangement for cooperation. An arrangement is considered to be operational if it has regular communication with respect to data and information, a joint body or organization, and a joint management plan or objectives.[27]

While both indicators (6.5.1 and 6.5.2) promote management that can help nation-states address the water crisis, the rest of this chapter will focus on Indicator 6.5.2 because it aims to measure progress toward transboundary water cooperation. The next question is, how does the Four Stages of Water Conflict Management Framework help us understand the capacity of Indicator 6.5.2 to address the challenges of managing shared waters?

THE FOUR STAGES OF WATER CONFLICT TRANSFORMATION FRAMEWORK

Thus far, we have covered the challenges presented by the global water crisis and noted that political borders make addressing these challenges even harder. To resolve the additional challenges presented by political boundaries, we need better management and cooperation in dealing with water resources. The concepts of sustainability and sustainable development can guide conversations and management practices to be more sustainable in the long term by supporting cooperation and reducing the overall crisis.

Aaron Wolf, a renowned water scholar, regularly states that "water management is conflict management." Therefore, to manage mutual waters, we need to address, resolve, and acknowledge the conflict inherent in sharing these vital resources. Chapter 2 presents the Four Stages of Water Conflict Transformation (see Table 9.1 for a summary), which is a tool for building skills that enable the resolution of conflicts and disputes over water at many scales, including internationally.

The Four Stages of Water Conflict Management was developed by Doermann and Wolf (2012) and draws from the ARIA model developed by Rothman (1989).[29] Consequently, the Four Stages of Water Conflict Transformation Framework identifies four ways of interpreting a water dispute, which correspond to the actions, scope, focus, and type of communication that occur in a negotiation between or among parties sharing surface or groundwaters. These stages are not necessarily linear and can exist simultaneously:

- Stage 1: Adversarial, which is focused on rights, positions, past events, precedence, and actions that may be defensive and competitive
- Stage 2: Reflexive, which begins the shift from rights to interests and needs; motivation behind positions starts to emerge and negotiation becomes less resistant.
- Stage 3: Integrative is consensus building, where group interests coalesce, and discussions become more collaborative and centered on relationships among participants.
- Stage 4: The last, but not necessarily final given their non-linear nature, is Action, which focuses on capacity-building and how the mutual goals are achieved. Potentially, the structures of governance are created or adapted to meet the group's requirements for management.

TABLE 9.1
Four Stages of Water Conflict Transformation Framework.

Summary of four stages of water conflict transformation framework table adapted from doermann and wolf (2012), which draws from rothman's ARIA model (adversarial framing, reflex reframing, inventing, agenda setting)[28]

Type of Process/ Negotiation Stage	Focus of Process	Collaborative and Transformational Skills	Context, Geographic Scope, or Framing for Outcomes	Focus of Process and Participants
Adversarial	Rights	Trust-building; deepening understanding of conflict	State, federal, tribal land, and water laws; priority, jurisdiction, and supremacy/sovereignty of rights	Apply laws and policies to reach a decision; control information to be selective and tactical
Reflexive	Needs and interests	Skills-building in listening for and identifying positions, needs, and interests	Watershed/basins	Content-centered
Integrative	Benefits/values/reframing	Consensus-building; relationship-building	"Problem-shed"/"Benefits-shed"	Relationship-centered; engages the systems within which relationships are embedded; focus shifts to listening/sensing an already existing wholeness; share information
Action	Governance in relation to dynamic systems; equity	Capacity-building; community-building	Networked systems across state, region, and/or country	Create or re-create institutions, policies, structures, and networks from which communities/society can express their new basis of shared meaning, goals, and principles

Much of this book focuses on using this framework to evaluate conversations, negotiation, and conflict scenarios at various scales; however, this tool can also be adapted to evaluate the progress nation-states are making in cooperatively managing their shared resources from a water conflict transformation lens. Now, we are going to take a slightly different approach and consider how a method used to encourage nation-states to cooperate (Indicator 6.5.2) melds with the framework and then evaluate how well it captures what is happening to conflict transformation by using a case study.

INDICATOR 6.5.2 METHODOLOGY

Indicator 6.5.2 measures the "proportion of transboundary basin area with an operational arrangement for water cooperation."[30] To apply the Four Stages of Water Conflict Transformation Framework, we first need to unpack this indicator and the methodology used to measure it.

The indicator's goal is to capture in-place, formal arrangements for sustaining cooperation over transboundary waters. Formal agreements, such as treaties, have been shown to be resilient and maintains cooperation, even in the face of hostile conflict between riparian States over other issues.[31] Historically, cooperation has been more prevalent than conflict over internationally shared waters.[32] Cooperation enables nation-states to negotiate, identify common interests, and prevent any loss of their water resources.[33] We can see these shared interests and benefits in past treaties and negotiated agreements between countries.[34] For example, the Columbia River Treaty, signed between the United States and Canada in 1961, centers on two main benefits to the two countries—the production of hydropower and flood control. These reciprocal benefits are still in place today.

Given the importance of cooperation in overseeing communal water and resolving disputes, teamwork is more likely to be maintained if there is adequate institutional capacity to handle physical and political changes.[35] *Institutional capacity* refers to the treaties, agreements, river basin organizations, and even positive relationships between or among countries.[36] This is an important concept for establishing the potential for resolving disputes or the likelihood that nation-states will be able to continue cooperating in the face of change, such as infrastructure development, alterations in the political system, or a natural disaster.

Therefore, Indicator 6.5.2 aims to capture an interpretation of the institutional capacity for cooperative arrangements between and among nation-states. The agencies responsible for monitoring and reporting on Indicator 6.5.2 (the United Nations Economic Commission for Europe Water Secretariat and the United Nations Educational, Scientific, and Cultural Organization's International Hydrological Programme under the UN-Water's Global Expanded Water Monitoring Initiative) have established two main elements for evaluating this capacity.

First, a shared water resource—either surface or groundwater—must have an arrangement for cooperation. An arrangement, in this sense, is defined as: "a bilateral or multilateral treaty, convention, agreement, or other arrangement, such as a memorandum of understanding, between riparian States that provides a framework

A Global Water Solution

for cooperation on transboundary water management."[37] The arrangement is the formal mechanism signed between nation-states, but it does not mean that cooperation cannot be informal, where there is no signed treaty or agreement between the governments. Informal cooperation can help to build trust, establish positive relationships, and effectively manage communal waters; however, research has shown that formal, signed, legal agreements are more resilient over time and are more likely to be maintained than informal declarations by themselves.

The other element for evaluating cooperation in the indicator is the concept of operational arrangements. For an arrangement to be considered operational, it must have *all* of the following criteria:

1. A joint body or mechanism for transboundary water cooperation
2. Regular, formal communication at the political or technical level at least once per year
3. Joint or coordinated water management plan(s) that provide guidance on combined actions, a common strategy or objective for the status or conditions of the mutual waters
4. Regular exchange of information and data on an annual basis, at a minimum[38]

These criteria are based on the procedural aspects of establishing cooperation and are derived from principles within international water law, specifically: (1) the 1992 Convention on the Protection and Use of Transboundary Watercourses and International Lakes and (2) the 1997 U.N. Watercourses Convention.[39] It is important to reiterate that an arrangement is only considered operational under Indicator 6.5.2 if it meets *all* of the criteria listed previously.

The indicator is calculated by totaling the surface area of the transboundary river basins and aquifers within the country that have an operational arrangement for cooperation, then dividing that number by the total amount of surface area in the country within a transboundary river basin or aquifer. This results in a percentage of the country's transboundary area that has operational cooperation present, which is the indicator's value (see Equation 9.1). It is important to remember that this indicator is focused on a country-level analysis; therefore, the only areas totaled are those within the country the indicator is being calculated for. This does not include the area of the river basin or aquifer in the other riparian countries that share the basin.

$$\text{Indicator 6.5.2}(\%) = \left[\frac{(\text{sum of transboundary area with an operational arrangement})}{(\text{Total transboundary area in the country})} \right] \times 100 \qquad (9.1)$$

INDICATOR 6.5.2 AND THE FOUR STAGES OF WATER CONFLICT TRANSFORMATION

Recall from Chapter 2 that when applying the Four Stages framework to a dispute or negotiation, we begin with identifying the interactions or focus of the interactions between or among the parties, such as content or relationship-centered interactions.

Then we can classify the style of process or negotiation that is occurring, whether it is in the Adversarial, Reflexive, Integrative, or Action stage. Finally, we can identify the skills needed to help transform the conflict and resolve the dispute. When considering the methodology for Indicator 6.5.2, we must take a different approach since we are evaluating the arrangements, which may be the outcome of a previous negotiation(s).

The Sustainable Development Goal Framework, and, subsequently, Indicator 6.5.2, is based solely on the country or nation-state scale. This means that the indicator is inherently going to have a country-specific focus, rather than basin-wide, placing the methodology within the Adversarial stage. From a transformative lens, we ideally want to shift from emphasis on national borders to the watershed, problemshed, or an integrated networked system. This transition is not possible, given the limitations of the framework, as it is an international, country-based initiative. In addition to considering Indicator 6.5.2, let us examine the two components of the methodology: an arrangement and the operational criteria.

Recall that an arrangement is a formal mechanism providing an agenda for transboundary water cooperation. This can fit within any of the Four Stages of the Water Conflict Transformation Framework. For example, in the Adversarial stage, a treaty can legally enshrine the positions and rights of a country, such as detailing the precise volume of water needed for each country in the basin. Alternatively, an arrangement could identify the allocation and timing needed to support domestic and agricultural demands of the countries—their respective interests or needs in the Reflexive stage.

The criteria for determining whether an arrangement is operational for water cooperation could also fit within any of the four stages depending on the content of the arrangement and the context of the cooperative process. However, certain criteria have the potential to promote different stages within the Four Stages of Water Conflict Transformation Framework:

1. *A joint body or mechanism for transboundary water cooperation*: Depending on the context, the creation of a joint body, such as a river-basin organization, has the potential to help States shift into the Integrative and/or Action stages of the framework. Establishing a joint body can help to build trust, establish working or diplomatic relationships (depending on the scale), and help to build capacity for managing the communal waters in a sustainable and equitable manner. However, a joint body could also be explicitly created to control the sharing of information and data, sitting within the Adversarial stages, which could enable States to push for their positions and exert power in the relationship.
2. *Regular, formal communication at the political or technical level at least once per year*: From the water conflict transformation perspective, communication is the heart of shifting from conflictive interactions toward cooperation. While this criterion can fit within any of the four stages, it has the potential to encourage actors to have regular communication, hopefully building trust and relationships, while encouraging active listening to the other actors. Therefore, this criterion has the potential to help States move into the Reflexive and/or Integrative stages.

A Global Water Solution

3. *Joint or coordinated water management plan(s) that provide guidance on combined actions, a common strategy or objective for the status or conditions of the mutual waters*: This criterion fits squarely within the Integrative stage. To achieve this component of operationality, the states must begin to have common goals and think of consensus-building between and among parties. The Four Stages of Water Conflict Transformation Framework can aid nation-states in achieving this criterion. It can help participants develop collaborative processes by shifting their thinking from that of a perceived problem to potential benefits, where joint values are identified, and innovative solutions can be developed that reach beyond defended positions and rights. Ideally, these would be the collaborative management plans or objectives that fulfill the criterion.
4. *Regular exchange of information and data on an annual basis, at a minimum*: Mutually disclosing data and information is a necessity for the cooperative processes to function; however, the quality of data, the extent of data, and the timing of sharing will all impact where data and information exchange falls within the Four Stages of Water Conflict Transformation. Disclosing minimal data on an infrequent timescale could be seen as an adversarial interaction, where trust between the parties is limited. Whereas, data collected in the same manner and openly revealed supports the Action stage. This would create a data/information networked system throughout a river basin or aquifer.

There are two important points to remember when considering the Indicator 6.5.2 methodology through a water conflict transformation lens. First, each element can be within any or multiple of the Four Stages of Water Conflict Transformation, as this will be dependent on the type of arrangement, the cooperative process in place, and the context of the shared-water resource—from both a political and physical context. The hydrology and climate, as well as the political relationships and types of government, can all influence the stage of the arrangement and the criteria for operational cooperation. We will see this exemplified in the case study in the next section. The second point is that the Four Stages of Water Conflict Transformation Framework provides a method for evaluating the degree of conflict transformation in the cooperative process measured by the indicator.

Sustainable Development Goal Indicator 6.5.2 considers operational arrangements for water cooperation to be the same if they meet all four of the criteria. However, not all cooperation is equal or comparable. As shown in the bulleted list previously, interactions that fulfill a criterion are not necessarily equivalent, as they can fall within multiple stages. Using the Four Stages of Water Conflict Transformation Framework to evaluate the results of Indicator 6.5.2 for a particular cooperative process will provide an assessment of the type of cooperation occurring and provide recommendations regarding collaborative and transformative skills that can help to shift how sharing the water is perceived and encourage more constructive outcomes. We will examine this in more detail in the following case study.

CASE STUDY: INDICATOR 6.5.2 AND UGANDA

As we learned in the previous section, there is a significant amount of variability when applying the Four Stages of Water Conflict Transformation Framework to the methodology of Indicator 6.5.2. This section will evaluate the cooperative processes occurring in Uganda over the country's shared river basins and aquifers. Remember, Indicator 6.5.2 is focused on determining the level of operational arrangements for cooperation present at a country level; therefore, this case study is focused on Uganda rather than on a specific river basin or aquifer. First is a brief overview of Uganda's shared water resources and cooperation, then the calculation of the indicator, followed by the application of the Four Stages of Water Conflict Transformation Framework.

BACKGROUND ON UGANDA'S INTERNATIONAL SHARED WATERS AND COOPERATION

Uganda is located in east-central Africa, just north of Lake Victoria. It is a landlocked country, where 100 percent of its land area is within an internationally shared river basin. Uganda is a water-rich country, considering the availability of its renewable water resources. It is heavily dependent on rainfall; therefore, water availability and stress are present, depending on the location and timing of the precipitation.[40] Groundwater is also a primary source for many of the rural and arid areas, where the rate at which water is being pumped from aquifers is lower than the rate at which the aquifers recharge.[41]

Most of the country resides within the Nile River Basin. The other two transboundary surface waters are the Lotagipi Swamp and Lake Turkana[42] (Figure 9.2). Uganda is a middle-stream country in the Nile River Basin, meaning that it is upstream to South Sudan, Sudan, and Egypt and downstream to Burundi, the Democratic Republic of the Congo, Kenya, Tanzania, and Rwanda along the White Nile. The White Nile is one of the two main tributaries (the other is the Blue Nile, which originates in the highlands of Ethiopia) that feed the main stem of the Nile River. In terms of groundwater, three transboundary aquifers have been mapped: Mount Elgon Aquifer, Kagera Aquifer, and Aquifere du Rift.[43] There are likely additional transboundary aquifers, and studies are still ongoing to further define the country's groundwater resources.[44]

Of the three international river basins, the Nile River has had numerous arrangements signed over the last century for sharing its waters. The other two international river basins do not have any endorsed arrangements for cooperation that include Uganda. Prior to the independence of Uganda, several agreements were signed by the British on their behalf that are affecting cooperation over the Nile today. The two most relevant to this discussion are the 1929 Nile Water Agreement, which was created to protect the "natural and historic" rights of Egypt, and the 1950 Agreement for the Cooperation Between the United Kingdom and Egypt, which established cooperation through meteorological and hydrological surveys.[45]

The key aspect of these treaties, and others signed on Uganda's behalf by the British, is that they do not acknowledge the right of Uganda to use the shared water.[46] In 1959, the independent countries of Egypt and Sudan signed an agreement for the

A Global Water Solution 193

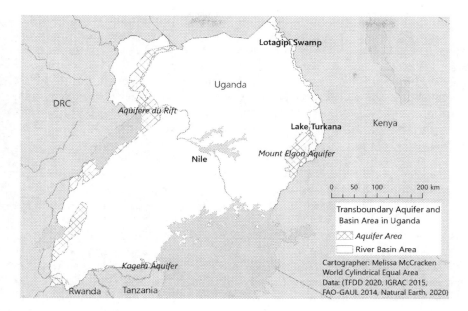

FIGURE 9.2 Transboundary river basins and aquifers in Uganda.
Source: (Data from TFDD 2020, FAO-GAUL 2014, and IGRAC and UNESCO-IHP 2015).

full utilization of the Nile's waters, which excludes the other countries sharing a transboundary river or aquifer and reinforces the dominant positions of Egypt and Sudan in the use of the Nile's waters.[47] Uganda, as well as the other independent countries in the Nile Basin, are in disagreement with the pre-independence treaties and began to develop new cooperative arrangements on the Nile that recognize the rights of all countries within the basin.

After several early agreements were signed, the Technical Cooperation Committee for the Promotion and Development of the Nile was created in 1992 to help the Nile-Basin countries use the river in an integrated manner.[48] This transitional agreement was replaced by the Nile Basin Initiative in 1999. This Initiative is important as it is the first time all the Nile-Basin countries have come together for the development and management of the river. It serves as a transitional arrangement that has the objective of creating a cooperatively agreed-upon framework that is inclusive of all in-basin countries.

Although the task was successful in creating the Cooperative Framework Arrangement, which Uganda signed in 2010, the Democratic Republic of the Congo, Egypt, South Sudan, and Sudan have yet to sign the agreement, which means it still has not entered into force. Egypt and Sudan want a provision included recognizing that the current uses and rights of any basin country would not be adversely affected.[49] This statement essentially attempts to enshrine the dominance of Egypt and Sudan in the use of the Nile and maintain the rights established in the pre-independence agreements.

The upstream nations, including Uganda, reject the inclusion of this provision, arguing that it is inconsistent with the goals of the Nile Basin Initiative, which remains the institutional body on the Nile that Egypt and Sudan—the major opponents of the Cooperative Framework Arrangement—are party to. Therefore, it is still unclear how the disagreement over the Arrangement will be resolved. Transboundary groundwaters hydrologically connected to the Nile River are mentioned briefly in the Arrangement. However, it is not apparent if there is any formal cooperation occurring on both the groundwaters hydrologically connected to the Nile and those not connected to the Nile.

In addition to basin-wide initiatives for cooperation, Uganda is also party to agreements at the sub-basin level. These include the creation of the East African Community, which promotes sustainable growth and equitable development while protecting the environment.[50] Through this organization, Uganda, Kenya, and Tanzania signed the Protocol for Sustainable Development of the Lake Victoria Basin of 2003. Lake Victoria and its watershed are a sub-basin to the great Nile River Basin. This protocol is the foundation for the Lake Victoria Basin Commission, which is responsible for the management of the Lake Victoria watershed and its sustainable use. The indicator includes sub-basin arrangements in its calculation, so both the basin-wide agreements and the sub-basin agreements must consider when calculating the indicator.

CALCULATING SDG INDICATOR 6.5.2 FOR UGANDA

Under the Sustainable Development Goal Framework, nations are asked to report their progress toward achieving the goals, targets, and indicators. For Indicator 6.5.2, the first data collection and reporting exercise were conducted in 2018, with the second data collection currently underway at the time of this writing in 2020.[51] To calculate the indicator, we are going to use the data provided by Uganda in the 2018 reporting exercise.[52] Recall that Indicator 6.5.2 measures the "proportion of transboundary basin area with an operational arrangement for water cooperation" and is calculated through Equation 9.1 listed earlier.

First, we need to identify the transboundary river basins and aquifers in the country and their area. Drawing from the reported numbers used in the official calculation of the indicator for the 2018 assessment in Uganda,[53] we have the areas of the basins and sub-basins in Table 9.2. However, the area of an aquifer is significantly more difficult to determine than the area of a river basin, and area measurements are not as readily available. Consequently, the report uses an estimated area for transboundary aquifers, which does not add up to the total area of the aquifers reported in Table 9.2.

The next step is to determine if the basin or aquifer has an operational arrangement for cooperation by meeting the four criteria defined in the *Indicator 6.5.2 Methodology* section. Of the two river basins identified in the report, only that of the Nile has an arrangement that meets all four criteria for operationality. There are several signed agreements that address the area of the Nile Basin in Uganda, including the Nile Basin Initiative and the Cooperative Framework Agreement (although this is not yet in force).

TABLE 9.2
Transboundary River Basins and Aquifers in Uganda and Their Estimated Areas.

As reported in the 2018 Reporting Exercise for Sustainable Development Goal Indicator 6.5.2. Drawn from Tindimugaya (2017).

Transboundary River Basin/Aquifer Name	Sub-basin name	Surface Area (km²) within Uganda	Is It Covered by an Operational Arrangement for Cooperation within Uganda?
Nile River Basin		126,389	Yes
	Lake Victoria	61,665	Yes
	Lake Edward	18,991	Yes
	Lake Albert	18,068	Yes
	Aswa	27,665	Yes
Kidepo Basin		3,185	No
Mount Elgon Aquifer*		5,398	No
Kagera Aquifer*		5,779	No
Western Rift Valley Sediments*		44,632	No
Total transboundary area with an operational arrangement for cooperation (km²)		126,389	
Total transboundary area (km²)		151,264	
SDG Indicator 6.5.2		84%	

Aquifers noted with an * have an *estimated* area listed. The report does not use these numbers for the calculation of the indicator. Instead, it uses an estimate that 9 percent of the country is underlain by a transboundary aquifer, which is equal to 21,690 km²[254]

With respect to the criteria for operationality, Uganda is a member of the Nile Basin Initiative, which is the current joint body for cooperation on the river. There is regular and formal communication through the Initiative, which meets annually, and through the Technical Advisory Committee of the Cooperative Framework Arrangement, which meets twice per year. Various other sub-groups and committees also meet regularly. Under the Initiative, the countries have developed several policies and joint management strategies on various topics, including gender, environment, and social issues. Lastly, there is regular exchange of data and information, as explicitly outlined in the Arrangement and has been occurring through the Nile Basin Initiative.

There are no arrangements in place on the groundwater aquifers in Uganda. The Cooperative Framework Arrangement acknowledges the hydro-connectivity of surface water and groundwater and that they need to be managed in conjunction. In the future, this could be used to extend the Arrangement to hydrologically connected groundwater underlying the Nile River Basin. Currently, there are some limited projects being conducted through the Initiative, but these do not meet the criteria for operational cooperation.

Now that we have the basin and aquifer areas and know which have an operational arrangement for cooperation, we can calculate the value of the Indicator 6.5.2, as shown in Table 9.2. Under the 2018 reporting exercise, Uganda's Indicator 6.5.2 is 84 percent. This means that 84 percent of the area within a transboundary river basin or aquifer has an operational arrangement for cooperation.

Applying the Water Conflict Transformation Framework to the Case Study

With Indicator 6.5.2 for Uganda calculated, we can apply the Four Stages of the Water Conflict Transformation Framework. The indicator value from the 2018 reporting exercise is 84 percent for the total transboundary basin area, but this can be broken down into values for surface water only (98 percent) and groundwater only (0 percent). Regardless of whether the value is presented in an aggregated or disaggregated state, the indicator is only showing the extent of the area with operational arrangements for cooperation in Uganda.

This outcome is inherently centering the indicator within the Adversarial stage, as the methodology limits the focus on cooperation to the nation—irrespective of whether the cooperative process is taking a basin-wide or integrated approach. Therefore, to better understand the indicator results for Uganda through the transformative lens, we again have to look at the components of the indicator's calculation: the arrangements and the criteria for operationality.

To briefly reiterate, there are several formal arrangements signed by Uganda or signed by the British prior to Uganda's independence. For the purpose of the calculation, the Nile Basin Initiative and the Cooperative Framework Arrangement are the two agreements cited as having the criteria for operational cooperation in the Nile River Basin, which is the only transboundary surface or groundwater area in Uganda that meets all four of the criteria. As described in the section on *Background on Uganda's International Shared Waters and Cooperation*, the Initiative is the first time all the countries within the Nile Basin came together to sign a transitional arrangement focused on drafting a permanent arrangement for the management and use of the river. While the Arrangement, to which Uganda is a signatory, is the outcome of efforts within the Initiative, it is not currently enforced.

The stage these agreements fit within differs on paper vs. in practice. On paper, based on the outlined goals of the agreements, they fall within the Reflexive and Integrative stages. However, in practice, the Cooperative Framework Arrangement has not been signed by all of the countries, primarily due to the rights-based issue described in the *Background on Uganda's International Shared Waters and Cooperation* section, placing the Arrangement within the Adversarial stage. Nevertheless, the wording and intent behind the agreements, as well as the relationships among some of the participants, highlights the potential for these agreements to shift in practice from the Adversarial stage to the Reflexive and Integrative stages.

A Global Water Solution 197

After considering the arrangements as a whole, it is time to consider the four criteria and their stages within the Four Stages of Water Conflict Transformation Framework for Uganda:

1. *A joint body or mechanism for transboundary water cooperation*: Uganda is a member of the Nile Basin Initiative, which is also the institution for consultation and coordination among the concerned parties. The institution has several main objectives, including "to ensure cooperation and joint action between the riparian countries, seeking win-win gains."[55] This institution generally falls within the Reflexive and Integrative stages, depending on the functions considered.

    One of its three core functions is developing trust and confidence by providing a neutral, inclusive forum wherein the participants can engage one another, demonstrating a focus on relationship building.[56] Other functions, such as the projects on management and development, highlight the content-centered goals of the Initiative. This joint body is a good example of how the Four Stages of Water Conflict Transformation Framework can exist simultaneously and not necessarily be in a linear progression. The stage reflects the context of the negotiation or process among the representative of the various countries.

2. *Regular, formal communication at the political or technical level at least once per year*: Communication is the heart of water conflict transformation and is a core criterion for Indicator 6.5.2. This criterion measures the frequency of formal consultations. The Cooperative Framework Arrangement outlines specific mechanisms for formal discussions, such as mandating that the Technical Advisory Committee of the Cooperative Framework Arrangement meet twice a year. In addition, various committees and subgroups meet within the framework of the Nile Basin Initiative, including Uganda. Ideally, regular communication supports trust and builds compatible relationships, placing these personal values within the Integrative stage.

    However, the interactions and negotiations that occur within these mandates are highly contextual and will depend on who is involved and what the topics for discussion are. Consequently, we must be cautious about asserting that a mechanism for communication equates to having positive trust and relationship-building interactions. Whereas this aspect of the case study demonstrates the ability of the Four Stages of Water Conflict Transformation Framework to critique the outcomes of the Indicator 6.5.2, it also shows that, just because a method directing a formal exchange of ideas is present, it does not mean beneficial, transformative interactions are occurring.

3. *Joint or coordinated water management plan(s) that provides guidance on the joint actions, a common strategy or joint objective for the status or conditions of the shared waters*: As discussed in the section concerning *Indicator 6.5.2 and the Four Stages of Water Conflict Transformation*, this criterion fits within the Integrative stage. Uganda, in conjunction with other members of the Nile Basin Initiative, has developed several joint objectives and strategies.

For example, the Initiative has a "Shared Vision Objective," which is "to achieve sustainable socio-economic development through equitable utilization of, and benefit from the shared Nile Basin water resources."[57] The Initiative has developed a 10-Year Strategy with six goals addressing water security, energy security, food security, environmental sustainability, climate change adaptation, and transboundary water governance to help with the achievement of this objective.[58] These objectives and goals are shared, which demonstrates that joint values have been established for the basin, ideally by a shift in thinking about the basin and its mutual benefits.

4. *Regular exchange of information and data at least once per year*: The exchange of data and information have been occurring between Uganda and the other countries through the Nile Basin Initiative. In addition, there are specific mechanisms for sharing data in the Cooperative Framework Arrangement. The disclosing of data and information centers around each country's environmental conditions, the transboundary impacts from current and future projects, and water discharge and extraction through projects managed by the Initiative.[59] Data and information exchanged through these specific projects fall within the Reflexive stage.

This exchange is limited, however, to specific projects conducted through the Initiative, which might indicate an emphasis on the needs and interests of the within-basin countries. Although these needs and interests could be established jointly, indicating the Integrative stage, further exploration and examination of the specific projects is needed to clearly determine whose interests are represented. In addition to this regular exchange of data and information, there is joint monitoring of hydrological elements on the main stem of the Nile, which has a harmonized monitoring protocol.[60] This process would fall within the Action stage, as there is a common network for collecting, monitoring, and sharing information among the countries within the Initiative's protocol.[61]

As shown in this case study, applying the Four Stages of Water Conflict Transformation Framework to evaluate the methodology and results of Indicator 6.5.2 requires a different approach than when applying the framework to a dispute or a negotiation. Instead of contemplating an interaction, we are considering formal, legal mechanisms and arrangements, which are often an outcome of a negotiation process. This is due to the Indicator's focus on the procedural elements of cooperation—e.g., regular meetings and the exchange of data and information.

Applying the water transformation lens allows us to see more nuance in these elements. As we saw in the Uganda case study, meeting all four criteria can be done in a variety of ways. This yields the same result in the calculation of the indicator—fulfillment of the criteria, but will be represented differently when viewed through the Four Stages of Water Conflict Transformation Framework. For example, the two different methods of data and information exchange in the Nile River Basin, which are in two different stages of the framework, both equally satisfy the methodology of

Indicator 6.5.2. In addition, this case study highlights that the Four Stages of Water Conflict are not necessarily a linear progression, so multiple stages can exist simultaneously, as we can see in the discussion of the Nile Basin Initiative.

Ultimately, it is important to remember that the place and context of the shared water resource will impact the type of arrangement and its procedures, thereby influencing its stage within the framework. Understanding of the context, hydrology, and political relationships are necessary to appropriately apply the Framework in evaluating the results of Indicator 6.5.2 or a particular outcome of a cooperative process.

SUMMARY

In this chapter, we have been focusing on how the Four Stages of Water Conflict Transformation Framework can be applied to the results and methodology of Sustainable Development Goal Indicator 6.5.2, which measures the extent of arrangements with operational cooperation in a particular country of interest. As we can see in the case study of Uganda, the Framework provides more nuance and detail in the interpretation of the results of the Indicator's calculation. While the Indicator measures the presence of procedural elements dealing with institutional capacity, the lens of water conflict transformation helps us, as well as practitioners and stakeholders, evaluate the type of communication and the focus of the process of cooperation, e.g., rights, needs, and interests.

However, such evaluation requires a slightly different approach to using the Four Stages of Water Conflict Transformation Framework, since we are evaluating the results of the Indicator's calculation, rather than a specific conflict or dispute. Therefore, when applying the Framework to appraise the methodology of a Sustainable Development Goal Indicator, we need to consider: (1) What is the focus of the criteria that fulfills the indicator? Is it rights, needs, or benefits? and (2) What are the context, geographic scope, and framing of the aspects that fulfill the indicator's criteria? By applying the framework through these guiding questions, we can identify the stage of the component that satisfies the Indicator's methodology. Once the stage has been recognized, collaborative and transformative skills can also be verified. These skills can aid in transforming a nation's cooperative arrangement to be more equitable and sustainable, as well as satisfying the criteria for Indicator 6.5.2.

Indicator 6.5.2 is one of over 150 indicators that have been developed to monitor and encourage countries to increase their sustainable development, as a part of the Sustainable Development Goal Framework. The application of the Four Stages of Water Conflict Transformation can help achieve the goal of Indicator 6.5.2, which is to globally increase the extent of cooperation on transboundary waters by encouraging countries to increase aspects of their institutional capacity. Along with the other indicators and targets developed to support Sustainable Development Goal 6 on water and sanitation, Indicator 6.5.2, when strengthened by the Four Stages of Water Conflict Transformation Framework, has the potential to increase transboundary water cooperation, support sustainable development, and ultimately provide a method for addressing the global water crisis at the global scale.

FURTHER READING

United Nations, 2015. *Transforming our world: The 2030 Agenda for Sustainable Development*. Available at: https://sustainabledevelopment.un.org/post2015/transformingourworld/publication

United Nations: Water, 2019. *Progress on Integrated Water Resources Management: Global Basins for Sustainable Development Goal Indicator 6.5.1* Available at: www.unwater.org/publications/progress-on-integrated-water-resources-management-651/

United Nations: Water, 2019. *Progress on Transboundary Water Cooperation: Global Baseline for Sustainable Development Goal Indicator 6.5.2* Available at: www.unwater.org/publications/progress-on-transboundary-water-cooperation-652/

EXERCISES

1. Countries have submitted the first round of data for the 2018 reporting exercise of the *Sustainable Development Goal Framework*. Of the 153 countries that share transboundary river basins, Indicator 6.5 2 has been calculated for 62 countries around the world.[62] You can access the summary in the *Progress on Transboundary Water Cooperation: Global Baseline for Sustainable Development Goal Indicator 6.5.2* report.[63] This report finds the most common criterion lacking in basins with non-operational criteria to be that nations had neither synchronized management plans nor objectives.[64] What collaborative and transformative skills would you recommend to nations trying to develop both joint management plans and objectives to meet this criterion for Indicator 6.5.2?

2. In addition to Indicator 6.5.2, Indicator 6.5.1, which measures the "degree of integrated water resource management implementation." It also helps to promote water management and tools to sustainably address the global water crisis. Likewise, management at the subnational scale encounters conflicts and disputes that can be supported by the Four Stages of Water Conflict Transformation Framework. Read more about the methodology for measuring integrated water resource management through Indicator 6.5.1 here: www.sdg6monitoring.org/indicator-651/.

    You can also read the report: *Progress on Integrated Water Resources Management: Global Basins for Indicator 6.5.1*. After looking at the methodology, how do you think the Four Stages of Water Conflict Transformation can be applied to Indicator 6.5.1? In what ways can the Framework support nations in developing strategies for integrated water resources management?

3. The *Sustainable Development Goal Framework* is meant to be integrative and holistic; when taken together, the goals help countries increase their sustainable development. Several of the other goals, targets, and indicators could help support Sustainable Development Goal 6 on water and sanitation (www.sdg6monitoring.org/) in addressing the global water crisis.

    Explore the other 17 Goals and their targets on https://sdgs.un.org/goals. What other goals, targets, or indicators do you think could support countries in their collaborative management of transboundary surface and groundwaters? Are there other goals, targets, and/or indicators that could support conflict management and cooperation over national or domestic waters? What about at the local or community scale?

NOTES

1 World Economic Forum and Zurich Insurance Group, *Global Risks 2019: Insight Report*, 2019, www3.weforum.org/docs/WEF_Global_Risks_Report_2019.pdf.
2 Ibid.
3 E. Erik Swyngedouw, *Social Power and the Urbanization of Water: Flows of Power*, Oxford Geographical and Environmental Studies (Oxford and New York: Oxford University Press, 2004); Azad Henareh Khalyani, Audrey L. Mayer, and Emma S. Norman, "Water Flows Toward Power: Socioecological Degradation of Lake Urmia, Iran," *Society & Natural Resources* 27, no. 7 (July 1, 2014): 759–767, https://doi.org/10.1080/08941920.2014.905890; Ranran Wang, Edgar Hertwich, and Julie B. Zimmerman, "(Virtual) Water Flows Uphill toward Money," *Environmental Science & Technology* 50, no. 22 (November 15, 2016): 12320–12330, https://doi.org/10.1021/acs.est.6b03343.
4 Melissa McCracken and Aaron T. Wolf, "Updating the Register of International River Basins of the World," *International Journal of Water Resources Development* 35, no. 5 (March 29, 2019): 732–782, https://doi.org/10.1080/07900627.2019.1572497; IGRAC and UNESCO-IHP, "Transboundary Aquifers of the World Map 2015," *International Groundwater Resources Assessment Centre*, 2015, www.un-igrac.org/resource/transboundary-aquifers-world-map-2015.
5 McCracken and Wolf, "Updating the Register of International River Basins of the World."
6 FAO-Aquastat, *Contribution of Transboundary Water to the Total Renewable Water Resources (%)* (FAO, 2015).
7 Jeremy L. Caradonna, *Sustainability: A History* (New York: Oxford University Press, 2014), https://ebookcentral.proquest.com/lib/orbis/detail.action?docID=1745809.
8 Ibid.; Charles V. Kidd, "The Evolution of Sustainability," *Journal of Agricultural and Environmental Ethics* 5, no. 1 (March 1992): 1–26, https://doi.org/10.1007/BF01965413.
9 Caradonna, *Sustainability*.
10 Brundtland Commission, *Our Common Future* (World Commission on Environment and Development, 1987), https://sustainabledevelopment.un.org/content/documents/5987our-common-future.pdf.
11 Ben Purvis, Yong Mao, and Darren Robinson, "Three Pillars of Sustainability: In Search of Conceptual Origins," *Sustainability Science* 14, no. 3 (May 2019): 681–695, https://doi.org/10.1007/s11625-018-0627-5.
12 Brundtland Commission, *Our Common Future*.
13 Caradonna, *Sustainability*; Edward B. Barbier and Joanne C. Burgess, "The Sustainable Development Goals and the Systems Approach to Sustainability," *Economics: The Open-Access, Open-Assessment E-Journal*, 2017, https://doi.org/10.5018/economics-ejournal.ja.2017-28; Purvis, Mao, and Robinson, "Three Pillars of Sustainability"; Jacobus A. Du Pisani, "Sustainable Development—Historical Roots of the Concept," *Environmental Sciences* 3, no. 2 (June 2006): 83–96, https://doi.org/10.1080/15693430600688831.
14 Erling Holden, Kristin Linnerud, and David Banister, "Sustainable Development: Our Common Future Revisited," *Global Environmental Change* 26 (May 1, 2014): 130–139, https://doi.org/10.1016/j.gloenvcha.2014.04.006.
15 Brundtland Commission, *Our Common Future*.
16 United Nations, *Transforming Our World: The 2030 Agenda for Sustainable Development* (New York: United Nations, 2015).

17 United Nations, *The Future We Want: Outcome Document of the United Nations Conference on Sustainable Development* (Rio de Janeiro: Rio+20 United Nations Conference on Sustainable Development, June 20, 2012), https://sustainabledevelopment.un.org/content/documents/733FutureWeWant.pdf.
18 U.N. General Assembly, "United Nations Millennium Declaration," A/RES/55/2 § (2000).
19 United Nations, *The Millennium Development Goals Report 2015* (United Nations, 2015).
20 United Nations, *Transforming Our World: The 2030 Agenda for Sustainable Development*.
21 Barbier and Burgess, "The Sustainable Development Goals and the Systems Approach to Sustainability."
22 United Nations, *Transforming Our World: The 2030 Agenda for Sustainable Development*.
23 UN-Water, "Integrated Monitoring Guide for SDG 6: Targets and Global Indicators" (UN-Water, July 19, 2016).
24 Paul Taylor, "National Stakeholder Consultations on Water: Supporting the Post-2015 Development Agenda," *The Post-2015 Water Thematic Consultation* (Stockholm: Global Water Partnership, 2013), https://sustainabledevelopment.un.org/content/documents/1815nationalstakeholder.pdf; Schweizerische Eidgenossenschaft, "Swiss Position Paper on Water in the Post-2015 Agenda" (Schweizerische Eidgenossenschaft, December 20, 2013), www.swisswaterpartnership.ch/wp-content/uploads/2014/07/2013.12.20_Swiss_Position_on_Water_in_Post2015_Agenda.pdf; UN-Water, "A Post-2015 Global Goal for Water: Synthesis of Key Findings and Recommendations from UN-Water" (UN-Water, January 27, 2014), www.un.org/waterforlifedecade/pdf/27_01_2014_un-water_paper_on_a_post2015_global_goal_for_water.pdf.
25 UN-Water, "Integrated Monitoring Guide for SDG 6: Targets and Global Indicators."
26 Ibid.
27 Ibid.
28 Julia Doermann and Aaron T. Wolf, *Sharing Water, Building Relations: Managing and Transforming Water Conflict In the U.S. West—A Professional Skills-Building Workbook* (Denver, Colorado: U.S. Bureau of Reclamation, September 2012); Jay Rothman, "Supplementing Tradition: A Theoretical and Practical Typology for International Conflict Management," *Negotiation Journal* 5, no. 3 (1989): 265–277, https://doi.org/10.1007/BF01000672; Jay Rothman, "The ARIA Contingency Approach to Identity-Based Conflicts," in *The Encyclopedia of Peace Psychology* (Blackwell Publishing Ltd, 2011), http://onlinelibrary.wiley.com/doi/10.1002/9780470672532.wbepp133/abstract.
29 Doermann and Wolf, *Sharing Water, Building Relations*; Rothman, "Supplementing Tradition"; Rothman, "The ARIA Contingency Approach to Identity-Based Conflicts."
30 UN-Water, "Integrated Monitoring Guide for SDG 6: Targets and Global Indicators."
31 Aaron T. Wolf, "Conflict and Cooperation along International Waterways," *Water Policy* 1, no. 2 (April 1998): 251–265, https://doi.org/10.1016/S1366-7017(98)00019-1; Shira B. Yoffe and Aaron T. Wolf, "Water, Conflict and Cooperation: Geographical Perspectives," *Cambridge Review of International Affairs* 12, no. 2 (March 1999): 197–213, https://doi.org/10.1080/09557579908400256; Aaron T. Wolf, "Shared Waters: Conflict and Cooperation," *Annual Review of Environment and Resources* 32, no. 1 (November 2007): 241–269, https://doi.org/10.1146/annurev.energy.32.041006.101434.
32 Wolf, "Conflict and Cooperation along International Waterways"; Aaron T. Wolf, Shira B. Yoffe, and Mark Giordano, "International Waters: Identifying Basins at Risk," *Water Policy* 5, no. 1 (February 2003): 29–60, https://doi.org/10.2166/wp.2003.0002.
33 Sara McLaughlin Mitchell and Neda A. Zawahri, "The Effectiveness of Treaty Design in Addressing Water Disputes," *Journal of Peace Research* 52, no. 2 (March 1, 2015): 187–200, https://doi.org/10.1177/0022343314559623.

A Global Water Solution   203

34 Mark Giordano et al., "A Review of the Evolution and State of Transboundary Freshwater Treaties," *International Environmental Agreements: Politics, Law and Economics* 14, no. 3 (February 25, 2013): 245–264, https://doi.org/10.1007/s10784-013-9211-8.
35 Wolf, Yoffe, and Giordano, "International Waters."
36 Wolf, "Shared Waters."
37 UNECE Water Secretariat, *Step-by-Step Monitoring Methodology for SDG Indicator 6.5.2 2020* (UN-Water, January 25, 2020).
38 Ibid.
39 U.N. Statistics, *Metadata Goal 6 Ensure Availability and Sustainable Management of Water and Sanitation for All* (United Nations, March 31, 2016), http://unstats.un.org/sdgs/files/metadata-compilation/Metadata-Goal-6.pdf.
40 Francis N. W. Nsubuga, Edith N. Namutebi, and Masoud Nsubuga-Ssenfuma, "Water Resources of Uganda: An Assessment and Review," *Journal of Water Resource and Protection* 6, no. 14 (2014): 1297–1315, https://doi.org/10.4236/jwarp.2014.614120.
41 Nicholas Kilimani, "Water Resource Accounts for Uganda: Use and Policy Relevancy," *Economic Research Southern Africa* (August 2013), www.up.ac.za/media/shared/61/WP/working_paper_365.zp39427.pdf.
42 McCracken and Wolf, "Updating the Register of International River Basins of the World."
43 IGRAC and UNESCO-IHP, "Transboundary Aquifers of the World Map 2015."
44 FAO, "Uganda" (FAO AQUASTAT, 2015), www.fao.org/nr/water/aquastat/countries_regions/UGA/print1.stm.
45 Emmanuel Kasimbazi, "Uganda: Sovereignty and International Water Agreements," in *A History of Water*, ed. Terje Tvedt, Owen McIntyre, and Tadesse Kassa Woldetsdik, Vol. 2, Series III (London: I.B. Tauris & Co. Ltd., 2015), 686–707; Emmanuel B. Kasimbazi, "The Impact of Colonial Agreements on the Regulation of the Waters of the River Nile," *Water International* 35, no. 6 (December 7, 2010): 718–732, https://doi.org/10.1080/02508060.2010.533642.
46 Kasimbazi, "Uganda: Sovereignty and International Water Agreements."
47 Kasimbazi, "The Impact of Colonial Agreements on the Regulation of the Waters of the River Nile."
48 Richard Paisley and Taylor W. Henshaw, "Transboundary Governance of the Nile River Basin: Past, Present and Future," *Environmental Development* 7 (July 2013): 59–71, https://doi.org/10.1016/j.envdev.2013.05.003.
49 Salman M.A. Salman, "The Nile Basin Cooperative Framework Agreement: A Peacefully Unfolding African Spring?," *Water International* 38, no. 1 (January 2013): 17–29, https://doi.org/10.1080/02508060.2013.744273.
50 EAC, *Treaty Establishing the East African Community (EAC)* (2000), www.eac.int/treaty/.
51 UNECE Water Secretariat, "Reporting under the Water Convention and Sustainable Development Goal 6.5.2," *UNECE Water Convention* (2020), www.unece.org/water/transboundary_water_cooperation_reporting.html.
52 If you want to see what other countries reported for their SDG Indicator 6.5.2. you can do so here: www.unece.org/water/transboundary_water_cooperation_reporting.html
53 Callist Tindimugaya, *Reporting on the Global SDG Indicator 6.5.2—Uganda* (Geneva: UNECE Water Secretariat and UNESCO-IHP, September 26, 2017), www.unece.org/fileadmin/DAM/env/water/activities/Reporting_convention/All_countries/UGANDA_Reporting_SDG652_final_29.09.2017.pdf.
54 Ibid.
55 Nile Basin Initiative, *Who We Are | Nile Basin Initiative (NBI)* (2020), www.nilebasin.org/nbi/who-we-are.

56 Ibid.
57 Nile Basin Initiative, *NBI Strategy | Nile Basin Initiative (NBI)* (2020), www.nilebasin.org/what-we-do/nbi-strategy.
58 Ibid.
59 Tindimugaya, *Reporting on the Global SDG Indicator 6.5.2—Uganda*.
60 Ibid.
61 Ibid.
62 United Nations, *Progress on Transboundary Water Cooperation 2018: Global Baseline for SDG 6 Indicator 6.5.2* (U.N., 2019), 2, https://doi.org/10.18356/f6afa45b-en.
63 The report Progress on Transboundary Water Cooperation: Global Baseline for SDG Indicator 6.5.2 can be accessed at: www.unwater.org/publications/progress-on-transboundary-watercooperation-652.
64 United Nations, *Progress on Transboundary Water Cooperation 2018*.

10 Religious Worldviews, Environmental Values, and Conflict-Management Traditions

Josiah J. Shaver

CONTENTS

Introduction 206
   Building on Shared Values 207
   Ancient Conflict Management Principles with Modern Applications 208
   Trying to Summarize the Complexity of Religions 208
Native American Traditions 209
Familial Environmental Ethics 209
Community Environmental Ethics 210
   Conflict Resolution Traditions of the Native Americans 211
      Peacemaking Circles: Equality and Agreement 211
      Connections to the Four Stages 212
   Conclusion 212
Hinduism 212
   Introduction 212
   Reincarnation, Karma, and Hindu Environmental Principles 213
   Historical and Modern Hindu Environmental Movements 213
      The Chipko Movement: Tree Huggers 213
      Climate Change and Modern Actions 214
   Hindu Conflict Resolution Teachings 214
      Peacefulness: Three Meanings of Śanti 214
      The Four Steps of Conflict Progression 215
      Divine Sandals in the Room 215
   Vishnu's Four Stages 215
   Conclusion 215
Buddhism 216
   Environmental Teachings of the Buddha 216
   Ecological Momentum in Contemporary Buddhism 217
      From the Dalai Lama 217
      Saving Trees by Ordaining Them 217

DOI: 10.1201/9781003032533-11

The Time to Act Is Now: A Buddhist Declaration
on Climate Change 218
Buddhist Nonviolence and Conflict Resolution Paradigm 218
    Extreme Nonviolence: A Teaching 219
    Intense Reflection 219
    The Story of a War Averted with a Question 219
The Four Stages and the Four Noble Truths 220
Conclusion 220
Islam 220
Environmental Standards from the Qur'an 220
Words of the Prophet 221
Islamic Declaration on Climate Change 222
Conflict Management Dynamics in Islam 222
Four Stages within Islam 224
Conclusion 224
Judaism 224
Judeo-Christian Foundations in Environmental Ethics 224
    The Role of Humans: A Question of Interpretation 225
    Biblical Stewardship Environmental Ethics 225
    Further Jewish Teachings on Nature 226
    Jewish Response to Climate Change 226
Judaism and Conflict Management 227
Judaism and the Four Stages of Water Conflict Transformation 228
Conclusion 228
Christianity 228
A Christian View of Nature: Scriptural Foundation with Judaism 228
    Catholic Statements on Environmental Issues 229
    Evangelical Voices on Climate Action 229
Christian Conflict Resolution Principles 230
    Seven Seeds of Peace: Resolving Conflict with Pastor Rick Warren 230
The Four Stages Applied to Christianity 232
Conclusion 232
Epilogue 233
Notes 233

INTRODUCTION

> *In the Western world it is widely held that only positivistic reason and the forms of philosophy based on it are universally valid. Yet the world's profoundly religious cultures see this exclusion of the divine from the universality of reason as an attack on their most profound convictions. A reason which is deaf to the divine and which relegates religion into the realm of subcultures is incapable of entering into the realm of cultures.*
> —Pope Benedict XVI, The Regensburg Lecture, 2006[1]

The vast majority of the world is religious. Data from the Pew Research Center (2017) documenting the human population in 2015 indicates that close to one third is Christian and approximately one quarter is part of the Islamic faith. Sixteen percent of the world claim no religious affiliation and 15 percent are associated with Hinduism. The other world denominations are characterized as Buddhism (6.9 percent), Folk religions (5.7 percent), other religions (0.8 percent), and Judaism (0.2 percent).[2] This information may prove useful in addressing questions such as: How can we best work with religious groups? More specifically, how can we address conflicts over natural resources when the stakeholders are primarily religious? And, what do religions have to offer environmental conflict management?

These are two main questions this chapter explores. The first centers around major world religions and how they view nature, especially in regard to climate change. The second is how world religions approach conflict.

In a world brimming with traditional religious values, the importance of understanding religion, as cultural conditioning, cannot be overstated. Consider what is likely to happen if we tried to work with a religious group without first understanding their values and traditions. The result could be confusion; misunderstanding; perceived insult; dishonor to their customs, religion, and people; or even open conflict.

In a world full of challenges that require teamwork, we cannot afford to repeat the mistakes of history. We must find a better way.

BUILDING ON SHARED VALUES

This chapter explores the environmental standards and traditional approaches to conflict of six major groups: Native Americans, Hindus, Buddhists, Muslims, Jews, and Christians. Here's the main idea: there's more that unites us than divides us. We have more in common than we often think.

In 2019, I helped organize an event at Oregon State University called *Deeper than Science: A Panel of Environmental Ethics Perspectives.* We hosted a local Zen Buddhist leader, a Muslim community member, a Jewish rabbi, and a Christian pastor. As they shared parts of their stories and values about nature, I noticed two common threads. First, all of these religious leaders felt an obligation to protect the environment, reflecting an idea that most of them called "stewardship." And, second, they wanted to make sure their children would have a healthy planet to live in. They wanted to preserve nature for future generations. Despite all the things that divide us, there are some values that we can all get behind. Whether we realize it or not, many of us share the same values: kindness, justice, peace, integrity, and love.

What we may disagree about is how those values should be applied in the practical world. That is to be expected. The world is a complicated place with a lot of moving parts. However, if we have similar core values, and if we have a similar idea of what we want the world to be like for our children, what is to stop us from coming together to create that world?

While this may sound too optimistic, contemplate the role religious leaders play in the world. Consider how many people will get behind an idea if a religious leader (like the Pope or the Dalai Lama) endorse it. Millions can rally behind a common cause when they know how it relates to their core values. Author Eric Weltman was right when he said, "Faith leaders have an extraordinary amount of credibility on any issue that they care to address. They have the capacity to reach out to their congregants and mobilize, engage, recruit and involve them."[3]

ANCIENT CONFLICT MANAGEMENT PRINCIPLES WITH MODERN APPLICATIONS

While the first major topic of this chapter focusses on worldviews of nature, the second focusses on worldviews of *conflict*. What are the main values that drive the various strategies of conflict resolution? What steps are outlined for resolving conflict? And how can those principles help us today, as we deal with conflicts over natural resources, water, and the impacts of climate change?

Dr. Aaron Wolf, an experienced, international water conflict mediator, wrote, "Both faith and water ignore separations and boundaries. Thus, they offer vehicles for bringing people together, and because they touch all we do and experience, they also suggest a language by which we may discuss our common future."[4]

The same logic applies to most conflicts over natural resources. Do trees follow national borders? How about fish? Diseases? Climate conditions? Storms? Therefore, as we work with religious communities on these issues, we would do well to learn from their traditional models of conflict resolution. Not only will they be more open to those approaches but also there is plenty that all of us can learn from their teachings.

TRYING TO SUMMARIZE THE COMPLEXITY OF RELIGIONS

The Four Stages of Water Conflict Transformation is a framework introduced in Chapter 2, which facilitates creative solutions to mitigate disputes. In Table 10.1, the negotiation stages (adversarial, reflective, integrative, and action) in the framework are correlated with the physical, emotional, mental, and spiritual "levels of holiness." In Table 10.1, the spiritual, transformative expression of conflict management demonstrates that faith-based traditions can be an instrument to harmony through community building, fostering collective action, and shared visions. However, while studying these worldviews, I found it difficult to apply the framework in a way that fits perfectly.

It is easier to notice trace elements of the Four Stages of Water Conflict Transformation sprinkled throughout the various aspects of each cultural worldview. Although a number of connections to the Four Stages of Water Conflict is included at the end of every section, there are many connections that I have not made.

Each of these intricate worldviews has been around for thousands of years. There are nuances in every religion that people have studied all of their lives and not fully understood. With this in mind, please understand that I am only able to scratch the surface of these worldviews in this chapter, and there is much more to discover within each.

Worldviews are like an orchard. Imagine different religions like different fields with different fruit. Apples, oranges, bananas . . . But there are also different kinds of apples in the Apple Field. And these are not uniform apple trees in uniform rows. The trees are different, old and young, tall and short. And the fruit is different. Red apples, yellow apples, green apples. Moreover, no apple is identical to another.

So, it is with religions. Tribes, denominations, sects, subgroups of subgroups, and so on all have their own nuanced views, which often come down to a person's individual perspective.

TABLE 10.1
The Four Stages of Water Conflict Transformation and "Levels of Holiness".[5,6,7,8,9,10]

Negotiation Stage[11]	Common Water Claims[12]	Collaborative Skills[13]	Geographic Scope	Levels of Holiness (Sinai, Temple, Prayer Service)[14]
Adversarial	Rights	Trust-building	Nations	Physical
Reflexive	Needs	Skills-building	Watersheds	Emotional
Integrative	Benefits	Consensus-building	"Benefit-sheds"	Mental
Action	Equity	Capacity-building	Region	Spiritual

Source: This framework is built mainly on the works of Jay Rothman,[15,16,17] Kaufman,[18,19] and Wolf.[20] This table is modified from Figure 6.1 in Jerome Delli Priscoli and Aaron T. Wolf. *Managing and Transforming Water Conflicts.* Cambridge University Press, New York, New York, 2009, 354 pp. It also includes work from Table 10.1 in Lynette de Silva L., and Aaron T. Wolf. Lessons from Transformative Practices for Water Diplomacy, In *Handbook of Water Resources Management*, Edited by Bogardi J.J., Bandalal K.D.W., van Nooyen R.R.P., and Bhaduri A. Springer International Publishing *(in press).*

With all these differences, this chapter paints with broad strokes. I have used generalizations and highlighted common themes. I have also relied heavily on the words of experts and religious leaders, or even gone back to the original religious texts themselves. Hopefully, with this approach, I have avoided making my own, incorrect interpretations or speaking wrongly on behalf of a major worldview. But, even then, I have probably made some mistakes.

In reading this chapter, I encourage you to further explore anything that catches your eye. There is much more under the crust of this pie.

NATIVE AMERICAN TRADITIONS

"The frog does not drink up the pond in which he lives."

—Lakota proverb[21]

"Treat the earth well: it was not given to you by your parents, it was loaned to you by your children. We do not inherit the Earth from our Ancestors, we borrow it from our Children."

—Crazy Horse, a Lakota tribal leader[22]

FAMILIAL ENVIRONMENTAL ETHICS

The Lakota Native American Tribe (also known as the Sioux, pronounced "soo") once lived in modern-day Minnesota, Wisconsin, Iowa, North Dakota, and South Dakota. *Relationships* define the Lakota view of nature because they hold a genuine respect for other life form believing they are related to nature through a deep, familial bond. According to Lakota lore, the sky is a great father figure and the earth is a mother figure. With the sky and earth as parents, everything else—the mountains, the rivers, the trees, the animals—become part of a large, extended family.

The implications of this view are profound and long-lasting. It sets the foundation for a relationship defined by mutual dependency and mutual care between people and nature. Natural unity and a sense of oneness with the environment are key defining traits of the Lakota worldview.

When pressured to give up native land and adopt a more "American" lifestyle, the Wanapum spiritual leader, Smohalla, made this dramatic reply:

> You ask me to plow the ground. Shall I take a knife and tear my mother's bosom? You ask me to dig for stone. Shall I dig under her skin for bones? You ask me to cut grass and make hay and sell it, and be rich like white men. But how dare I cut off my mother's hair?[23]

This quote illustrates the intensity with which many Native American tribes hold as their convictions about nature.

"Pantheism" is the idea of many gods that together compose the universe. Some philosophers would describe this environmental worldview as "Pan*en*theism", meaning not that elements of nature *are* gods, but that divine spirits *reside inside* elements of nature, like the trees, earth, and animals. J. Baird Callicott, author of *Earth's Insights: A Multicultural Survey of the Ecological Ethics from the Mediterranean Basin to the Australian Outback*, is one such scholar.[24]

However, at the same time, the Lakota do not just see the spiritual world as a list of distinct spiritual entities inside separate elements of nature. Every member is part of the whole, which they call the Great Spirit. This Great Spirit is part of everything—every plant, animal, and mineral—and gives life and consciousness to all. Thus, every member of this natural family plays its part in the intricate, beautiful dance of life in harmony. Some would describe this worldview as Animism.

One final Lakota tradition I will mention is their Vision Quest. Lakota spiritual leaders would fast in remote locations and wait for a kind of epiphany or revelation from the Great Spirit. The purpose was to "contact with a power broker from the spirit world in the form of a bird, animal, or natural phenomenon (such as thunder), experienced in an altered state of consciousness like a dream or hallucination."[25]

Thus, we see that Lakota tradition requires honor and protection for nature because natural elements contain both family members and divine spirits, which mutually guide leaders and tribes.

COMMUNITY ENVIRONMENTAL ETHICS

The Ojibwa are a First Nations tribe with large populations in Canada and northern midwestern United States, around Lake Superior. Although the Ojibwa had similar standards to the Lakota for interacting with the environment, the legends behind those standards are quite different. The Ojibwa essentially view nature and animals as trading partners. This means there is a give and take dynamic between people and

Religious Worldviews, Environmental Values

the elk, the deer, and the trees. When an Ojibwa hunter killed an animal for food, there was a deep sense of respect and reverence. These creates a sense of balance between natural-resource consumption and the needs of the tribe. While the tribe must take enough to survive, stripping too much from the earth would offset the fairness of this respectful relationship and could bring misfortune.

Therefore, to ensure favorable trading relationships with nature, the Ojibwa would take negotiations a step further. Their legends describe *intermarriage* between their people and animals to secure favorable relationships. J. Baird Callicott describes the idea like this,

> just as intertribal social relations and mutual goodwill were cemented my intermarriage between tries, so the interspecies social relations and mutual goodwill—on which the Ojibwa felt their survival to depend—were cemented by intermarriage between species in the ambiguous past/present of story time.[26]

These marriages often resulted in the human coming back occasionally to offer some wisdom about nature. Consider the message behind this legend called "The Woman Who Married a Beaver":

> Thereupon she plainly told the story of what happened to her while she lived with the beavers. She never ate a beaver. . . . And she was wont to say: "Never speak you ill of a beaver! Should you speak ill of a beaver, you will not be able to kill one."
>
> Therefore such was what the people always did; they never spoke ill of the beaver, especially when they intended hunting them. . . . Just the same as the feelings of one who is disliked, so is the feeling of the beaver. And he who never speaks ill of a beaver is very much loved by it; in the same way as people often love one another, so is one held in the mind of the beaver; particularly lucky then is one at killing beavers.[27]

Thus, we see both the intricate relationship between nature and the Ojibwa people, as well as the implied consequences of damaging this relationship.

CONFLICT RESOLUTION TRADITIONS OF THE NATIVE AMERICANS

Peacemaking Circles: Equality and Agreement

As the modern, Western framework of litigation, trials, and arbitration leaves many participants exhausted of resources and sometimes also real resolution, a number of traditional, indigenous groups have looked back to their native traditions for resolving disputes, wondering if there might be a better way forward by examining the past. The Native American people are certainly one such group of searchers.

Peacemaking Circles stand in stark contrast to the modern legal framework of aggressive trials and hierarchy, as Smith Carson, summarizes for the Choctaw Nation of Oklahoma:

> Peacemaking Circles, a form of indigenous conflict resolution, have been traditionally used in several Native American communities and continue to be used in a variety of settings today; such models challenge the adversarial processes we often see in the western courtroom, which inevitably shapes the American understanding of conflict.

Instead, this system relies on all impacted parties to join together and openly air their grievances of a conflict, while being moderated by a third-party, participant—the Peacemaker. The case has only been settled when all participants can unanimously agree on a resolution.[28]

This conflict resolution framework has even gained a favorable reputation among some tribal judicial authorities, including the Chickasaw Nation. Tribal members of the Chickasaw Nation have, in some cases, incorporated Peacemaking Circles in their communities and courts. This approach is especially favored when dealing with small-scale conflicts, such as domestic disputes.[29]

Connections to the Four Stages

At this point in the book you are probably quite familiar with the Four Stages of Water Conflict Transformation, so I will numerically summarize the applications within conflict resolution, as practiced by some tribes.

While there are still plenty of legal battles between native tribes and national and state agencies, some tribes have been dissatisfied with this adversarial (Stage 1) approach to fighting over legal rights, especially for small-scale disputes. Alternatively, Peacemaking Circles offer a chance for all parties to express their needs (Stage 2), build consensus (Stage 3), and hopefully agree on a mutually beneficial path forward (Stage 4).

CONCLUSION

Native Americans often illustrate the value of nature through analogies, such as "Mother Earth." The Lakota people viewed elements of nature as family members, whereas the Ojibwa people saw elements of nature as honored trading partners. These cultural views reflect the core values of respect, balance, peace, and harmony between people and nature. As for strategies of conflict resolution, we can learn from peacemaking circles, where everyone's voice is heard and resolutions must be unanimously agreed upon.

HINDUISM

> "Ether, air, fire, water, earth, planets, all creatures, directions, trees and plants, rivers and seas, they are all organs of God's body. Remembering this a devotee respects all species."
>
> —Srimad Bhagavatam (11.2.41)[30]

INTRODUCTION

Summarizing the beautiful intricacies of a religion as deep and broad as Hinduism is indeed a daunting task. Here we will merely glance briefly into Hindu thought and tradition. We will take a quick look at reincarnation, karma, and the holiness of Ganges River, and then shift toward the clear framework and applications for conflict resolution in the Hindu scriptures. We will also look at a few examples of these ancient values on modern practice.

Reincarnation, Karma, and Hindu Environmental Principles

Hinduism is defined by religious pluralism. More specifically, some Hindus (but not all) believe in polytheism, the belief in multitude gods and spiritual beings. These deities often take the form of natural elements, like fire, water, and wind. This idea inherently places value on these natural elements, since harming them can be seen as harming the god within them.[31]

In Hinduism, there is a fundamental concept called *Rtam* (equivalent to truth in action, Cosmic rhythm, equilibrium, echo-system), where everything is connected to and balanced by others. It simply means that everything is united. Not a single atom can move without taking the whole universe with it. *Rtam* denotes the unity of Existence. Therefore, we are related with our environment, and if we harm our environment, we harm ourselves.

Another core principle of Hinduism is *reincarnation*. For some Hindus, this simply means humans today may have taken the form of other living things in past lives—such as trees, worms, or other animals—and they will likely take the form of another life form in future lives. Reincarnation implies the concept that *all* life has inherent unity and must be treated with reverence. This ethic is reflected in the Hindu principle of *ahimsa*:

> The term ahimsa, of non-injury to all living creatures, is cast in the negative, *a-himsa*, but its import is clearly positive. It calls for a loving care of everything in nature. It demands that we accept responsibility for being guardians of, as well as participants in, the natural order and balance of things.[32]

Karma is another closely linked principle. It means that, "every action has consequences and that there is a causal relationship between one's actions and one's future fate, even in subsequent lifetimes."[33]

Hindus also consider all rivers to be sacred, especially the Ganges River in India. The Ganges is the site of many Hindu religious practices, including bathing to remove sins, worshipping, drinking the water, and the depositing of ashes from the remains of the deceased. As you might expect, these traditions raise some health concerns. They also raise some environmental concerns. In an environmental analysis of Hindu tradition, it was noted that:

> Religious activities do constitute a part of those problems, especially when it comes to the pollution of bodies of water that hold religious and ritualistic significance to the Hindu communities. There have been various studies on how worshipping activities like the Kumbh Mela festivals, the annual Ganesh Chaturthi festivals, or the daily aarthi ceremonies contribute to the pollution problem for rivers such as the Ganges and the Yamuna, especially with the use of religious offerings that are usually non-biodegradable and often contain heavy metals or plastic.[34]

Historical and Modern Hindu Environmental Movements

The Chipko Movement: Tree Huggers

The most popular example of Hindu environmental values in action is perhaps the famous Chipko movement of the 1970s, when the needs of rural villagers in India were being severely overlooked. Government-backed foreign timber companies were preparing to harvest vast areas of forest that held significant importance to the native Hindu people there. Aside from the spiritual significance, these forests were also key elements of the local water purification system, helped stabilize slopes in very landslide-prone areas, and helped to prevent flooding. At one point, the government summoned all the men from a village to another area, possibly foreseeing some kind of a protest, as the logging company moved in to cut trees down. With the men of the village gone, the women rose to the occasion. As the word *chipko* means "to hug," that is exactly what the women did.

They put themselves between the loggers and the trees, hugging the trees. In addition to Hindu principles, they followed the nonviolent principles pioneered by Mahatma Gandhi, a devout Hindu. And it worked! The trees were not cut, and, in most cases, the loggers had to move on.

In addition to the "tree hugging" strategy, the members of the Chipko movement also used such strategies as fasting, bandaging trees with sap-collecting tape around them, and stealing the tools of loggers.

As the movement spread, more than 159 villages were involved and more than 12 major protests were organized, not including many other smaller protests. The results included large-scale logging bans in India, the formation of the "Save Himalaya" movement, and the planting of over 1 million trees.[35]

Climate Change and Modern Actions

At the 2009 Parliament of World Religions, the Convocation of Hindu Spiritual Leaders adopted the inaugural Hindu Declaration on Climate Change to make an official statement about climate action. The declaration was reiterated in preparation for the Paris Climate Conference in 2015, when it gained recognition from Hindu leaders around the world. This statement incorporated *dharma*, a Hindu term often translated as "duty." It describes standards for people to live by in good standing with everything and everyone. The Hindu Declaration on Climate Change stated that it is a, "dharmic duty [to ensure that] we have a functioning, abundant, and bountiful planet."[36]

Like-minded Hindu groups have taken it upon themselves to make Hindu traditions more sustainable, like the Bhumi Project, which created a Green Temples Guide to encourage green, renewable, infrastructure and energy.[37,38]

HINDU CONFLICT RESOLUTION TEACHINGS

"An eye for an eye will only make the whole world blind."

—Mahatma Gandhi

"The weak can never forgive. Forgiveness is the attribute of the strong."
—Mahatma Gandhi, All Men are Brothers: Autobiographical Reflections

Peacefulness: Three Meanings of Śanti

Hindus often will end their prayers with the phrase, "Om Śanti Śanti Śanti," a phrase that reinforces the three meanings behind the word "Śanti." This concept

Religious Worldviews, Environmental Values

incorporates principles of resolution, peace, gentleness, and avoiding unnecessary disputes. The three meanings are:

1. *Adhidaivika*: Sorrows from natural calamities, e.g., earthquake, famine, flood
2. *Adhibhautika*: Sorrows from other creatures, like snake bite or an attack by an enemy army
3. *Ādhyātmika*: Sorrows due to our mental or physical diseases, like fever and epilepsy or due to our spiritual ignorance that can cause feelings of delusion, etc.[39]

The Four Steps of Conflict Progression

Hindu tradition offers four steps to be followed when dealing with conflicts. They say this progression should be followed so the world is not overwhelmed with conflicts:

1. *Sāma*: Counseling, appealing to reason and rationale
2. *Dāna*: Offer sops, or forgive, or let go
3. *Bheda*: Threats of bad consequences if the opponent does not concede or mend his ways
4. *Danda*: Punishment through violence or other means[40]

Divine Sandals in the Room

Hindu gods are considered to be the *legal owners* of their temples in modern India. This creates a unique relationship between parties when a conflict arises, because the god must be involved if all parties are to reach a mutually agreeable solution. The god is a key stakeholder in the situation.

Thus, Hindu monks will often bring sandals with them to the resolution meetings. They will simply place the sandals on a chair during the stakeholder meeting to remind participants of the god's presence. Members of these meetings have reported much different feelings during the negotiation process.

VISHNU'S FOUR STAGES

Consider this section on Hinduism and the Four Stages from Dr. Aaron Wolf's *The Spirit of Dialogue*:

> In Hinduism, we learn about the sequence as body, mind, intellect, and AUM, or unity. Each deity can express each of these four aspects. Consider Vishnu's four totems—a mace (physical strength), a lotus flower (the glory of existence), a discus (representing the mind *chakra*), and the conch (representing the AUM through the primeval sound of creation).[41]

CONCLUSION

So, does Hinduism provide a sufficient platform to resolve conflicts over natural resources? Absolutely. Hindu traditions and Holy Scriptures paint a world where everything and everyone have inherent value. One of the main goals is a beautifully intricate world in complete harmony. Divine beings live alongside mortal creatures, watching. There are even supernatural consequences for misconduct and incentives for harmonious living. As for guidance on conflict resolution, Hinduism offers structure, principles, and examples. And, while the goal is complete harmony, Hinduism provides specific provisions when confrontation is necessary. Nevertheless, it was Mahatma Gandhi, a humble Hindu, who developed the art of nonviolent protesting with world-changing effect.

BUDDHISM

> Many problems that confront us today are created by man, whether they are violent conflicts, destruction of the environment, poverty or hunger. These problems can be resolved thanks to human efforts by understanding that we are brother and sister and by developing this sense of closeness. We must cultivate a universal responsibility toward each other and extend it to the planet that we have to share.
>
> —His Holiness the XIV Dalai Lama

ENVIRONMENTAL TEACHINGS OF THE BUDDHA

Buddhism is comparable to Hinduism in some respects. Similar to the Hindu concept of reincarnation, Buddhists Both believe in *rebirth* as the continuation of karmic tendencies. Both religions originated in India, and believe in forms of karma and ahimsa, and recognize the interconnectedness of all things. Thus, the environmental standards derived from each are parallel, but with differences.

We will start with what the Buddha taught in India in the sixth century. While the people of that time were not faced with ecological disasters on the scale of modern climate change, the Buddha still taught simple principles for both human and ecological health, such as making sure human waste stayed far from water sources.[42]

The Buddha also taught that all life is sacred. In fact, this is one of Buddhism's *Five Precepts of ahimsa* (meaning *harmlessness*). Some Buddhists take this precept quite literally and take extra measures to make sure they do not cause *any* death at all, even going so far as to carefully remove worms from excavation sites. The principle is quite clear: causing damage to any plant, animal, or person is unacceptable.[43]

The second of the Five Precepts condemns stealing. What you might not expect, however, is the way some Buddhists apply this standard to the ecological world. They consider disturbing an ecosystem to be *stealing* the resources, environment, and chances for life of the impacted species.

Buddhists believe in rebirth, which means that they will be directly influenced by their conduct here in this life. The Buddha taught that the origin of all pain and suffering is *desire* (wanting, longing). Desire for wealth, power, self-promotion, and so on causes all the unpleasant things in the world, including conflict, war, and disease. Therefore, part of the path to enlightenment includes seeing the nature of desire within oneself, which Buddha did to reach enlightenment.

So, can Buddhism provide a solid foundation for environmental stewardship? Certainly. According to Bhikku Bodhi, a contemporary Buddhist philosopher:

> With its philosophic insight into the interconnectedness and thoroughgoing interdependence of all conditioned things, with its thesis that happiness is to be found through the restraint of desire, with its goal of enlightenment through renunciation and contemplation and its ethic of noninjury and boundless loving-kindness for all beings, Buddhism provides all the essential elements for a relationship to the natural world characterized by respect, care, and compassion.[44]

Ecological Momentum in Contemporary Buddhism

From the Dalai Lama

As the figurehead of modern Tibetan Buddhism, His Holiness the XVI Dalai Lama has incredible potential to direct Buddhist standards around the world. And, he has been using his platform effectively for decades. In fact, the Dalai Lama has been quoted in saying that, "If science proves facts that conflict with Buddhist understanding, Buddhism must change accordingly. We should always adopt a view that accords with the facts."[45] This statement is a surprise to some people because it appears to place proven scientific facts on a higher level of truth than contradictory Buddhist beliefs.

Concerning environmental standards, the Dalai Lama made this public statement from New Delhi, India, in 1992:

> if in our generation we exploit every available thing: trees, water, mineral resources or anything, without bothering about the next generation, about the future, that's our guilt, isn't it? So if we have a genuine sense of universal responsibility, as the central motivation and principle, then from that direction our relations with the environment will be well balanced. Similarly with every aspect of relationships, our relations with our neighbors, our family neighbors, or country neighbors, will be balanced from that direction.[46]

Two years later, in 1994, on Tibetan Democracy Day, the Dalai Lama urged his followers to take several practical steps toward conservation. He encouraged them to plant a diverse variety of trees wherever they could, to plant flowers also, to teach their children to protect (and not harm) the trees and flowers, and to reexamine their waste-disposal habits and live more sustainably. Moreover, the Dalai Lama is not the only Buddhist leader to make a stand for saving the environment.

Saving Trees by Ordaining Them

For over 25 years, a Buddhist monk in northeast Thailand, named Phrakru Pitak Nanthakthun, has been "ordaining" trees. In the face of mass deforestation and ecosystem destruction, this monk found that giving such an honorable status to a tree, along with a cloth robe to represent its new position, was enough to dissuade people from cutting the trees down. So that is what Nanthakthun does. He and his followers perform the ceremonial rites and wrap a holy robe around the trees facing danger. For these Buddhists, this is a practical application of the faith that they live by.

Concerning this movement, Susan M. Darlington wrote this explanation in her 1998 essay "The Ordination of a Tree: The Buddhist Ecology Movement in Thailand":

> The "ecology monks" are those actively engaged in environmental and conservation activities and who respond to the suffering which environmental degradation causes. A major aim of Buddhism is to relieve suffering, the root causes of which are greed, ignorance, and hatred. The monks see the destruction of the forests, pollution of the air and water, and other environmental problems as ultimately caused by people acting through these evils, motivated by economic gain and the material benefits of development, industrialization, and consumerism. As monks, they believe it is their duty to take action against these evils. Their actions bring them into the realm of political and economic debates, especially concerning the rapid development of the Thai economy and control of natural resources.[47]

The Time to Act Is Now: A Buddhist Declaration on Climate Change

In conjunction with the 2015 Paris Climate Conference, thousands of Buddhist teachers around the world, including the Dalai Lama, signed a decisive statement titled: "The Time to Act Is Now: A Buddhist Declaration on Climate Change." Some highlights are:

> warming from reaching catastrophic "tipping points." For human civilization to be sustainable, the safe level of carbon dioxide in the atmosphere is no more than 350 parts per million (ppm). This target has been endorsed by the Dalai Lama, along with other Nobel laureates and distinguished scientists. Our current situation is of profound concern since the level is already 400 ppm, and has been rising at 2 ppm per year. We are challenged not only to reduce carbon emissions, but also to remove large quantities of carbon gas already present in the atmosphere.
>
> As signatories to this statement of Buddhist principles, we acknowledge the urgent challenge of climate change. We join with the Dalai Lama in endorsing the 350 ppm target. In accordance with Buddhist teachings, we accept our individual and collective responsibility to do whatever we can to meet this target, including (but not limited to) the personal and social responses outlined above.
>
> We have a brief window of opportunity to take action, to preserve humanity from imminent disaster and to assist the survival of the many diverse and beautiful forms of life on Earth. Future generations, and the other species that share the biosphere with us, have no voice to ask for our compassion, wisdom, and leadership. We must listen to their silence. We must be their voice, too, and act on their behalf.[48]

BUDDHIST NONVIOLENCE AND CONFLICT RESOLUTION PARADIGM

> When we face problems or disagreements today, we have to arrive at solutions through dialogue. Dialogue is the only appropriate method. One-sided victory is no longer acceptable. We must work to resolve conflicts in a spirit of reconciliation and always keep in mind the interests of others.
>
> —Dalai Lama[49]

Religious Worldviews, Environmental Values 219

Extreme Nonviolence: A Teaching

Peace is paramount for the Buddhist. According to a BBC report, "Nothing in Buddhist scripture gives any support to the use of violence as a way to resolve conflict."[50]

A Vietnam veteran was overheard rebuking the Vietnamese Buddhist monk, Thich Nhat Hanh, who was asked how he would respond if he were the last Buddhist on Earth and his life was at risk, and he could save himself and his religion by killing the challenger. Thich Nhat Hanh said, "in killing I would be betraying and abandoning the very teachings I would be seeking to preserve. So, it would be better to let him kill me and remain true to the spirit of the Dharma."[51]

Intense Reflection

Buddhists believe that our own desires cause suffering in the world. This is the problem that every person has to deal with. Thus, before addressing external conflicts, Buddhist teaching requires examining personal, internal conflicts that may stem from greed, desire, and so on. It is also recommended to stay open-minded and try to avoid seeing things as purely black and white, or exclusively right and wrong because of the incredible diversity found in real-life conditions, relationships, and disagreements. Conflict rarely impacts just two people.[52]

On a similar note, it is recommended to neither criticize nor compliment people. Like the *ad hominem* rhetorical strategy, arguments for or against the person (rather than the actions of that person) are not encouraged. In an essay on conflict resolution, the Buddhist mediator Andrew Olendzki wrote, "Both praise and blame evoke a sense of self, and the self always shows up ready to fight." He goes on to encourage a more rational, impersonal approach:

> It may be a modest contribution, but let's see whether following the Buddha's suggestion of using depersonalized language to critique harmful thoughts, words, and deeds, rather than attacking the people who wield them, can help end some of the fighting and muffle the call to battle.[53]

The Story of a War Averted with a Question

Reframing a scenario with excellent questions is another strategy that Buddhists employ to aid conflict resolution. Consider this quote from Dr. Aaron Wolf's *The Spirit of Dialogue* that states,

> asking the right question at the right time can have just the impact.... Phra Paisan Visalo, the Buddhist monk and mediator, often poses this question to affect a shift: "If you get what you are asking for, what will be the impact on the community?" He says he models his approach on that of the Buddha, who was able to stop a war with just one question.[54]

The story centered around two communities, the Sakyans and the Koliyans, that shared the waters of the Rohini River. However, when water availability started to decline, both communities claimed ownership of the water resource and were prepared to go to war over it. The Buddha hearing of this, asked the community leaders, "is water worth more than the blood of your subjects?" And thus, the war was averted.[55]

The Four Stages and the Four Noble Truths

The Four Noble Truths are core principles that provide overarching guidance to Buddhists in their pursuit of enlightenment. Dr. Wolf points out the clear connections to our Four Stages of Water Conflict Transformation in the Four Noble Truths given in the following:

1. All is impermanent (physical).
2. The source of suffering is craving (emotional).
3. *Nirvana* is the cessation of suffering (knowing).
4. The path to *nirvana* is the eightfold path (spiritual).[56]

Conclusion

The principles of Buddhism have incredible potential to help us resolve conflicts over natural resources and climate change. The intrinsic value of all life, the implications of karma, and the Buddhist's view of everything as interconnected all provide environmental values with which to build trust. And, while Buddhism might not provide a cut-and-dry, step-by-step process for conflict resolution, the principles of self-reflection, finding harmony, and asking the right questions are great advice. Perhaps, the most encouraging factor is that contemporary leaders, like the Dalai Lama, have been forcefully applying Buddhist principles to modern problems.

ISLAM

> *"Do not waste water even if you were at a running stream."*
> —Prophet Muhammad (peace be upon him) Sunan Ibn Majah 425[57]

> *"And the retribution for an evil act is an evil one like it, but whoever pardons and makes reconciliation—his reward is [due] from Allah. Indeed, He does not like wrongdoers."*
> —Ash-Shura 42:40 (Sahih International)[58]

Environmental Standards from the Qur'an

> *"There is no joy in life unless three things are available: clean fresh air, abundant pure water, and fertile land."*
> —Imam Sadiq[59]

The Qur'an, which is the central text of Islam, lays out standards for environmental interactions. In Islam, there is just one supreme God, Allah. Messages and standards were passed from Allah to his Prophet Muhammad and then to the people. The

Qur'an recognizes the interconnectedness and interdependence of all life and alludes to a "Mother Earth." In Islam, people are *more important* than plants and animals. While Allah created all life, it is only the humans who have eternal souls, which sets them apart from all other creatures. Further, Earth is not the final destination of a Muslim. Earth is a temporary place, where a person's actions may, or may not, allow them to enter Paradise when they die.[60]

In the analysis of human-environmental relations from Islam, some Muslims conclude the following, considering the coming judgment from Allah:

> how we [Muslims] respond to local and global environmental challenges as a community is critical. When we enter the court of The Almighty and are called to trial, witnesses will be brought forth, I wonder whether the Earth will act as a witness for us or against us?[61]

Given these fundamental dynamics for the Muslim, there are at least two common views on nature and the environment. First, there is the Mastery Perspective, which views all natural resources and animals as the subjects of the humans, there to do their bidding and support people at all times. Second, is the Stewardship Perspective, which still sees people as the authority over nature, but requires humans to *take care* of the environment as temporary trustees, managers, or stewards of the land. Humans are discouraged from exploiting nature and animals. In fact, the Qur'an gives a detailed list of requirements for how animals must be treated. This list includes providing food and water for one's animals, providing favorable locations for feeding and watering them, and inflicting minimal pain when hunting/killing animals.[62] If these principles are scaled to the ecosystem level, this implies the obligation to maintain healthy ecology.

In a clearer directive, the Qur'an maintains that all creatures display the glory of Allah. Thus, people should preserve this glory for others to observe, even for future generations. While some Muslims might hesitate to make sacrifices for the sake of the environment alone, making sacrifices for the benefit of future generations is highly encouraged. Planting trees is considered an act of worship for Muslims.[63] In fact, Allah promises rewards for good deeds like these.[64] When asked about rewards, the Prophet said, "There is a reward in doing good to every living thing."[65]

WORDS OF THE PROPHET

Consider the emphasis on justice and natural balance in the following excerpt from the Qur'an:

> The All-Merciful has taught the Qur'an. He created man and He taught him the explanation. The sun and the moon to a reckoning, and the stars and trees bow themselves; and heaven—He raised it up and set the balance. Transgress not in the balance, and weigh with justice, and skimp not in the balance. And Earth—He set it down for all beings, therein fruits and palm trees with sheaths, and grain in the blade, and fragrant herbs. Which of your Lord's bounties will you deny?

(Qur'an 55:1–12)[66]

In addition to encouraging gratitude for our natural resources, this passage establishes the principle of balance in nature. It also supports the idea of harmony among our natural systems.

Water resources management is another topic the Qur'an touches on. When addressing a conflict between a camel and the Thamud people, according to the historian, Ibn Kathir, the Prophet responded by saying, "And tell them the water shall be shared between them" (Qur'an 54:28).[67] This reinforces the idea that natural resources must be shared with all creatures.

ISLAMIC DECLARATION ON CLIMATE CHANGE

In the summer of 2015, Muslim leaders from 20 countries gathered to write a unified statement on climate change from the Islamic community around the world. Here is just a piece of their bold statement:

> We are in danger of ending life as we know it on our planet. This current rate of climate change cannot be sustained, and the earth's fine equilibrium (mīzān) may soon be lost.
>
> We particularly call on the well-off nations and oil-producing states to lead the way in phasing out their greenhouse gas emissions as early as possible and no later than the middle of the century.[68]

CONFLICT MANAGEMENT DYNAMICS IN ISLAM

وَإِنْ خِفْتُمْ شِقَاقَ بَيْنِهِمَا فَابْعَثُوا حَكَمًا مِنْ أَهْلِهِ وَحَكَمًا مِنْ أَهْلِهَا إِنْ يُرِيدَا إِصْلَاحًا يُوَفِّقِ اللَّهُ بَيْنَهُمَا إِنَّ اللَّهَ كَانَ عَلِيمًا خَبِيرًا {35}

[Al-Nisaa 4:35] If ye fear a breach between them twain, appoint (two) arbiters, one from his family, and the other from hers; if they wish for peace, Allah will cause their reconciliation: For Allah hath full knowledge, and is acquainted with all things.[69]

This passage from the Qur'an introduces the strategy of having mediators help find resolution between groups, which is one of most recommended traditions for conflicts in Islam. Claudia Maffettone, a modern conflict mediator, further explains the role of mediation in Islamic culture:

> ... the objective of the third party is to restore order and harmony rather than change power relationships; conflict resolution is a community priority that involves elders, local leaders and family members who put pressure on the parties and guarantee the implementation of the agreement; the process is guided by established norms that include honor restoration, face saving, avoiding shame, saving dignity; relationships are key and their restoration is paramount.[70]

The process for conflict mediation has been further itemized by researcher Siraj Islam Mufti:

1. Appointment of a Justice of Peace (Qadi as Sulh) to oversee the processes of mediation, arbitration, and reconciliation to achieve settlement and peace

Religious Worldviews, Environmental Values

2. Parties in conflict have the option of resolving their dispute through a Wasta or third-party mediator who would ensure that all parties were satisfied with the outcome.
3. Other practices could use tahkeem, or using intermediaries to represent the parties. These intermediaries should be able to represent the parties' position as clearly as possible to negotiate on their behalf, and guarantee that the parties receive a fair settlement.

A settlement could include[:]

   a. Financial compensation
   b. Service to the family
   c. Service to the community
   d. Specific gestures of sympathy, or public demonstration of reconciliation[71]

One complication factor in most Islamic culture is the firm social roles that different people play, which clearly indicates who has authority. This power imbalance makes finding a mutually agreeable resolution to a dispute particularly difficult, since the party with authority can just make demands. Maffettone summarizes these social roles including,

> age hierarchies (the young submits to the old), familial hierarchies (the son submits to the father), gender hierarchies (women submit to men), and constrain parties in a weaker position to submit to what is considered right by the elders and the community.[72]

The United States Institute of Peace noted that *peace* and *justice* are almost interchangeable concepts for most Muslims. There is no peace without justice. To help define the Islamic approach to conflict management, the United States Institute of Peace also generated this list of key dimensions in justice and peace:

1. The first is in the metaphysical-spiritual context, in which peace as one of the names of God is seen as an essential part of God's creation and assigned substantive value.
2. The second is the philosophical-theological context, within which the question of evil is addressed as a cosmic, ethical, and social problem.
3. The third is the political-legal context, the proper locus of classical legal and juristic discussions of war, rebellion, oppression, and political order and disorder.
4. The fourth is the socio-cultural context, which reveals the parameters of the Muslim experience of religious and cultural diversity in communities of other faiths and cultural traditions.[73]

Lastly, one final Muslim conflict resolution tradition is called *sulha*, and is a ritual ceremony of forgiveness, where the parties that have reached an agreement will share a large meal together. Honor is restored to everyone involved, hostilities are forgotten, wrongs are forgiven, and peace returns to the community. In fact, this tradition requires that the parties forget about the disagreement and never bring it up again, whether to their own groups, for history to remember, or if disagreements arise again between the same groups. It is as if the disagreement never happened at all. This is the practical application of the Arabic word *tarrahidhin*, which means "resolution of a conflict that involves no humiliation." It stands in juxtaposition with common, Western approaches, which often involve blaming, taking responsibility, detailed records of faults, and some degree of shame.[74]

FOUR STAGES WITHIN ISLAM

Demanding justice from a place of authority is the obvious example of Stage 1, which is sometimes hard to move beyond because of the strong social hierarchy in Islam. But, when parties can meet, possibly with the help of mediators, needs can be privately addressed (Stage 2) and a mutually agreeable deal, with benefits to both parties, can be reached (Stage 3). It is then the responsibility of the parties to move forward with the action items of their agreement (Stage 4), and authority figures help hold those parties accountable to their agreements.

CONCLUSION

By following the moral standards set forth in the Qur'an, opposing parties can move forward while maintaining honor and respect on all sides, particularly with the mediation framework so familiar in Muslim culture. With the looming challenges of climate change and water scarcity, particularly in many countries with high Muslim populations, we are going to need our best approaches to conflict management. Shared values can be the starting point for discussion. These values include justice, peace, harmony, balance, and the value of human life. With shared values and mutual respect, we have the foundations for working on complex natural resources issues.

JUDAISM

> *So God created man in his own image, in the image of God created he him; male and female created he them.*
>
> *And God blessed them, and God said unto them, Be fruitful, and multiply, and replenish the earth, and subdue it: and have dominion over the fish of the sea, and over the fowl of the air, and over every living thing that moveth upon the earth.*
> —Genesis 1:27–28 King James Version[75]

JUDEO-CHRISTIAN FOUNDATIONS IN ENVIRONMENTAL ETHICS

It starts off with people being made in the "image of God," as quoted in the passage. Thus, people are immediately elevated above plants and animals, although the latter were also created by God in the biblical story of creation. People are the grand finale of God's creation. And, unlike the plants and animals, humans have eternal souls, as taught in Islam. Thus, it could be said that Judaism, Christianity, and Islam all share a *homocentric* view of nature, where people are the most important form of life, although some subgroups would disagree with this generalization.

It is worth noting the *environmental setting* that God originally created for Adam and Eve, the first man and woman. They were in a garden. For some unspecified amount of time, Adam and Eve lived in the Garden of Eden, eating the fruit, naming the animals, taking care of the garden, and living in complete harmony with all of nature. If any picture can encapsulate the Judeo-Christian view of nature, this one can. But this was before Adam and Eve disobeyed God's one command and had to leave this perfect garden environment.

The real controversy stems from the translation of the word "dominion" in Genesis 1:28. What does that mean? What relationship between people and nature can we extract from this word? The New Jewish Publication Society (NJPS) translates this section as ". . . fill the earth and master it; rule the fish of the sea . . ."[76] The New Living Translation (NLT) translates it as ". . . Fill the earth and govern it. Reign over the fish in the sea . . ."[77]

The Role of Humans: A Question of Interpretation

There are at least three major views of nature that stem from this first chapter of Genesis. J. Baird Callicott summarizes each view with the following titles:

The *Despotic Interpretation* only sees value in nature when nature can benefit people. Thus, natural resources should be collected, as long as it is helping (and not harming) people. This authority comes directly from God when he gave people "dominion" over every living thing.[78]

The *Stewardship Interpretation* also recognizes the authority of man over nature, but assumes that we humans have responsibility for the welfare of nature. Since Earth is not the permanent residence of humans, we are the *temporary* stewards of the environment. We are guardians, keepers, and protectors of nature. This obligation is derived from the original role as gardeners and from the fact that God declared that all of his creation was "good."[79]

Finally, the *Citizen Interpretation* puts much more intrinsic value in non-human life and originates from the idea that the animals were created to be potential companions for people. This position takes a much more "ecocentric" view of nature, in which the goal is the collective harmony of all life, not just humans. Humans are rightful citizens of Earth, just as much as the animals are.[80]

Of these, the Stewardship Ethic is probably the most popular.

Biblical Stewardship Environmental Ethics

"The earth is the Lord's, and everything in it."

—Psalm 24:1 New Living Translation.[81]

As the passage clearly states, people are not really the owners of anything. God is. Thus, even though we are given authority over nature, we are not allowed to do whatever we want with it. As the ultimate owner and authority, God has delegated some of his authority to us, which became part of our job as humans on Earth.[82] We are accountable to God for how we use natural resources and how we treat life.

These are the foundational views of the Biblical Stewardship Ethic for both Jews and Christians.

But here is the delicate aspect. We have to balance our human needs with the needs of the environment. The rules and standards set in the rest of the Bible, and other Jewish texts, help clarify how our priorities should be balanced.

For example, the Bible contains a mandate for the Israelites' use of trees during times of war. It has become known as the law of *Bal Tash'chit* to the Jews, and prohibits the careless destruction of nature. Quoted as the direct command of God, this passage is found in both the Hebrew and the Christian Bible:

> When you are attacking a town and the war drags on, you must not cut down the trees with your axes. You may eat the fruit, but do not cut down the trees. Are the trees your enemies, that you should attack them? You may only cut down trees that you know are not valuable for food. Use them to make the equipment you need to attack the enemy town until it falls.[83]

Further Jewish Teachings on Nature

There are two agricultural Jewish laws worth mentioning here. The first required that harvesters leave a small portion of their crop unharvested. This was to allow poor people to collect the crop and thus sustain themselves, which reflects the community ethic of Judaism.[84]

According to the Talmudic sages, this law reflected the importance of preserving the environment, preventing pollution, and maintaining a pleasant relationship with nature. It states that, "It is forbidden to live in a town which has no garden or greenery" (Jerusalem Talmud Kiddushin 48b).[85]

Additionally, Jews teach this story from Ecclesiastes Rabbah 7:13 to illustrate the importance of the environment:

> In the hour when the Holy one, blessed be He,
> created the first man,
> He took him and let him pass before all the trees of
> the Garden of Eden and said to him:
> "See my works, how fine and excellent they are!
> Now all that I have created, for you have I created.
> Think upon this and do not corrupt and desolate My World,
> For if you corrupt it, there is no one to set it
> right after you.[86]

Jewish Response to Climate Change

A group called the Jewish National Fund has been raising money to plant trees and do other restoration efforts in Israel since 1901. They have also collaborated on tree planting efforts in Australia, including the approach road to Olympic Park and Bondi-Bronte Beach coastal walk.[87]

Additionally, over 50 Jewish leaders from various religious and political affiliations have signed the Jewish Environmental and Energy Imperative, an ambitious goal to reduce 2005 greenhouse gas emissions in Jewish communities by 83 percent by 2050. The Rabbinical Assembly has also made an audacious commitment to use only sustainable products at their religious events.[88] Some other Jewish groups worth noting are the Coalition on the Environment and Jewish Life and Hazon: The Jewish Lab for Sustainability.

Rabbi Saul Berman has written the following forceful response to climate change and the balancing act between human and environmental needs:

> The rights of nature need to be carefully balanced, calibrated, against human interests; and in that balancing, it will be the human interests which will have the priority. . . . it has become abundantly clear that the real risk in our continued pollution of the environment is not the Earth—but rather it is humankind. The Earth will undoubtedly survive our depredations and will continue to swarm with life, but humankind may be extinguished and end this stage of God's experiment on the Earth. If we love humanity, then we must now act to save it from ourselves.[89]

Rabbi Berman also appeals with the Jewish principle of *Hatzalah*, which requires that people help each other when they need it. This rule stems from Leviticus 19:16, which commands, "You shall not stand idly by the blood of your neighbor."[90] Then he adds an extension of this rule that requires people to do something if their neighbor's *property* is being harmed. After which, he applies this concept to our environment. If our neighbor's environment is harmful to them, are we not obliged to help them?

To conclude this argument for stewardship, Rabbi charges his audience with this noble objective:

> The challenge ahead of us is the common challenge of science and religion together—to discover and implement the means of assuring the physical survival of humanity on Earth, to discover and implement the means of assuring the spiritual survival of a more humble and more modest humanity on this, God's earth.[91]

JUDAISM AND CONFLICT MANAGEMENT

סוּר מֵרָע, וַעֲשֵׂה-טוֹב בַּקֵּשׁ שָׁלוֹם וְרָדְפֵהוּ.
Depart from evil, and do good; seek peace, and pursue it.

—Psalms 34:15[92]

The concept of mediation has been central to Jewish culture and religion, since at least the time of Moses and Aaron, as laws of compromise and justice known as *p'shara*. Many Jews recognize Aaron, the brother of Moses, as Judaism's first mediator, since he is called a "pursuer of peace" or *rodef shalom*.[93]

Central to the Jewish faith is the idea that God will someday bring complete justice and peace to the world. This anticipation is reflected in the writings of the Jewish prophet, Isaiah, as quoted here from Isaiah 2:4 in the New Living Translation:

> The Lord will mediate between nations and will settle international disputes. They will hammer their swords into plowshares and their spears into pruning hooks. Nation will no longer fight against nation, nor train for war anymore.[94]

This scripture depicts peace in the vivid imagery of repurposing weapons into tools, a clear declaration of the intent for peace and not conflict. This scripture inspired the Soviet sculptor Yevgeny Vuchetich to create a striking statue of a man hammering a sword into a plowshare, which was given to the United Nations as a gift in 1959 by the USSR government, and now stands in the North Garden of the UN Headquarters in New York City.

JUDAISM AND THE FOUR STAGES OF WATER CONFLICT TRANSFORMATION

While there are many connections to the Four Stages of Water Conflict Transformation within Judaism, Dr. Aaron Wolf has applied the framework to Moses' path to holiness to receive the Ten Commandments on Mount Sinai. Moses had built an altar at the foot of the Mountain and purified all the people in a 3-day process. This is the connection to physical holiness, representing Stage 1. Stage 2 is represented by the emotional holiness and joy that was shared between Moses, Aaron, and 70 of Israel's elders, as they ate and drank a meal with God himself. Stage 3 is represented when Moses receives the Ten Commandments from God, a form of perceptual or intuitive holiness. Finally, spiritual holiness is represented by the thickness of the cloud that surrounded the mountaintop, 'av ha'anan, which is Stage 4: spiritual holiness.

CONCLUSION

In Judaism, people are given the prerogative to exercise mastery over plants, animals, and the rest of nature. However, many Jews consider themselves as stewards (or temporary guardians) over nature, with the goal of preserving it for the benefit of others and for future generations, because that is the command of God. These values provide an excellent foundation for resolving conflict over natural resources. Furthermore, Jewish tradition, scriptures, and prophets place a high value on peace. Among other traditions, mediation is fundamental. Conclusively, Jewish values and approaches to conflict management may provide solid insights into modern natural resources conflicts.

CHRISTIANITY

> "Do to others whatever you would like them to do to you. This is the essence of all that is taught in the law and the prophets."
> —Jesus Christ (Matthew 7:12 New Living Translation)[95]

A CHRISTIAN VIEW OF NATURE: SCRIPTURAL FOUNDATION WITH JUDAISM

As stated in the section on Judaism and nature, most Christians have a very similar view on nature compared to most Jews, since both religions share the same foundational scriptures. Thus, many Christians believe that people are the most important life form, and adhere to either: (1) the Despotic view of nature for the sole benefit of nature, (2) the Stewardship view where people must take care of nature, or (3) the Citizen view where all life has the same value and right to preservation. Christians also view Earth as only a place of temporary residence place. Please review the sections on Judeo-Christian environmental ethics for further details on foundation for environmental ethics derived from the Old Testament scriptures.

Catholic Statements on Environmental Issues

Like many religious leaders, the Pope, head of the Catholic Church, has significant influence. In 2007, Pope Benedict XVI made a public statement reflecting on the collaboration that led to the Montreal Protocol, the international treaty to cut back on chemicals harming the ozone hole. This is part of Pope Benedict XVI's statement on this global success on the 20th anniversary of the Montreal Protocol:

> In the past two decades, thanks to exemplary collaboration between politicians, scientists and economists within the international community, important results have been obtained with positive repercussions on present and future generations. I desire that, on the part of everyone, cooperation intensify to the end of promoting the common good, development, and the safeguarding of creation, returning to the alliance between man and the environment, which must be a mirror of God the Creator, from whom we come and toward whom we are journeying.[96]

Pope Francis has also made a significant push toward environmentalism in the last few years, including his encyclical letter on ecology, Laudato Si', or "Praised Be." He even addresses climate change. Consider this excerpt from his letter, in which he describes some of the consequences of climate change, as well as humanity's responsibility to change our habits accordingly:

> A very solid scientific consensus indicates that we are presently witnessing a disturbing warming of the climatic system. In recent decades this warming has been accompanied by a constant rise in the sea level and, it would appear, by an increase of extreme weather events, even if a scientifically determinable cause cannot be assigned to each particular phenomenon. Humanity is called to recognize the need for changes of lifestyle, production and consumption, in order to combat this warming or at least the human causes which produce or aggravate it.[97]

Evangelical Voices on Climate Action

While some Evangelical Christians do not yet see climate change as a significant concern, many do. I, Josiah J. Shaver, am one such Evangelical Christian that sees the imperative need to steward the Earth and find real solutions to climate change. The tide is turning. Many Christian groups have rallied to share the need for climate action with their fellow Christians. The Evangelical Environmental Network is one such group. They published a statement titled "An Evangelical Declaration on the Care of Creation," which states:

> As followers of Jesus Christ, committed to the full authority of the Scriptures, and aware of the ways we have degraded creation, we believe that biblical faith is essential to the solution of our ecological problems.[98]

Dr. Katharine Hayhoe is an outspoken Christian climate scientist. As an excellent science communicator and speaker, Dr. Hayhoe has recently gained international attention and numerous awards for her excellent work, including a "Champion of the Earth" award from the United Nations.[99] Dr. Hayhoe wrote an article for the New York Times in 2019 in which she explained some of her spiritual motivations as a Christian climate scientist:

> . . . climate change disproportionately affects the poor and vulnerable, those already most at risk today. To me, caring about and acting on climate was a way to live out my calling to love others as we've been loved ourselves by God.
>
> By beginning with what we share and then connecting the dots between that value and a changing climate, it becomes clear how caring about this planet and every living thing on it is not somehow antithetical to who we are as Christians, but rather central to it. Being concerned about climate change is a genuine expression of our faith, bringing our attitudes and actions more closely into line with who we already are and what we most want to be.[100]

There are a number of other Christian leaders and organizations addressing climate change, such as Operation Noah, A Rocha, and Young Evangelicals for Climate Action. As part of their mission statement, Young Evangelicals for Climate Action simply says, "We are young evangelicals in the United States who are coming together and taking action to overcome the climate crisis as part of our Christian discipleship and witness."[101]

Christians often act to protect the environment because of the biblical mandate for environmental stewardship and because there is a direct, positive impact on other people, which is a great way we can show God's love to others.

CHRISTIAN CONFLICT RESOLUTION PRINCIPLES

> "God blesses those who work for peace, for they will be called the children of God."
> —Jesus Christ (Matthew 5:9 New Living Translation)[102]

The authors of the Bible paint a world of principles that balance full justice with infinite grace, and hard truth with compassionate love. Communities and relationships are a very high priority. Thus, reconciliation (the restoration of relationships) is also a high priority when working toward resolution.

Seven Seeds of Peace: Resolving Conflict with Pastor Rick Warren

Rick Warren is the lead pastor of Saddleback Church, an evangelical megachurch affiliated with the Southern Baptist Convention in Lake Forest, California. The following is an outline for a sermon he gave on conflict resolution in 2014, which identifies seven biblical principles for dealing with disagreements.[103]

1. *Make the first move.* Conflict is never resolved accidentally. Letting the problems remain unsolved is not good, because time does *not* heal all wounds. The only way to resolve a conflict is to face it. Somebody has to take the initiative and start the resolution process. Matthew 5:23–24 indicates that it is often better to reconcile a personal conflict before coming to church.

2. *Ask God for wisdom in dealing with the conflict.* Since God created everything and understands everyone, he may give you an idea or advice that would help tremendously. This wisdom could come from reading the Bible, from a friend, or from the Holy Spirit directly.
3. *Begin with what's your fault.* When you open up and are honest enough to admit your mistakes, it sends a significant message to the others involved. If you aren't pretending to be perfect and infallible, they probably won't feel like they have to pretend to be perfect either. This reflects the biblical concepts of *self-reflection* and *humility*. Jesus encouraged self-reflection in Matthew 7:3–5 when he asked,

> "And why worry about a speck in your friend's eye when you have a log in your own? How can you think of saying to your friend, 'Let me help you get rid of that speck in your eye,' when you can't see past the log in your own eye? Hypocrite! First get rid of the log in your own eye; then you will see well enough to deal with the speck in your friend's eye."[104]

4. *Listen for their hurt and perspective.* This is huge. We think we argue over ideas, but we actually often argue over emotions. Sometimes the problem is mainly an emotional reaction. And hearing other perspectives is important because no one is perfect, so we need to listen to each other, not only to show respect, but also to get a better picture of the situation.
5. *Speak the truth tactfully.* It may help to make a list of triggering words or phrases that are better not to use because they are too triggering or offensive. Call these WMDs, Words of Mass Destruction. The Bible puts heavy emphasis on finding the right balance between truth and love, as the Apostle Paul commands in Ephesians 4:15. Sometimes the truth is very hard for people to hear, which is why communicating with love, care, and kindness is so important.
6. *Fix the problem, not the blame.* It might be their fault, but rubbing it in their face probably won't help. Rather, focus on fixing the present situation and moving forward into the future, with less emphasis on who is at fault.
7. *Focus on reconciliation, not resolution.* Restoring trust and a good relationship is usually more important than fixing the problem itself.

(These are some key points from Pastor Rick Warren's sermon on conflict resolution and the full video on YouTube.)[105]

Another key biblical framework for conflict resolution comes from Matthew 5, which describes a process for dealing with conflict between Christians. Jesus commands the following:

> If another believer sins against you, go privately and point out the offense. If the other person listens and confesses it, you have won that person back. But if you are unsuccessful, take one or two others with you and go back again, so that everything you say may be confirmed by two or three witnesses. If the person still refuses to listen, take your case to the church. Then if he or she won't accept the church's decision, treat that person as a pagan or a corrupt tax collector.[106]

Although trying to resolve disputes privately before taking it to higher authorities is something anyone can apply, many people, who claim to be Christians, do not follow the biblical principles for conflict resolution. Some would even say that church organizations have not taught conflict resolution sufficiently, which is a huge tragedy. Rachel Anderson and Shannon Allen, who run a Christian mediation firm out of Denver, Colorado, are disappointed by how many Christians take their disputes straight to the legal courts, without first trying biblical approaches like mediation.[107]

When a conflict arises between Christians, Anderson and Allen recommend finding a mediator within the local Christian community, such as a pastor or elder. They caution that going straight to the legal system is costly, very adversarial, and often neither restores the relationship nor ends in a favorable outcome. On the other hand, this is what they say about mediation:

> Christian mediation focuses on identifying the heart issues underlying the dispute and providing a forum for gracious restoration of offenses. The mediator can help the parties identify mutually beneficial outcomes to a conflict, or negotiate a settlement to a legal dispute, that is satisfactory to both parties.
>
> The process of Christian mediation endeavors to restore relationships in a manner that glorifies God and honors the other person.[108]

Finally, Christianity is a religion that not only emphasizes peacemaking, but also discourages vengeance. Referencing the writings of Jewish authors from the Old Testament, the Apostle Paul gave these specific instructions to the Christians living in Rome, as written in Romans 12: "Do all that you can to live in peace with everyone. Dear friends, never take revenge . . . Don't let evil conquer you, but conquer evil by doing good."[109]

THE FOUR STAGES APPLIED TO CHRISTIANITY

Christianity normally only encourages adversarial confrontation (Stage 1) only after all other means of reconciliation have failed. Conflicts must be approached with love, kindness, and grace to care for the emotional needs of the participants (Stage 2). The full picture of the situation should be understood by getting the perspective of others to gain knowledge (Stage 3). And, finally, conflicts should be resolved not only to reconcile human relationships but also to maintain a personal relationship with God (Stage 4).

CONCLUSION

The Christian view of nature builds on the Jewish view of nature. Many Christians see themselves as stewards of the environment, obligated to take care of it because of God's command, and as an expression of their love for fellow people, who are all made in the image of God. In the face of climate change and other environmental issues, some Christian leaders have taken a bold stand for environmental stewardship, and many Christian groups are actively working to help solve environmental problems.

In regard to conflict, the Christian Bible gives a comprehensive picture of conflict resolution, which includes personal reflection, justice, peacemaking, private conversations, more formal actions, forgiveness, grace, and building personal relationships.

EPILOGUE

We have seen the peacemaking circles of the Native Americans, where everyone's voice is heard. We have learned the history of Hindus tree-huggers and Buddhists ordaining trees to save them. We have read statements on climate change from Muslim leaders around world, as well as from other religious leaders. And we have explored the role of people from the Judeo-Christian scriptures and the implications for modern environmental ethics.

Looking at the big picture, a number of similarities in the core values of these worldviews becomes evident. Among these shared *core values* are: harmony, peace, interdependence, justice, honor, and care for fellow human beings. Additionally, we all care about the future of our children.

Together with the conflict management strategies from each worldview, these core values provide an excellent foundation for bringing people together. Solving problems and disagreements is much easier when we realize that we share many of the same fundamental human values. In a world where we humans are so often reminded about what divides us, it is important to remember what brings us into harmony. This foundational approach will be instrumental when addressing conflicts over natural resources, water, and climate change.

NOTES

1 Wolf, T. Aaron. *The Spirit of Dialogue: Lessons from Faith Traditions in Transforming Conflict*. Island Press, Washington, DC, 2017, p. 14.
2 Mcclendon, David and Conrad Hackett. Christians Remain World's Largest Religious Group, But They Are Declining in Europe. *Pew Research Center*. April 5, 2017. Accessed June 4, 2020. www.pewresearch.org/fact-tank/2017/04/05/christians-remain-worlds-largest-religious-group-but-they-are-declining-in-europe/
3 Halpert, Julie. Judaism and Climate Change. *Yale Climate Connections*. February 29, 2020. Accessed May 28, 2020. www.yaleclimateconnections.org/2012/02/judaism-and-climate-change/
4 Wolf, T. Aaron. *The Spirit of Dialogue: Lessons from Faith Traditions in Transforming Conflict*. Island Press, Washington, DC, 2017, p. 33.
5 Rothman, Jay. Supplementing Tradition: A Theoretical and Practical Typology for International Conflict Management. *Negotiation Journal*, 5(1989):265–277.
6 Rothman, Jay. Pre-Negotiation in Water Disputes: Where Culture is Core. *Cultural Survival Quarterly*, 19(1995):19–22.
7 Rothman, Jay. *Resolving Identity-Based Conflicts in Nations, Organizations, and Communities*. Jossey-Bass, San Francisco, CA, 1997, 224 p.
8 Kaufman, Edward. Chapter 9: Sharing the Experience of Citizen' Diplomacy with Partners in Conflict. Pp 183–222. In: *Second Track/Citizens' Diplomacy* (John Davies and Edward Kaufman, Eds.). Lanham, MD: Rowman & Littlefield, 2002.
9 Kaufman, Edward. Chapter 10: Toward Innovative Solutions. Pp 223–264. In: *Second Track/Citizens' Diplomacy: Concepts and Techniques for Conflict Transformation* (John Davies and Edward Kaufman, Eds.). Rowman & Littlefield, Lanham, MD, 2002.

10 Wolf, Aaron T. Criteria for Equitable Allocations: The Heart of International Water Conflict. *Natural Resources Forum*, 23(1999):3–30.
11 These stages build primarily on the work of Jay Rothman, who initially described his stages as ARI—Adversarial, Reflexive, and Integrative (Rothman 1989). When ARI become ARIA, adding Action, Rothman's terminology (1997) also evolved to Antagonism, Resonance, Invention, and Action. We retain the former terms, feeling they are more descriptive for our purposes.
12 These claims stem from an assessment of 145 treaty deliberations described in Wolf (1999). Rothman (1995) too uses the terms rights, interests, and needs, in that order, arguing that "needs" are motivation for "interests," rather than the other way round as we use it here. For our purposes, our order feels more intuitive, especially for natural resources.
13 These sets of skills draw from Kaufman (2002), who ties each set of dynamics specifically to Rothman's ARIA model in great detail, based on his extensive work conducting "Innovative Problem Solving Workshops" for "partners in conflict" around the world.
14 The four worlds are described in Wolf, Aaron T. *The Spirit of Dialogue: Lessons from Faith Traditions in Transforming Conflict*. Island Press, Washington, DC, 2017, 205 p.
15 Rothman, Jay. Supplementing tradition: A Theoretical and Practical Typology for International Conflict Management. *Negotiation Journal*, 5(1989):265–277.
16 Rothman, Jay. Pre-Negotiation in Water Disputes: Where Culture is Core. *Cultural Survival Quarterly*, 19(1995):19–22.
17 Rothman, Jay. *Resolving Identity-Based Conflicts in Nations, Organizations, and Communities*. Jossey-Bass, San Francisco, CA, 1997, 224 p.
18 Kaufman, Edward. Chapter 9: Sharing the Experience of Citizen' Diplomacy with Partners in Conflict. Pp 183–222. In: *Second Track/Citizens' Diplomacy* (John Davies and Edward Kaufman, Eds.). Rowman & Littlefield, Lanham, MD, 2002.
19 Kaufman, Edward. Chapter 10: Toward Innovative Solutions. Pp 223–264. In: *Second Track/Citizens' Diplomacy: Concepts and Techniques for Conflict Transformation* (John Davies and Edward Kaufman, Eds.). Rowman & Littlefield, Lanham, MD, 2002.
20 Wolf, Aaron T. Criteria for Equitable Allocations: The Heart of International Water Conflict. *Natural Resources Forum*, 23(1999):3–30.
21 Indian Country Today. *Every Day Is Earth Day: Quotable Native Wisdom About the Environment*. Published April 23, 2012. Accessed May 21, 2020. https://indiancountry-today.com/archive/every-day-is-earth-day-quotable-native-wisdom-about-the-environment-SwPjXdbtEU-Tbw4lDfqfLA
22 Wolf, T. Aaron. *The Spirit of Dialogue: Lessons from Faith Traditions in Transforming Conflict*. Island Press, Washington, DC, 2017, p. 14.
23 Mooney, James. *The Ghost Dance Religion and the Sioux Outbreak of 1890*. Fourteenth Annual Report of the Bureau of Ethnology, 1892–1893. Washington, DC, 1896. See Gill, Sam D. *Mother Earth: An American Story*. University of Chicago Press, Chicago, 1987 for context and critical discussion.
24 Callicott, J. Baird. *Earth's Insights: A Multicultural Survey of Ecological Ethics from the Mediterranean Basin to the Australian Outback*. University of California Press, Berkeley, CA, 1994, pp. 122–128.
25 Ibid.
26 Ibid.
27 Ibid.
28 Smith, Carson. Peacemaking Circles: Justice in Tribal Communities. *The Bill Lane Center for the American West*. Stanford University, October 17, 2017. Accessed May 21, 2020. https://west.stanford.edu/news/blogs/out-west-blog/2017-peacemaking-circles-smith

Religious Worldviews, Environmental Values 235

29 Smith, Justice Barbara and Jason Burwell. *Peacemaking: A Way of Life*, October 23, 2007. The Chickasaw Nation. https://peacemaking.narf.org/wp-content/uploads/2018/09/peacemaking-way-life.pdf
30 McDermott, Mat. 7 Hindu Quotes about Nature for Earth Day. *Patheos.com*. Published March 20, 2018. Accessed on August 2, 2020. www.patheos.com/blogs/samudra/2018/04/7-hindu-quotes-about-nature-earth-day-world-environment-day/
31 Callicott, J. Baird. *Earth's Insights: A Multicultural Survey of Ecological Ethics from the Mediterranean Basin to the Australian Outback*. University of California Press, Berkeley, CA, 1994.
32 Ibid., p. 50. Ryali cites Swearer, Donald K. "Ecological Perspectives from Asian Religion." Unpublished MS., n.d., p. 1., as quoted by Callicott on pages 49–50.
33 Tay, Priscilla. Can Religion Teach Us to Protect Our Environment? Analyzing the Case of Hinduism. *Ethics & International Affairs, Carnegie Council*, April 2019. Accessed May 25, 2020. www.ethicsandinternationalaffairs.org/2019/can-religion-teach-us-to-protect-our-environment-analyzing-the-case-of-hinduism/#easy-footnote-bottom-5-56833
34 Ibid.
35 Ibid.
36 Oxford Centre for Hindu Studies, The, Hindu Declaration on Climate Change.
37 Tay, Priscilla. Can Religion Teach Us to Protect Our Environment? Analyzing the Case of Hinduism. *Ethics & International Affairs, Carnegie Council*, April 2019. Accessed May 25, 2020. www.ethicsandinternationalaffairs.org/2019/can-religion-teach-us-to-protect-our-environment-analyzing-the-case-of-hinduism/#easy-footnote-bottom-5-56833
38 Bhumi Project website, the. Accessed August 2, 2020. www.bhumiproject.org/
39 Hindupedia. *Ideals and Values/Peacefulness (Santi)*. Hindupedia: The Hindu Encyclopedia. Accessed May 19, 2020. www.hindupedia.com/en/Ideals_and_Values/Peacefulness_(%C5%9Aanti)
40 Ibid.
41 Wolf, T. Aaron. *The Spirit of Dialogue: Lessons from Faith Traditions in Transforming Conflict*. Island Press, Washington, DC, 2017, p. 43.
42 BBC. *What Does Buddhism Teach about the Environment?* Accessed May 26, 2020. www.bbc.co.uk/bitesize/guides/z4b42hv/revision/3
43 Ibid.
44 Bhikku Bodhi. *Forward* in Kalas Sandell, edl, Buddhist Perspectives on the Ecocrisis (Kandy, Sri Lanka: Buddhist Publication Society, 1987), p. vii., as quoted by Callicott on page 65.
45 Zetter, Kim. *Scientists Meditate on Happiness*. Accessed September 16, 2003. www.wired.com
46 Dalai Lama. *A Buddhist Concept of Nature*. His Holiness, the 14th Dalai Lama of Tibet. Transcript of an address on February 4, 1992, at New Delhi, India. Accessed May 26, 2020. www.dalailama.com/messages/environment/buddhist-concept-of-nature
47 Darlington, Susan M. *The Ordination of a Tree: The Buddhist Ecology Movement in Thailand*. Ethnology. Published by the University of Pittsburgh: Commonwealth System of Higher Education. Vol. 37, No. 1 (Winter, 1998), pp. 1–15.
48 One Earth Sangha. *The Time to Act is Now: A Buddhist Declaration on Climate Change*. A statement for COP 21 in Paris in 2015. Accessed May 26, 2020. https://oneearthsangha.org/statements/the-time-to-act-is-now/
49 Dalai Lama Quotes About Reconciliation. *AZ Quotes*. Accessed August 3, 2020. www.azquotes.com/author/8418-Dalai_Lama/tag/reconciliation
50 BBC. *Buddhism and War*. Accessed on May 26, 2020. www.bbc.co.uk/religion/religions/buddhism/buddhistethics/war.shtml

51 Ibid.
52 Nadimpalli, Harshita. *Buddhism: A Pathway to Peace and Conflict Resolution*. Georgetown University Berkley Center, June 24, 2016. Accessed May 26, 2020. https://berkleycenter.georgetown.edu/posts/buddhism-a-pathway-to-peace-and-conflict-resolution
53 Olendzki, Andrew. *Advice for Conflict: Lessons from the Buddha about How We Can Use Our Speech to Reduce Instead of Provoke Hostility*. Tricycle: The Bhuddist Review. Summer 2017. Accessed May 26, 2020. https://tricycle.org/magazine/advice-for-conflict/
54 Wolf, T. Aaron. *The Spirit of Dialogue: Lessons from Faith Traditions in Transforming Conflict*. Island Press, Washington, DC, 2017, pp. 158–159.
55 Ibid.
56 Wolf, T. Aaron. *The Spirit of Dialogue: Lessons from Faith Traditions in Transforming Conflict*. Island Press, Washington, DC, 2017, p. 42.
57 Karim, Fatima. *Do Not Waste Water Even If You Were at a Running Stream*, July 11, 2018. Accessed 31 January 2021. https://marytn.medium.com/do-not-waste-water-even-if-you-were-at-a-running-stream-ea5cdf737e79.
58 Tanzil.net. *Ash-Shura*. . Accessed 31 January 2021. http://tanzil.net/#trans/en.sahih/42:40.
59 Fasahah, Nahj al. *Our Duty to the Environment Starts at the Mosque*, August 7, 2017. Accessed January 31, 2021. https://imam-us.org/islam-and-the-environment.
60 Callicott, J. Baird. *Earth's Insights: A Multicultural Survey of Ecological Ethics from the Mediterranean Basin to the Australian Outback*. University of California Press, Berkeley, CA, 1994, pp. 30–36.
61 Redwan, Afsan. When the Earth Speaks Against Us: Environmental Ethics in Islam. *Yaqeen Institute*, September 20, 2018. Accessed May 27, 2020. https://yaqeeninstitute.org/afsan-redwan/when-the-earth-speaks-against-us-environmental-ethics-in-islam/
62 Redwan, Afsan. Animals Have Rights Over Us | Animation. *Yaqeen Institute*. December 17, 2018. Accessed May 27, 2020. https://yaqeeninstitute.org/afsan-redwan/animals-have-rights-over-us-animation/
63 Shomali, Mohammad. Aspects of Environmental Ethics: An Islamic Perspective. *Thinking Faith*, November 11, 2008. Accessed May 27, 2020. www.thinkingfaith.org/articles/20081111_1.htm
64 Ahlulbayt TV. *The Environment an Islamic Perspective*, April 30, 2014. Accessed May 27, 2020. www.youtube.com/watch?v=5ybGH94xbMg
65 Redwan, Afsan. When the Earth Speaks Against Us: Environmental Ethics in Islam. *Yaqeen Institute*, September 20, 2018. Accessed May 27, 2020. https://yaqeeninstitute.org/afsan-redwan/when-the-earth-speaks-against-us-environmental-ethics-in-islam/
66 Ibid.
67 Ibid.
68 Nelsen, Arthur. Islamic Leaders Issue Bold Call for Rapid Phase Out of Fossil Fuels. *The Guardian*, August 18, 2015. Accessed May 27, 2020. www.theguardian.com/environment/2015/aug/18/islamic-leaders-issue-bold-call-rapid-phase-out-fossil-fuels
69 Iqbal, Khalid. *Islamic Mediation. Rahmaa Institute*. No publishing date given. Accessed May 27, 2020. www.rahmaa.org/domestic-violence/islamic-mediation/
70 Maffettone, Claudia. Principles and Practices of Peace and Conflict Resolution in Islam. *The Case of Morocco*. Mediate.com, August 2016. Accessed May 27, 2020. www.mediate.com/articles/MaffettoneC2.cfm
71 Mufti, Siraj Islam. Peacebuilding and Conflict Resolution in Islam. *IslamiCity*, November 12, 2014. Accessed May 27, 2020. www.islamicity.org/6351/peacebuilding-and-conflict-resolution-in-islam/

72 Maffettone, Claudia. Principles and Practices of Peace and Conflict Resolution in Islam. *The Case of Morocco*. Mediate.com, August 2016. Accessed May 27, 2020. www.mediate.com/articles/MaffettoneC2.cfm
73 United States Institute of Peace. *Crescent and Dove: Peace and Conflict Resolution in Islam*. No publication date given. Accessed May 27, 2020. www.usip.org/publications/crescent-and-dove-peace-and-conflict-resolution-islam
74 Wolf, T. Aaron. *The Spirit of Dialogue: Lessons from Faith Traditions in Transforming Conflict*. Island Press, Washington, DC, 2017, p. 31.
75 BibleGateway. *Genesis 1: King James Version (KJV)*. Accessed May 2020. www.biblegateway.com/passage/?search=genesis+1&version=KJV
76 Sefaria.org. *Genesis 1*. Accessed August 14, 2020. www.sefaria.org/Genesis.1.28-29?lang=bi&aliyot=0
77 Ibid.
78 Callicott, J. Baird. *Earth's Insights: A Multicultural Survey of Ecological Ethics from the Mediterranean Basin to the Australian Outback*. University of California Press, Berkeley, CA, 1994, pp. 14–24.
79 Ibid.
80 Ibid.
81 BibleGateway. *Psalms 24: New Living Translation*. Accessed May 29, 2020. www.biblegateway.com/passage/?search=psalm+24&version=NLT
82 Sefaria.org. *Genesis 2:15*. Accessed August 14, 20. www.sefaria.org/Genesis.2.15?lang=bi&aliyot=0
83 BibleGateway. *Deuteronomy 20: New Living Translation*. Accessed May 29, 2020. www.biblegateway.com/passage/?search=Deuteronomy+20&version=NLT
84 Lacey, Josie. Environmental Ethics in Judaism. *Israel & Judaism Studies: The Education Website of the NSW Jewish Board of Deputies*, 2006. Accessed May 28, 2020. www.ijs.org.au/environmental-ethics-in-judaism/
85 Ibid.
86 Ibid.
87 Ibid.
88 Halpert, Julie. Judaism and Climate Change. *Yale Climate Connections*, February 29, 2020. Accessed May 28, 2020. www.yaleclimateconnections.org/2012/02/judaism-and-climate-change/
89 Berman, Saul. Israel Environment & Nature: Jewish Environmental values—The Dynamic Tension Between Nature and Human Needs. *Jewish Virtual Library*. No date given. Accessed May 28, 2020. www.jewishvirtuallibrary.org/jewish-environmental-values-the-dynamic-tension-between-nature-and-human-needs
90 Ibid.
91 Ibid.
92 Mechon-Mamre.org. *Psalms Chapter 34*. No date given. Accessed May 28, 2020. www.mechon-mamre.org/p/pt/pt2634.htm#15
93 Ben-Zvi, Daniel. Mediation's Deep Jewish Roots. *Jewish Journal*, December 12, 2013. Accessed May 28, 2020. https://jewishjournal.com/commentary/opinion/125372/
94 Bible Gateway. *Isaiah 2: New Living Translation*. Accessed May 30, 2020. www.biblegateway.com/passage/?search=Isaiah+2%3A4&version=NLT
95 Bible Gateway. *Matthew 7 New Living Translation*. Accessed August 2, 2020. www.biblegateway.com/passage/?search=Matthew+7&version=NLT
96 Alliance of Religions and Conservation. *Christian Quotes*. Accessed June 2, 2020. www.arcworld.org/faiths.asp?pageID=97

97   Catholic Climate Covenant. *Respond to Pope Francis's Call to Action on Climate Change. Online PDF.* No date given. Accessed May 30, 2020. https://catholicclimate covenant.org/files/inline-files/CatholicClimateCovenantencyclicalexcerpts.pdf
98   Evangelical Environmental Network. *On the Care of Creation: An Evangelical Declaration on the Care of Creation.* Accessed May 30, 2020. https://creationcare.org/what-we-do/an-evangelical-declaration-on-the-care-of-creation.html
99   United Nations Environmental Programme. *Canadian Professor Katharine Hayhoe named UN Champion of the Earth.* Press Release, September 16, 2019. Accessed June 2, 2020. www.unenvironment.org/news-and-stories/press-release/canadian-professor-katharine-hayhoe-named-un-champion-earth
100 Hayhoe, Katharine. I'm a Climate Scientist Who Believes in God. Hear Me Out. *The New York Times,* October 31, 2019. Accessed June 2, 2020. www.nytimes.com/2019/10/31/opinion/sunday/climate-change-evangelical-christian.html
101 Young Evangelicals for Climate Action. Website. Accessed May 30, 2020. https://yecaction.org/about-us/what-we-do.html
102 Bible Gateway. *Matthew 5 New Living Translation.* Accessed June 2, 2020. www.biblegateway.com/passage/?search=Matthew+5&version=NLT
103 Saddleback Church. *Learn How to Resolve Conflict & Restore Relationships with Rick Warren.* YouTube video published on July 28, 2014. Accessed June 2, 2020. www.youtube.com/watch?v=I1udN6OShf4&t=501s
104 Bible Gateway. *Matthew 7 New Living Translation.* Accessed June 4, 2020. www.biblegateway.com/passage/?search=Matthew+7&version=NLT
105 Saddleback Church. *Learn How to Resolve Conflict & Restore Relationships with Rick Warren.* YouTube video published on July 28, 2014. Accessed June 2, 2020. www.youtube.com/watch?v=I1udN6OShf4&t=501s
106 Bible Gateway. *Matthew 7 New Living Translation.* Accessed June 4, 2020. www.biblegateway.com/passage/?search=Matthew+18&version=NLT
107 Bernero, Laura. *Biblical Conflict Resolution.* Denver Institute for Faith & Work. August 28, 2017. Accessed June 2, 2020. https://denverinstitute.org/the-process-of-biblical-conflict-resolution/
108 Ibid.
109 Bible Gateway. *Romans 12 New Living Translation.* Accessed August 2, 2020. www.biblegateway.com/passage/?search=Romans%2012&version=NLT

Conclusion

Lynette de Silva

Everyone knows the necessity of water and that no substitute exists. Nevertheless, as global citizens, our decisions concerning the ecosystem and water, as a foundational resource, have been reckless. Our choices jeopardize the Earth's biophysical systems, life forms, and our own existence. Our thinking is, too often, linear. For example, such a singular approach manifests itself by: (1) letting geopolitics—based on economics—determine access to required resources, (2) ruling through the supremacy of personal rights, (3) focusing on surface water to the detriment of groundwater, and (4) addressing the interests of one community while neglecting and/or negating the necessities of a neighboring one. This kind of thinking does not consider: (1) the pervasive, unintentional effects across a unit, be it at the ecological, and ultimately climatological, expanse; and (2) the level of social systems, beginning at the community or household level and descending to the personal (individual) scale. Such superficial thinking addresses an infinitesimal, symptomatic part of a system, often spanning but a decade or so into the foreseeable future—taking for granted the value of water; the sustainable, biophysical balance of the environment; and the systemic consideration of all generations, *present and future*. To achieve social-environmental sustainability for all generations, it is ultimately necessary to honor *the inviolable consequences of decision making*.

Similarities exist among environmental conflicts, yet each is unique—steeped in its own history, with varying levels of stakeholder engagement and communication. The presented case studies exemplify these complexities from cooperation to conflict across the water spectrum. This workbook demonstrates actionable ways, that each of us, as individuals and communities, can take—to enhance our biophysical/social understanding and connectivity of systemic relationships across landscapes and through time, in a way that allows us to cooperatively mitigate environmental crises. Will we practice these tools? Will we do the work? We can only answer these questions through our actions.

New collaborative skills, frameworks, and transformative practices abound. Some of the corrective measures presented come from United Nations strategic goals, national directives, mediators, lessons learned from environmental interactions, and ancient cultural and faith-based practices. Such approaches can be used to broaden our individual and collective perspectives, allowing us to move forward together by strengthening our cooperative relationships, as we share the Earth's resources on a progressively sustainable basis for the benefit of all life.

Index

Note: Boldface page references indicate tables. Italic references indicate figures and boxed text.

A

Aaron (brother of Moses), 227–228
accessibility to water, 6
Action negotiation stage
  description of, **38**, 40–42, **41–42**
  Sustainable Development Goal Framework and, 186, **187**, 190–191
  techniques in, **43**
  Uganda and Indicator 6.5.2 and, 198
  in Vanport African American community, 158, **159**
adaptability, simplicity as key to, 25
Adversarial negotiation stage
  description of, 37–39, **38**, **41–42**
  in Flint African American community, 167
  Native American traditions and, 212
  Sustainable Development Goal Framework and, 186, **187**, 190–191
  techniques in, 43, **43**
  Uganda and Indicator 6.5.2 and, 196
  in Vanport African American community, 158, **159**, 161–162, **161**
African American communities and water insecurities, 8, 149–150, *see also* Flint African American community; Vanport African American community
Agenda 2030 for Sustainable Development, 182–183
Agreement for the Cooperation Between the United Kingdom and Egypt (1950), 192
ahimsa, 213, 216
Allen, Shannon, 232
Amazon Cooperation Treaty, 63
American Prairie Reserve, 93
American Rivers (organization), 94
Anderson, Rachel, 232
Army Corps of Engineers (Corps), 79, 106, 154–156
Ashu-Shura, 220
Aswan High Dam, 8, 27–29
Atiyeh, Victor, 109
Atrato River, 97
availability of water, 12, 67–68

B

Bakun Dam, 29
Bal Tash'chit law, 226
Batang Ai Dam, 29

Benedict XVI, 206, 229
Berman, Saul, 227
Bhagavatam, Srimad, 212
Bhikku Bodhi, 217
Bhumi Project, 214
Bible, 225, 226–228, 231
bilharzia, 27
biodiversity, 12, 27
Blue Heron paper-mill site, 118
Bolivia, 33, 87
Bonneville Power Administration, 107
Brazilian water management (Singreh)
  availability of water in various regions and, 67–68
  Civil Law Code and, 63
  Constitution of 1988 and, 64
  Federal Consumers' Rights Law and, 67
  Federal Law 9433 and, 64
  importance of, 63
  international profile in water and, 68
  National Agency of Water and Basic Sanitation and, 66–69
  National Information System on Water Resources and, 66
  National Water Agency and, 66, 69–72
  National Water Management Council and, 66
  National Water Policy and, 64–68
  negotiation and, 69, 71–72, 74, 76
  overview, 8, 62–63
  power generation and, 67
  quality of water and, 63–64
  role of Brazil in South America and, 63
  sanitation services and, 66–67
  scarcity of water and, 64
  success of, key to, 81–82
  system framework, 64–65, *65*
  Transparency Law and, 67
  U.S. water management versus, 61–62, 76
  Water Code and, 63
  Water Law of 1997 and, 64, 66, 70
  water uses and, 74
  water withdrawal and, total, 67
  see also Federal District of Brasilia; São Paulo Metropolitan Region
Brundtland Report (1987), 181–182
bubonic plague, 29
Buddha, 22, 216–217
Buddhism
  ahimsa and, 216
  climate change and, 218

241

conflict resolution in, 218–220
contemplative movement and, 43–44, **43**
ecological momentum in, 217–218
environmental teachings of Buddha and, 216–217
Five Precepts and, 216
Four Noble Truths and, 220
Four Stages of Water Conflict Transformation and, 220
nonviolence and, 218–220
ordaining trees to save them and, 217–218
overview, 220
pollution and, 218
reflection and, intense, 219
reframing scenarios with questions and, 219–220
Zen, 43
bundled rights, 171
Busch, Steven, 166
butterfly effect, 20

C

Callicott, J. Baird, 210–211, 225
Capra, Fritjof, 54
Carson, Smith, 211–212
Cascades Locks Casino, 114
Cascades Tribes, 116–117
Catholic statements on environmental issues, 229
Celilo Village, 106–107
Centers for Disease and Prevention, 165
change
consistency of, 22
irreversibility of, 19–20
systemic, 20, *21*, 22
Chesapeake Bay watershed, 55–56
Chickasaw Nation, 212
Chief Kiesno, 105
children, world's commitment to, 16, *16*
Chipko movement, 213–214
choices, 22, *see also* decision making
Christianity
Catholic statements on environmental issues and, 229
climate change and, 229–230, 232
conflict resolution in, 230–232
evangelical voices on climate action and, 229–230
Four Stages of Water Conflict Transformation and, 232
nature and, 228–230, 232
overview, 232
peace and, 230–231
Churchill, Winston, 12–13
Citizen Interpretation of nature, 225–226
Citizens Advocating for Clean Healthy Environment, 91
Civil Law Code (1916), 63

Clackamas River, 115
Clackamas Tribe, 113–115
Clean Air Act, 77
Clean Water Act (CWA) (1972), 49, 51–52, 56, 76–78, 86
climate
Buddhism and change in, 218
challenges of changing, 6–7
Christianity and change in, 229–230, 232
evangelical voices on action toward, 229–230
Francis's encyclical letter on change in, 229
Hinduism and change in, 214
impact of change in, 6
Islam and change in, 222
Judaism and change in, 226–227
oceans and, 2
Clowewalla Tribe, 113–115
Coalition on the Environment and Jewish Life, 227
Coast Reservation, 112
Collier, John, 106
Colombia, 97
Colorado River, 80–81
Columbia Gorge National Scenic Act, 110
Columbia Gorge National Scenic Area, 109–110
Columbia River, 109, 117, 150, *151*, 154–155
Columbia River Basin, 150–152, *151*
Columbia River Inter-Tribal Fish Commission (CRITFC), 110, 117–118
Columbia River Trade Network, 104–105
Columbia River Treaty (1964), 40–41, 110, 120n32
Columbia Slough Watershed, 151, *151*
"command-and-control" style of water management, 124
Community Bill of Rights ordinance (2013), 91
competition, 14
composition of people/systems, 18
Comprehensive Environmental Response, Compensation, and Liability Act (1980), 51
Confederated Tribes of Grand Ronde, 113
conflict, defining, 125
conflict management, *see* conflict resolution
conflict resolution
in Buddhism, 218–220
in Christianity, 230–232
in Ferghana Valley, 137–138
governance of water under U.S. law and, 50
in Hinduism, 214–215
in Islam, 222–224
in Judaism, 227–228
in Native American traditions, 211–212
principles, 208
shared values and, 233
see also Four Stages of Water Conflict Transformation
conflict transformation, 36–37, 42–44, **43**, *see also* Four Stages of Water Conflict Transformation
Congo River Basin, 6

Index

consensus building technique, **43**, 44
Constitution of 1988, 64
contemplative movement technique, 43–44, **43**
contentment, simplicity as key to, 25
Convention on the Protection and Use of Transboundary Watercourses and International Lakes, 189
Convocation of Hindu Spiritual Leaders, 214
Cooperation Benefits on International Rivers framework, 37
Cooperative Framework Arrangement, 193–198
Cowlitz Tribe, 105
Crazy Horse, 209
creation story, 225
Cross-border Cooperation for the Sustainable Peace and Development Project, 136
cumulative effects of systems, 18–19
cycle of water, 1–3, *2*

D

Dalai Lama, 216, 217–218
Dalles Dam, 106
dam building trend, 128
dam removal projects, 94, *94*, *95*, 96
Darlington, Susan M., 218
decision making
  all relationships are all inclusive and productive of an outcome (Rule 2), 16–17
  all relationships have one or more trade-offs (Rule 6), 18
  all relationships involve a transfer of energy (Rule 4), 17–18
  all systems are based on composition, structure, and function (Rule 5), 18
  all systems have cumulative effects, lag periods, and thresholds (Rule 7), 18–19
  Aswan High Dam and, 27–29
  change is an irreversible process of eternal becoming (Rule 8), 19–20
  collective, 26
  dynamic disequilibrium rules all systems (Rule 10), 22
  eternal parade of, 22
  every legal citizen deserves the right to vote (Rule 16), 26
  everything is a relationship (Rule 1), 13–16
  impact of, 239
  inviolable, 12–13, 239
  linear, 239
  nature, environmental/cultural wisdom, and human well-being are paramount (Rule 15), 25–26
  only true investment is energy from sunlight (Rule 3), 17
  outcome of, magnitude of, 12
  overview, 8, 29
  past reckless, 239
  people must be equally informed if they are to function as a truly democratic society (Rule 12), 23
  simplicity is the key to contentment, adaptability, and survival (Rule 14), 25
  success or failure lies in the interpretation of an event (Rule 11), 23
  systemic change is based on self-organized criticality (Rule 9), 20, *21*, 22
  this present moment, the here and now, is all we ever have (Rule 17), 26–27
  trade-offs in, 18
  we must consciously limit our "wants" (Rule 13), 24–25
Deeper than Science event, 207
democratic society, 23, 26
Deschutes River Basin
  Four Stages of Water Conflict Transformation and, 124–125, 140
  gender representation of water-related institutions in, 131–132
  geography of, 128–130, *129*
  issues addressed in study of, 127–128
  lessons learned from study of, 138–140
  overview, 124
  selection for study, 124
  water management in, 130–131, 141
Deschutes Water Alliance, 130
Despotic Interpretation of nature, 225
dharma, 214
disenfranchised communities, 139, 167, 171, *see also* African American communities
disequilibrium, dynamic, 22
distribution of water on Earth, 1–2
Douglas, William O., 86, 93
drought
  Federal District of Brasilia water crisis and, 68, 74–75
  Mexican Treaty of 1944 and, 80–81
  São Paulo Metropolitan Region and, 62–63, 68, 70
  water use rights and, 50–51
Dublin Principles, 64

E

Eban, Abba, 22
Ecclesiastes Rabbah, 226
ecological governance, 96–98
economic well-being, 26
ecosystem-based water management, 54–55
Ecuador, 86–87
Egypt, 27–29, 192–194
electricity production, 67
Elwa Dam removal, 94, *94*
energy, 17–18
Environmental Law Institute, 53–54
environmental movements, 213–215

Environmental Protection Agency (EPA), 5, 51–53, 56, 76, 167
environmental values, *see* religious worldviews and environmental values
environment-people relationship, 14–15
eternal moment, 26–27
Ethiopia, 33
"Evangelical Declaration on the Care of Creation, An," 229
Evangelical Environmental Network, 229
evangelical voices on climate action, 229–230
evaporation, oceanic, 2
evapotranspiration, 2
events, interpretation of, 23

F

fairness, economic and social, 153, 163, 211
faith-based practices, *see* religious worldviews and environmental values
false premises/thinking, 7
Federal Consumers' Rights Law, 67
Federal District of Brasilia water crisis (2016–2018)
  context of, 73–74
  drought and, 68, 74–75
  lessons learned from study of, 75–76
  location of, 69
  results of study, main, 75–76
  Water and Sanitation Agency and, 74
  water conflict and, 62–63, 74–75
  water consumption and, 68, 74
Federal Law 9433, 64
Fee, Chief Judge, 155
feminine, 125
Ferghana Valley
  conflict resolution in, 137–138
  emancipation of Central Asia's women and, 135–136
  Four Stages of Water Conflict Transformation and, 124–125, 140
  geography of, 133, *133*
  issues addressed by study of, 132
  lessons learned from study of, 138–140
  overview, 124, 132–135
  peace in, 136–137
  selection for study, 124
  transboundary water conflict resolution and, 137–138
  water management in, 133–135, 141
Fessenden, William Pitt, 26–27
"first in time, first in right" system, 77
Fish and Wildlife Service, 131
fishing protocols, 116
fishing rights, 108, 112, 118, 120n28, *see also* intertribal fishing conflicts and federal obstruction in Oregon
Five Precepts, 216

Flint African American community
  adversarial negotiation stage of water conflict transformation in, 167
  background information, 164
  current situation of, 166–167
  Flint River water supply treatment and, 164–166
  Four Stages of Water Conflict Transformation and, 167–168, 170
  government's service role and, 171
  lead in drinking water and, 150, 165–167, 170
  lessons learned from study of, 171
  reflective negotiation stage of water conflict transformation in, 167
  water crimes and, 166
  water use rights and, strengthening, 167–168, *168*, **169–170**, 170
Flint River, 164–166
flooding, 6, 20, *21*, 106, *see also* Vanport African American community
Florida v Georgia
  agreement attempts and, 78
  context of, 78
  lessons learned from study of, 78–80
  new approaches and, designing, 79–80
  results from study of, main, 79–80
  water conflict and, 78–79
  Water Resources Reform and Development and, 78–79
flow of water, 1–3, *2*
Forest Service, 86
foundation resource, water as, 1, 239
Four Noble Truths, 220
Four Stages of Water Conflict Transformation
  Action negotiation stage, **38**, 40–43, **41–42**
  Adversarial negotiation stage, 37–39, **38**, **41–42**
  Buddhism and, 220
  Christianity and, 232
  Deschutes River Basin and, 124–125, 140
  Ferghana Valley and, 124–125, 140
  Flint African American community and, 167–168, 170
  function of, 37
  gender in water conflicts and, 124, 140–141
  Hinduism and, 215
  Indicator 6.5.2 and, 189–191
  Integrative negotiation stage, **38**, 39–40, **41–42**
  Islam and, 224
  Judaism and, 228
  Native American traditions and, 212
  Reflective negotiation stage, **38**, 39, **41–42**
  religious worldviews and environmental values and, 208–209, **209**
  Sustainable Development Goal Framework and, 181, 186, **187**, 188–191
  Uganda and Indicator 6.5.2 and, 196–199

Index

Vanport African American community and, 156–158, **159–160**, 160–161, **161**
in water conflict transformation, 37
see also specific stage
Framework Law on Mother Earth and Integral Development for Living Well, 87
Francis, Pope, 229
function of systems, 18

G

Gandhi, Mahatma, 214
Ganges-Brahmaputra-Meghna Basin, 6
Ganges Rights of Nature, 97
Ganges River, 97, 213
Garden of Eden, 225
gendered approach to water conflict, 140–141
gender in water conflicts
  Action negotiation stage and, 140
  Adversarial negotiation stage and, 140
  conflict and, defining, 125
  data and, lack of, 127–128
  emancipation of Central Asia's women and, 135–137
  Four Stages of Water Conflict Transformation and, 124, 140
  gender and, defining, 125
  gendered approach to move forward and, 140–141
  inequities and, 123–124
  Integrative negotiation stage and, 140
  man's domain of water sector and, 126–127
  Ministerial Declaration and, 126–127
  overview, 8, 124–125, 141–142
  Reflective negotiation stage in, 140
  representation of women and, lack of, 127–128
  transboundary water conflict resolution and, 137–138
  water conflict and, defining, 126
  women's role in water sector and, 124, 126–127
  see also Deschutes River Basin; Ferghana Valley
General Electric Company, 91–92
General Motors, 164–165
Genesis, Book of, 224
Geological Service, 49
Geological Survey, 5, 155
geopolitics of water, 3–6
glass half empty/half full concept, 23, *24*
Glines Dam (Washington State) removal, 94, *95*
global water crisis, 180–181
Goggins, David, 166
governance of water under U.S. law
  Chesapeake Bay watershed and, 55–56
  Clean Water Act and, 49, 51–52
  Comprehensive Environmental Response, Compensation, and Liability Act and, 51
  conflict resolution and, 50
  groundwater, 50–51
  legal rights to use of water and, 50–51, 57
  legal system and, 50
  litigation and, 50
  National Pollution Discharge Elimination System and, 51
  National Resources Defense Council et al. v Train and, 51
  overview, 8, 56–58
  Resource Conservation and Recovery Act and, 51
  surface water, 50–51
  sustainability and, 54–55
  Total Maximum Daily Load Program and, 51–52, 55–56
  water conflict and, 50, 56
  Watershed Approach Framework and, 52–54, 57
  water use and, 49–50
Grand Ronde Reservation, 111, 116–117
Grand Ronde Tribe, 103, 107–115, 118
Grant Township (Pennsylvania), 90–92
Great Lakes Water Authority, 166
Green Temples Guide, 214
groundwater, 50–51, 77, 192
Gyalwang Karmapa Ogyen Trinley Dorje, 25

H

Hanna-Attisha, Mona, 165–166
Hatzalah, 227
Hawaiian Tradition, 43
Hayhoe, Katherine, 229–230
Hazon, 227
Highland Township (Pennsylvania), 90–92
Hindu Declaration on Climate Change, 214
Hinduism
  ahimsa and, 213
  Chipko movement and, 213–214
  climate change and, 214
  conflict resolution in, 214–215
  dharma and, 214
  environmental movements of, 213–215
  environmental principles and, 213
  Four Stages of Water Conflict Transformation and, 215
  karma and, 213
  overview, 212, 215–216
  peacefulness and, 214–215
  pollution and, 213
  reincarnation and, 213
  Rtam and, 213
  sandals and conflict resolution and, 215
  Śanti and, 214–215
  steps in conflict resolution and, 215
  sustainability and, 214
  Vishnu's four stages and, 215

Home Rule Charter, 91–92
Hood River Wascos, 116
Ho'oponopono technique, 43, **43**
Housing Authority of Portland, 152
human activities and river basins/Earth, 3, 6
human well-being, 25–26
hydraulic fracturing, 91–92
hydrologic units, 5
Hydro-Trifecta framework, 37

I

Iban people, 29
Ibn Kathir, 222
iceberg analogy of interests/positions, 35–36, *35*
India, 97, 213–214
Indian Head Casino, 114
Indian policy in U.S., 106, *see also specific legislation*
Indian Rehabilitation Project, 106
Indian Reorganization Act (1934), 118
Indicator 6.5.2, 189–191, *see also* Uganda and Indicator 6.5.2
indigenous people, *see specific name*
information, equal access to, 23
Information System for Follow-Up and Assessment of the Water Management Policy Implementation (Siapreh), 66
institutional capacity, 188
Integrative negotiation stage
  description of, **38**, 39–40, **41–42**
  Sustainable Development Goal Framework and, 186, **187**, 190–191
  techniques in, 43–44, **43**
  Uganda and Indicator 6.5.2 and, 196–198
  in Vanport African American community, 158, **159**
interconnectivity of river basins, 3
interests and water conflict, 34–36, 155
Intergovernmental Panel on Climate Change, 6
International Conference on Freshwater (2001), 126–127
International Conference on Water and the Environment (1992), 126
inter-personal relationship, 13–14
intertribal fishing conflicts and federal obstruction in Oregon
  Celilo Village and, 106–107
  change to tribal culture and, 105–106
  Clackamas Tribe and, 113–115
  Clowewalla Tribe and, 113–115
  conflicts between tribes and, 105
  contemporary water issues and, 113–118
  fishing protocols and, 116
  fishing rights and, 108, 112, 118, 120n28
  "fishing wars" and, 108–109
  fish species, 104
  Grand Ronde Tribe and, 103, 107–115, 118
  Indian policy and, 106
  Indian Reorganization Act and, 118
  negotiation and, 114–115
  in 1950s, 106
  Oregon tribes and, 103–106, *104*, 112
  overview, 8, 103
  Public Law 588 and, 111
  Rogue River Tribe and, 107
  Siletz Tribe and, 107–109, 118
  Task Force Ten Commission findings and, 108
  Termination policy and, 106. 108
  trading network and, 104–105
  Umpqua Valley Tribe and, 107
  Warm Springs Reservation and, 106, 113–116
  Willamette Valley Treaty and, 107–111, *107*, 120n28
  Yakima Reservation and, 106, 115, 117
intra-personal relationship, 13
irreversibility of change, 19–20
irrigation, 28, 50, 67, 93–94, 130–136
Irwin v Phillips, 77
Isaiah, Book of, 227
Islam
  climate change and, 222
  conflict resolution in, 222–224
  environmental standards from Qur'an, 220–221
  Four Stages of Water Conflict Transformation and, 224
  Muhammad and, 221–222
  overview, 224
  tarrahidhin and, 224

J

Jesus Christ, 228, 230–231
Jewish Environmental and Energy Imperative, 226–227
Jewish National Fund, 226
Judaism
  Bal Tash'chit law and, 226
  biblical stewardship environmental ethics, 225–226
  climate change and, 226–227
  Coalition on the Environment and Jewish Life and, 227
  conflict resolution in, 227–228
  environmental ethics and, 224–225
  Four Stages of Water Conflict Transformation and, 228
  Hatzalah and, 227
  Hazon and, 227
  humans' role in life and, 225
  interpretations of nature and, 225–226
  Jewish Environmental and Energy Imperative and, 226–227
  overview, 228
  pollution and, 226–227

Index 247

p'shara and, 227
sustainability and, 227
Talmud and, 226
teachings on nature and, 226

K

Kah-nee-ta casino, 114
Kaiser, Edgar, 152
Kaiser, Henry John, 152
Kalapuya Etc. Treaty (1855), 107–108, *107*, 110
karma, 213
Killmann, Wulf, 29
Klamath Hydropower Settlement Agreement, 94
Klamath River, 94, 109
Klamath River Renewal Corporation, 94
Klamath Tribe, 109

L

lag periods of systems, 18–19
Lake Huron, 164, 166
Lake Mead, 81
Lake Nasser, 27
Lake Turkama, 192, *193*
Lake Victoria Basin Commission, 194
Lake Victoria watershed, 194
Lakota Tribe, 209–210
La Plata River Basin, 6
Laudato Si' ("Praised Be"), 229
leadership, true social-environmental, 26–27, *see also* decision making
lead in drinking water, 33, *see also* Flint African American community
legal pluralism, 167
Libby Dam, 40
linear decision making, 239
listening skills, 38, 163–164
litigation, 50, *see also specific case*
Little Mahoning watershed, 91–92
Local Financial Stability and Choice Act 436 (2012), 166
long-term trends, 14–15, 20
Lotagipi Swamp, 192

M

Māori, 89
masculine, 125
Matthew, Book of, 231
Mattole River, 23
Meganck, Dr. R., 63
Meinzen-Dick, Ruth, 167
Mexican Treaty (1944), 80–81
Millennium Declaration, 183
Millennium Development Goals, 183
Ministerial Declaration (2001), 126–127
Montreal Protocols, 229

Morales, Evo, 87
Moses, 227–228
Mother Earth, rights of, 87, *see also* Rights of Nature
Muhammad, Prophet, 220–222
multidimensional learning, 16–17

N

Nanthakthun, Phrakru Pitak, 217
narrative water quality standards, 51
Nasser, Gamal Abdel, 27
National Agency of Water and Basic Sanitation, 66–69
National Green Tribunal, 97
National Information System on Water Resources (SNIRH), 66
National Pollution Discharge Elimination System (NPDES), 51
National Research Council, 4
National Resources Defense Council et al. v Train, 51
National Water Agency (ANA), 66, 69–72
National Water Council, 72
National Water Management Council (CNRH), 66
National Water Management Policy, 64
National Water Policy, 64–68
Native American traditions
    Adversarial negotiation stage and, 212
    community environmental ethics, 210–211
    conflict resolution, 211–212
    familial environmental ethics and, 209–210
    Four Stages of Water Conflict Transformation and, 212
    Lakota proverb and, 209
    overview, 212
    Peacemaking Circles, 211–212
    social relations between tribes and, 211
    see also specific tribe
Native American water use rights, 77
natural areas, rights of, 86
nature
    Christianity and, 228–230, 232
    Citizen Interpretation of, 225–226
    Despotic Interpretation of, 225
    homocentric view of, 224–225
    importance of, 25–26
    interpretations of, 225–226
    Jewish interpretations of, 225–226
    Jewish teachings on, 226
    Stewardship Interpretation of, 225–226
Nature Conservancy, 53–54
nature-people relationship
    dam removal projects and, 94, *94*, *95*, 96
    destruction of rivers and, moving beyond, 93–94, 96
    dichotomy of, 7

ecological governance and, 96–98
Elwha Dam removal project and, 94, *94*
functioning of, 87–89
Glines Dam removal project and, 94, *95*
Grant Township in Pennsylvania, 90–92
Highland Township in Pennsylvania, 90–92
importance of water and, 85
legal system and Rights of Nature, 92–93
overview, 8, 98–99
PacifiCorp dams removal project and, 94, 96
pollution and, 85
restoring, 93–94, 96
Rights of Nature and, 86–88, 91–93, 97
river protection and, local and global, 96–97
scarcity of water and, 85–86
Walt Disney Enterprises resort and, 86
water conflict in ecological governance framework and, 98
water use and, 86
Whanguanui River in New Zealand, 89–90, *90*
negotiation
Brazilian water management and, 69, 71–72, 74, 76
bundled rights and, 171
Columbia River Treaty and, 40, 110, 120n32
iceberg analogy of interests/positions in, *35*
intertribal fishing conflicts and federal obstruction in Oregon, 114–115
laws as bargaining power and, 168, **169–170**, 171
of Māori claims, 89
of Ojibwa Tribe, 211
parties, selecting, 137, 141
of Portland harbors' cleanup, 120n29
style, 189–190
techniques, 43–44, **43**
understanding conflict and, 61
U.S. water management and, 78, 80
Water Resources Management System and, 64
see also Four Stages of Water Conflict Transformation; *specific stage*
network of rivers and their tributaries, 3
Newark (New Jersey) drinking water, 33
New Zealand, 5, 89–90, *90*
Nez Perce tribe, 105
Nile Basin Initiative (1999), 193, 195–198
Nile River, 27–29, 33, 192–195, *193*
Nile River Basin, 192–194, *193*, 196
Nile Water Agreement (1929), 192
non-sustainable development, 15
Nubian people, 28
numeric water quality standards, 51

O

oceans, 2
Ojibwa Tribe, 210–211

Olendzki, Andrew, 219
Olson, Terese, 165
ordaining trees to save them, 217–218
Oregon City Cultural Coalition, 113
Oregon Department of Fish and Wildlife, 112
Oregon tribes, 103–106, *104*, 112, *see also* intertribal fishing conflicts and federal obstruction in Oregon
Our Common Future (Brundtland Report) (1987), 181–182

P

Pacific Fur Traders, 105
PacifiCorp dams removal project, 94, 96
pantheism, 210
Paris Climate Conference (2015), 218
Parliament of World Religions (2009), 214
Paul, Apostle, 232
Peacemaking Circles, 211–212
Pennsylvania Department of Environmental Protection, 92
people-environment relationship, 14–15
people-nature relationship, *see* nature-people relationship
Pew Research Center, 206–207
Pipiripau Watershed, 75
Piracicaba, Capivari, and Jundiaí (PCJ) Watershed, 71
pluralism, legal, 167
pollution
    Buddhism and, 218
    Clean Air Act and, 77
    Clean Water Act and toxic, 51–52, 77, 86
    ending/reducing, 98, *185*
    of Ganges River, 97
    Hinduism and, 213
    impact of, 85
    industrial, 70
    Judaism and, 226–227
    nature-people relationship and, 85
    nonpoint source, 52
    Rights of Nature to live without, 87–88
    sewage overflows, 52
    U.S. management of, 49
    of water with religious significance, 213
Portland harbors' cleanup, 120n29
portmanteau technique, **43**, 44
power generation, 67
Pradhan, Rajendra, 167
precipitation, 2, 6, 50, 52, 128, 154, 192, *see also* rainfall
present-future people relationship, 15–16
present moment, 26–27
prior appropriations doctrine, 50, 76–77, 130
privatization of water, 33

Index

Protocol for Sustainable Development of the Lake Victoria Basin (2003), 194
Prysby, Michael, 166
Psalms, 225, 227
p'shara, 227
public good, water as, 64
Public Law 588, 111
Pulido, Laura, 166

Q

quality of water, 51, 55–56, 63–64
Qur'an, 220–222

R

Rabbinical Assembly, 227
rain drop, 20, *21*
rainfall, 70, 74, 80, 154, 192, *see also* precipitation
re-allocation of energy, 17
Red River, 6
Reflective negotiation stage
    description of, **38**, 39, **41–42**
    in Flint African American community, 167
    gender in water conflicts and, 140
    Sustainable Development Goal Framework and, 186, **187**
    techniques in, 43, **43**
    in Vanport African American community, 158, **159**
reframing, 167
reincarnation, 213
re-investment of energy, 17
relationships
    decision making rule that everything is a relationship, 13–16
    dichotomy of, 7
    energy transfer in, 17–18
    inclusive and productive of outcome, 16–17
    interpersonal, 13–14
    intra-personal, 13
    between people and environment, 14–15
    people-environment, 14–15
    between people in present and those in future, 15–16
    self-reinforcing feedback loops and, 23
    trade-offs in, 18
    see also nature-people relationship
religious worldviews and environmental values
    ancient conflict management principles with modern applications, 208
    background information, 206–207
    Buddhism, 216–220
    Christianity, 228–233
    complexity of religions and, 208–209
    conflict transformation and, 42–43
    Four Stages of Water Conflict Transformation and, 208–209, **209**

Hinduism, 212–216
Islam, 220–224
Judaism, 224–228
Native American, 209–212
    shared values and, building on, 207, 233
remedies for water conflict, degrees of, 34
Renaissance Dam, 33
Resource Conservation and Recovery Act (1976), 51
Resource Management Act (1991) (New Zealand), 5
restoration of watersheds, 56
Rhine River Basin, 6
Rights of Nature, 86–88, 91, 91–93, 96–97
Rio+20 Conference on Sustainable Development (2012), 183
Rio Grande River, 80–81
riparian ecosystems, 27, *see also specific system*
riparian water use rights, 76
rivalry, 14
river-basin approach to water management, 4
River Basin Authorities (UK), 4
river basins, 3–6, *5*, *see also specific name*
river protection, local and global, 96–97
rivers and their tributaries, network of, 3, *see also specific river name*
Rogue River Tribe, 107
Rohini River, 219–220
Rtam, 213
Ruhr River Association (Germany), 4

S

Sabesp (São Paulo utility company), 71–72
Safe Drinking Water Act (1974), 51, 77, 165–166
salmon, 104, 118
Salmon River, 112
Salmon River Highway (formerly Wagon Road), 112
saltwater, 2
sanitation services, 66–67, 71
Śanti, 214–215
São Paulo Metropolitan Region (RMSP) water crisis (2014–2015 <or2016?>)
    Brazilian Water Law and, 70
    Cantareira Reservoir and, 70–71
    composition of, 62
    context of, 69–70
    drought and, 62–63, 68, 70
    lessons learned from study of, 72–73
    location of, *69*
    National Water Agency and, 69–72
    results of study of, main, 72–73
    Sabesp and, 71–72
    water conflict in, 62–63, 71–72
    water use and, 68
scarcity of water, 64, 85–86
schistosomiasis, 27
sea water, 2

self-organized criticality, 20, *21*, 22
Seneca Resources (gas-drilling company), 91
sewage overflows, 52
shared values, building on, 207, 233
Shaver, Josiah J., 229
short-term trends, 14–15
Shuttle, John H., 155
Sierra Legal Defense Fund, 86
Siletz Tribe, 107–109, 118
simplicity as key to contentment, adaptability, and survival, 25
Sioux Tribe, 209–210
situation maps, 157–158, *158*
Slusky, David, 166
Smith, Greta, 153
Smohalla, 210
snowmelt, 6, 154
Snyder, Rick, 164
social-environmental practices, 3, 6
Sohappy, David, 108
solar energy, 17
Sous, Matthew, 166
South Africa, 33
Spain, 4
Spirit Mountain Casino, 114
standards, water quality, 51
steady-state economics, 22
steelhead trout, 104
Steindl-Rast, David, 19
Stewardship Interpretation of nature, 225–226
Stone, Christopher, 86, 89, 93
Straub, Robert, 109
structure of systems, 18
Sudan, 192–194
surface water, legal rights to use of, 50–51
survival, simplicity as key to, 25
sustainability
 ecosystem-based management and, 55
 governance of water under U.S. law and, 54–55
 Hinduism and, 214
 Judaism and, 227
 people-environment relationship and, 14
 principles of, 181, *182*
 social-environmental, 26
 sustainable development versus, 181–182
sustainable development, 15, 181–183, *see also* Sustainable Development Goal Framework
Sustainable Development Goal Framework
 Four Stages of Water Conflict Transformation and, 181, 186, **187**, 188–191
 goals, 183–184, *183–184*
 Indicator 6.5.2 and, 188–191
 Millennium Development Goals and, 183
 overview, 8, 199
 resolution, 182–183
 water and sanitation, 184–186, *184–185*
 see also Uganda and Indicator 6.5.2

Sustainable Development Goals, 183–186, *183–184*, *184–185*
symptomatic approaches, 17
systemic change, 20, *21*, 22
systems
 composition of, 18
 cumulative effects of, 18–19
 dynamic disequilibrium ruling all, 22
 function of, 18
 lag periods of, 18–19
 structure of, 18
 thresholds of visibility of, 18–19

T

talking stick technique, 43, **43**
Talmud, 226
tarrahidhin, 224
Task Force Ten Commission findings (1975), 108
Technical Advisory Committee of the Cooperative Framework Agreement, 195
Technical Cooperation Committee for the Promotion and Development of the Nile (1992), 193
Ten Commandments, 228
Tennessee River Basin, 4
Tennessee Valley Authority (U.S.), 4–5
Termination Policy, 106, 108
Texas, 80
Thich Nhat Hanh, 219
thresholds of visibility of systems, 18–19
"Time to Act Is Now" climate statement, 218
topographic boundaries, 3
Total Maximum Daily Load Program, 51–52, 55–56
trade-offs, 18
trading network of Oregon tribes, 104–105
transboundary river basins, 5–6, *5*, 192, *193*, **195**, *see also specific name*
Transboundary Water Interactions Nexus (TWINS) Matrix framework, 37
transfer of energy, 17–18
Transparency Law, 67
Treaty of Middle Oregon, 116
Treaty of the Río de la Plata (Prata), 63
Treaty of Waitangi (1840), 89
Truman, Harry, 156
trust building, 38, 163
Tuhoe people, 89
Twitchell, James B., 25

U

Uganda and Indicator 6.5.2
 Action negotiation stage and, 198
 Adversarial negotiation stage and, 196
 background information, 192–194, *193*
 Cooperative Framework Arrangement and, 193–198

Index

Four Stages of Water Conflict Transformation and, 196–199
Integrative negotiation stage and, 196–198
Nile Basin Initiative and, 193, 195–198
overview, 180, 192, 199
shared waters and cooperation and, 192–194, *193*
Sustainable Development Goal Framework and, 194–196, **195**
transboundary river basis and, 192, *193*, **195**
water cooperation and, 192–199, **195**
Umpqua Valley Tribe, 107
United Nations Development Programme, 136
United Nations Entity for Gender Equality and the Empowerment of Women, 136
United Nations Secretary General's Peacebuilding Fund, 136
United Nations Water, 127
United Nations Watercourses Convention (1997), 189
United Nations Women, 137–138
United Nations World Commission on Environment and Development, 181
United States
 Army Corps of Engineers, 79, 106, 154–156
 Buddha parable and, 19
 Clean Air Act, 77
 Clean Water Act, 49, 51–52, 56, 76–78, 86
 Environmental Protection Agency, 5, 51–53, 56, 76, 167
 Fish and Wildlife Service, 131
 Forest Service, 86
 Geological Service, 49
 Geological Survey, 5, 155
 National Research Council, 4
 pollution management and, 49
 Watershed Approach Framework in, 5, 52–54
 see also governance of water under U.S. law; U.S. water management
United States Institute of Peace, 223
Universal Declaration of the Rights of Mother Earth, 87
Upper Tietê River, 71
Urewara National Park, 89
U.S. water management
 Brazilian water management versus, 61–62, 76
 Clean Air Act and, 77
 Clean Water Act and, 76–78
 federally reserved water rights and, 77
 Florida v Georgia and, 78–80
 groundwater rights and, 77
 Mexican Water Treaty of 1944 and, 80–81
 Native American water rights and, 77
 overview, 8, 76
 prior appropriations doctrine and, 76–77
 Safe Drinking Water Act and, 77
 success of, key to, 81–82

Watershed Protection Approach Framework and, 76
water use rights and, 76–77

V

Vanport African American community
 Action negotiation stage and, 158, **159**
 Adversarial negotiation stage and, 158, **159**, 161–162, **161**
 background information, 150
 discharges in Columbia and Willamette Rivers and, 154–155
 flooding of, 155–156
 Four Stages of Water Conflict Transformation and, 156–158, **159–160**, 160–161, **161**
 geography of, 150–152, *151*, *152*
 house building in, 153
 Integrative negotiation stage and, 158, **159**
 lessons learned from study of, 161–163, 171
 listening skills and, 163–164
 location of, significance of, 150–152, *151*
 movement of African Americans and, 161–162
 Reflective negotiation stage and, 158, **159**
 shipbuilding in World War II and, 152–154
 situation maps of crisis, 157–158, *158*
 trust building and, 163
Vanport Interracial Council, 156, 158
voting rights, 26

W

Walt Disney Enterprises resort, 86
"wants," limiting, 24–25
Warm Springs Reservation, 106, 113–116
Warren, Rick, 230–231
Water and Sanitation Agency (Adasa), 74
Water Code (1934), 63
water conflict
 complexities of, 239
 defining, 126
 drivers of, 50
 examples of, 33
 in Federal District of Brasilia, 62–63, 74–75
 Florida v Georgia and, 78–79
 gendered approach and, 140–141
 governance of water under U.S. law and, 50, 56
 Grant Township in Pennsylvania, 90–92
 Highland Township in Pennsylvania and, 90–91
 incidences of, 33
 interests and, 34–36, 155
 issues related to, 33
 Mattole River, 23
 Mexican Treaty of 1944 and, 80–81
 overview, 8, 44–45

remedies for, degrees of, 34
in São Paulo Metropolitan Region, 62–63, 71–72
tools, 36–37
transformation, 36–37, 42–44, **43**
Whanganui River in New Zealand, 89–90, *90*
see also Four Stages of Water Conflict Transformation; *specific conflict*
water cooperation, 5–6, 34, 37, 126, 139, 181, 185–186, *185*, 188–191, 239, *see also* Uganda and Indicator 6.5.2
water crimes, 166
water crises, 179–182, *see also specific type*; Sustainable Development Goal Framework; Uganda and Indicator 6.5.2
Water Event Intensity Scale of Basins at Risk framework, 36–37
water insecurities, 8, 149–150, *see also* Flint African American community; Vanport African American community
Water Law (1997), 64, 66, 70
water management
"command-and-control" style of, 124
as conflict management, 186
corrective measures, 239
in Deschutes River Basin, 130–131, 141
ecosystem-based, 54–55
in Ferghana Valley, 133–135, 141
integrated, 4
river-basin approach to, 4
science-based, 53
see also Brazilian water management; U.S. water management
Water Mark Project, 65
Water Producer Project, 75
Water Resources Management System (Singreh), 64
Water Resources Reform and Development Act, 78–79
Watershed Approach Framework, 5, 52–54, 57, 76
Watershed Protection Approach Framework, 76
watersheds, 5, *see also specific name*

water use/consumption, 49–50, 68, 86
water use rights
drought and, 50–51
federally reserved, 77
"first in time, first in right" system and, 77
Flint African American community and, strengthening, 167–168, *168*, **169–170**, 170
groundwater, 77
Native American, 77
prior appropriations doctrine and, 50, 76–77
riparian, 76
U.S., 76–77
well-being of humans, 25–26
Whanganui (River People), 89
Whanganui River Claims Settlement Agreement, 89
Whanganui River in New Zealand, 89–90, *90*
Wheeler-Howard Act, 106
White Salmon Reservation, 117
Wickiup Reservoir and Dam, 130
Willamette Falls Heritage Area Coalition, 113
Willamette River and Falls, 103–104, *104*, 111–112, 115, 151, 154–155
Willamette Valley Treaty (1855), 107–111, *107*, 120n28
Williams, Chuck, 110
Winters v the United States, 77
wisdom, environmental/cultural, 25–26
Wolf, Aaron, 186, 208, 215, 219, 228
World Bank, 127
World Economic Forum, 179–180
World People Conference on Climate Change, 87

Y

Yakima Reservation, 106, 115, 117
Yamhill River, 111–112
"Yes, And" technique, **43**, 44

Z

Zen Buddhism, 43